Praise for *White Male Privilege: How This Happened and Why It's Even Worse than We Thought*

"This is a courageous book. . . . David Goldenkranz has taken on one of the most controversial aspects of race in America and addressed it with intellect, boldness, and compassion. It is also a deeply personal book, as Goldenkranz shares his own journey from blindness to awareness and offers it as an inspiration and road map for the rest of us. Do not choose this book if you are looking for simplistic polemic or political correctness. Goldenkranz draws from history, psychology, and sociological research to build the case that we live in a system of race that traps all of us in roles that are toxic and self-defeating, and, most importantly, he charts a path for the possibility of a new future. This is a deep and intelligent book and a worthy read for people of all races."

—Howard Ross, Author of *Everyday Bias: Identifying and Navigating Unconscious Judgments in Our Daily Lives*

"As a Black man who has navigated the complexities of a society deeply ingrained with systemic inequalities, I am thrilled to offer my most enthusiastic endorsement for Goldenkranz's groundbreaking book, *White Male Privilege: How This Happened and Why It's Even Worse Than We Thought.* In a time when the world demands a candid and sincere exploration of privilege, Goldenkranz's work shines as a beacon of illumination and inspiration.

"His willingness to confront the uncomfortable truths surrounding White male privilege sets him apart as a courageous ally in the ongoing fight for equality and justice. Through meticulous research, thought-provoking analysis, and a deeply empathetic narrative, he delves into the roots of this pervasive issue, unraveling its origins and tracing its evolution through history. His dedication to uncovering the harsh realities is commendable and essential in our pursuit of a more equitable society.

"What sets this book apart is Goldenkranz's unwavering commitment to self-reflection and accountability. He unflinchingly acknowledges his own privilege, demonstrating that the journey toward equality is one we must all embark upon, regardless of our background. This is not a book written from an ivory tower; it is a testament to the power of personal growth and transformation.

"*White Male Privilege* is not just a book; it's a road map for change. Goldenkranz's thoughtful insights and actionable recommendations offer a path forward for dismantling the structures that perpetuate inequality. His call for intersectional solidarity is a call to action for all of us, regardless of our race or gender, to come together in the name of progress.

"In these pages, Goldenkranz challenges us to confront the uncomfortable truths, but he does so with compassion and hope. He understands that acknowledging privilege is not an indictment but an opportunity for change. His book reminds us that we all have a role to play in the fight for justice, and it is through dialogue, understanding, and unity that we can create a more equitable world for future generations.

"*White Male Privilege* is a testament to Goldenkranz's courage, wisdom, and commitment to social justice. It is a must-read for anyone who seeks a deeper understanding of privilege and a brighter future for all."

—Dameon Brown, Professional Learning and Mentorship Program Coordinator, Association of Washington School Principals

"In my work with White women around sexism and racism, I am often asked, 'But what about White men?' Fortunately, *White Male Privilege* gives me, and all of us, an accessible and useful resource to help answer that question. Goldenkranz has created a holistic framework to help us better understand the history, politics, cultural context, and actual mechanics of White male privilege. With his comprehensive research, conversational tone, and dry wit, Goldenkranz makes complicated issues approachable and understandable while also offering practical and constructive ways forward. What a relief to have this book available at a time when it is so urgently needed."

—Tilman C. Smith, Coauthor of *What's Up with White Women? Unpacking Sexism and White Privilege in Pursuit of Racial Justice*

"David Goldenkranz offers a much-needed invitation to White men to take an active role in unlearning racist and sexist ideas and finding a path to healing. In this extensively researched book, Goldenkranz is skilled in connecting with the reader, taking complex ideas and historical facts and folding them into an easy-to-read narrative. His humor throughout clearly illustrates the joy that is possible when we confront racist systems and work together for collective liberation."

—Ilsa Marie Govan, Cofounder of Cultures Connecting, Coauthor of *What's Up with White Women? Unpacking Sexism and White Privilege in Pursuit of Racial Justice*

"*White Male Privilege* is a candid and introspective approach to addressing racism, sexism, and their intersections. Goldenkranz leverages his own Whiteness to provide a comprehensive examination of the insidious ways in which racism and sexism persist, as he confronts his own biases as an advocate for change. He underscores the importance of self-awareness, humility, and taking accountability as essential steps toward dismantling oppressive systems and engaging in difficult conversations to strive for positive change."

—Dr. Batsheva Guy, Prosci® Certified Change Practitioner and Certified Diversity Professional®

"In our globalized and yet still so polarized world, David Goldenkranz provides a welcome call to action to critically examine White male privilege. . . . It's refreshing to see this call coming from inside the house of our privilege; for too long, the burden of calling for change has rested much too heavily on the marginalized, especially Black, Indigenous, and other persons of color.

"We may not have created the harmful systems of marginalization and oppression which rule our world, but as primary beneficiaries of those systems, White men have a critical role in addressing and dismantling them. The stakes have never been higher for our collective identity and humanity. *White Male Privilege* shows us, with unflinching honesty, how we got here, why we urgently need change, and how White men can play their necessary part in this shared responsibility."

—Warren Stapley, Lawyer, Diversity, Equity, and Inclusion Strategist & Disability Rights Advocate (London, England)

"Reading this extraordinarily well-researched book will make it impossible to ignore the ravages that White male privilege have had on our society. David Goldenkranz knows we don't have time to beat around the bush. His immediate and direct style is sure to challenge every White man who reads it, and we will be better for it."

—James Boutin, Anti-Oppression Educator, Facilitator, and Coach

"There's not a more important conversation to be having today than to get at the root of the issues we see and do it with honesty, transparency, and a human-centric approach. Goldenkranz brings these issues to light in a way that allows us to examine ourselves while also seeking accountability for those who choose to ignore the reality of oppression within our society."

—Elisa Stampf, Cofounder and CEO of Insure Equality

"*White Male Privilege: How This Happened And Why It's Even Worse Than We Thought* is a candid exploration of the history, reality, and pervasiveness of racism and sexism in the US. Despite the fact that the context for the book is the United States, the insights are widely generalizable. Goldenkranz's self-awareness and accessible style encourages reflection long after one is finished reading, making the book thought provoking and authentic."

—Laura Germishuys, Disability Consultant (Capetown, South Africa)

"In order for DEI to take its rightful place as a mainstream business strategy, the involvement of White men is essential. David Goldenkranz courageously and unapologetically steps into the fray with *White Male Privilege: Why This Happened and Why It's Even Worse Than We Thought.* He skillfully holds up a mirror that allows us to see why we are the way we are and then describes the heavy lifting we will all need to do—for and with each other—to break free of stereotypes and norms. Goldenkranz debunks the pseudoscience, rumors, and misinformation that have made their way into our ways of thinking about Whiteness . . . without preaching or overprescribing what we need to do to foster change for the better."

—Jim Morris, Strategist, Speaker, Interventionist, Writer, and DEI Advocate, Author of *Gaslights and Dog Whistles: Standing Up to Facts over Fiction in a Fearful and Divided World*

"*White Male Privilege* is a well-researched exploration of Whiteness, White supremacy, its implications, and possibilities. David Goldenkranz dives deep into history, science, social movements, and politics to reveal, unpack, and counter racist arguments with clarity."

—Keith E. Edwards, PhD, Speaker, Coach, and Author of *Unmasking: Toward Authentic Masculinity*

"Every White American man will discover knowledge and insight they didn't know in this extensive history of what created our privilege in America. Goldenkranz invites us deeper into nuances of grasping the complexities of what it will take to move beyond the superficial and truly heal ourselves and our country."

—Michael Welp, PhD, Cofounder, White Men as Full Diversity Partners, Author of *Four Days To Change: 12 Radical Habits to Overcome Bias and Thrive in a Diverse World*, TEDx Presenter

"David Goldenkranz offers up an easy-to-read integration of history, language, and science in this groundbreaking book to provide context for how and why White men are in positions of power and dominance in the United States. This book is for anyone who wants to unpack societal structures such as healthcare, higher education, or the military from a racialized lens to understand how we got to where we are and how White people can move forward in a more accountable, thoughtful, collaborative manner."

—Rebecca J. Evan, Associate Professor, Metropolitan State University, Minnesota

"David Goldenkranz's new book *White Male Privilege* is a great example of why we need more White men to speak to their experiences of racism and sexism and the price they pay when they uphold those systems. With a straightforward tone and a healthy dose of humility, he provides a sweeping historical account of Whiteness, its current manifestations, and the steps White men can take to move towards a more connected and fulfilling life not based on the oppression of others. This is an important resource for anyone interested in how White privilege and oppression operate and what we can do about it."

—Elizabeth Denevi, PhD, Author of *Learning and Teaching While White: Antiracist Strategies for School Communities*

"We can't solve these societal problems that impact all of us without clearly understanding the problem and our role in it. Goldenkranz has written a well-researched book that allows you to take tangible steps in understanding the challenges underrepresented minorities face and how we can all acknowledge our bias and do better."

—Karin Moore, Software Executive and Global Change Leader

"Powerful. David Goldenkranz codifies in *White Male Privilege* what those of us who identify or have been labeled as Blacks, Africans, Coloreds, and Negroes, both men and women, have known for generations. . . . Every literate American should have this book in their personal library."

—Peter J. Gravett, Major General, US Army (Ret.), Author of *Battling While Black: General Patton's Heroic African-American WWII Battalions*

"For white men who have experienced the anxiety, the overwhelm, the sense of isolation, that lead far more of us, than any other group, to deaths of despair, this book is for you. For white men who want to be on the right side of history, and who want a world of dignity, peace, and fairness, this book is for you. For white men who desperately hope that there is something better than the nightmare of division, of feeling pitted against others, pitted against people and communities we love, this book is for you. David Goldenkranz has given us a crucially important guide to make sense of the historical, institutional, and culture dynamics that intimately impact our lives, families, workplaces, and communities. This isn't just a book to help us be better people, but to also get free from what is holding us back."

—Chris Crass, Author of *Towards Collective Liberation: Anti-Racist Organizing, Feminist Praxis, and Movement Building Strategy*

White Male Privilege:
How This Happened and Why It's Even Worse than We Thought
by David Goldenkranz

© 2023 David Goldenkranz

ISBN 979-8-88824-141-7

All rights reserved. No part of this publication may be reproduced, stored in a retrieval system, or transmitted in any form or by any means electronic, mechanical, photocopy, recording, or any other except for brief quotations in printed reviews, without the prior written permission of the author.

Published by

3705 Shore Drive
Virginia Beach, VA 23455
800-435-4811

WHITE MALE PRIVILEGE

How This Happened and Why It's Even Worse than We Thought

DAVID GOLDENKRANZ

VIRGINIA BEACH
CAPE CHARLES

TABLE OF CONTENTS

INTRODUCTION | 1
    To My Fellow White American Men | 13

PART 1: What Is Whiteness, and How Did It Begin?

CHAPTER 1 "Primary Colors" | 19
    Words Create Worlds | 19
    White = Good | 21
    Black = Bad | 23
    Brown = Apparently Not Worth Discussing in Detail | 25
    "Creating" Meaning | 26
    Webster Defines America | 29
    Politically Correct(ing) Labels | 32

CHAPTER 2: "US" Versus Them: The Story of Whiteness | 35
    A "White" Lie | 35
    Slavery "Evolves" in America | 38
    A Population Paradox | 41
    (Legally) A Slave Forever | 42
    Who's Your ~~Daddy~~ Mommy | 43
    Fear of Power and the Power of Fear | 46
    Bacon Frightens the Elite | 47
    The One Race to Rule Them All | 48
    Heathens, Pagans, and Bastard Children | 50
    Whiteness Takes Root | 53

CHAPTER 3: White Pseudoscience | 55
    Self-Vindication | 55

The Dark Side of the Enlightenment | 56

Bigger (Skulls) = Better (Intelligence) | 57

The Purest White | 61

Heil Whiteness | 63

A Disturbing Parallel | 65

CHAPTER 4: "Our" Genes and
"Their" Genes: "Biological Whiteness" | 66

How the Sun Created "White" Skin | 68

The Euro Nose | 71

Alt(ernative) Right Science: The Neanderthal in Us All | 72

Okay, Race Is Not Scientific; So What? | 76

CHAPTER 5: "Purebred" White | 78

Race and Breed: A Harmful Correlation | 78

Dog "Races" | 79

Pit Bull Prejudice | 81

Deliberate Breed Bias | 83

Categorical Confusion | 85

CHAPTER 6: "Natural" Abilities | 88

Born Athletes | 88

Labeled Promiscuous | 94

Better in Bed? | 97

Racial Fetishization | 100

Intellectually Gifted | 102

Racism Starts Young | 103

CHAPTER 7: Racialized Heathcare: A Lethal Outcome | 105

An African American "Mutation" | 106

A "Vitamin D-ficiency" | 108

Black Diseases? | 110

White Diseases? | 112

Deracializing Healthcare | 115

PART 2: How Whiteness Works

CHAPTER 8: Name-Calling: Dividing Us and Them | 119

Racialized Data | 119

Racial Hierarchy | 121

"Fractioned" Identities | 122

"Hispanic Origin" Story | 127

Which Box *Do* I Check? | 130

"Disassembling" Asian | 131

White (Only) on Paper | 134

A Superior Form of Asian | 135

Noninterchangeable Terms | 138

Black Is Back | 138

Black (Gains) Power | 141

"Safe" Labels | 143

CHAPTER 9: A Word Made "Just" for Me | 145

The Top Tier of Whiteness | 145

What Exactly Is White Privilege? | 147

(Un)earned and (Un)deserved | 149

My Skin Color Keeps Me Safe | 151

White Convenience | 158

A World that Looks Like Me | 159

Coloring in Textbooks | 161

Made in *Our* Image | 163

PART 3: A Whitewashed World: Extract and Assimilate

CHAPTER 10: The Power of White Language | 171

    Literacy = Power | 172

    "Black English" | 174

    Ebonics: A Primary Language? | 176

    Inferior Language, Inferior Intellect | 180

    The Litmus Test | 183

    White English | 186

    How English Evolved | 189

    White Enough to Go to College | 192

    The Toll of Conformity | 193

    When Only We Speak, Everyone Misses Out | 197

    White Code-Switching | 199

    What's in a Name? Access, Privilege, and Power | 201

    "Whitened" Credentials | 203

CHAPTER 11: The World Is Our Oyster:
                  Taking What Doesn't Belong to Us | 205

    The Purveyors of Western Civilization | 206

    Context Is Key | 207

    Cultural Appropriation: One-Way Street | 209

    "Borrowing" Other People's Stuff | 210

    We Love Their Things . . . but Not Them | 213

    Desecrating an Icon | 214

    The (Stolen) Crown Jewel | 216

    Imposter Yoga | 219

    Yoga Heads West | 220

Hot Yoga, Goat Yoga, Wine Yoga, White Yoga | 221

Real Practitioners Get Pushed Out | 222

The "Riches" of Yoga | 223

Musical Appropriation: Adjusting the "Dial" of Whiteness | 226

Whitewashing Hip-Hop | 230

But What If It Doesn't Offend Them? | 234

CHAPTER 12: Our Society, Our Rules:
    Making "Them" More Like "Us" | 236

Forced Assimilation | 237

Dressing the Part | 243

No Hats in the Building | 245

Sit Up Straight! | 246

Appropriation and Assimilation: Two Sides of the Same Coin | 249

PART 4: Who Are We?

CHAPTER 13: White "Culture" | 255

From NASCAR to NPR: The Spectrum of the White Male Persona | 255

Rugged Individualism | 257

What White American Men Have in Common | 258

A Divine Permission Slip | 261

CHAPTER 14: The "White Spectrum" | 266

The (Dis)United States of America | 268

Whiteness Across America | 272

What the Hell Are We? | 274

Recent Arrivals | 276

"We ~~Hold~~ Pretend These Truths to Be Self-Evident" | 277

All (White) Men Are Capable of Self-Governance | 278

Does *Our* God Pick Favorites? | 279

CHAPTER 15: Fight for What's ~~Right~~ White | 283

    "Targeting" People of Color | 283

    Camouflaged Colors | 284

    Wounded Warriors | 286

    Fighting for Equality | 287

    The War for White Power | 290

PART 5: The Fall of Whiteness?

CHAPTER 16: The War on Whiteness | 297

    Strangers to Our Own Race | 298

    "Hyphenated Americans" | 299

    "Becoming" White | 300

    White All Along | 305

    The Jewish Confederacy | 306

    Kicked out of the Club | 310

    Whiteness Gets a Rude Awakening | 313

    With or Against US | 316

    Cultural Demise | 318

    Losing Our Purpose | 321

    Nationalism on Steroids | 321

CHAPTER 17: The Loss of White Power | 325

    Bountiful Inheritance | 325

    Who's in Charge Here? | 327

    The KKK Still Holds Sway | 329

    Influencing the "White" House | 332

    Political Domination | 335

    "Minority" Rule | 336

    Power by Ratio | 337

    "Allowing" Political Diversity | 339

"Make America ~~Great~~ White Again!" | 342
The Right to Fight | 344

CHAPTER 18: White Extinction Theory | 349
    The Great Replacement | 349
    Population Overrun | 353
    Procreation + Globalization = Destabilization | 354
    Race Is *Not* A Fraction | 356
    Racial Play Doh? | 358
    Whiteness "Restored" | 361
    Forced Evolution | 363

PART 6: Trauma, Self-Harm, and Healing

CHAPTER 19: What Does It Really Mean to Be White? | 369
    Race Supersedes Ethnicity | 370
    Teaching (White) Kids Their Place | 371
    "What do you like about being White?" | 372
    Whiteness Spreads throughout America | 373
    Involuntary Hosts: Internalized Racism | 377
    Masking the Symptoms (i.e., Coping with Whiteness) | 379
    Radical Patriots | 380
    Radical Liberals | 382
    Radical Deniers | 387
    Can Whiteness Ever Become Good? | 388
    Restoring White to Its "Intended" Meaning | 391
    A Hypothetical Conundrum: Letting Our Whiteness Go | 391

CHAPTER 20: Tortured and Traumatized | 395
    Tortured Souls | 397
    The Indentured and Indebted Pilgrims | 399

Trauma Travels, Bloodlust Abounds | 406

   Self-Inflicted Suffering | 409

   Traumatized and Trigger Happy | 411

   Self-Induced PTSD | 413

   Uprooted | 417

CHAPTER 21: Healing from Whiteness | 419

   Facing Our Demons | 420

   Building a New Self | 422

   Waking Up | 423

   Resurrecting Our History | 426

   Growing New Roots | 431

   Joining the Movement | 433

   Recovery from Whiteness | 436

ACKNOWLEDGMENTS | 441

ENDNOTES | 442

INTRODUCTION

What if I told you that the book you are about to read was written by someone who admittedly holds racist and sexist beliefs? Would you shove this book into a recycling bin? Maybe you would frantically try to return it. Or maybe, just maybe, you would decide to keep reading.

If you still have this book in your hands, chances are you have chosen the latter. But allow me to provide some context for why a self-proclaimed racist and sexist individual has taken it upon himself to write a book on the role that White men play in upholding racism and sexism—and what we can do to overcome it. While this book is not about me, I still need to qualify why *I* am writing such a book.

My journey into anti-oppression work was a result of my upbringing. Growing up in an upper-middle-class progressive Seattle home, I was raised with the implied belief that everyone is created equal; yet race and gender disparities were never explicitly talked about in my household. While I was fortunate enough to attend uniquely diverse schools with significant ratios of BIPOC (Black, Indigenous, and people of color) students all the way through the end of high school, I was unaware of how segregated my classes and friend groups were.

Despite having many friends of color, I went through my childhood and teenage years proclaiming that I did not see color, naively assuming that I could magically treat everyone equally and have no racial bias or prejudice whatsoever. I still cringe when I think of an exceptionally corny line I often used in high school: "Skin is only skin, but we are all the same within." I thought that this sentiment was somehow profound. I resolutely believed that racism was a problem outside of me, completely blind to my own privilege, prejudices, and biases.

During those formative years, I was convinced that I treated all people, especially women, with respect and dignity. I often bristled at the machismo and hypermasculinity of many of my male counterparts, believing myself to be one of the "good guys" who understood the struggles of women and LBGTQ+ folks. Never mind that I was terrified of the slightest inkling of a nonhetero fantasy creeping into my thoughts or that I constantly objectified both women and men by watching pornography throughout high school and college.

It was not until I was accepted into a graduate program to begin my master's degree in teaching (fueled in part by a deep savior complex) that my "White man in shining armor" facade came crashing down around me, leaving me feeling naked and exposed—and mad.

Back in August 2013, I was sitting in a stiflingly hot and cramped classroom with thirty of my educator-to-be peers. As part of a lesson on the inequalities of our education system, one of our professors showed us a cheesy animated video about White male privilege and the irrefutable need for affirmative action.

In the video, two Black athletes and two White athletes stand at the start of a racetrack. Adjacent to the track is a stopwatch set at 1492 (Columbus's arrival in America). When the race begins, the White athletes surge ahead, while the Black athletes are physically held back. The clock progresses, and the White runners steadily widen the gap between themselves and the Black athletes, lapping them multiple times. It is not until the stopwatch hits 1964 (after the signing of the Civil Rights Act) that the Black athletes are finally released from the starting line. However, by then, their chances of closing the gap are downright impossible.

I had seen this kind of stuff before, but for some reason, this time it finally sank into my overly intellectualizing brain. My cheeks became flush, my heart raced, and my palms sweated profusely as I gawked at the screen, filled with righteous indignation. A visceral level of defensiveness, denial, and rage bubbled up inside of me. It was as if someone had pulled off a blindfold and exposed me to my own reflection for the first time. I was not one of the "good ones" after all. I was just one of the many people existing in willful ignorance and bitter denial.

I didn't know it at the time, but to use a trite cliché, this simple video was my "Matrix moment." Only unlike Neo, the main character in the 1999 blockbuster movie *The Matrix,* instead of bravely swallowing the red pill, I fumbled, choked on it, and swallowed without knowing it. Also unlike Neo, I was not able to download my new reality and immediately "kick ass" in my new role, instinctively knowing what to do. It was a messy process, to say the least. I asked *many* ignorant and awkward questions of people of color and women, made *many* assumptions, and wanted to talk more than I wanted to listen, something I am still working on. Yet from that moment on, I began peeling off layer after layer of my Whiteness and toxic masculinity, exposing each fresh, pus-filled wound to the light.

So how exactly did I get here and decide to write a book about White men? After spending nearly a decade working with underserved youth and BIPOC communities as an educator, I became fed up with trying to "fix" the system from within. Not to mention that I completely burned out. But more on that later. Despite leaving the classroom, my desire to work toward social justice only grew, and I made a significant career pivot to take on more systemic and structural-level reform.

When I finally made the difficult decision to leave teaching in 2019, I began building my current practice as a DEI (diversity, equity, and inclusion) consultant, coach, and facilitator, supporting White men as well as organizations (especially those run by primarily White men) in eliminating structural, institutional, and systemic racism and sexism in the workplace.

In 2021, I was hired for a newly created role at an education-based nonprofit where I was tasked with creating and implementing a program specifically designed for White leaders in education to build anti-racist and culturally responsive practices into their leadership as well as within their school environments. I went from being a teacher with minimal influence on school leadership to leading workshops for principals, district officials, and senior-level administration who needed help figuring out why their schools and districts were not only failing their Black, Indigenous, and people of color (BIPOC) students but also unable to hire or retain BIPOC educators and administrators. For context, White people still account for over 80 percent of education leadership roles across the nation, even in schools and districts where the reverse is true of the student demographics they serve.

In addition to my full-time role, I continue to provide freelance coaching and consulting, working with several DEI firms to support leadership teams from internationally recognized companies and organizations. My job involves a bit of bait and switch. Company leaders tend to assume that I am going to train employees to fix specific "racial issues" within their organization. Instead, I help the individuals within the organization, particularly the leaders themselves, begin to overcome a culture rooted in toxic patriarchy and Whiteness itself. My role primarily centers on helping White folks, especially other White men, explore the insidious ways in which racism and toxic masculinity negatively impact our ability to experience compassion, empathy, and humility while also stunting our growth and hindering our ability to be part of a more collective society.

Let me be real with you. For starters, I hate the phrase "diversity, equity, and inclusion." It is a trite way of trying to encapsulate the incredibly complex and nuanced work that most people in this profession do, particularly those who hold marginalized identities themselves (i.e., BIPOC folks, women, LGBTQ+ individuals, etc.).

It should come as no surprise that this work looks different for every practitioner in this field. However, if we do not explicitly mention the widely used acronyms D&I or DEI, most people have no clue what we do for a living. I should pause to point out that there are now several newer iterations of this acronym, including diversity, equity, inclusion, and belonging (DEIB), and justice, equity, diversity, inclusion (JEDI)—yes, like *Star Wars*.

People often ask me why a White man is doing this type of work in the first place. Here is my overly simplistic response: My personal belief is that when White men fail to show up in DEI efforts (which, let's face it, we often do), we put a significant burden on those whom we have already marginalized and oppressed to do *more* to continue to fight for what we took from them. Expecting people of color, women, or LGBTQ+ folks to always "lead the charge" on diversity, equity, and inclusion not only is unfair but also minimizes the whole reason why these efforts are needed to begin with. Bluntly put, White men are primarily the ones who created this mess, and yet we expect those who have been most harmed to clean it all up.

I believe that when it comes to returning rightful power to marginalized groups, White men are either a part of the problem or part of the solution. There is no such thing as neutral when it comes to upholding the status quo.

At this point you might be wondering just why I decided to begin this book by outing myself as racist and sexist. Well, in the few decades I've been on this earth, three things have become very apparent to me:

I am a man, and therefore privileged.
I am White, and therefore privileged.
I am American, and therefore privileged.

These three qualities have profound meaning when it comes to my core beliefs, my values, as well as my understanding of my status. Yet, like most White men, I have been deliberately conditioned by American society *not* to see these collective parts of my identity but instead to take them for granted and to view my privileged disposition as the status quo. More importantly, I have been taught to see myself as a unique individual and to always value rugged individualism, even though I share a collective identity that was literally designed to give me a distinct advantage over everyone else in America.

Rather than dismiss, deny, or disown my identity as a White male, I must understand my complicit role in upholding something much more powerful than myself. Simply put, the first step to changing this about myself is to accept reality: I am a privileged White American male.

Even in writing this book, I'm touting my White-guy privilege. I state my opinions as fact (as many White men so often do) and give you lengthy descriptions under the assumption that you don't know what I'm talking about. I also tell you how I feel about things, validating that my way is the right way.

As you read this book, I encourage you to challenge my assumptions, my ignorance, and shortsightedness, as well as my biases, prejudices, and racist and misogynistic beliefs. Trust me when I say that White American men need more people holding us accountable for this stuff on a regular basis. Humility is not exactly our defining feature.

I should also state up front that this book is going to be filled with generalizations, stereotypes, and biases. I also use words like "our" and "us" throughout the book. I do this because, as the title would imply, this book is written primarily about White American men, and I am a White American man. When I use the words "we," "us," "you," and "your," I am typically addressing the White American males reading this book.

That said, if you are not a White American male, please do not close the book just yet. Just because this book is written by a White American man, about White American men (as are most pieces of literature in our society, unfortunately), that does not mean that this book is of no use to you. I hope the opposite is true. While I want to illuminate for my fellow White American men what many of us either ignore or simply don't see, I also hope to give those outside our gilded bubble some insight into the power structure and oppressive mindset of arguably the most powerful group of people on the planet. Let's call it a glimpse into the inner workings of a house of cards that we have convinced ourselves is made of steel-reinforced concrete.

Returning to the opening of this introduction, I want to be clear that I do not carry the types of racist thoughts that would lead me to march down the street wielding a tiki torch with my fraternity brothers, yelling, "Blood and soil!" Nor do I insist that a woman's place is in the home. Rather, in outing myself as having racist and sexist thoughts, I am talking about the types of prejudices, stereotypes, and unconscious biases that lead me to make naive and misguided assumptions and snap judgments about others. These thoughts and beliefs get in the way of my ability to truly connect with people I see as different than me. These thoughts and beliefs also cause me to commit small (and not-so-small) microaggressions on a daily basis that offend those around me without my being aware of it.

This is the part that makes most of us squirm: darker thoughts and beliefs often creep in. They percolate deep within my subconscious, bubbling up to the surface when I feel my status as a White male being challenged. While I want to justify these thoughts and beliefs by writing some lengthy diatribe about how I was raised in a culture that saturated me in an unwanted, subjective reality of entitlement and superiority, instead I choose to own these thoughts and not minimize the impact they have on those around me. To be clear, the fact that I *have* these thoughts and beliefs is not my fault, but they are my responsibility to do something about.

So, let me get real with you right now and qualify myself as an unfortunately typical chauvinistic White American male. During my life, I have done the following:

- I have labeled, judged, and ostracized almost everyone who isn't a part of *my* culture.

- I have considered White people—White men in particular—to be more capable, more in control of our behavior, and as having superior intellect.

- I have suspiciously eyed Muslim men at airports.

- I have mockingly imitated accents while telling jokes among my White friends.

- I have crossed the street when I saw a group of Black men ahead of me.

- I have made assumptions about why a woman or a person of color got a position instead of me.

- I have doubted the overall competence of both my female colleagues and colleagues of color.

- I engaged in "locker room talk" when I was in high school.

The painful truth is that disturbing racist and sexist fodder often creep into my mind when I feel that I am not receiving the treatment I am "entitled" to as a White American man. And I would be lying if I said that I have never experienced the urge to utter outright racist and sexist slurs when I felt directly attacked or threatened because of my race or gender.

Okay, take a breath. Still with me?

Am I proud of these thoughts? Absolutely not! Ashamed and embarrassed would be a much better description. Yet rather than grappling with these thoughts and beliefs to try to overcome their stranglehold over me, I have spent most of my life mentally torturing and punishing myself. I outright hated myself at times because of these thoughts. I spent years feeling like my mind was possessed and hoping the "demons" would simply go away if I ignored and denied them.

Because of this, I often overcompensated and tried to be the refined, socially savvy White guy I thought the "progressive world" wanted me to be. This typically ended in embarrassing faux pas and awkward social blunders, particularly around women and people of color. I made more than my share of awkward apologies and placations on behalf of my entire race and gender, to many people who were likely beyond tired of hearing it. Never mind the fact that I was not doing anything to change the oppression happening all around me—and often because of me.

I also spent nearly two decades of my life playing the "I don't see color" card, justifying this by saying that I went to diverse public schools and had plenty of friends of color growing up. And of course, I also must own my embarrassing savior complex—which lasted through most of my twenties—toward both people of color and women. Like Sandra Bullock's character in *The Blind Side*, I thought I was the cure for the woes of racism and misogyny in our culture.

I've tried just about every approach to address racism and sexism based on the common assumption that these ailments of society had nothing to do with me. If I could just tell the whole world how sorry I was on behalf of all the "bad White men" out there, I would be vindicated, and everyone would lovingly applaud me. In other words, I was doing what White males often do: putting myself at the center of the narrative and making everything about me.

Suffice it to say that the seeds of racism and misogyny, like termites in an attic, burrowed further into the rafters of my mind and caved the roof in, ruining my veneer of privileged denial.

Now, my dear White men, I don't mean to throw you under the bus (or maybe I do), but I'm also willing to bet that 99.99 percent of you (especially those who are choosing to read this book) have had similar racist and sexist thoughts and beliefs. I guarantee that some of you are now saying, "Who do you think you are to be accusing me of being racist and sexist just because you are?!"

So why bother sharing all of this? And why assume that many other White American men are unwittingly sharing a similar reality? Is it because I want to let go of my guilt and be exonerated for my sins? No. I insist on revealing these uncomfortable truths about myself because I believe that racism and misogyny are inherently woven into the fabric of White American culture, and that for us as men to overcome them, we must face these hidden racist and sexist parts of ourselves.

As uncomfortable as it may be, owning up to these thoughts and addressing them candidly with other White men is a crucial way for us to overcome them. The problem is that most White people (particularly progressive White men) are absolutely terrified of being labeled as racist or sexist. We slap ourselves on the wrist every time we have a "bad" thought, the same way we would if we had a sexual fantasy about a cousin. We punish, suppress, deny, or ignore. We also seek scapegoats or attack those who we deem worse than us—the *real* bad guys.

In our progressive culture, most White folks are more afraid of being *accused* of being racist than *being* racist. As Heather Dalmage, an assistant professor of sociology at Roosevelt University, so eloquently puts it, "To admit to [our] racism would mean questioning [our] own identity."[1] For White men, the same could be said about admitting our misogynistic beliefs. It is extremely difficult to do, but it is a vital first step toward overcoming the bigger systemic issues that are oppressing all those around us. By choosing not to admit our part, we remain dismissively complicit in White male supremacy.

Let me be clear: This has nothing to do with confessing our sins, being exonerated, or seeking forgiveness. It is also not about guilt-tripping or self-flagellation. It is about bringing our deep-seated fears and internalized biases and prejudices into the light to take away the power they hold over us. As the old saying goes, "We are only as sick as the secrets we keep."

I am holding up a mirror for anyone willing to look. If you choose to look away, I can't blame you, nor will I hold it against you. You may not be ready yet. However, I encourage those of you who are brave enough to look to stare more closely into this mirror. Examine the blemishes and imperfections that go beyond the surface. Are you *really* willing to look at what's underneath? Are there thoughts and beliefs that you've been hiding from the world, or from yourself? If so, the next question is simple: what do you intend to *do* about it?

Bringing these thoughts and beliefs to the surface is not easy, and it does not feel cathartic. However, I challenge you to open up to these painful parts of yourself to better understand your identity as a White American man. Again, I cannot say this enough: we cannot begin the fight against structural and systemic racism and sexism if we are not first willing to address how they reside within us both collectively *and* as individuals.

This book is all about taking a hard look at ourselves—challenging us to own up to our individual racism and sexism, as well as our collective sense of power, entitlement, and supremacy. It also aims to assist in confronting our shame, defensiveness, and entrenched racial and gender insecurities by offering tangible methods for White American men to break our fraternal solidarity and begin the necessary and tough conversations about our role in upholding the status quo.

In this book, we will begin by examining how this oppressive system came to be in the first place, as well as the role we played, and still play, in upholding it. Next, we will explore many of the overt—as well as more subtle and insidious—effects of racism and misogyny on others and on ourselves. In the final portion of the book, we will focus on what we can do about racism and misogyny as White men, examining ways we can become less complicit in perpetuating oppression and how we can finally begin to heal from the pain and trauma that we collectively hold as White men.

To My Fellow White American Men,

If you haven't been formally welcomed, I would like to extend a special invitation to you that is reserved *only* for us. Whether or not we choose to accept the invitation, we are already executive-card-carrying members with benefits, perks, immunity—the works. I would like to welcome you to privilege. And not just any run-of-the-mill privilege. I'm talking about White American male privilege.

Look around you. It's in the very air we breathe and the water we drink. When we go to work, go for a jog, turn on the TV, tie our shoes, or go to the bathroom, we are benefiting from a deliberate and treacherous form of power that likely no other group of people has experienced in human history. Despite how it may seem or feel to us as individuals, our identity as White American males—and the privilege that entails—exudes from our very being, on display for all to see.

Many of our not-so-distant European male ancestors endured a few generations of "ritual hazing" to join this elite fraternity. And while they may not have become full-fledged members themselves, we as their successors are guaranteed entry for three simple reasons: the lack of melanin in our skin, our gender, and our place at the helm of Western imperialism.

Regardless of our political affiliation and religion or whether we enjoy fine wine and listen to NPR or drink PBR and watch NASCAR, *all* of us benefit from this unmerited status in one way or another. We are collectively in charge of the nation, able to write our own as well as other peoples' history, shaping the world in *our* image for *our* best interests.

However, our status and privilege have come at a cost beyond measure. We live in a self-created world full of violence, corruption, trauma, and mental illness. America is tearing itself apart at the seams while our entire planet is on the brink of an ecological collapse, and there seems to be no way out. How did we get here? And most importantly, what can we do about it?

For starters, it's time to address one of the primary causes of the current state of our world: the fear, anger, paranoia, and neuroses at the heart of White male supremacy.

At this point, you may already want to put down this book. Maybe the subject does not interest you, or you disagree with my above sentiment. Maybe you feel as if you already carry enough guilt and don't need more. Maybe you simply don't want to read yet another text that makes you feel like you are at fault for something your ancestors did. But I assure you that despite how educated in "progressive ideology" we believe ourselves to be, every single one of us (myself included) is sorely lacking in our understanding of how much our privilege both serves and harms us.

It is imperative that we learn not only *how* but also *why* we inherited our position and status in the first place. Otherwise, we are choosing to partake in an ongoing system of oppression and subjugation that benefits us. Privilege in the United States is a powerful weapon that was designed (yes, designed) to keep us in charge, by ensuring that power was hoarded among White men in America. Most of us don't fully grasp how powerful the "weapon" of privilege can be.

Our society is a bed of oppression on which we lie. It is filled with jagged metal springs of anger, fear, hatred, paranoia, and unresolved trauma. We hurt others with this self-imposed hierarchy, but we also hurt *ourselves*. It is ultimately in our own best interest to finally face these truths. This book is simply a chance to recognize and acknowledge a fact that many of us have known, lived according to, and created our lives around, yet often deny: As White men, we are the embodiment of privilege itself. We have been unfairly exalted to the highest level of our species based on the oppression of others, resulting in the loss of our own humanity. Until we own this painful truth, and begin working to change it, we will continue to be a part of the problem.

If we choose to let go of the corrosive forces of power and control, we stand a shot at finding out who we really are underneath our falsified racial and gender identity. More importantly, we stand a shot at healing some of the pain and trauma that is eroding the society we designed for ourselves at the expense of others. Otherwise, we are likely to face the catastrophic collapse of America.

It is time to face our current reality. It is time to let go of the anger, pain, and fear that comprise the heart of both toxic masculinity and Whiteness itself. Perhaps most importantly, it is time for us to begin to decenter White men as the self-proclaimed protagonists in the "Westernized" narrative that we have created.

PART 1

What Is Whiteness, and How Did It Begin?

CHAPTER 1

"Primary" Colors

WHITE = GOOD. BLACK = BAD.

Does the above statement seem racist? While it may seem like a gross overgeneralization, *Merriam-Webster's Dictionary*, one of America's most esteemed dictionaries, suggests otherwise with these two definitions: White is a symbol of moral purity.[2] Black means thoroughly sinister or evil.[3]

But just because some old-school dictionary uses these definitions doesn't mean it reflects how we all feel about race, right? After all, we are objective, thoughtful, and unique individuals who can form our own opinions.

Unfortunately, it's not that simple—especially when it comes to how we define the world around us. While it may seem implausible, American English, which most of us inherit, predisposes us to racism. Since we are marinated in an inherently racist language, we remain unable to see it unless we unpack the meaning of the words that define our culture.

• • •

WORDS CREATE WORLDS

Dictionaries exist to store our collective vocabulary and shared understanding of the world. Dictionaries do not create words, nor do they come up with the initial definitions; we do. They mirror how we feel about each thing we have labeled. In her book *Becoming Wise*, author and journalist Krista Tippet explains how the "words we use shape how we understand ourselves, how we interpret the world, how we treat others."[4] Ultimately, "words make worlds."

The problem is that once we have collectively agreed on the meaning of a particular word and inserted it into our shared terminology, we become trapped in a myopic feedback loop of preconceived biases. When we first define or learn terminology, it is nearly impossible to detach from the associations that already exist for every word we use to define the next; we are forced to construct our entire perspective of the world using only the vocabulary we have available to us, regardless of the associations those words already carry.

A simple example would be the word "fat." There is nothing inherently wrong with the word "fat," yet outside of the scientific community, this word, like so many others, carries stigmas, associations, and biases. But words like this only scratch the surface of how our language is weighed. Many words we take for granted don't even exist within other languages and cultures. These untranslatable words give us insight into our understanding of the world.

A powerful example of this is the word "poverty." While we currently discuss poverty as an ongoing crisis affecting Native American communities, before Europeans arrived, Indigenous Americans did not have a concept of what it meant.[5] Both the word and poverty itself did not exist to those who are now most impacted by it.

In *Decolonizing Wealth*, Native American author Edgar Villanueva describes a revealing interview with Dana Arviso, executive director of the Potlatch Fund. When discussing strategies to reduce poverty among Native Americans in the Cheyenne River Territory, the tribes explained to Arviso that the concept that someone could be "so isolated and so without any sort of a safety net or a family or a sense of kinship that they would be suffering from poverty"[6] was unfathomable to them. In fact, "the closest thing that they had as an explanation for poverty was 'to be without family.'" This speaks volumes about Western society and our familial values and demonstrates just how subjective our language and conceptual understanding can be.

How does this all apply to race? Essentially, our subjective understanding of the world is exemplified by the *words* we currently use to describe skin color—namely black, white, and brown.

When it comes specifically to race, the terminology we have chosen/been provided with sets the stage for how we are likely to feel about the people who fit into the categories created by those who came before. In an article about the power of language and colonialism, Robin Kimmerer, environmental professor and member of the Citizen Potawatomi Nation, describes how "many linguists and psychologists agree that language reveals unconscious cultural assumptions and exerts some influence over patterns of thought."[7] To see how this plays out when it comes to race, let's take a look at a few examples of the definitions of "white" and "black." While we are at it, let's just peek at "brown" and see what that tells us as well.

• • •

WHITE = GOOD

A copy of *Merriam-Webster's Dictionary* provides us with myriad definitions for the word "white." And all of them are extremely positive. On the surface, many of these definitions may feel sterile and innocuous. However, when we dig deeper, inevitable biases present themselves.

Here is the first example: "Free from color"; "Of the color of milk or fresh snow"; "synonyms: colorless, unpigmented, bleached, natural."[*] According to *Merriam-Webster*, my skin resembles the "color of milk

---

[*] It should be noted that these definitions, examples, and synonyms were still in print as of early 2020. However, since publishing this book, Merriam-Webster has been editing a number of their definitions that pertain to race—most likely in response to the changing political climate and the Black Lives Matter movement. This further proves the point about the impact of word associations and biases. The term "natural" was omitted in the late 2020 version of Merriam-Webster Online. But why was "natural" there in the first place?

or fresh snow." These are certainly flattering descriptors. Let us look at by far the most revealing bias: the word "natural" is listed as a synonym for "white." What exactly about the color white is inherently considered natural? Can we comfortably say that snow, vanilla ice cream, milk, or the inside of an Oreo are "natural" colored?

One can only make sense of this strange correlation when used in the context of race. White is considered a "natural" or "neutral" skin color, implying that any other skin color is unnatural. If that seems like a stretch, try describing the two colors of an Oreo as "natural" and "black."

Okay, next definitions: "Belonging to or denoting a human group having light-colored skin (chiefly used of peoples of European extraction)"; "of, relating to, characteristic of, or consisting of White people or their culture"; "synonyms: Caucasian, European." "From the former stereotypical association of good character with Northern European descent: Marked by upright fairness. [Example:] That's mighty white of you."

I think that my favorite part of the definition would have to be the word "former," as if adding that single word somehow asserts or justifies that this assumption/association only existed in the past. But *Merriam-Webster* does not stop there: "Free from spot or blemish: such as . . . free from moral impurity: innocent . . . a symbol of purity. [Example:] the pure White heart of the devout; not intended to cause harm. [Example:] a White lie; White magic; favorable; fortunate. [Example:] One of the white days of his life—Sir Walter Scott."[8]

Notice any positive biases that might stem from our understanding of the word "white"? My skin color is the very "symbol of purity." And, of course, who doesn't fondly recall those "white days of our lives"? Or maybe Sir Walter Scott was simply referencing the almost all-White cast of the infamous television soap opera *Days of Our Lives*?

At this point, you might be thinking, *Okay, I get it! Enough already!* Or perhaps you are not convinced that this means anything about how we perceive race. I don't blame you. But stay with me here because without looking at the definition of the other two words, "black" and "brown," we are not able to truly see how "white" holds such power in our culture. Pun intended.

Recognizing that most of us are prone to seeing binaries, the next set of definitions should not be surprising.

● ● ●

BLACK = BAD

Let's start off with a bang, shall we?

The definition: "of the color black"; "[examples:] a black sweater . . . a black dog."

Interesting how the search for "white" did not use a dog in the first example of the word. Not to mention that dogs and sweaters are not inherently black. So how on earth does referring to two things that often are not black help someone picture the color black? That's like trying to teach a child the color red by describing a red ball without providing a picture. Couldn't they have used crows, the night sky, coal, or any other example that is actually black?

Okay, on to the next definition: "of or relating to any of various population groups having dark pigmentation of the skin . . . of or relating to the African American people or their culture"; "[examples:] Black Americans; black literature; a black college; Black pride; Black studies."

There is certainly a lot to unpack here. It is worth noting that the very fact that some colleges define themselves as "Black colleges" derives from that fact that other colleges were (and mostly still are) primarily for White people; just as "Black literature" implies that most literature in our country is predominantly for White people.

I guess both statements should be obvious considering how for most of our country's history, almost everything catered to White people. Just imagine for a second that you are trying to figure out what college to attend, and you must select among "White colleges" (what most elite universities were intended to be up until recently). Or imagine that you walk into a library and see a section labeled "White literature." In this instance, one could claim that "White" is already implied when we look across the span of America's authors, especially when considering that between 1950 and 2018, White authors accounted for 95 percent of all American fiction books.[9]

The next definition is also intriguing: "Typical or representative of the most readily perceived characteristics of Black culture; [example:] trying to sound Black."

By default, doesn't that mean that there is also such a thing as trying to sound White? If you don't know what I'm talking about, think about a time when you've called a customer-support line and spoken with a Mark, Tom, or Nancy at a call center somewhere in South Asia. These individuals have painstakingly learned to speak with a more "American-sounding" accent—in a process known as accent reduction or accent neutralization training—just so that we feel more at ease talking to them.[10] In a sense, it's easiest to recognize what it means to "sound White" when we are provided with obvious examples of what Whiteness does not sound like.

At this point, we begin to see a marked shift in the definition of black. We go from color and culture to characteristics. The subsequent definitions are not exactly flattering of blackness: "distorted or darkened by anger; [example:] his face was black with rage."

When does someone's face ever become "black with rage"? If anything, faces like mine become a shade of pink or red. Why use a useless metaphorical example linking "black" with "rage" in the first place?

The next definition is "of propaganda: conducted so as to appear to originate within an enemy country and designed to weaken enemy morale . . . characterized by or connected with the use of black propaganda"; then "characterized by hostility or angry discontent: sullen"; "[example:] black resentment filled his heart."

Is it worth pointing out that this last example has an unintended double meaning given much of White America's historical (and arguably current) sentiment toward Black folks (i.e., resentment)?

Alas, the next few definitions get darker: "Distorted or darkened by anger"; "Indicative of condemnation or discredit"; "[example:] got a black mark for being late"; "Dirty; Soiled"; "[example:] hands black with grime"; "Thoroughly sinister or evil: wicked"; "Connected with or invoking the supernatural and especially the devil"; "[example:] black magic; the black arts"; "Characterized by grim, distorted, or grotesque . . . [example:] black humor."

These definitions are abysmal. And we wonder why we have so many ingrained associations around White people versus Black people. Also, as a side note, I'm pretty sure that *Merriam-Webster* and I differ on our understanding of what black humor means. But going back to my earlier point, from merely seeing these definitions in a vacuum, it would be logical to assume that an alien species encountering our dictionary for the first time would come to the obvious conclusion that everything white is good, whereas everything black is bad.

Oddly, "brown" seems to be a little hard to pin down. It starts out promisingly, then quickly takes a turn for the worse.

• • •

BROWN = APPARENTLY NOT WORTH DISCUSSING IN DETAIL

Let's move on to our last word. I guess I should say last *and* least because, based on this definition, it is the least discussed. This is literally the only thing *Merriam-Webster* has to say about the adjective "brown": "Of the color brown"; "especially: of dark or tanned complexion"; "Any of a group of colors between red and yellow in hue, of medium to low lightness, and of moderate to low saturation"; "A brown-skinned person"; "brown trout."

And that is all *Merriam-Webster* wrote. Four definitions to describe the entirety of the word "brown"—one of which just provides a link to an invasive European fish. It's like "brown" was given the "honorable mention" award in the double entendre word Olympics. Fortunately, when I scrolled all the way down to the bottom of the page, there was an English-language learner's definition: "Having a color like coffee or chocolate."

I can't help but think that those are two of the best descriptors anyone could have ever produced. After all, who doesn't like coffee or chocolate? But then I found the examples of brown used in a sentence, and true to form, "brown" quickly proved its place in the negative-bias bin: "Example of brown used in a sentence: Adjective— workers whose backs are *brown* from long hours in the sun."[11]

People with brown backs working long hours in the sun. Hmm, nothing comes to mind . . . oh, except for migrant laborers, slavery, and people of color being forced to do backbreaking labor.

Seriously, Merriam-Webster? You almost redeemed yourself with "coffee and chocolate," and then you steered the ship right back toward the giant racist iceberg!

• • •

"CREATING" MEANING

Now that we have unpacked some of these bias-loaded terms, it is time to examine whether we can consciously change some of these predetermined negative associations embedded within our terminology.

Why can't we just change the definition of existing words to make them more positive? Or what about creating novel words to describe old concepts, as Crayola and Band-Aid did in rebranding "flesh-colored" crayons and bandages? Unfortunately, it's not that simple. While new words are invented all the time, undoing the negative meaning of already established words is much less common, if not impossible. The converse does not hold true; when it comes to injecting negative meanings into previously benign or positive words, it only takes a mutual agreement or shared experience to "hijack" a meaning and make it into something harmful. Case in point, Isis used to be an Egyptian goddess. Or take the word "f*ggot"—originally meant to indicate a bundle or bunch (of sticks).[12]

The term "f*ggot" has now become charged with such a level of animosity that outside of its use within the gay community, people often cringe when they hear it. *I am censoring the word here to try to avoid upsetting my readers*. Moreover, we have given this word the power to brand a person in a way that can compromise their status, their livelihood, and their safety.

But unlike this kind of standalone word, the words "black" and "white" are integral to our shared understanding of the world around us—and we can't simply change their meaning. This unfortunately means that the word "black" has rarely, if ever, been used in a positive context.

A few basic examples:

- "A black cloud above my head"
- "Blackness in his heart"
- "The Black Plague"
- "A black mark"
- "Pitch black"
- "Black market"
- "Black magic"
- "Blackmail"
- "Black skin"

Did that last one throw you off? If you believe you were able to dismiss the negative connotation solely for the "black skin" example, I challenge you to dig a little deeper. Even if you did find yourself offended by it, that was likely a secondary reaction. But it's not your fault; I intentionally built upon negative associations already in place to slip what should have been a benign example into your unconscious. This is what happens to us every day.

For over three centuries, White people have been deliberately conditioned to form negative biases and prejudices toward "black." We cannot collectively or individually turn this conditioning on or off at will for the same reason that we cannot simply redefine the word "black" to make it mean something more positive. Often unconsciously, we have an inherently unfavorable view of everything that falls within that category, people included.

Sadly, and perhaps more concerning, the same is true for our understanding of the word "white." Only, in this case, we have been conditioned to see it as a representation of something both positive and superior. In our culture, it has been deemed the very symbol of purity. Moreover, when our dictionaries reinforce this skewed understanding of ourselves as well as those around us, we become susceptible to manipulation. As described by a 2018 article, "The Nationalist Roots of *Merriam-Webster's Dictionary*," published in the *Paris Review*,

> Nearly two centuries later [after the publication of Webster's dictionary], at a time when truth is increasingly undervalued and American exceptionalism is widely embraced, the dictionary takes on fresh significance. Words, like the dictionaries that define them, have little intrinsic meaning. Those in power can wield them as an instrument for untruthful, or even tyrannical, ends. In a time of fake news and alternative facts, the usage of even simple words can serve to ensnare the listener rather than to educate him.[13]

Our definitions and understanding of the terms "white" and "black" ensure that we have an "us versus them" mentality. While the other colors that fall within this spectrum also elicit fear and hatred for many White folks, this still is a black-and-white matter on a more fundamental level.

We have undeniably been conditioned to see ourselves in the word "white." It is not a coincidence that we chose this word to collectively define ourselves over three centuries ago. One particular definition enshrined in America's most prestigious dictionary confirms this, so I will return to it: "free from spot or blemish . . . free from moral impurity: innocent . . . a symbol of purity."[14] This definition encapsulates our conflated understanding of ourselves.

When it comes to understanding how our shared vocabulary upholds biases, those who define our words must also be understood. In this case, one man single-handedly took it upon himself to create a standardized form of American English, beginning in the late eighteenth century: Noah Webster.

• • •

WEBSTER DEFINES AMERICA

Noah Webster had perhaps the single greatest influence on American English of any person in US history. He was a staunch nationalist who genuinely believed that it was his ordained mission to "purify" the English language, encouraged by none other than God himself.[15]

Yet Noah Webster wasn't a mere religious zealot who randomly decided to write a dictionary. Some scholars have referred to him as the "father of American scholarship and education."[16] Born in 1758, Webster came from a family of little wealth and suffered a series of significant failures and setbacks in his early career as a teacher and a writer. However, after graduating from Yale in 1778, he eventually rose among the ranks of the White men who were shaping the early-American colonies.

Webster became well connected and influential, corresponding with the likes of George Washington, Benjamin Franklin, and Alexander Hamilton.[17] He became obsessed with America's growing power as a nation and believed the United States to be a successor to the Roman and Greek empires. As part of his staunch nationalistic vision, he sought to create a version of the English language that would surpass that of England.

According to the *Paris Review* article on Webster's nationalist roots, "Webster's dream of American exceptionalism underscores how the act of making a dictionary is by its very nature political, dictating the ways in which people communicate. Webster's particular political agenda was an authoritarian one, and it veered into a total intolerance of difference."[18] A self-prescribed language expert, Webster detested all dialects that did not mirror that of his prominent Yale counterparts. He denounced pronunciation in the American South as "repugnant" and referred to their schools as "disgraceful" for teaching such an inferior form of English.

While it would be easy to excuse Webster as a product of his time, his sharp criticisms of any part of American culture that he didn't like led one of his modern-day biographers, Joshua Kendall, to call him "one of the most politically incorrect men alive,"[19] comparing him to former Fox News anchor Sean Hannity.

Webster believed he was working to preserve America's fragile union. One of his greatest fears was that the differences in dialects and influence of other languages would "corrupt the national language" and further fragment the nation. He saw his work as vital to uphold not just an identity of language but also, more importantly, preserving an identity based on shared ideology.[20] Webster's understanding of America's *shared* identity did not factor in anyone of non-European descent. This can be seen clearly in his nonchalant definition of a plantation as a farm "where the labor is performed by slaves."[21]

While it may seem as if most of Webster's work is now obsolete, written over by the ensuing centuries, he created some of America's most influential history and literacy textbooks. Kendall, despite his disdain for the man, referred to Webster as "the forgotten founding father,"[22] arguing that what the authors of the Constitution did for American politics, Webster did for American education.

First published in 1828 and selling nearly 100 million copies throughout the 1800s, (second only to the Bible itself),[23] Webster's seminal textbook, *A Grammatical Institute of the English Language*, taught all White American children the fundamentals of literacy. It remained *the* defining text in all American schools for over 100 years.[24]

Building off his success, Webster then authored one of America's first history textbooks, published in 1832. As a born-again Christian and Bible literalist, Webster wove religion seamlessly into American history. In one of the very first chapters, Webster describes in physical detail what he presumes to be the most accurate depictions of the "varieties" of the different types of descendants of Adam and Eve. You can probably guess which "variety" he favored.

At best, his anthropological work is disturbing. Webster describes the swollen lips, outwardly bent legs, and protruding heels of Africans. He also describes "Hindoos . . . [as] wrinkled at thirty years of age"[25] as well as "cowardly and effeminate." When it came to his own kind, he indulged in quite a bit of self-flattery. Besides referring to himself as a member of the "most distinguished variety of men," he also highlights the perfect "symmetry of the body, the strength of the limbs, the vigor of understanding, and . . . [Europeans'] improvements in science and the arts."[26] Not to mention that in Webster's historical account of the United States, he "somehow" ignored the abolitionist movement entirely and explicitly believed that Africans didn't have a history worth discussing.[27]

Nonetheless, on the "About Us" page of their own website, Merriam-Webster Online shows reverence for his invaluable contributions to American society by referring to this "great man's"[28] death in 1843. The Noah Webster House and Museum (located at Webster's house of birth) echoes this sentiment, describing him as "an American hero";[29] never mind that he was driven by an elitist, narcissistic attitude, hell-bent on shaping all of American culture to fit his perfect vision.

While Webster may have been responsible for "defining" nineteenth and twentieth-century America, many are now trying to undo the harm of the labels that have shaped our society. One of the common approaches to fixing this "baked-in bias" is to try to either get rid of or "fix" the words themselves. However, this often doesn't go as planned.

• • •

POLITICALLY CORRECT(ING) LABELS

In the twenty-first century "politically correct" has become a go-to phrase in many conversations about race. However, political correctness doesn't encapsulate the whole story when it comes to the labels we use for ourselves or others (not to mention what *they* want to be called). Despite our best attempts to be "culturally sensitive," there remains a lot of confusion about what White folks can and can't say. This hesitation undeniably comes from a place of discomfort and fear. While it may seem that the only driving force here is a desire not to offend, there is often a more substantial underlying reason: our own egos. Simply put, self-described progressive White Americans (like me) can become fanatical about not wanting to appear ignorant, or worse, unknowingly racist.

The term "politically correct" has essentially become a euphemism for "not offensive to anyone in any way, shape, or form." Consequently, many of us progressive White folks go about our lives afraid of tripping over our own verbal shoelaces. Despite our best efforts, we often miss certain social cues while reading *way* too far into others. Many of us also have a knack for making interactions more awkward and forced than they need to be, by censoring ourselves and condescendingly correcting our peers.

Still others roam about with a self-appointed savior-complex badge that reads "PC Police," believing it is our sworn duty to protect all BIPOC folks from those "other" White people. However, in these instances, there is typically a motive other than wanting to legitimately "protect" BIPOC folks. We want to seem like the cool White people who already "get it" and don't have to be educated about the injustices people of color continuously experience, unlike all those other White people who (we believe) need to be educated by us.

Consequently, each time we say something that offends someone, rather than simply acknowledging and owning our impact, apologizing, and moving on, the faux pas becomes a crippling blow to our ego as we are confronted by our own ignorance and arrogance.

You might be asking yourself, *So what should we call other people so that I don't offend them?* Not surprisingly, this is something I struggled with in writing this book.

Welcome to the world of socially constructed categorization. There isn't a simple answer to such a complicated question. Just as people of color are not a monolith, there is no one term that everyone wants to be called. Some terms are certainly more universally accepted than others, but if we aren't brave enough to ask *individuals* how they would like to be addressed, we will continue to flounder in social situations.

I must admit, though, that I love watching politically correct White people get tongue-tied while trying to describe Black people who don't live in the United States. Terms like African Swedish or Black Scottish just don't have the same ring to them, do they?

Regardless of what terms currently feel safest, comfortable, or normal, as racial categories shift and evolve, ultimately so will the terms by which we try to grapple with these kaleidoscopic racial identities we have unleashed on the world. This leaves us with an interesting paradox. While most terms used to label people based solely on their color have become defunct (due primarily to their lack of political correctness), one term has remained essentially untouched since it was first conceived over three centuries ago: "White." This is far from an accident.

By calling *our* racial category into question, we force ourselves to face the inherently oppressive label that defines us both as individuals and as a collective. The continued use of the term "White" has allowed us to sustain and validate our self-appointed place within society, at the apex of humankind.

Yet for us to fully understand this, we must look at how this word came to define our racial identity in the first place. This isn't about etymology or Webster's attempts to define America. What we need to examine is not only how but also when and why we started calling ourselves White. Similarly, we must look at how this term was coupled with gender to ensure that one group acquired the indisputable position of power in this country: White men.

CHAPTER 2

"US" Versus Them: The Story of Whiteness

WHEN IT COMES to the United States and the formation of the "New World," the demand for labor created race as we know it today. Or as Suzanne Plihcik, cofounder of the Racial Equity Institute, puts it, "The story of race is the story of labor."[30] Consequently, the story of slavery in America is also the story of race, which was created for one purpose: to justify slavery.

Slavery did not occur because of race or racism. The creation of race served as the basis for legalized human exploitation and subjugation, and the two became inescapably intertwined throughout the American colonies.

Let's get one thing clear before we go any further: Whiteness is not simply a racial identity. By design, it is a social and political designation rooted in power and the deliberate, sanctioned oppression of non-Whites.

• • •

A "WHITE" LIE

The version of American history that I learned in school was the one in which the "good guys" (America) won, and now democracy is spreading and setting everyone else free. Even at an early age, I could tell that a big part of the story was missing. However, without the internet at my fingertips to discover how much had been deliberately omitted from our textbooks, I found American history incredibly boring. It read like a watered-down epic full of clichés, idealism and glory, patriotism and valor, and grit and survival.

The portion of the textbook covering slavery in America was typically a one-off chapter, making it seem like it was just a big mistake and we had learned our lesson. The mass genocide of Indigenous peoples was more like an accidental byproduct of the "heroic" White expansion to the West—not to mention that it was completely overshadowed by the story of Pocahontas (a "love story") and Lewis and Clark (a "heroic adventure"), both of which involved the kidnapping and rape of underage girls. The first was a blatant case of child abduction (Pocahontas, whose real name was Amonute, was between nine and eleven years old).[31] The second, rather than a daring adventure of rugged men in coonskin caps, was a military-sponsored mission.[32] During the arduous journey, men were court-martialed and severely punished for not wearing uniforms, going AWOL, or not abiding by strict discipline.[33] The mission was guided in part by a teenager making the best of a shitty situation: Sacagawea had been kidnapped, then sold (or acquired through gambling) and forced into a nonconsensual marriage by a man who was then hired as a guide by Lewis and Clark.[34]

Of course, who could forget the fictionalized holiday about White people and "Indians" peacefully sitting at a long table, eating an oversized pheasant and some squash together. Thanksgiving has become an occasion on which present-day White folks can unapologetically let go of our guilt and justify an atrocious genocide by highlighting a single civil meal between White men and Native Americans that may not have occurred in the first place. The traced hand of a young child to create a turkey, alongside precious little cutout pilgrims and adorable "Indians," still seems to be a staple of American "refrigerator art." Never mind that these "Indians" are often depicted wearing the feathered headdresses of the American Plains tribes, which are located over a thousand miles away from the Atlantic shores.

Alas, although more White Americans have wakened to the fictionalized aspects of this holiday, we now just say Thanksgiving is a chance to spend time with family, watch football, be grateful, and to stuff ourselves silly—never mind the genocide part.

Columbus, the *Mayflower*, the Boston Tea Party, the Revolutionary War, and the Civil War (where the non-racist good guys from the North freed the poor slaves) are still cast in a positive light in our schools. It's almost like we feel this pressing need to teach the "American Dream" before teaching the "American reality"—as if it's as innocuous as avoiding telling children that Santa Claus is not real. But teaching a deliberately concocted lie about how our nation became great comes at an incalculable cost.

What we White people (White men in particular) learn in our childhood serves as the foundation for understanding the world and our "rightful" place within it. So, when we teach White kids the whitewashed version of the American story, we further establish a sense of White pride and Manifest Destiny.

Our entire history gets condensed into this:

Some bad stuff was going on in Europe, so our ancestors left and came here to be free. But the bad guys in Europe still wanted to be in charge, and they treated us badly, so we bravely fought a war against them. A little bit later, there were some racist bad guys in the South doing mean things to other people and forcing them to be slaves because of the color of their skin. So, the not-racist good guys from the North had to fight another war against the mean Southern guys to make sure that the slaves were set free.

Once things settled down a bit, many people decided to get into big wagons and go west to "undiscovered" lands and start happy new lives. They bravely fought against the Indians and

Mexicans who tried to stop them on their perilous journey. They eventually succeeded, and America became one big, united country.

Much later, some other racist bad guys—again, mostly in the South—decided they still didn't want some people to be free, and so Martin Luther King Jr. made important speeches and convinced them, and now everyone is really free. Today America is the best country in the world, and all the other countries look up to us because we let every citizen vote!

The end.

However, that version of American history cannot be further from the truth.

• • •

SLAVERY "EVOLVES" IN AMERICA

While 1776 marks the official birth of our nation, 1619 marks the beginning of the United States' participation in a globalized empire that allowed White American males to seize power on an unprecedented scale for centuries to come.

By this point the Portuguese and the Spanish had been engaged in the transatlantic slave trade for nearly a century—transporting kidnapped Africans from West Central Africa to mines and plantations that had been set up on the Caribbean Islands. These Africans were brought in on ships by the hundreds to replace the Indigenous people who had nearly died off from brutal work conditions and disease.[35]

In the summer of 1619, one of those ships, the *San Juan Bautista*, was on its way to Vera Cruz, Mexico, carrying 350 captured Africans. It was attacked by two British privateer ships: the *White Lion* and the *Treasurer*. At that time, British privateering was a form of legally sanctioned piracy, as means of acquiring more wealth.[36]

After robbing the *San Juan Bautista* of somewhere between fifty and sixty Africans, the *White Lion* and the *Treasurer* set sail northward. On August 20, 1619, the *White Lion*, in desperate need of supplies, arrived at a port in the British colony of Point Comfort, Virginia. A simple exchange was made: twenty human beings unwillingly disembarked the vessel to be sold as property in exchange for basic supplies so that the ship could make its return voyage to Europe. While these were certainly not the first Africans to be purchased or enslaved, this particular transaction is marked as the preliminary exchange in what became America's involvement in the transatlantic slave trade.[37] However, it would take decades for chattel slavery (i.e., slavery in which a person of color can legally be considered property) to become the primary economic backbone of the early colonies.

Prior to the advent of outright enslavement, indentured servitude was the foundation on which America began building its fledgling labor force. Most Europeans arriving in America did not have enough money to finance their own voyages or purchase their own land. But labor was in high demand, so a system was designed in which wealthy land or business owners, either in Europe or in the new colonies, would pay for the trip in exchange for a set term of servitude once the travelers arrived. These "subsidized laborers" were expected to work for a designated length of time to pay back the cost of their voyage.

Many of them agreed to longer contracts so that they could earn a land grant as additional compensation for their servitude. While indentured servitude was fraught with corruption, exploitation, and discriminatory practices, the overall system still functioned based on contracts and predetermined labor agreements.

This system was so effective that somewhere between one- and two-thirds of the entire population in the colonies during the fifteenth through seventeenth centuries consisted of indentured servants from Europe.[38] Nevertheless, while Europeans made up the bulk of the labor force, "imported" Africans quickly became an indispensable component of the labor needed to build the colonies.

During the early 1600s, while many Africans were purchased as slaves from the Portuguese and Spanish, a large number of African Americans in the colonies were provided with the same terms of indentured servitude as their European counterparts. They worked side by side in the fields, sometimes even alongside their masters.[39] Improbable as it may seem, after completing their requirement of servitude, many Africans were granted basic rights, land, and their freedom.[40] Despite their forced servitude, they often became landowners themselves, and some even built sizable wealth.

At that time, any man who was "free of indenture faced the same opportunities as a matter of law,"[41] describes author and historian Jacqueline Battalora. "Free men of African descent could own servants or slaves[,] . . . they could vote[,] . . . [and] they could marry persons of the opposite sex[,] . . . regardless of national origin. In fact, marriages between men of African descent and women of British descent were not uncommon at all." Consequently, many African Americans in the early 1600s received far better treatment and more liberties than their successors would over the next three centuries.

Of course, unlike most of their European counterparts, these early African captives did not have a choice in coming to America, and in addition to being stripped away from their families, many faced significant obstacles when it came to forced assimilation once their terms of servitude ended. Not to mention that converting to Christianity was a nonnegotiable requirement to receive freedom from servitude.⁴² This was in part because many British colonists were against enslaving practicing Christians. However, that would soon change.

Wealthy European colonists ultimately recognized that the system of indentured servitude could not meet the needs of the growing colonies. Faced with a soaring labor demand to keep up with the shifting industrialized economy in the North and the gluttonous demand for cotton and other essential commodities, the transition to outright slavery became essential. With the "onslaught" of African immigrants, the cost of labor was artificially driven down, and providing livable wages for indentured servants became impossible. As more ships of captured Africans arrived, the balance of power shifted, and the practice of chattel slavery took root in the colonies.

• • •

A POPULATION PARADOX

From an economic standpoint, indentured servitude of captured Africans didn't make sense. Why go through all the trouble of kidnapping, trafficking, and forcing people to work for a few years if they were just going to be set free afterward? Many wealthy landowners and businessmen saw this as a waste of potential unlimited free labor. Moreover, the desire to provide freed Africans with land that could otherwise be profitable to European colonists quickly diminished. Aside from the economic motives for slavery, from a societal and political standpoint, indentured servitude was unsustainable and considered self-destructive by the wealthy elite.

An unavoidable cycle was created. More Africans brought to America meant additional free Africans once their terms of servitude ended. This becomes even more significant when taking into account that once an African servant was granted freedom, all of their descendants were automatically born free (as long as they were Christian), creating an exponentially growing population of free Americans of African ancestry. The higher the demand for labor, the higher the number of free Africans and Black Americans there would be in the colonies.

This growing "other" population concerned wealthy European colonists. Left unchecked, freed Africans could potentially surpass the number of European colonists. Many colonists simply could not accept a society in which people of African ancestry were allowed to hold any amount of land, wealth, or power. With entire ships jammed full of captive Africans consistently arriving in the newly forming colonies, a different labor structure would be required to ensure that European colonists unequivocally maintained the balance of power in their favor.

• • •

(LEGALLY) A SLAVE FOREVER

In 1640, three indentured servants working in Virginia became fed up with servitude and decided to run away. And they lived happily ever after—except that they were immediately captured and returned to their "rightful master." When brought before a judge, the first two were given four additional years of servitude—a moderate sentence. The third wasn't quite so lucky and was sentenced to perpetual servitude. Why? Because John Punch didn't share the same ancestry as his two runaway companions. His dark complexion unfairly landed him a life of "labor without parole."

John Punch is arguably the first American to become a victim of legally sanctioned permanent enslavement in the United States. Looks like discriminatory sentencing goes back quite a ways; Black Americans still face substantially harsher sentencing than their White counterparts for the exact same crimes.[43]

• • •

WHO'S YOUR ~~DADDY~~ MOMMY

Judges were not the only ones drawing up the terms of what became the transatlantic slave trade. Unlike today's government, which has multiple branches and institutions, the pseudonational colonial government consisted primarily of members of one house. The House of Burgesses was the meeting place of our first "democratically elected" and the longest-running lawmaking body in America: the Virginia General Assembly, established in 1619.[44] When it came to creating laws and establishing who was granted what rights within the colonies, this was the institution to which most deferred.

Now, one particular member of the House of Burgesses had fathered a child, Elizabeth Key, with an enslaved African woman; of course, he was not the only White guy in that body of lawmakers who had forced himself upon a Black woman and then took zero responsibility for his own child. As any reasonable father who doesn't care would do, plantation owner Thomas Key decided to make a "reasonable" compromise. After some deliberation, he decided that his own daughter should be placed into indentured servitude for the first fifteen years of her life and then be set free. And the 1630 "Crappy American Father of the Year Award" goes to—drumroll, please—Thomas Key, a man who thought that fifteen years of forced, backbreaking labor was a fair start for his own daughter!

Long story short, Elizabeth Key's father thankfully died in 1636, and her racist owner (John Mottram) kicked the bucket about twenty years later. Having served well beyond the term of her contract, Elizabeth requested freedom for her young son and herself. However, Mottram's heirs decided that Key and her young son were no longer indentured servants but rather slaves that officially belonged to the Mottram Estate.[45]

Elizabeth wasn't about to back down. A fierce, educated woman, Elizabeth was in a relationship and had a child with William Greensted, one of Mottram's former European indentured servants, who was now practicing law. With his help, Elizabeth sued her owner for her and her son's freedom and won the case. She subsequently lost her case in the court of appeals but was not deterred. She took her plight to the Virginia General Assembly, and in 1656, they decreed that "Elizabeth ought to be free and that her last Master should give her Corn and Clothes and give her satisfaction for the time she hath served longer than She ought to have done."[46] Take that, greedy racist Mottrams!

But wait, there's more. As is the case with most trials where a person of color goes up against a powerful White entity, this story has a far from happy ending. While Elizabeth successfully gained her deserved freedom, this trial had significant unforeseen consequences. A bunch of old White dudes were not happy that a person of color—and a woman, at that—had bested them!

Elizabeth's release had been granted on the grounds that she was both a practicing Christian and the daughter of a man with European ancestry. The Virginia General Assembly stated, "By the Common Law the Child of a Woman slave begot by a freeman ought to be free. That she hath been long since Christened."[47] So, up until that point, if you had any African ancestry, the two big questions to establish your status as a servant, slave, or free person were "Who's your daddy?" and "Do you accept Jesus Christ as your Lord and Savior?" As long as your answers to these two questions were "A man with pale skin" and "Amen! Hallelujah!" nobody could *legally* keep you as a slave. After all, it was clearly unethical to enslave a practicing Christian, particularly one that had a European father— because that goes against God's will. Obviously.

Alas, the wealthy elite decided to reinvent God's will and make a few simple changes that would have profound consequences for every person of African descent from that point forward. After several other slaves used the same appeal to try to gain their freedom from lifelong servitude, plantation owners took action and appealed to the Virginia Assembly.

In 1662, the assembly did an about-face and with the swipe of the pen surreptitiously changed the question from "Who's your daddy?" to "Who's your mommy?" By simply declaring that "Negro womens['] children [are now] to serve according to the condition of the mother,"[48] every child born to a woman of *any* degree of African descent was now automatically a slave, regardless of who the father was.

A lot of free labor was created by simply switching the word "father" to "mother." The change piqued the interest of many wealthy landowners of European descent, who realized that there was now a simple way to bypass indentured servitude altogether to build their wealth. Rape and forced "breeding" became a guaranteed means of creating an unlimited source of free labor; never mind that these men were enslaving their own children!

But there was still one loophole that needed to be closed: how to go about enslaving Christians. After all, most plantation owners wanted their slaves to be Christian (primarily to assimilate them and make them more "docile"); however, by the very act of baptizing them, the owners stood the risk of someday having to set those Christian slaves free.

The Virginia Assembly quickly put fears to rest when they passed a subsequent law in 1667 that abolished the Christian loophole. The new law stated that "the conferring of baptism does not alter the condition of the person as to his bondage or freedom."[49] The Virginia Assembly explicitly noted that slaves were baptized only "by the charity and piety of their owners" and that "now freed from this doubt, [these owners] may more carefully endeavor the propagation of Christianity." In other words, blessed be these powerful men, who so generously spread Christianity among their "faithful" servants.

• • •

FEAR OF POWER AND THE POWER OF FEAR

It could be argued that there were two primary defining elements in the creation of both slavery and race—power and fear. As is the case now, back during colonial times, the wealthy elite wanted to take any actions necessary to increase and secure their own power. Yet for their power to be protected, they had a big problem to solve.

To put it simply, the problem was that there were a whole bunch of pissed-off European colonists who did not like the lopsided power structure one bit. Obviously, those people were not the ones living on huge estates, sleeping in posh beds, eating with silver cutlery, and attending lavish parties.[50] To these folks, the colonies still reeked of European aristocracy.

The heroic version of American history that we like to teach students describes how all the early settlers worked together to keep the colonies alive, and that our Founding Fathers rolled up their sleeves along with the rest of them. But wealth was siphoned into the pockets of the rich, with the top 10 percent possessing nearly 60 percent of the total income.[51] Meanwhile, many European colonists, most of whom had no voting rights because they possessed no land, struggled to keep food on the table and a roof over their heads.

For most of our ancestors, colonial America was not a great place to live. If we were living back then, most of us would have toiled our lives away with the meager promise that someday, we might possess a smidgen of land and possibly "free laborers" of our own. Inequality has always been the driving force of both politics and economics in America.[52] Indentured servants were not allowed to marry, and any woman unfortunate enough to get pregnant during her term of servitude was automatically given an additional seven to nine years of indentured status.[53]

Understandably, the countless human beings living under these terrible labor conditions often became restless and angry, and the elite constantly worried that their underlings would revolt. Their concerns were not without merit; those they were exploiting vastly outnumbered them. Small revolts and uprisings were a regular occurrence in the early colonies, and skin color was secondary when it came to workers' rights. Whether day laborers, farm workers, builders, or seamstresses, workers of all colors and genders banded together and instigated intense, if not outright violent, protests against their overlords.

One such uprising stands out among others—because the elites seized it as an opportunity to create America's first distinct racial divide.

• • •

BACON FRIGHTENS THE ELITE

In September 1676, an angry mob burned Jamestown to the ground, and the governor barely escaped with his life. Nathaniel Bacon was the man at the front of the charge.

A wealthy young aristocrat with significant flaws and blatant prejudices, Bacon was not against taking up arms with people of African ancestry. His hatred was directed toward the "real enemies" of early America: those "pesky Indians"! An instigating circumstance in the rebellion itself was that Bacon was denied a commission by Jamestown's elite for his "noble attempts" to drive out the savages.[54] I will spare you the details about him and his traitorous men slaughtering an allied Native American force that had previously helped Bacon capture another, more "hostile" tribe. Suffice it to say, this dude is anything but an American hero. A selfish, stubborn mass murderer would be a more fitting title.

I do not profess to be a history teacher, and many other precipitating events and causes (e.g., trade disputes, financial misfortunes, policy disagreements, etc.) ultimately led to this rebellion. But the reason it began isn't all that important in the context of defining race; the lasting effects of this rebellion are what matter most.

Bacon's Rebellion created significant concern among the wealthy elite, especially because it sent a governor fleeing from his own town. They recognized the tenuousness of this exploitative system and knew that without taking drastic action, the early colonies would likely unravel, and they themselves might be in danger. As Professor Chenjerai Kumanyika—journalist, scholar, and collaborator on the NPR series *Seeing White*—put it, the elite feared that Bacon had demonstrated a successful "multi-racial rebellion that showed the possibility of class solidarity across racial lines."[55]

As more and more indentured servants and enslaved African descendants banded together to rebel, the ruling class deemed it a matter of survival to alienate the two struggling parties from one another. Therefore, a divisive strategy was put into effect, which laid the framework for explicitly racialized slavery.

• • •

THE ONE RACE TO RULE THEM ALL

It should come as no surprise that Whiteness was conceived directly out of deceit and manipulation by those in charge—the goal being to create the illusion of solidarity between the top echelon and the struggling masses of poor European colonists against a shared "enemy." This political tactic remains common to this day.

Although hideous curly wigs, fancy buckled shoes, and strong wooden teeth were primarily reserved for the crème de la crème of society, the rich recognized the usefulness of convincing the

European masses that they too could have these treasures if they behaved and played nice. For this to happen, the wealthy needed to create the illusion of a shared sense of identity, pride, and ownership. What better way to do that than to grant them some basic rights and give them land that was already inhabited by millions of Indigenous peoples? It's not like they had to pay for that land, so why not?

The wealthy's need to ensure that poor, working European colonists saw themselves as superior to workers of African ancestry was the defining element in the initial conception of race. As Plihcik describes, giving laborers of European descent even the slightest advantages over those with traces of African ancestry "switched their allegiance from the people in their same circumstance to the people at the top. It eventually created a multi-class coalition of people who would later come to be called White. . . . This was a divide and conquer strategy. It was completely brilliant."[56] By giving the working-class European colonists *just* enough to keep them satisfied and give them something to work toward, the wealthy elite ensured their loyalty in perpetuity. Moreover, they could leverage that loyalty to maintain the idea of a shared collective identity.

The newly formed colonial government began guaranteeing limited rights to indentured servants of European ancestry while they were still working. These same rights did not apply to their African counterparts. These privileges included a limited term of service (typically four to seven years) as well as room and board and a freedom package that guaranteed land upon completion of their contract.[57] This was done strategically to ensure that European servants worked hard to maintain their now slightly elevated status and would no longer equate themselves to Africans in the pecking order.

Moreover, indentured servants of European ancestry now had a lot to lose from joining forces with their African counterparts to take down their "oppressors." If any of the terms of servitude were violated or they attempted to overthrow a corrupt master, these "guaranteed" rights became null and void, and they forfeited their chance at economic freedom. Meanwhile, if they played by the rules, they could potentially join the general population and become wealthy and own slaves (and women) of their own.

As European colonists were granted more rights, the use of indentured African servants was quickly phased out in favor of unlimited free labor that also upheld this worker stratification. Most African descendants were stripped of their already limited freedoms as new laws and restrictions went into effect.

Now that a clear distinction had been made, it was necessary to make explicit the distinction between those *entitled* to a life of freedom and those who would be enslaved for the entirety of theirs. This required a polarization that was easy to identify, and thus, the foundation for the racial concepts of Black and White were born.

● ● ●

HEATHENS, PAGANS, AND BASTARD CHILDREN

In 1682, the Virginia Assembly passed a law that created a nonnegotiable prerequisite for citizenship. Simply put, one had to be of European ancestry. Furthermore, the new law, which included the term "imported" in reference to non-Europeans who were brought here, also listed distinct categories for these noncitizens: Negroes, Moors, mulattoes, and Indians—designating them as fair game for enslavement. According to the law, which smacked of unapologetic racial superiority, anyone "borne of and in heathenish, idollatrous, pagan [or] mahometan [Muslim] parentage and country . . . may be purchased, procured, or otherwise obteigned as slaves . . . out of their heathenish country by some well disposed christian."[58]

The law went on to explicitly clarify that even if these "procured" slaves were converted to Christianity by an "upstanding" Christian or someone else who purchased these slaves from him, they were not to receive freedom from servitude at any point in time. This law not only defined the terms of citizenship but also, and more importantly, enshrined legalized slavery based on ancestry or place of origin.

However, the Virginia Assembly had to overcome a significant problem: countless people of European ancestry were still choosing to befriend, marry, and, worst of all, have children with these "inferior" noncitizens. Those in power decided that it was time to put an end to this once and for all.

In 1691, the first recorded law in US history to include the word "white" was passed. Simply put, this law was "the invention of the human category white,"[59] describes author and historian Jacqueline Battalora. While it was not the first time the word "white" had ever been used to label someone, it now became codified in the American legal system and mainstreamed into America's vocabulary and racialized understanding of itself. I'm not exaggerating when I say that this law would have made Adolf Hitler incredibly proud. In essence, it was one of many racial purification laws designed to prevent "racial contamination" of the newly conceived White race.

The law clearly stated, "And for the prevention of that abominable mixture . . . it is hereby enacted, that for the time to come, whatsoever English or other white man or woman, being free, shall intermarry with a negro, mullato, or Indian man or woman, bond or free, shall within three months after marriage be banished and removed from this dominion forever."[60] This law necessitated further codifying racial categories and barriers in order to ensure that people were not doing something now considered illegal.

A similar law passed three decades earlier had outlawed fornication between Europeans and Africans. This new law was designed to tighten the reins and ensure that European colonists had no way to foster *any* type of relationship with a non-European person other than within the confines of a slavery-based relationship.

Battalora advises, "Anytime we look at law and study [American] history and you see a break from British common law, you always want to pay attention because it tells us something about the needs and desires of those who wielded power in the colonial context."[61] This is critical in understanding how the concept of Whiteness evolved in America. Laws are made to stop something that is already happening. There were innumerable instances of sex, friendship, and intermarriage between the newly delineated races. Fines and imprisonment were clearly not enough of a deterrent— nor was the fact that any offspring "conceived illegally" would likely be enslaved.

Not surprisingly, the rich White men who wrote this law seemed to be the only ones exempt from the penalties; it was designed not to punish or deter White men so much as it was to ensure that White women were not sleeping with, falling in love with, or marrying Black men—a fear that still lingers among many White males in the US.

As is the case today, women unduly bore the brunt of punishment and chastisement for having "unwanted" children. If a "bastard child" was born to a father of African descent, the (White) woman was expected to pay a sum of fifteen pounds of sterling (almost $5,000 in today's currency) to the church or parish to which the baby was born. If unable to pay, the law stated that "she should be taken into the possession of the said church wardens and disposed of for five years, and such bastard child should be bound out as a servant by the church wardens until he or she should attain the age of thirty years"[62]—or more likely never if they were dark skinned. For *anyone* now designated as White, whether they saw themselves as belonging to this category or not, marrying someone who was not considered White had serious consequences: steep fines, imprisonment, forced servitude, and banishment.

More ludicrous, Black women who had children by White men were subject to the same punishment. While this may at first seem obvious, the implications of this scenario are disturbing. This meant that any Black women who were raped by a White man and then became pregnant not only would have their children enslaved but were also subject to a fine.

If we have a hard time understanding why women of color are so disrespected and why women's rights in general in this country are incredibly stunted, particularly pertaining to childcare, maternity leave, and abortion, we need look no further than a couple hundred years ago. It was enshrined in our laws that pregnant women—including women who were raped—were legally obligated to suffer the burden of the outcome.

● ● ●

WHITENESS TAKES ROOT

By the 1700s, Whiteness had already begun to "refine" and further distinguish itself from the other racial categories White men created. The Virginia Slave Codes of 1705 unequivocally codified slavery as well as encapsulated the imbalance between "Whites" and "Blacks," designating the latter as property that could be captured, punished, and legally murdered (as long as it was done in the context of punishment).[63]

These laws were not simply about defining skin color or designating one's ancestral origins. This was a deliberate move by those in power to uphold racial solidarity through means of methodical oppression. Once the concept of race had taken root, it became the indispensable nexus used to justify the brutal exploitation and subjugation of millions of human beings, allowing slavery to become the backbone of America's rise to power.

As John Biewin, host of the NPR series Seeing White, puts it, "Race, and Whiteness, were not created by nature and simply observed by people. They were man-made, built, for reasons that had entirely to do with power and greed. . . . The institutions that built slavery American style are inseparable from the construction of Whiteness as we know it today."[64] Whiteness was invented to make sure that White people would never again have to question our place in the world. More importantly, we granted ourselves the inalienable "right" to subdue, subjugate, exploit, and, until recently, own, punish, and murder anyone we deemed beneath us.

This offers us two pertinent facts about Whiteness:

1.) Whiteness is not (scientifically or legally) real. It was, and remains to this day, a social construct, not a fact of nature.

2.) White supremacy and racism, however, are very real. They are the entire basis on which Whiteness was created in the first place.

CHAPTER 3

White Pseudoscience

SELF-VINDICATION

Beginning in the eighteenth century, a new category of science took root: race science.

Despite America's bold and beloved declaration that "all men are created equal," the fundamental goal of race science was to prove that members of the human race were *not at all* created equal. Race science further contradicted the Declaration of Independence by justifying stripping our fellow human beings of the "unalienable rights" we claim are at the heart of our American democracy. While it may outwardly appear that people from Africa were exploited *because* they were Black, the idea of Blackness instead came directly from the economic and social "need" to justify oppression and slavery.[65]

This may seem counterintuitive to many of us White folks, but consider for a moment that the terms Black and White in reference to race did not come into existence until almost a century after Africans first "arrived" in the colonies. These colorized terms stemmed solely from the desire to justify human trafficking and exploitation by creating an "us" and "them" mentality. Believing that the "heathens" they were brutally kidnapping, trafficking, exploiting, enslaving, torturing, raping, and murdering were not fully human made it easier for White folks to go to bed at night. How else could these respectable Christians justify their unspeakable violations of what they proclaimed to be God's will?

THE DARK SIDE OF THE ENLIGHTENMENT

White folks like to think of the Enlightenment as the great awakening of Western civilization. We are told from an early age that this was a golden era where science and reason triumphed over the rule of the Catholic Church. Our textbooks sing the praises of John Locke, Immanuel Kant, Jean-Jacques Rousseau, Adam Smith, and Voltaire. However, they leave out key figures from this critical era in Western science and philosophy—namely the founding fathers of race science, including Carl Linnaeus, the man who established the categories of race that still serve as the basis of our racialized identities nearly three centuries later.

While the Enlightenment undeniably brought about the beginnings of liberalism, freedom of speech, and the separation of church and state, it also sowed the seeds of racial oppression, dehumanization, and global exploitation. Once we "awoke" and threw off the shackles of tyrants and religious doctrine, we unleashed our bottled-up anger, neuroses, and trauma upon the rest of the world.[66] I'll speak more on that later.

Prior to the Enlightenment, religion and place of birth had been the primary classifiers of our ancestors. Christianity was the arbiter of civilized versus uncivilized people throughout the seventeenth century.[67] From the Enlightenment onward, science took over this responsibility and redefined the parameters of classification based on physical characteristics and appearance alone. As the transatlantic slave trade became the backbone of the economy in both Europe and America, race science rose to center stage.

BIGGER (SKULLS) = BETTER (INTELLIGENCE)

The erroneous, research-driven race science of the eighteenth century focused primarily on physical qualities such as skin color, hair, facial features, and skull sizes. At that time, the size and shape of one's skull was thought to directly correlate to one's intelligence (i.e., bigger meant better). Multiple scientists were on a ceaseless quest to prove that high levels of intelligence were reserved exclusively for the brains of their European contemporaries.

During the mid-1700s, world-renowned Swedish scientist Carl Linnaeus, known as the father of modern taxonomy, concocted *the* name for our entire species that remains to this day: *Homo sapiens*. *Homo sapiens*, or "wise man" in Latin, almost seems to be a misnomer considering that Linnaeus himself clearly did not see different "types" of humans as equal yet still recognized all of us as belonging to one species. As one whose job it was to name, rank, and classify organisms, Linnaeus divided the human population into four subgroups. He decided that there were four distinct categories of humans based on appearance and geography: Red American (Native Americans), Brown Asian (which he later changed to Yellow), Black African, and, of course, White European.[68]

About a century later, American scientist Samuel George Morton took Linnaeus's work one step further, not only redefining the categories of people but also exclusively working to prove that White people were biologically superior. Technically, he backtracked on a lot of pseudoscientific work, dismissing many of his predecessors' conclusions while proposing his own radical theories as the basis for his studies—which were astonishingly inaccurate even compared to what his predecessors believed.

Morton was convinced that he had discovered a foolproof method to show how Europeans were inherently superior. Unlike Linnaeus, Morton was a polygenist, believing that Black people and White people did not originate from the same species.[69] He likened interracial mixing to hybridization of entirely different species. Even though this stood in stark contrast to the widely accepted Adam-and-Eve version of human history, many White people were more than happy to support his theories and finance his primary work of craniometry (the measurement of skulls).

Collecting almost a thousand skulls over a twenty-year period starting in the 1830s, Morton performed detailed measurements of every skull he collected, pouring lead shot into each and then using a graduated cylinder to compare the volume. He was operating under the assumption that a larger brain indicated more intelligence and was intent on proving that the "White species" had the largest volume of all the skulls he collected.

Any scientist who invests twenty years of their life testing a flawed hypothesis for which they have already drawn a conclusion will either be sorely disappointed or simply become a victim of their own confirmation bias. Not to mention that Morton's literal rewriting of history and steadfast belief that the rulers of ancient Egypt were actually White didn't help his objectivity. While Morton's results were inconclusive at best, he presented his heavily skewed data to the Western world as fact, giving yet another boost to the morale of powerful White men hell-bent on proving their biological superiority.

What makes this more frustrating is that many scientists during this period were conducting *real* research. According to science and environmental writer, Michele Berger, one such scientist, a German anatomist named Friedrich Tiedemann, conducted very similar work to Morton, hoping to prove the exact opposite in order to "fight for equality and the abolition of slavery, and against the idea that different races were created separately."[70] Whereas Tiedemann's work fell into obscurity, scholars celebrated Morton's work for nearly two centuries after he passed.

Upon his death in 1851, the *Charleston Medical Journal* sang Morton's praises: "We can only say that we of the South should consider him as our benefactor, for aiding most materially in giving to the negro his true position as an inferior race."[71] The notion that Morton gave Black people "their true position" is viscerally disturbing. It took genetic scientists well over a century to show how wrong his findings were, proving that all humans share 99.9 percent of the same genes—none of which are linked to intelligence.[72] "Today Morton is known as the father of scientific racism,"[73] writes journalist Elizabeth Kolbert in a 2018 *National Geographic* special issue about race. "So many of the horrors of the past few centuries can be traced back to [his] idea[s]." Kolbert goes on to say that "to an uncomfortable degree we still live with Morton's legacy."

Morton's work—along with that of many other incredibly biased, racially motivated White scientists—became part of the connecting thread between biology and anthropology that remains at the heart of why many White folks have been so fascinated with studying "primitive" civilizations and cultures.

In Decolonizing Methodologies: Research and Indigenous Peoples, Linda Tuhiwai Smith argues that "of all the disciplines, anthropology is [still] the one most closely associated with the study of the Other and with the defining of primitivism. . . . [A]nthropology has collected, classified, and represented other cultures to the extent that anthropologists are often . . . perceived by the indigenous world as the epitome of all that is bad with academics."[74] This should come as no surprise considering that most of the funding and research that went into early taxonomy—and what was later to become anthropology—was rooted in proving that certain people were biologically superior to others.

As a result of Morton's (and other race scientists') celebrated work, anthropology became a purveyor of unspeakable atrocities that targeted what were now considered "inferior" forms of our species. Human zoos, referred to as "ethnological expositions," became commonplace around the turn of the twentieth century, drawing in hundreds of thousands of White visitors eager to see captured human beings displayed in their "natural" state.[75] In a 2018 article, anthropologist and author Shoshi Parks describes how "human rarities agents, the men who acquired human 'specimens' for circuses, expositions, and other events in the West," would traffic countless individuals from "primitive" tribes all over the world. The 1904 World's Fair in St. Louis had nearly 3,000 "primitive" human beings on display for an audience of close to twenty million White visitors.[76]

Well into the twentieth century, countless books, newspapers, and, later, magazines and television shows were also full of exotic depictions of the so-called "primitive" world. The frequent images of topless and naked women of color further eroticized, objectified, and dehumanized non-White bodies. Both anthropology and media made an explicit distinction between those observing and those being observed (i.e., the civilized and the uncivilized). Take a moment to imagine the uproar that would have occurred if a single White woman had been displayed topless in a "nature magazine."

By its own admission, National Geographic Magazine, founded in 1888, was filled with racist articles, drawings, and photographs of what it considered to be more primitive peoples. In a full-issue article in 1916, the magazine referred to Aboriginal Australians as savages who "rank lowest in intelligence of all human beings."[77]

For nearly a century, National Geographic unabashedly displayed non-American people of color for the Western world's enjoyment. Yet up "until the 1970s National Geographic all but ignored people of color who lived in the United States, rarely acknowledging them beyond laborers or domestic workers,"[78] describes a 2018 NPR story entitled "National Geographic Reckons With Its Past: 'For Decades, Our Coverage Was Racist.'" Traces of this exoticism remain a staple of Western media, allowing this paternalistic form of anthropology to continue.

However, this is not simply a matter of how people of color were treated and perceived by the Western world. Toward the end of the nineteenth century, once the belief in White superiority had been "scientifically proven" by the experts, the focus took yet a darker turn. The desire to label and categorize human beings shifted to wanting to "create" a superior form of the White race—and thus, eugenics was born.

● ● ●

THE PUREST WHITE

The term "eugenics" (meaning "well born") was first coined in 1883 by British scholar Sir Francis Galton, Darwin's cousin.[79] Galton was convinced that it was in mankind's best interests to influence the direction of our evolution by selectively breeding our most "desirable" traits. Eugenics was not simply about eliminating minorities; the intent was to refine Whiteness to its purest form— kind of like putting White people through a Brita filter.

Across the Atlantic, powerful White American men took a strong liking to Galton's ideas. This was probably because many of them were scared about the repercussions of recently freed slaves now dispersing around the country—and expecting to be treated with more dignity. The American Breeders' Association (later changed to the American Genetics Association) was founded in 1903. A "pedigree registry" was established under the Race Betterment Foundation, started by none other than John Harvey Kellogg.[80] Yes, the cereal guy! His outlandish "scientific" claims were not limited to race, however. In addition to his "cereal entrepreneurship," Kellogg was a renowned nutritionist and physician during his time. To grasp just how far off the mark Kellogg was about race, it is necessary to examine some of his more absurd beliefs about human health.

Among his claims, Kellogg insisted that masturbation was destructive to the human body and mind, potentially leading to impaired vision, memory loss, heart disease, epilepsy, and insanity.

His suggested cure for this potential killer only got weirder. Kellogg believed that bland foods—including his flagship cereal, Corn Flakes—would help steer Americans away from this unforgivable sin.[81] He also suggested tying one's hands, wrapping one's "organ" in bandages, or, best of all, putting a metal cage over one's genitals. And if all that failed, there was always the fallback "cure" of circumcision without anesthetic![82]

While Kellogg's crusade against masturbation may sound like it belongs in a medieval torture chamber, he was not a fringe conspiracy theorist when it came to his health claims or steadfast beliefs about "refining" the human race through racial purification. In fact, Kellogg had the ear of many wealthy, elite Americans, including a number of US presidents, Henry Ford, and Thomas Edison.

Through his lectures, books, and magazines, during the early 1900s, Kellogg became an outspoken proponent of making humans as "healthy" as possible, even if it meant selectively breeding some populations while discouraging procreation by those that he saw as "unfit." As described by the Eugenics Archive database, "Kellogg was a vocal eugenicist, and he was particularly concerned with race degeneracy. He believed that race was threatened both by racial mixing and mental defectives."[83] Kellogg was also obsessed with the notion of "racial hygiene," advocating for national enforcement of eugenic legislation and explicitly encouraging people with "good pedigrees" to procreate with one another.

Kellogg's Race Betterment Foundation was established exclusively to promote his White-supremacist beliefs. His focus on effectively taking evolution into his own hands was certainly not a new idea, nor was Kellogg alone in his desire to "improve" the human race. While many of his absurd health claims were eventually dismissed, both his famous cereal and his legacy of racial purification became embedded in mainstream American culture.

As described by a 2017 article on History.com, once "the concept of eugenics took hold, prominent citizens, scientists and socialists championed the cause and established the Eugenics Record Office."[84] This office diligently "tracked [multiple] families and their genetic traits, claiming [that] most people considered unfit were immigrants, minorities or poor." This meant that supporters of eugenics in the early twentieth century took active steps to ensure that certain people were stopped from "muddying" goals of racial purity.

As eugenics catapulted into America's elite circles, many Europeans eyed this lucrative science with renewed interest. In the 1920s, one man fatefully took a strong liking to the concept of racial superiority.

• • •

HEIL WHITENESS

When Adolf Hitler and the Nazi party rose to power, Hitler's belief in the supremacy of the Germanic race, which he referred to as the Aryan race, became crucial to his policies. Created as much more than a political party, Nazism was designed to establish an identity that unified the German people behind a belief in their inherent superiority over all others. More importantly, it was used to justify exploitation, slavery, torture, experimentation, mass oppression, and ultimately genocide against those deemed inferior or a threat to the German race, including Jews, Roma (often known by the pejorative Gypsies), people with mental and physical disabilities, and LGBTQ+ individuals. Whiteness became a weapon.

While some would like to believe otherwise, America became Hitler's literal guidebook for his own vision of racial purity. Beyond a mere fascination, Hitler idolized the American legal systems and structures that had nearly exterminated Indigenous populations and systematically oppressed Black Americans. In *Hitler's American Model*, Yale professor of law James Whitman describes how early-twentieth-century "Nazi Germany looked to America for inspiration. . . . The United States was not just a country with racism[;] . . . it was *the* leading racist jurisdiction."[85] Hitler was inspired by one American author and avowed eugenicist in particular, personally thanking Madison Grant, who authored *The Passing of the Great Race* in 1916, and telling him, "The book is my Bible."[86]

Hoping to implement a similar legal caste system in his own country, Hitler appointed Nazi lawyers, who "carefully studied how the United States suppressed nonwhite immigrants and consigned minorities to second-class citizenship. In private hearings, they discussed how the U.S. model for white supremacy in the Jim Crow South could be transposed to Germany and inflicted on the Jews,"[87] describes Whitman.

As a result, a number of American and German eugenicists worked in close collaboration, leading to the 1933 sterilization law in Nazi Germany, much of which was borrowed directly from the American systems put in place to stop certain populations from procreating.[88] Adolf Hitler's vision of a purified White race led to the death of over twelve million people—many of whom would be unmistakably identified as White both now and back then.

While it is easy to point the finger at Hitler as a cruel, callous, and insane dictator, he was far from alone in his brutal beliefs and actions. He had the support of millions of White Germans, Europeans, and Americans. Far from being a disgrace, to certain demographics Adolf Hitler was and remains *the* champion of Whiteness. In his purification crusade, Hitler was willing to take ruthless steps that racial purists before him could have only dreamed of.

A DISTURBING PARALLEL

It is dangerous to fool ourselves into thinking that Whiteness is somehow linked to our ethnicity. Rather than Whiteness serving as an erroneous synonym for European ancestry, there is another, more disturbing parallel at play here. To simply say that White is a synonym for European ancestry is as misguided as saying that Aryan is a reasonable substitute for German.

Just as Nazism declared the Aryan race the indisputable apex of humanity, so too did Whiteness declare itself the superior form of the human species. Nazism can be viewed as a natural progression of the concept of Whiteness. It was built upon beliefs and practices that were already in place for centuries. Hitler was merely trying to "perfect" Whiteness. To borrow a phrase referenced by many social justice commentators regarding the effects of White supremacy on people of color, the Holocaust was a textbook example of Whiteness "working according to design."[89] Racial purity and the consolidation of power were the driving forces behind Hitler's seemingly maniacal plan. He and the Nazi party were not an anomaly—they were the direct manifestation of the "will of Whiteness," built upon a platform of racism, nationalism, bigotry, and xenophobia.

While it would be comforting to say that we learned our lesson after World War II about the dangers of racialized science, many remnants of this "science" continue to spill into the twenty-first century. This is especially prevalent in misunderstandings about race and genetics.

CHAPTER 4

"Our" Genes and "Their" Genes: "Biological Whiteness"

BOTH EVOLUTION and genetics played a defining role in shaping the physical appearance of people living on planet Earth. However, race scientists of centuries past created tremendous misunderstanding around the role that genetics currently plays in human appearance. This is the result of their attempts to consolidate hundreds of millennia of human evolution into entirely subjective categories created out of nothing more than prejudice mere decades before they began their "studies." *Real* genetic science tells a different story and paints a much clearer picture of the differences and similarities that make us *all* who we are.

As acclaimed scholar of race Dorothy Roberts points out, every single one of the visible genetic variations we have used to define race (skin color, hair texture, eye color, etc.) exist within a 0.1 percent spectrum of the entire human genome. While White folks tend to assume that the biggest "gap" in genetics is between us and those with vastly different appearances, the majority of genetic diversity actually exists among people on the African continent.[90] This is due to one simple fact: Homo sapiens evolved somewhere between 200,000 and 300,000 years ago yet spent the vast majority of their existence spreading throughout Africa—before finally venturing north only about 60,000 to 70,000 years ago. As a result, our species' most significant genetic variations exist among the different African populations who settled and remained throughout the enormous continent over the course of hundreds of thousands of years.[91]

The seemingly drastic genetic variations that have led to superficial changes, including pale skin, are relatively new in our evolutionary timeline. Perhaps more surprising is that recent genetic science has revealed that "all non-Africans today are descended from a few thousand humans who left Africa,"[92] writes journalist Elizabeth Kolbert. A combination of luck and circumstance (including a close call with a climate catastrophe that almost led to the extinction of our entire species) allowed the distant descendants of this small group to ultimately spread across the globe and populate almost every corner of the planet, finally reaching South America roughly 15,000 years ago.

This relatively small group took a fraction of our species' overall genetic diversity with them. Because every single non-African person on the planet is a direct descendant from this one specific group, all non-Africans are rather closely related, genetically speaking. This also means every non-African person, including White people, are more closely related to one specific group of Africans than most Africans are to one another. For example, we share significantly more genes with people of Somalian ancestry than people with Somalian ancestry share with many other populations in Africa.[93] While we often visually lump together all people of African descent under one broad racial category, genetically speaking, they are by far the most diverse people on the planet. This disproves every single biological claim about the existence of distinct racial categories.

An article published by *The Guardian* concerning the resurgence of flawed race science in the twenty-first century states that "as much as 95% of the genetic difference in our species sits *within* the major population groups, not between them."[94] This means that there is often more genetic variation within a fictitious, socially assigned racial category than there is between two entirely different racial categories.

This would have baffled race scientists and slave owners alike—whose entire justification for human exploitation was dependent on the assumption that all people from Africa were members of a singular inferior gene pool.

How does this information connect to modern White people? More importantly, why does it matter that our ancestors came from one small group in Africa? Well, that is where the sun comes into the picture.

* * *

HOW THE SUN CREATED "WHITE" SKIN

The diaspora of "modern humans" (within 70,000 years of present day) is what led to the distinct color gradient we see today. If you were to look at a map by skin color of our ancestors before globalization, you would see a band of dark color surrounding the equator that gets lighter the further north or south you go. Subject to natural selection, those who ended up in the farther reaches of the Northern and Southern Hemispheres underwent a series of random mutations. This led to the survival of those with lighter skin, who were able to absorb the necessary amounts of ultraviolet (UV) light to maintain healthy vitamin D levels—which is essential to human survival and proliferation.[95]

Conversely, those who either remained close to the equator or migrated and "horizontally settled" survived because of their darker pigmentation, which kept them shielded from the intensity of the sun's powerful UV radiation.[96] Thus, darker skin remains advantageous to many humans, but up in, say, Norway, pale skin has the advantage.

There are many exceptions to this equatorial UV relationship, due primarily to variations in altitude and abnormal regional genetic mutations (including a blue-skinned family in Kentucky that occurred as a result of six generations of inbreeding with a rare blood condition called methemoglobinemia).[97]

The foundation of White people's assumption that we are genetically and intellectually superior is simply a biological fluke that led to our survival living further north. In fact, "the mutation that is most responsible for giving Europeans lighter skin is a single tweak in a gene known as SLC24A5.... [I]n one position where most Sub-Saharan Africans have a G, Europeans have an A,"[98] explains Kolbert. More startling, this particular G-to-A genetic substitution likely didn't show up in Western Europe until only about 8,000 years ago, and was brought by a small group migrating north from the Middle East. This group is likely also responsible for bringing farming to the more "primitive" Europeans up north—which allowed this genetic variation to sustain itself. So the main culprit of our vast differences in skin color is a single genetic anomaly that helped us survive the carcinogenic cosmic radiation of an enormous ball of gas ninety-three million miles away.

Wait a minute—doesn't that prove that there *is* something that makes White people genetically different? Couldn't we argue that our lack of melanin was the defining factor in the genetic evolution of Whiteness? Not so fast. This color gradient spills across every continent. This is not a matter of Africans and Europeans or Black and White. Color categories remain entirely subjective. There are plenty of White people with darker skin than someone from, say, mainland China or many parts of South America; if lack of melanin were the only determining factor of Whiteness, then surely many folks from mainland China should be welcome in our tribe, right?

These skin-deep differences do not provide any genetic proof of Whiteness. They simply show that mutations can work to our advantage or disadvantage. In some cases, a mutation leading to less melanin benefited populations. Moreover, populations that left Africa and whose descendants ended up settling closer to the equator reacquired a darker hue via natural selection.

Keep in mind that none of this evolution happened within a

visible time span. To put it in perspective, in the mere 60,000 to 70,000 years that our species has been traversing the planet, some groups hit an impasse that lasted for roughly a quarter of that time. While we often imagine a long and perilous journey across an icy land bridge that spanned between modern Asia and North America, the journey was not continuous. The so-called "bridge" was a wide swath of land that was temperate, hospitable, and filled with plants and animals. The most recent developing theory is that the ancestors of all Indigenous Americans settled on this enormous land mass for thousands of years before some of them chose to move on into what is now North America—likely driven by climate.[99]

In other words, it was a slow, multigenerational crawl by which humans moved across continents and settled down. Our species' evolution, including our various features, has occurred at a still slower pace, based simply on where our ancestors decided to stay (or were forced to stay because of climate or geographical barriers). While many groups remained where they were, and their features evolved accordingly over generations, others decided to move on, and their features also slowly evolved to better suit their surroundings.

The ancestors of all modern-day White people are a mix of some of the groups who chose not to continue the multigenerational journey across the continents. These individuals instead remained in what is now Europe. Consequently, the survival of those with a G-to-A genetic mutation leading to lighter skin roughly 8,000 years ago was favorable to this group, who received less sunlight than those who ventured further toward the equator.

So, what exactly makes us White? If our skin color does not set us apart, there must be some other components of the (subjectively) agreed-upon characteristics of a "White appearance." As it turns out, there is another potential feature that, combined with our skin color, supposedly qualifies us as White: our noses.

● ● ●

THE EURO NOSE

Let's start by getting a common stereotype out of the way. Black people have flatter noses than most of us. But so do many Asians, Aborigines, South Indian people, Southeast Asian populations, Pacific Islanders, and many people native to Central and South America, as well as plenty of other populations. Maybe we should be looking not at "their" noses for the thing that makes them different but instead at our own noses as a defining feature of Whiteness. What makes our noses so different?

While noses may sound like a trivial component of Whiteness, race scientists of previous centuries would beg to differ. Nose shape has been a defining feature of physical beauty throughout Europe's history, often considered a marker of genetic superiority. Case in point: the "Roman nose," as it was referred to, with its prominent bridge and hooked appearance, was considered the standard of beauty by many Europeans for centuries. That is, of course, until the Nazis targeted it as a primary characteristic of Jewish people.[100] Moreover, throughout the nineteenth century, race scientists specifically included the distinct shapes of noses in many of their cranial studies.

However, what they assumed to be a defining feature of superiority may just be a way for us to stay healthy in colder climates. Recent research has shown that, surprisingly, the sun could be the culprit here as well. Regardless of shape, noses serve a common function besides smell—to warm and infuse humidity into air on its passage into the lungs.[101] It is now thought that people with ancestors who lived in colder and/or drier regions have evolved with longer, expanded nasal cavities to better heat and moisturize the air.[102]

Lauren Butaric, a biological anthropologist at Des Moines University, explains that "what [we] see in the cartilaginous structure, which matches up with the internal structure, is that individuals from cold, dry environments tend to have tall and narrow nasal cavities.... In the wide noses often seen in individuals with tropical ancestry... the air flow is much smoother, traveling straight back with less warming and humidification."[103] So, like every other feature on our body, noses evolved to best suit the climate in which people settled.

However, it is important not to broadly apply this evolutionary "rule." As is the case with skin variations, local climate isn't always the determining factor in the shapes of noses. Some are likely the result of simple coding "errors" that were passed along within specific populations. Significantly reshaping the human face can take thousands of years and many generations—or it can happen by virtue of small groups with distinctive features or mutations spreading their dominant genes within a given population. For these reasons, elongated, hooked, or pointy noses are not limited to people of European descent, nor does every person of European descent have the once-idolized "Roman nose."

One could argue that the further our ancestors evolved from our place of origin (Africa), the more coding errors (i.e., mutations) we embedded in our DNA. However, evolution doesn't tell the whole story when it comes to our species' physical characteristics. Humans have also selectively "created" or perpetuated some traits within our population.

• • •

ALT(ERNATIVE) RIGHT SCIENCE: THE NEANDERTHAL IN US ALL

In the process of procreation, many of our ancestors had sexual encounters with a group that many researchers now argue were an entirely different species altogether: the Neanderthals.

The alt-right (Alternative Right) movement—whose entire

existence is centered around the core belief that whiteness is under attack by the combined forces of social justice, political correctness, and intermixing alongside overpopulation by other races and ethnicities[104]—has glommed onto an absurd theory about our lingering Neanderthal DNA to make a case for our supposed superior intellect. What are they basing this on? The same thing that "big-headed" race scientists of centuries past based it on: horribly inaccurate cranial science.

As it turns out, Neanderthals happened to have larger skulls than *Homo sapiens*. Alt-right supporters have made the argument that Europeans and Asians have inherited larger brains than people of strictly African ancestry and therefore have higher intellect.[105] They believe that when our ancestors "crossed paths" with Neanderthals, we inherited the seeds of Whiteness's primary component: our "stunning" intellect.

According to this logic, though, we are smart *in spite* of being *Homo sapiens* ("wise man")—only intelligent because of our sexual escapades with Neanderthals. Whatever the circumstances behind the countless occurrences of interbreeding, one thing is certain: there is zero scientific evidence that it made *Homo sapiens* smarter.

Scientists have already debunked the "brain size = intelligence" myth. If a larger brain meant a higher intellect among mammals, then sperm whales should have colonized Mars centuries ago with their thirteen pounds of sheer intelligence compared to our meager three pounds. I guess someone should also tell the alt-right "skull aficionados" that there is now research to show potential links between Neanderthal DNA and negative health effects in current *Homo sapiens*. As it turns out, one of the only things that we, along with countless other populations with Neanderthal ancestry, gain from our genetic inheritance is a possible predisposition for autoimmune diseases and metabolic disorders, including diabetes and obesity.[106] And while some evidence indicates that our Neanderthal genes may potentially increase our vitamin D levels, those same genes also increase our risk of schizophrenia and extra belly fat.[107] How exactly does that make us superior?

Moreover, to argue that having Neanderthal ancestry is what makes us White, we would also have to account for the fact that countless other populations also carry this far-from-unique genetic marker. In some Asian populations, Neanderthal DNA is even more prevalent than it is in many Europeans—accounting for as much as 4 percent in some groups.[108]

There are also detectable amounts of Neanderthal DNA in many African populations as well, likely due to humans migrating back into Africa during the past 20,000 years.[109] In other words, Neanderthal DNA is not a unique feature to people with European ancestry.

Lastly, Samuel Morton—whose inaccurate cranial studies are the basis for this bigger=better theory—was unable to prove that the skulls of Europeans were any larger than skulls from other regions. Tellingly, he himself could not distinguish which skulls were which unless he was provided with an attached label indicating the specific region of origin.

Unlike skin color or nose shape, which make specific groups of humans better suited to their local climate, the shape of human skulls is more likely a result of random mutations, not Neanderthal DNA. According to one study published in the *American Journal of Physical Anthropology*, "much of the skull variation in today's human populations is explainable more by distance from Africa than by adaptation to the local environment."[110] As described by Todd Rae, an anthropologist at the University of Roehampton in the UK, "the further you get, the more a population will start to develop differences from copying errors in DNA."[111] Simply put, our variations of skull shape and size are due to malfunctions in our genetic replication—far from a divinely imparted gift to hold more intellect.

Guess the alt-right theory of large-brained Neanderthals doesn't hold up after all. Yet the alt-right movement is certainly not to blame for this absurd theory. They are merely continuing the legacy of what race science has always been about—cherry-picking facts and molding them to fit a desired assumption.

Ultimately, "the few [physical] differences that do exist reflect differences in environments and external factors, not core biology."[112] It has been proven that the genetics that determine variations in physical appearance are not correlated with those that potentially influence intellect or behavior. Whether from random mistakes in our DNA, natural selection based on climate, experimental, or selective breeding, the differences in human DNA that lead to physical changes are not indicators of race; rather, the fluidity of our genes indicates that they *do not* reflect racial categories. Variations that do exist overlap and intersect in ways that have and will continue to "evolve us" as a species.

As genetic science continues to improve in the twenty-first century, what is truly astonishing is the lack of variation in our genetics. While our brains have been hardwired as well as socially programmed to look for visual differences in our species, causing our prefrontal cortex to form resulting biases and prejudices, what we have discovered under a microscope tells a very different story— one in which we are much more biologically united than divided.

However, at this point, it's easy to find ourselves at a crossroads when it comes to the actual importance of disproving the science behind race. Even if we concede that there is no biological basis for race, we are still left with the undeniable fact that race already exists in our society.

OKAY, RACE IS NOT SCIENTIFIC; SO WHAT?

Trying to disprove the validity of race using only a scientific argument is often where we hit a dead end. Many people counter with "So what? I still see lots of people that look very different than me but very similar to each other; doesn't lumping people into larger categories make things a lot easier? What does it matter if science can't back it up?"

Frankly, race doesn't have to be scientifically proven to be real. Individuals and institutions continue to uphold its merit, and it has very real and measurable consequences on human lives. Race still serves its original intended function of establishing a hierarchy to divide and conquer. Moreover, "to the victims of racism, it's small consolation to say that the category [of race] has no scientific basis,"[113] writes Elizabeth Kolbert. Paradoxically, the very fact that race was born out of a scientifically unproven belief is what makes it so real in our society.

Humans believe in and live according to plenty of unproven things. Our ability to rely on faith, intuition, and "our gut" has unfortunately also allowed us to build our entire society upon the premise that race is real. Therefore, for me to say that race is not scientifically real is about as effective as saying that "I am colorblind" and expecting racism to resolve itself. Acknowledging race is not only important but also necessary when describing the effects of systemic and structural racism, which is very real.

People who are perceived as White are going to receive unmerited status, material wealth, opportunities, and privileges. Conversely, people who are perceived as not White are likely going to face discrimination and obstacles—not to mention measurable effects on the overall quality of their lives, including their health and safety.

Because race is *not* rooted in science, it can easily be modified on a whim to serve political interests and influence the racial hierarchy in our society. Currently, Whiteness continues to serve us, so White we shall remain. As long as our belief in our Whiteness remains firm, we can continue to enforce its "realness" upon all those we deem beneath us.

CHAPTER 5

"Purebred" White

EVOLUTIONARY BIOLOGIST J. B. S. Haldane once posed a famous question to his fellow anthropologists back in 1956: "Are the biological differences between human groups comparable with those between groups of domestic animals such as greyhounds and bulldogs?"[114]

While on the surface this inaccurate comparison may seem like a simple folly, Haldane's question highlights an insidious and pervasive misunderstanding of race and is fundamental to how the concept of race evolved in America. More importantly, there are significant consequences to this belief when it comes to how we view ourselves and others.

• • •

RACE AND BREED: A HARMFUL CORRELATION

When it comes to the intellect and athleticism of our canine companions, we shamelessly and playfully share our biases for and against certain breeds among our peers. Most of us openly prefer certain breeds to others—and while there is arguably nothing wrong with this, a deliberate connection made between breed and race during the nineteenth and twentieth centuries created damaging beliefs about people who do and don't look like us.

Researcher and professor of anthropology Holly Dunsworth explains that this popular analogy "may sound innocent and [even] scientific on the surface, but carries deep racist undertones."[115] Besides the fact that it is a scientifically inaccurate way to interpret our visual differences, it also invokes connotations of racial superiority, racial hierarchy, purebred lineage, and even selective breeding. As a result, this seemingly innocuous comparison has huge ramifications for the scientific community and the general population alike, particularly in the United States.

An extensive study published in BioMed Central explains, "In the U.S., and likely beyond, the human race-dog breed analogy is not merely an academic question about patterns of variation; today, it factors substantially into the popular debate about whether race is fundamentally biological as opposed to a social construct, and it carries forward an ugly American tradition. Inherent to the analogy is the transference of beliefs about pure-bred dogs onto notions of human racial 'purity' (e.g. Castle 1942; Harrington 2009)."[116]

Simply put, the comparison between dog breeds and race inherently creates a system in which we perceive similarities and differences among our species that are not actually there—particularly pertaining to our physical abilities, character traits, and intelligence. While for most of us there is no intentional malice in equating race and breed, nor a conscious awareness that we do so, that has not always been the case. For most of our country's history, race and breed were believed to be one and the same.

● ● ●

DOG "RACES"

During the eighteenth century, many European and American scientists spearheading racial taxonomy embraced the comparison of dogs and people. But this connection was far from coincidence. The notions of breed and race have been intertwined for centuries. The word "race" itself may have originated in reference not to humans but to dogs and other domesticated animals.[117]

As author Dickey Bronwen describes in his book *Pit Bull: The Battle Over an American Icon*, "hunters and falconers [in Medieval

France] classed their animals according to function, like the English, but also according to 'nobility,' in a quasi-caste system. The hounds belonging to French royalty were placed in the 'highest' race, and the common guard dog belonged to the 'lowest.' For several hundred years thereafter, writers across Europe referred to races, rather than breeds, of dog."[118] Brown explains how this term was then likely adopted for humans by the English sometime during the Enlightenment, as taxonomists began to group humans into what they genuinely believed were scientifically accurate categories.

Co-opting the term "race" was an easy way to not only classify but also determine rank, status, and characteristics of the newly established categories. This false correlation became the foundation for how the scientific world came to view the visible differences within our species, perplexing the man who proposed evolutionary theory itself—Charles Darwin.

During the 1800s, Darwin spent much of his adult life laboring over the question of whether racial varieties were the same as breed varieties. A 2019 research article titled, "Human Races Are Not like Dog Breeds: Refuting a Racist Analogy," describes how "dogs factored greatly into Darwin's conception of evolution . . . and he specifically pondered the similarities of human races and dog breeds in [his seminal book] *The Descent of Man*, published in 1871."[119] Unfortunately, like most scientists, Darwin was confined by the scientific knowledge available to him in his day, and his particular field of study was among those at the epicenter of misguided and erroneous race science.

The consequences of this scientific era have had profound lasting effects. Many of us are still likely to unconsciously equate certain breeds with certain people at a surface level. This can be exemplified by examining one specific racial/breed association that has endured for well over a century: the damaging comparison of Black Americans to the American pit bull.

● ● ●

PIT BULL PREJUDICE

The troubling history behind racial notions of "purebred" ancestry—including its incursion into eugenics—has left us impressionable when it comes to how we view race.

Consider the following excerpt from a 2016 *Current Affairs* article titled "Racism and the American Pitbull: The fear of certain breeds of dogs mirrors the fear of certain people": "The link made between savage beasts or dangerous animals and black humans is as old as the history of enslavement."[120] This is far from an accident. One of the easiest ways to dehumanize other human beings is to compare them to animals that we fear. As actor Michael B. Jordan memorably phrased it: "Black males, we are America's pit bull. We're labeled vicious, inhumane, and left to die on the street."[121] This is not simply a matter of how we *feel* about pit bulls or Black Americans. This association has a direct impact on the health and safety of Black communities, specifically pertaining to breed bans and discriminatory practices.

As described in a 2008 article titled "Are Pitbulls the Black People of Dogs?," "not only are pitbulls more likely to be affiliated with 'inner city' communities, but their [negative] behavior is reported at a dramatically higher rate than other breeds. Similar to the underreporting of Whites committing drug crimes, rapes, and other violent crimes, dogs thought of as 'good for children' (*Beagles! Labs! Golden Retrievers!*) are unlikely to generate the communal hatred so easily sparked by the independent action of a [single] pitbull."[122] While this quote speaks for itself—and can easily be verified by a visit to a local dog park—it is especially worth noting how the author highlights that the individual actions of one pit bull affects people's impressions of the entire breed. This invokes the same burden of "unwanted ambassadorship" that many Black Americans experience daily, particularly when it comes to negative stereotypes.

The issue of racially discriminatory breed bans has even made it to the Ohio Supreme Court.

In a 2018 research article titled "The Black Man's Dog: The Social Context of Breed Specific Legislation," published in Animal Law Review, Ann Linder, Associate Director of Policy & Research at Harvard University, describes a 2015 Ohio Supreme Court ruling that upheld breed bans in multiple cities and communities which unfairly targeted pit bulls and disproportionately harmed communities of color—particularly African Americans and Latinos. Similarly, she emphasizes how when it comes to punishment and discrimination, pit bulls are subject to much harsher penalties and police involvement than most other breeds, as are the Americans of color who own them.[123]

Alas, it should come as no surprise that such a link exists in many White American minds between African Americans and a breed that we have unfairly demonized and labeled as violent, dangerous, and unpredictable. Yet despite no current data to show a higher percentage of Latinos or African Americans owning pit bulls, the association has become intrinsic (and deliberate). While the American pit bull was indeed primarily bred to fight other dogs and animals, according to the United Kennel Club they are also "great family dogs and exceptionally noted for loving children[,] . . . [and] aggression towards humans is uncharacteristic."[124] This fact is consistently overlooked or ignored.

Pit bulls invoke the same fear that causes many White folks to cross the street when they see a Black man ahead of them. The editor of *City Magazine*, Brian C. Anderson, aptly sums up this connection. In his 1999 opinion piece titled "Scared of Pit Bulls? You'd Better Be!," Anderson describes how pit bulls "wreck a neighborhood's quality of life as surely as prostitutes or drug dealers."[125] He explains that due to his fear for his wife's safety, "pit bulls drove [his] family from the Bronx." While this may seem like merely an unfair criticism piece against pit bulls, his description of their owners as "thugs" and his statement that "all men may be created equal, but not all dogs" clearly shows there's more to the story. His words highlight the deep racial prejudices and fears that unconsciously equate the two, and Anderson is far from alone in feeling this way. Over two decades later, many White Americans still feel the same.

This link leads to further stereotypes, discriminatory practices, and the unnecessary endangerment of both an entire race and a breed of dog that have nothing in common—other than both being the targets of prejudicial biases carried by many White people.

However, the enduring connection between people and dogs goes far beyond targeting one breed or one race. There are more nefarious and deliberate reasons why this link is still espoused when it comes to upholding beliefs in White supremacy.

● ● ●

DELIBERATE BREED BIAS

Beyond the historically instilled misconception, the association between race and breed has been used as a ploy to ensure the oppression of certain groups of people and to dictate who gets to remain in charge from a societal and political standpoint. As described by Holly Dunsworth, maintaining "the assumption that human races are the same as dog breeds is a [deliberate] racist strategy for justifying social, political, and economic inequality."[126]

Throughout the mid-twentieth century, notions of racial purity were firmly upheld by the American Breeders' Association, as well as by the pedigree-based "eugenic registry" created under the Race Betterment Foundation in the early 1900s.[127] The comparison of race and breed served as a fundamental way in which racial scientists and White supremacists ascribe credibility to the notion of biological race. Throughout the early days of "racial taxonomy," this analogy was an effective means of convincing the public that inherent differences in our "bloodlines" accounted for differences in physical appearance. In modern times, some have taken it one step further. Richard Spencer, a leading White supremacist, said in a 2016 interview, "Race is something between a breed and an actual species. . . . It's that powerful."[128] He went on to compare the differences between White people and people of color to those between golden retrievers and basset hounds.

One of the major problems in this assertion is that different breeds of dogs *do* have varying degrees of physical abilities and intelligence. In the process of breeding and domesticating wolves, humans deliberately created dogs to carry out various tasks; we selected dogs based on appearance, temperament, and type of intellect.

Stanley Coren, a professor of psychology at the University of British Columbia, describes how the intelligence of dogs is quantified on three specific levels: instinctive intelligence (the purpose for which a dog was bred); adaptive intelligence (what a dog can learn to do on its own behalf/for its own purposes); and working and obedience intelligence (what a dog is capable of learning through explicit training and instruction by humans).[129] While the degree and type of intelligence does vary within a specific breed, these variations are much more dramatically observed across different breeds.

For example, border collies—because they were bred to autonomously herd sheep—need to be alert, adaptive, agile, and have complex problem-solving skills. Conversely, a breed such as the modern-day pug, which dates as far back as the first century BC, was originally "created" in Asia as loyal companions of royalty and aristocrats.[130] Border collies are part of a specific class of working-line dogs and require intense stimulation and enjoy challenging tasks. Pugs, on the other hand, were literally bred to be dependent and docile lapdogs. Because of the traits we deliberately selected among their ancestors, it would be cruel to expect a border collie to live the sedentary life of a pug and equally unpleasant for most pugs to be exposed to the working life of a border collie.

Obviously there are exceptions to this rule, but if you are thinking, *Oh yeah!? Well, my pug knows fifty different commands!* then you are missing the point.

This intellectual comparison has complex ramifications on how we humans compare ourselves to one another, consciously or not. Even if we completely understand the fallacy of the race and breed correlation, we are still heavily influenced by the belief that physical abilities and intellect vary among different races similarly to how they vary among different breeds.

But the analogy of race and breed quickly falls apart under further scrutiny.

● ● ●

CATEGORICAL CONFUSION

The analogy between race and breed is a poor one. Not only are the categories of race ever changing, but also the entire concept of race itself is driven by highly subjective social forces. This approach stands in direct opposition to that of the official list of breeds recognized by the American Kennel Club, which can only be updated by shared consensus using highly selective criteria, adding only a few carefully chosen breeds each year.

The American Kennel Club began its official classification of dogs in 1878 and as of the year 2023 recognized 200 distinct breeds of dogs.[131] Unlike breed, however, races cannot be counted or quantified—genetically or otherwise. Moreover, not only have individual or entire groups people been included or excluded from particular races at different points in history, but also the racial categories themselves have drastically changed over the past few centuries. Just look at the 2020 US census, which had over fifteen racial and ethnic categories to choose from.

The distinct breeds of dogs were "created" to serve a specific role and/or look a certain way. Whereas in the case of racial categories, the same function/form and name model does not apply. Instead, broad labels are assigned to large (and often diverse) groups of people who have existed independently for thousands of years. Moreover, since the inception of race as a concept only took hold a few centuries ago, many racial categories have either morphed into one another or disappeared entirely. This does not happen with the category of breed.

Take, for example, the "extinct" racial categories used to describe people who reside in present-day India. Once referred to (by White people) as "Hindoo"[132] back in the early 1800s, Indian people now fit under a generic subcategory (i.e., South Asian) that resides within the even more generic blanket category of Asian Pacific Islander—a category that didn't exist until a few decades ago. To equate that to breed would be the same as saying that a dog initially had its own distinct category of breed before then being reassigned into a new breed that became a subcategory of yet another, broader breed that didn't come into existence until nearly two centuries later. If that sounds confusing, that's because it is! This is how arbitrary the designation of most racial categories has been throughout our country's history.

While the categories of White and Black could be considered an exception in that they have remained a constant since they were invented, the people who fit into these categories have been anything but consistent. We only need to look to how the Jews or Irish were once ostracized to see how arbitrary Whiteness really is. More on that later. The equally nebulous category of Black—with its now defunct categories of quadroons, octoroons, or mulattoes—highlights the abstract nature of these politically and socially prescribed categories.

Race cannot, and should not, be equated to the intentional "crafting" of specific breeds of dogs over the course of centuries. There is simply too much genetic variability among different regional groups of people to be lumped into racial categories—particularly when those labels/categories may literally change tomorrow.

While the analogy between breed and race has been proven irrefutably false from a scientific and societal perspective, it still has many real-world consequences. In addition to the harmful stereotypes that linger, it plays a defining role in the assumption that certain bodies and brains are better designed to carry out certain tasks—especially tasks having to do with athleticism or intellect.

CHAPTER 6

"Natural" Abilitites

MANY OF US innocently talk about gifted athletes because it is built into our understanding of sports. However, "gifted athlete" holds a much darker connotation (pun intended) than is initially apparent. Moreover, our distinction between people who are more naturally sporty (i.e., athletic) versus scholarly (i.e., intelligent) is rooted in willfully racist propaganda that stems directly from race science of the eighteenth century. The popular adage "White men can't jump" should come with an unstated caveat: "because they don't *have* to."

• • •

BORN ATHLETES

Turn on ESPN, and you are likely to see enormous Black men exhibiting what appears to be supernatural talent. This is not some random phenomenon; it is the direct result of centuries of slavery, racial science, and a persistent belief that Black people are physically stronger and intellectually inferior. As a result, it was typically assumed that they were "built" to do physical labor for White Americans.

These false narratives deliberately positioned Africans and Black Americans as ideal candidates for slavery and underpin the reasons why the NFL and NBA still disproportionately employ Black athletes. Despite making up only about 13 percent of the total American population in 2022, Black athletes accounted for close to 60 percent of the NFL and over 70 percent of the NBA.[133] These institutions are still built on the assumption that Black people have superior strength and athletic ability; consequently, owners, coaches, teammates, and fans alike have overinflated expectations of Black athletes.

As described by a 1995 research study published in the *Journal of African American Men*, "the Black Body is again internally colonized by these institutions for physical exploitation.... [T]hough the exploitation is disguised at the professional level by designer clothes and multi-million-dollar contracts, the exploitation is even greater at the collegiate level . . . where these institutions benefit to a far greater extent than the athletes."[134]

It is far from coincidental that the vast majority of owners, managers, head coaches, and (until recently) quarterbacks in the NFL have been White men, while Black men were relegated to assistant coaching roles and field positions involving brute strength and/or speed.[135] To put it simply, this is a blatant example of self-proclaimed "intelligent" White men in powerful positions making a tremendous amount of profit by determining how strong Black men can be used for their own financial gain.

However, this isn't just about how White folks profit off of Black athletes. Studies going as far back as the 1970s show how sports have perpetuated significant negative stereotypes about Black American males.[136] Much of this can be observed in the language of sports commentators and media when it comes to discussing the athletes themselves.

As associate professor of journalism and sports history enthusiast John Carvalho says in a 2014 *Vice Magazine* article, "The overwhelmingly White sports media consistently uses terms that enhance the image of White athletes while dismissing Black athletes as being over-reliant on their natural gifts. White athletes are smart, hardworking, team players. Black athletes are freaks and beasts who get by on their natural gifts as opposed to their work ethic, which perpetuates the broader stereotype of Black people as lazy."[137] This is why White players like former Patriots quarterback Tom Brady are idolized as intelligent and tenacious all-American athletes, while someone like former San Francisco's cornerback Richard Sherman still has to prove that he didn't attend Stanford University only because of his athletic abilities.

A 2018 article in *The Guardian* titled "How the 'natural talent' myth is used as a weapon against black athletes" describes a study conducted by the University of Colorado in which "researchers asked [White participants] . . . across a wide range of ages and education levels . . . to rate paragraphs and photos of pro quarterbacks based on parameters like physical strength and leadership."[138] Not surprisingly, the study found that the White "participants wound up assigning negative stereotypes to the black quarterbacks, while assigning positive attributes such as leadership to white ones."

Taking it a step further, the term "beast mode" was used to describe the abilities of former Seahawks running back Marshawn Lynch because coaches, teammates, commentators, and fans assumed that he was nearly unstoppable and could run through any number of defensive linemen—never mind the chronic lower-back spasms (and presumed concussions) that plagued him throughout his short NFL career.[139]

While players like Richard Sherman and Marshawn Lynch were invaluable players on the field, the racial discrimination they faced off the field further emphasizes how their worth is equated to their athletic abilities. There is no excusing Richard Sherman's 2021 arrest for drunk driving and criminal trespass, but untreated suicidal depression and alcohol were partly responsible his unfortunate decisions.[140] However, his behavior was used to further stigmatize and reinforce the belief that Black athletes are deviant and violent by nature. Regardless of the circumstances, a White professional athlete behaving in the exact same manner would simply not have to reckon with the unwarranted "racial ambassadorship" nuances of his very human foibles.

This becomes even more depressing when we think about how many Black children are led to believe that professional sports such as football and basketball are a surefire way to success. Try as they might, only 0.08 percent of high school athletes in America will ever play football at a professional level. Of the few that do make it, most have an average career span of barely 3.5 years on a minimum starting salary. Moreover, with an estimated 80 percent of all retired players losing their entire earnings within their first three years off the field,[141] it is clear who the primary beneficiaries of professional sports are: powerful White men.

The NCAA tournament became the focal point of this financial exploitation in 2021. Whistleblowers highlighted the fact that wealthy universities were making billions off the unpaid labor of NCAA athletes—over 50 percent of whom identified as Black (and big-name revenue-generating athletes were almost 100 percent Black and brown).[142] For decades, these powerhouse schools continued to peddle the damaging narrative that "saving" Black students through education and "bringing them to college [was] enough,"[143] stated Louis Moore, associate professor of history at Grand Valley State University in Michigan, in a 2021 CNN interview. As it turns out, the no-pay policy was initially instated in the 1950s so that football players—coined "student athletes"—and their families were unable to file insurance claims for injuries or deaths sustained while playing.[144]

This ultimately created a multibillion-dollar enterprise in which primarily White commissioners, athletic directors, coaches, deans, administrators, and faculty benefit from the unpaid labor and injuries of financially disadvantaged athletes of color—as well as wealthy White students. A paper released by the National

Bureau of Economic research found that "nonrevenue" sports such as tennis, sailing, and crew—which are dominated by wealthy White athletes—are reliant on multimillion-dollar subsidies from the profits generated by football and basketball.[145] Similarly, many of these large universities, which still cater primarily to White students, rely on this "free money" to build infrastructure and pay staff and faculty, not to mention coaches' enormous salaries.

On top of all this, the few Black men who manage to thrive in spite of "collegiate exploitation" and become financially successful through professional sports face an additional problem once they retire. Coupled with bodily injuries, former NFL players are likely to suffer brain damage, and are three times more likely than the general population to die of neurodegenerative illness such as ALS or Alzheimer's.[146] In other words, Black NFL players have a tremendous amount to lose both physically and mentally from putting their brains and bodies at risk on the field. Similarly, those who manage to make it to the NBA are often a single leg injury away from losing a hard-won career built on athleticism.

Nonetheless, professional sports remain one of the only areas where White men will ever sing the praises of Black men, and not for their intellect but rather for their brute strength and "natural" athletic ability. White Americans reinforce the message to young Black males that if they want to be loved and respected by *our* society, they need to either dance, sing, or be an exceptional athlete[147]—and under no circumstances should they take a knee during the National Anthem!

A strange paradox presents itself here. Ironically, the belief in "natural athleticism" has made sports one of the main areas where White people feel disadvantaged compared to Black people. We have been inundated and brainwashed with antiquated science that inadvertently makes us doubt our own athletic ability and assume that our competitor is likely to physically dominate us. Combined with the fact that we have been conditioned to believe that Black men are not only stronger but also more aggressive, violent, and dangerous than us,[148] we often doubt ourselves long before the start of a match. Many White athletes (falsely) believe that they must work harder than athletes of color—believing that their place on the team was *earned* versus merely ordained by physical might.

This insidious stereotype also completely minimizes the effort and painstakingly acquired skills of Black professional athletes and forces them to continuously prove to the world that they have *earned* their place through hard work and dedication rather than their "athletic privilege." I'm honestly surprised we haven't seen a push for reverse affirmative action in professional sports.

Infamous sports commentator and prognosticator Jimmy "the Greek" Snyder said it best during a 1988 interview that ending up getting him fired from CBS. He did not beat around the bush, unabashedly stating that Black athletes were more successful simply because "during the slave trading, the slave owner would breed his big black to his big woman so that he would have a big black kid."[149] He then went on to describe how unfair he believed professional sports to be, expressing that "they've [Black athletes] got everything. . . . If they take over coaching like everybody wants them to, there's not going to be anything left for White people."

While Jimmy ultimately was sacked for his racist comments and even later apologized, stating that he thought he was just being "instructive," his sentiments remain engrained in White American culture. Jimmy merely said "the quiet part out loud," stating rather brashly what many misinformed White Americans believe to be true and yet would never say.

The irony is that our perceived disadvantage is entirely of our own making. Our own racism got us here—because in our desire to justify subjecting other human beings to brutal physical labor, early race science inadvertently implied that White people are athletically inferior. Consequently, we now feel at an athletic disadvantage, despite being in the racial demographic who laid the foundation for the exploitation of Black athletes—and in doing so, positioned them as "inherently" better than us.

Unfortunately, athleticism isn't the only area where White people have created a self-induced inferiority complex. We also created a parallel between what we perceive to be superior physicality in Black Americans and superior sexual abilities as well as hypersexuality.

• • •

> Note: Trigger warning! The following section contains descriptions of sexual violence.

LABELED PROMISCUOUS

While "historically, White women, as a category, were portrayed as models of self-respect, self-control, and modesty—even sexual purity . . . black women were often portrayed as innately promiscuous, even predatory,"[150] describes the Jim Crow Museum.

The belief that Black women were sexual objects has roots predating American slavery. According to professor of sociology David Pilgrim, early "European travelers to Africa found scantily clad natives. This semi-nudity was misinterpreted as lewdness. White Europeans, locked into the racial ethnocentrism of the 17th century, saw African polygamy and tribal dances as proof of the African's uncontrolled sexual lust. . . . The genesis of anti-black sexual archetypes emerged . . . : the black male as brute and potential rapist; the black woman, as Jezebel [i.e., a shameless and wicked woman] whore."[151] This became yet another justification for enslaving Africans, who were seen as less than human, intellectually inferior, and sexually barbaric—and therefore deserved to be subjugated. Consequently, rape and the violation of Black women's bodies is inextricably built into the fabric of American racism and slavery.

Violating Black women's bodies allowed White men to physically display their dominant position over all non-White women, as well as Black men, many of whom were forced to witness these acts. This was particularly the case among slave owners, who saw it as their right to rape any enslaved human being they chose, including children. One of the many ways that White men attempted to justify these unspeakable acts was to uphold and perpetuate the lie that Black women were overtly promiscuous and hypersexual. This began the Jezebel stereotype that persists to this day among many White men.[152]

Many White slave owners also leveraged a disturbingly false belief that Black women wanted their children to be lighter skinned in order to rationalize that Black women wanted to be raped. White American journalist James Redpath wrote in 1859 that many enslaved Black women were "averse to a sexual connection with persons of their own *shade*; but are gratified by the criminal advances of Saxons, whose intimacy, they hope, may make them the mothers of children almost White—which is the quadroon [quarter-Black] girl's ambition."[153]

On top of these barbaric beliefs, Black women were often seen as nothing more than breeding stock, so much so that "slave breeding" was a common dinner conversation in many plantation homes.[154] The Jim Crow Museum website explains, "Young black girls were encouraged to have sex as 'anticipatory socialization' for their later status as 'breeders.' When they did reproduce, their fecundity [fertility] was seen as proof of their insatiable sexual appetites."[155] But there was a darker side to all of this than simply a desire for more enslaved Black Americans. While labor demand was undeniably the primary reason for American slavery, the "Jezebel trade" (i.e., sex trafficking) wasn't far behind.[156]

An entire industry of sexual exploitation was created around Black and multiracial women and young girls. In what would later be known as the "fancy trade" during the nineteenth century, Black women (many of whom were still considered property) were forced into sex work explicitly for the pleasure of White men. In a 2015 research paper, social entrepreneur and nonprofit founder and president Tiye Gordon describes how rape was deliberately commodified in the "sexual economy of nineteenth century US slavery,"[157] stating that "the trilogy of 'pleasure-rape-desire' is as much a pillar of slavery as coerced labor." From the 1600s onward, untold numbers of Black women and children were sold to fulfill the lust and labor demands of White men.

Black sexual exploitation and victimization continued unabated well into the late 1900s. According to author and professor Deborah Gray White, "from the end of the Civil War to the mid-1960s, no Southern white male was convicted of raping or attempting to rape a black woman. . . . Black women, especially in the South or border states, had little legal recourse when raped by white men, and many black women were [also] reluctant to report their sexual victimization by black men for fear that the black men would be lynched."[158]

In addition to being exploited in real life, Black women were further exploited on the screen. During the 1970s, B-movie blaxploitation films became a hit among countless White moviegoers. Fans lusted after Black female characters on-screen, often depicted as deviant, eager, and sexually aggressive. While deliberately silly and often cheesy, these films reinforced a damaging stereotype about Black women rooted directly in stereotypes contrived centuries prior.

Another subset of the film industry has taken this damaging fetishization one step further in pornography. The Jim Crow Museum explains how the "pornography industry remains a bastion of explicit anti-black stereotyping—raw, obscene, and increasing mainstreamed. . . . [T]here are hundreds of pornographic movies that . . . depict black women as 'sexual things'—and as 'sexual animals.'"[159] The internet is filled with "videos with titles like *Black Chicks in Heat, Black Bitches, Hoochie Mamas, Video Sto' Ho, Black and Nasty, South Central Hookers,* and *Git Yo' Ass On Da Bus!* In the privacy of their homes or hotel rooms, [White] Americans can watch black actresses . . . 'validate' the belief that black women are whores."

While these extreme examples display how racial degradation and sexual exploitation can cause overt harm, this multicentury legacy has led to more subtle forms of dehumanization in modern White populations—including the racial fetishization of non-White people. One of the most common of these in America is linked to the historical taboo of Black men sleeping with White women.

> End trigger warning

• • •

BETTER IN BED?

Strange as it may seem, many White men are sexually aroused by the idea of White women being sexual with Black men.[160] As is the case with many forms of sexual aversions and taboos that later evolve into arousal patterns, the revulsion that many White men still have toward interracial sexuality has evolved into a common fetish. But how and why did this happen?

Throughout most of European and all of American history, most

White men have loathed the idea of White women "intermixing" with other races, both from a control and a purity standpoint. Nonetheless, as the anti-miscegenation laws have shown, interracial relationships have been around since day one.

During the twentieth century, politicians and media moguls alike deliberately stoked public fears, even creating national propaganda to stop this from happening. D. W. Griffith's *Birth of a Nation*, an infamous 1915 film shown in the White House, is perhaps the most glaring example. Not only is this film largely responsible for the rise in power of the Ku Klux Klan, but it also inspired the practice of burning crosses, something that was uncommon before the film.

In the film, Black men (played by White men wearing face paint) are deliberately portrayed as savage beasts that roam around chasing and raping helpless White women. While instilling sexual fear was part of the intent, this animalistic depiction was also meant to defend the horrific treatment of Black Americans as well as stop Black men from being allowed to vote or gain political power.

As for the Ku Klux Klan, this film tapped into the primal protector instinct of many White men who watched it, inspiring a resurgence in Klan membership. "White damsel in distress" savior complexes contributed to countless hate crimes, including castrations and public hangings of Black men and White women engaged in or accused of such relationships.[161] However, the vehement fear and disgust also reinforced a taboo, further entrenching a disturbing arousal pattern for many White men that is still prominent in America today.

This is not merely anecdotal. An entire fetishized pornographic genre of Black men and White women sexually engaged with one another—often in large groups—has evolved over the past few decades. Known as BMWW (Black men, White women), this "taboo genre" is highly searched by White men. "In an era of mass porn consumption, black male porn actors having sex with white women is a popular subgenre. . . . It's as if the online commercialization of sexual fantasy has globalized racial stereotypes and sent them freewheeling backwards,"[162] describes writer and broadcaster Afua Hirsch in a 2018 article for *The Guardian* about fetishized racism in the bedroom. There are entire online communities and swingers' clubs specifically for White men who want to watch their White partners having sex with Black men. Members of these communities "are active on Twitter, where they share pictures of exceptionally large black penises and rough sex in which a black man clearly dominates," describes Hirsch. In other words, many White men have become sexual voyeurs of something many of our predecessors tried desperately to stop from happening.

But this fetishization doesn't go one way. Equally disturbing is the fetishization of Black men by White women. Let me be clear: this is *not* to say that White women should not choose to be sexual with Black men—which was made explicitly illegal and punishable for most of America's history. However, engaging sexually with someone *exclusively* because of their race and the purported "benefits" (e.g., a larger penis, hypersexuality, sexual prowess, better rhythm, more passionate, more athleticism, etc.)[163] is inherently rooted in racist stereotypes because it further objectifies and dehumanizes an already marginalized group.

Unsurprisingly, this phenomenon is not new. It was very common in previous centuries. To the horror of the White men who inadvertently caused it, this desire was largely the result of White men's attempt to depict Africans as animalistic and inferior—unwittingly eliciting a primal sexual curiosity in many European women. Many Elizabethan-era travel books described African men as hypersexualized animals with enormous penises that were literally a burden to carry—or, in Elizabethan speak, "furnisht with such members as are after a sort burthensome unto them."[164]

Black men became a forbidden fruit, and the paranoia, oppression, and misogyny that White men frequently exhibited toward them only furthered these taboo desires. This desire was increased by countless "BMWW (black man white woman) erotic novels [that] specifically cater to the fantasy of crudely stereotyped black male aggression and sexual domination,"[165] explains Hirsch. Now many modern White women desire to sleep with a Black man to see what it feels like.

Ultimately, these sexualized forms of racism are not an accident. They are a direct byproduct of deliberate dehumanization and exploitation. Furthermore, they have become embedded as a taboo in American culture, not only making them uncomfortable to talk about but also allowing the same mistakes to be repeated because of misinformation.

Many interracial relationships and marriages are of course built on genuine love and affection *regardless* of race. Others, however, are rooted in unconscious stereotypes and fetishization. So, while many White Americans would like to believe that they are sexually liberated and racially progressive, some of us are just repeating centuries-old patterns of abuse and racial power dynamics.

When it comes to addressing these patterns of racial trauma, "sex and relationships are one of the last remaining bastions of unreconstructed racial prejudice,"[166] describes Hirsch. What we do in the bedroom tends to remain behind closed doors. Yet when it comes to our sexual "preferences," our racism might hide in plain sight, allowing us to believe that we are more "open minded" than our ancestors. This has become a mainstream topic of conversation.

● ● ●

RACIAL FETISHIZATION

Many of us have either said or heard a friend say something like "I have a thing for [insert race or ethnicity here] people." While this may initially seem like a harmless, albeit objectifying compliment, the reality is more complex. Because racial and ethnic fetishization is a direct legacy of centuries of dehumanization and sexual exploitation by White people, "saying that you are attracted to a specific ethnic group, or that you find particular racialized features sexually appealing, is not a compliment or something positive," explains Natalie Morris, deputy Lifestyle editor of UK's *Metro Magazine*. "This is [called] racial fetishization and it is a form of racism."[167]

While some would argue that this is the same as saying that you are attracted to hazel eyes, tall people, or "blondes," this argument "ignores the specific dynamics of racial power hierarchies that make racial fetishization different and more damaging than a simple romantic preference," Morris continues.

Beyond merely perpetuating stereotypes or this form of objectification, White people who hold such racial preferences are often subject to conscious and unconscious elements of White supremacy, which has characteristically determined who is and who is not considered sexually attractive. Many of us have inherited countless stereotypes about who is, say, more dominant, more submissive, or "better" in bed.

It is simply not possible to fully see someone as an equal if we have lumped them into a racialized "sexual preference" category. For example, a White man's statement that he *prefers* to date Black women is not indicative of him being more progressive or open minded; he is stating a racial fetish. Being attracted to someone *because* they are Black versus attracted to someone who happens to be Black are two extremely different things, but many White people have a hard time telling the difference. That is not the case, however, for the individual being fetishized.

While there may be no malintent on our part, the experience is extremely dehumanizing for the person being racially fetishized. It "can negatively impact a person [of color's] sense of personal safety, their sense of self, self-esteem and self-worth,"[168] Morris says. Not to mention that it "can also be demeaning and infuriating not to be seen as a real person who is multidimensional and who has lots of different things to offer a potential partner." Despite this, many White people continue to view their fetishized attraction to "certain people" as proof that they are not racist—when it proves that they are.

The choice to date or be sexual with someone because of their race or ethnicity from a "curiosity" standpoint positions them as an objectified novelty versus another human being.

However, the physical body is where this inflated belief about people of color ends—because while certain bodies may be frequently idolized (i.e., fetishized) when it comes to both sports and sexuality in America, the same does not hold true for intelligence.

● ● ●

INTELLECTUALLY GIFTED

While many of us have internalized the inadvertent message that we are physically inferior in terms of strength and sexuality to Black Americans, the opposite is true when it comes to our intellect. We have been conditioned to believe that we are naturally more suited for academia and corporate America.

As described by activist Peggy McIntosh, the woman who popularized the term "White privilege" in the 1980s, "I was taught that Whites have knowledge, Whites make more knowledge, Whites publish knowledge, Whites profess knowledge as professors, Whites run the big research universities, and Whites run the university presses. . . . I drank in the idea that knowledge is White, and White people are knowers."[169] We tend to conflate our learned predisposition that we are the creators, possessors, and spreaders of academic knowledge with having superior abilities, thereby assuming that we are naturally more qualified than others.

When encountering a person of color in a predominantly White space such as a college lecture hall or a boardroom, many of us White folks have found ourselves unwittingly wondering if that person is there primarily because of affirmative action. Our belief in both our intellectual superiority and our physical inferiority has allowed many of us to justify our resentment at supposedly having to work harder than people of color to earn our "rightful" spot. While we can objectively see that this is not true, we are often likely to experience feelings of frustration and entitlement when we feel that we have been slighted or given less than a fair chance.

■ ■ ■

RACISM STARTS YOUNG

An inexhaustible number of research studies conducted by institutions ranging from the American Psychological Association to Harvard University have confirmed how racial biases among students and teachers are one of the primary contributing factors to racial disparities in the American education system.[170] Needless to say, racism and internalized racism are rampant in our education system, regarding both athletics and academics.

Stepping away from generalizations and statistics, as a former teacher I watched the physicality-versus-intellect dynamic occur on an almost daily basis. It's not just adults who have internalized these beliefs; we pass them on to our children.

While the first children picked for kickball teams at recess were almost always Black, a different story played out when it came to picking partners or forming small groups in the classroom. Almost without fail, White students tended to gravitate toward one another. More concerning was that many students of color (particularly Black American and Latino students) would seek out White or Asian students to partner with because they automatically assumed that this would give them an advantage. The Black and Latino students had internalized the false belief that White and Asian kids were smarter than them, subconsciously reinforcing the White students' perception of their own intellectual superiority. This superiority complex is unfortunately common for many White children coming into diverse schools.

In an episode of the 2020 NPR special series *Nice White Parents*, which examines a sixty-year relationship between well-meaning White parents and a small Brooklyn school primarily serving students of color, a large cohort of 103 nearly all White children were enrolled by wealthy parents in 2015 with the promise of a dual-lingual program. The new arrivals quickly made assumptions about the previous condition of the school, passing judgment about the intellect of their peers of color.

In an interview with host Chana Joffe-Walt, one of the new boys, an eleven-year-old White male, casually described his "superior" cohort and the "positive" effect they'd had on the school: "The kids [referring to the *other* students] wouldn't pay attention, and they . . . zone[d] out [at] every little thing. And I bet they learned very little. And now, this generation, with us, I think we're doing a lot better, and I think that we're learning at a much faster pace."[171] He goes on to say that with the changes that are happening, he now believes that the school has a high status and is soon going to be one of the top choices in Brooklyn. Like so many other White children his age, this eleven-year-old boy unconsciously believes what White adults have taught him: that White people "improve" things wherever they go.

Unfortunately, teachers and students alike are no more immune to the effects of antiquated race science than the rest of us. We are taught from a very early age who we *should* want on our sports team versus who we *should* want on our research team.

CHAPTER 7

Racialized Healthcare: A Lethal Outcome

THE HEALTHCARE INDUSTRY is one of the primary perpetrators of erroneous and potentially fatal scientific beliefs. Both doctors and multibillion-dollar pharmaceutical industries still make decisions based on the assumption that race is a biological fact. Research published in 2003 by the National Academy of Sciences demonstrates how "racial and ethnic minorities tend to receive a lower quality of healthcare than non-minorities, even when access-related factors, such as patients' insurance status and income, are controlled."[172] This significantly contributes to patients of color—especially Black and Latino Americans—having poorer overall quality of health, meaning that they seemingly require more medical help than White Americans.

This chicken-and-egg scenario leads insurance providers, doctors, and drug companies to make assumptions about people's health based on race alone. As a result, many people of color are provided with less effective care and prescriptions and higher costs.[173] In fact, such a large body of data emerged on these racial disparities that in 1999, Congress requested that the Institute of Medicine carry out an extensive study to determine the "extent of racial and ethnic differences in healthcare . . . [and to] evaluate potential sources of racial and ethnic disparities in healthcare, including the role of bias, discrimination, and stereotyping at the individual (provider and patient), institutional, and health system levels."[174]

It didn't take the Institute of Medicine very long to prove that racism directly impacts our healthcare system. Yet despite the institute's conclusive findings on racial biases and unequal treatment, as well their concrete recommendations on how to combat the effects, our healthcare system remains rampant with racism more than twenty years later.

At the heart of this disparity lie the vestiges of racial science and unconscious assumptions about how race is directly related to biological health. The US National Library of Medicine published an article stating that "in spite of significant advances in the diagnosis and treatment of most chronic diseases, there is evidence that racial and ethnic minorities tend to receive lower quality of care . . . and that patients of minority ethnicity experience greater morbidity and mortality from various chronic diseases than non-minorities."[175]

It may be tempting to argue that unequal healthcare is the result of racism and discrimination at a societal and institutional level, unrelated to erroneous racial science. However, we have to take into consideration that Western healthcare is directly rooted in science. When large institutions fund research based on the assumptions that specific races suffer from more cases of a specific disease, that is undeniably racialized science. Why? Because these studies use socially constructed categories as the basis for determining how medicine should be practiced. This leads to policies as well as further categorization of people that impact the overall health of certain populations.

The irony is that specific ailments are disproportionately higher in certain communities of color, which reinforces these biased healthcare practices and leads to additional studies. However, this is a typical cause-and-correlation fallacy.

• • •

AN AFRICAN AMERICAN "MUTATION"

Two conditions that are frequently identified in Black communities are diabetes and hypertension. Up until 2022, the American Heart Association backed up this claim in an article titled "High

Blood Pressure and African Americans." The article stated that "the prevalence of high blood pressure (HBP or hypertension) in African-Americans in the United States is among the highest in the world. More than 40 percent of non-Hispanic African-American men and women have high blood pressure."[176]

The American Heart Association's initial explanation of this phenomenon included theories about higher rates of diabetes and obesity contributing to these ailments. However, the article then suggested a race-based, seemingly scientific explanation about why Black Americans have higher rates of hypertension: "Researchers have also found that there may be a gene that makes African-Americans much more salt sensitive."[177]* While this may seem like an innocuous, benign, and even potentially helpful theory, there were some serious problems with the article's generalization of genetic causes based on racial categories.

The implication of a salt-sensitivity gene in Black Americans automatically implied that all Black Americans shared the exact same genes. This is simply not true—for the same reason that not all White Americans share the exact same genes. It makes sense that certain populations from Africa have a salt-sensitivity gene. However, that does not mean that everyone who comes from Africa possesses that same gene.

What's the harm in assuming that this gene is present in all Black Americans? It ignores the fact that race is a socially constructed category by making a blanket biological claim about everyone with black skin. Consequently, specific treatments (that may be ineffective for those who do not possess this gene) and

---

*The AHA updated this specific page on their website in February 2022, removing any mention of a salt-sensitivity gene and adding that "historical and systemic factors play a major role in these statistics. . . includ[ing] lack of access to care, lack of access to healthy foods and other societal issues." It appears the AHA may have recognized the inaccuracy of this race-based scientific claim. However, a version of the article first appeared on their website as early as 2016, meaning that the AHA published this claim for nearly six years before it was updated.

targeted drugs could be given to *all* Black Americans suffering from hypertension, including those who do not possess this specific gene. Prescribing drugs that may cause harm and not considering all available treatment options that might be better for the intended recipient, based solely on a generalized racial assumption, is not only careless and irresponsible but also potentially deadly, especially considering that nearly 7,000 Americans die every year from completely preventable adverse drug reactions.[178]

I don't want to minimize the other points above, but if I was told to cut down on my salt intake because I might be at a high risk for hypertension, had to eat bland food for the rest of my life, and then found out that the prognosis was based on faulty racial assumptions, I would be pissed!

Another harmful component of treating obesity and diabetes in the Black population as a genetic disorder is that it overlooks the fact that there are known and preventable causes of these specific ailments in the Black population. The overall lower health of Black Americans is a direct consequence of systemic issues, including discriminatory housing, unaffordability, and lack of access to healthy foods, inadequate healthcare, and racial disparities—not to mention the intergenerational trauma and stress inherited from facing centuries of brutal oppression and racism.

• • •

A "VITAMIN D—FICIENCY"

Many of the ailments that disproportionately affect communities of color are caused in large part by systemic and societal inequities. However, one potential biological "culprit" could help improve the lives of millions of Black Americans if addressed properly.

Believe it or not, skin color matters when it comes to the health of darker-skinned people living in areas that they are not biologically adapted to—especially when many have only had a few centuries to cope with an abrupt shift in climate. While evolutionary traits often lead to advantages in populations who evolved according to the survival needs of their specific environment, modern globalization (as well as the transatlantic slave trade) over the past few centuries has contributed to some unforeseen health obstacles.

Vitamin D deficiency is much more prevalent in Black Americans than White Americans.[179] However, yet again, this is not a Black issue, nor does it provide any proof of biological Blackness. More melanin means a lower absorption of sunlight, leading to a lower production of vitamin D. Furthermore, as explained by Tufts University professor Jean Mayer, "it is becoming increasingly apparent that vitamin D protects against other chronic conditions, including cardiovascular disease, diabetes, and some cancers, all of which are as prevalent or more prevalent among Blacks than Whites."[180] In other words, kidnapping people who evolved to handle much higher levels of sun exposure and then transporting them to a continent with much lower UV levels has created distinct health problems over the past few centuries—as if Black Americans didn't already have enough to contend with.

It is also important to note that these scientific findings do not apply to people of African ancestry living in Africa or anywhere closer to the equator. The study encapsulated one specific group (Black Americans) currently living in a place with less-than-ideal levels of sunlight for their optimal health. This is yet another example of why we must be careful about using socially constructed labels for scientific findings. This condition is not suffered by one race. It affects *some* people of African ancestry specifically based on where they live. If the tables had been flipped and people of European ancestry had been captured as slaves and forced to work for years along the equator without any sunscreen, I'm pretty sure that we would be suffering from some significant ailments—skin cancer being one of them. To then claim that skin cancer is primarily a White ailment would be a complete correlation–causation fallacy.

Despite its problematic racial terminology, there is some promising data in this study that could potentially improve the lives of countless Black Americans. In her research, Professor Mayer encourages clinicians and educators to actively spread information about the need for improved vitamin D levels among African Americans.

Let's move on to another, iconic example of a disease that appears to only affect Black Americans: the so-called "Black disease" of sickle cell anemia.

• • •

BLACK DISEASES?

Despite the popular misconception, sickle cell anemia is not a Black disease (a myth that Johns Hopkins Children's Hospital chose to explicitly name on their "top 3 misconceptions about sickle cell disease").[181] This condition started as a random genetic mutation within a Sub-Saharan African population experiencing high rates of malaria.[182] The genetic trait that causes sickle cell anemia happened to make those who possessed it more immune to malaria—including those who only inherited the gene from one parent (meaning that they would not experience full-blown sickle cell anemia). This allowed them to survive and pass on the mutation to their descendants.

While many people carried on this single gene unscathed, those who received a copy of it from each parent were not so lucky, ending up with a debilitating, and often fatal, illness.

So, yes; some people of African descent are going to have the sickle cell trait and/or sickle cell anemia—but only if they inherit a specific mutation from a particular region in Sub-Saharan Africa. That does not qualify as a Black disease for three primary reasons:

1.) There is no such thing as biological Blackness.

2.) A regional mutation does not automatically translate to the people of an entire continent.

3.) Anyone can be a carrier of the sickle cell trait, including White people. How, you ask? Sex.

For anyone (regardless of their race) to have the sickle cell trait, one of their ancestors had to have been a carrier of the gene mutation. With as many as 300 million people carrying the sickle cell trait,[183] it has spread among the global population. Someone who currently presents as White can inherit it from one or more ancestors who also had it.

While sickle cell anemia affects about 1 in 365 Black Americans,[184] the American Academy of Pediatrics states that it is also common in "Mediterranean countries (such as Greece, Turkey, and Italy), the Arabian Peninsula, India, Spanish-speaking regions in South and Central America, and parts of the Caribbean. . . . [B]oth dark and light skin people can carry copies of the sickle cell genes."[185] As in America, this is a result of migration and intermixing of different populations.

Despite this simple scientific explanation, sickle cell anemia is often used as concrete proof that certain diseases disproportionately (or only) affect certain populations, furthering the belief that race is biological. Similarly, while the American Heart Association certainly did not state that *only* Black Americans suffer from elevated rates of obesity, diabetes, and hypertension, up until 2022, they were espousing the same racialized logic that applies to inaccurate conclusions about sickle cell anemia and Black Americans. As described by a 2016 research report titled "Taking race out of human genetics," "using 'race' as a variable . . . may simply obscure important variation within these socially-defined categories that can have significant [negative] implications."[186]

Besides the potential for ineffective treatments and potential adverse drug reactions, these false conclusions can lead to insurance companies adjusting risk factors based on "ethnicity," pharmaceutical companies spending untold millions specifically targeting Black Americans for (unnecessary and potentially ineffective) medications, and healthcare providers providing generalized recommendations based on skin color—all based on mistaken science.

If all that doesn't seem concerning to you, consider this fictional scenario for a moment: Researchers find a gene in certain people of Swedish descent that contributes to an increased risk of dementia and therefore conclude that *all* White people are more likely to have dementia. This would be considered unethical and irresponsible. This might lead not only to the creation of "White-targeted" pharmaceuticals but also to a significant increase in the cost of long-term-care insurance for all White people. Doesn't sound fair, does it?

We can clearly see that people of color have disproportionally suffered in terms of their health. So, does that mean that us White folks haven't had evolutionary "malfunctions" or disproportionate ailments?

● ● ●

WHITE DISEASES?

Let's briefly turn the lens back on ourselves. Hypothetically, if there are so-called racialized diseases, there must be some "White diseases" as well. Well, as it turns out, there is one! Cystic fibrosis (CF) is a potentially lethal disease that is substantially more common in the so-called "White population."

CF is a progressive genetic disease that causes damage to multiple organ systems, including the lungs and digestive system, often leading to persistent lung infections and inhibited breathing.

However, just like sickle cell anemia, CF is linked not to a race but instead to a small, localized region in Europe.

According to Dr. Philip Farrell, a neonatologist and pediatric pulmonologist, cystic fibrosis can be directly traced to "a group of distinct but mysterious Europeans who lived about 5,000 years ago."[187] He goes on to say that "CF is the most common, potentially lethal, inherited disease among Caucasians—about one in 40 carry the so-called F508del mutation." However, just like sickle cell anemia, CF is thought to have initially carried some adaptive advantages in that it may have provided resistance to certain infectious diseases, including cholera[188]—a bacterial disease that is spread through water and can often be fatal as a result of severe diarrhea and dehydration.

This primarily "Caucasian" disease does show up in other ethnic populations. However, while as many as 1 in 3,500 White children are born with CF, only about 1 in 17,000 Black Americans and only 1 in 31,000 Asian babies inherit CF.[189] Now, hold on a second; if it is a so-called "White disease," then why are babies of color being born with CF? In case you missed some of the stuff earlier about biracial relations, let's just say that some genes crossed paths along the way.

Similarly, Ashkenazi Jews, certain French Canadian communities, an Old Order Amish community in Pennsylvania, and the Cajun community (a socioeconomic classification of people of French descent who live in Louisiana) are more prone to a rare, progressive, fatal neurological disorder called Tay-Sachs, or Canavan disease.[190] Infants who inherit the genetic mutation are highly likely to die within the first few years of age. The lack of a certain enzyme allows toxic fatty substances to build up the brain, leading to a host of symptoms, including seizures, vision loss, mental impairment, and paralysis.[191] There are also less common forms: juvenile and late-onset Tay-Sachs.

Yet cystic fibrosis and Tay-Sachs disease are only the beginning of these seemingly White ailments. There are a whole host of other regional diseases from various parts of Europe associated with evolutionary advantages that spread within certain populations before making their way into the general population. One such congenital disorder, myasthenia gravis (a chronic autoimmune disease), makes people less susceptible to rabies. Another intriguing example is that women who are phenylketonuria carriers are less likely to have spontaneous miscarriages caused by one specific fungal spore. These miscarriages used to be a common phenomenon in Scotland and Ireland, where damp climates often led to growth of mold and fungi on bean and grain crops.[192] Similar to sickle cell, those who inherited phenylketonuria from both parents experienced significant health issues, including intellectual disabilities, behavioral symptoms, brain damage, and seizures due to a build-up of a specific amino acid in the blood.[193] But those who only inherited it from one parent were more likely to avoid miscarriage and successfully produce multiple offspring.

Ultimately, White people are not the only potential carriers of these diseases for the same reason that Black people are not the only potential carriers of sickle cell anemia or the salt-sensitivity gene. These are not racialized diseases; they are regional diseases that disseminated into the surrounding populations and eventually made their way across the globe.

The false correlation between illness and race has directly impeded medical progress and discovery. As described in 1962 by Theodosius Dobzhansky, a prominent geneticist and evolutionary biologist, race is "a blunt implement that does a poor job of explaining actual relationships between ancestry and genetics."[194]

By more accurately categorizing these illnesses as regional versus racial, we can study resistant populations for therapeutic purposes, including vaccine development and prevention of infectious diseases. This is not hypothetical: one such study led to the development of an anti-salmonella vaccine.[195] Fortunately, scientists are beginning to investigate how these regional genetic mutations might help us find cures for some of the world's deadliest diseases, including HIV and Ebola. But we still have a long way to go—and a lot of unlearning to do—before our healthcare system rids itself of racial fallacies.

• • •

DERACIALIZING HEALTHCARE

If race is such a problem in medicine, why not just eliminate this variable from healthcare altogether? Unfortunately, it's not that simple. While the concept of race can and does create significant confusion in the healthcare industry, acknowledging that race influences healthcare is essential when specifically addressing its health effects on certain communities for reasons that have nothing to do with biology. As described by the "Taking race out of human genetics" report, "in some cases using 'race' as a variable may be important, especially when exploring how social discrimination, structural racism, and other socially determined factors may be responsible for health disparities."[196] In this case, racism rather than race is the tool being used. For example, it is fair to say that Black people living in America more commonly suffer from high blood pressure *if* the connection is explicitly made to the effects of racism on their overall health. If we were to merely say that people of color often suffer from higher blood pressure, we would undermine the fact that specific communities are disproportionately affected. Differing levels of oppression are directly connected to differing levels of overall health.

However, in other instances, as the same study points out, race makes it more difficult to detect important patterns because the socially constructed category overshadows more accurate scientific categories. "Treating" people *because* of their race harms the people who are already most marginalized when it comes to their health. Consequently, many scientists, scholars, and doctors are adamant about removing any mention of race from biological sciences altogether. While this is a noble sentiment, because of systemic and structural disparities that exist within society as well as the healthcare system itself, we cannot simply eliminate race in Western healthcare.

While medical practices and technology have come a long way since the 1700s, the racial science on which much of it is based remains like an infected appendix—functionless, unnecessary, and potentially deadly. A concerned group of biologists in a 2019 article titled "Human races are not like dog breeds: refuting a racist analogy" sum it up best: "harm [is] caused when human biological variation is treated as a mere synonym for racial categories built on the hierarchical organization of people. . . . [W]hether one race is superior to another is not a scientific or biological issue."[197] Yet when it comes to medicine and healthcare in America, race is still treated as a biological fact.

PART 2

How Whiteness Works

CHAPTER 8

Name-Calling: Dividing Us and Them

WHEN DESCRIBING the US census in 1904, statistician Walter Willcox proclaimed that "there is no country in which statistical investigation of race questions is so highly developed . . . as the United States."[198] This quote remains as salient now as it was over a century ago.

Whether or not race can be scientifically proven, White America is still societally obsessed with trying to pin down who exactly "we" are, as well as who "they" are. While it may seem like the census is nothing more than annoying busywork that shows up every ten years, asking invasive questions about how we self-identify, the US census serves as the international epitome of racial categorization. Moreover, we have dedicated a statistical scientific approach to tracking a divisive social construct that has tremendous implications for the fate of every American—especially people of color. Not only does the census help establish the racial hierarchy in the United States, but it also serves as the basis for social, political, and societal organization.

• • •

RACIALIZED DATA

"Our census helps to construct and reconstruct an ethno-racial order in four ways: by providing the taxonomy and language of race; generating the informational content for that taxonomy; facilitating the development of public policies; and generating numbers upon which claims to political representation are made,"[199] explains Harvard professor Jennifer Hochschild. In other words, our census profoundly impacts not only social perceptions of one another but also social mobility and policy decisions.

The census is created and compiled by a combination of scientists, researchers, statisticians, and demographers—and, of course, politicians and policymakers. As a government-funded institution, despite an ongoing plight for autonomy and administrative control, the US Census Bureau has been under the watchful eye, and even direct influence, of Congress and the Supreme Court. The census is a tremendous undertaking, costing taxpayers over $6.3 billion in 2020 alone.[200]

The ten-year census reflects the current political and social order and often sets the terms for the following decade. As described by Hochschild, "a nation's census is deeply implicated in and helps to construct its social and political order. Censuses provide the concepts, taxonomy, and substantive information by which a nation understands its component parts as well as the contours of the whole; censuses both create the image and provide the mirror of that image for a nation's self-reflection."[201] This chicken–egg scenario becomes a self-perpetuating cycle, often leading to further confusion and an ever-shifting social order. Consequently, it most certainly does matter which box you check—whether you want it to or not.

As it currently stands, there are only two remaining categories on the census designated by a color: White and Black. The remaining races are no longer linked to a color in any way. Further scrutiny reveals that White and Black are the only bona fide categories of race still remaining on the census. This is not an accident; it is a byproduct of the integral role the racial designations of White and Black have played in our country's history. These titles are the vestigial organ of a time in which racism dominated—and perhaps created—Western society.

While it may be tempting to say that we should do away with

these two colorized labels on the census, that would be akin to saying we should simply get rid of race. If those labels could simply be dropped from the census, it would have been done decades ago. Rather than White and Black being the exception to the multiple distinctly ethnic categories available on the census, White and Black are the very categories on which the census was built.

Here's what we see in the categories of self-selection available on the very first US census conducted in 1790: "Free White males of 16 years and upward (to assess the country's industrial and military potential), Free White males under 16 years, Free White females, All other free persons, Slaves."[202] These categories are pulled directly from the Census Bureau's own website, in which they provide an overview of every ten-year census dating back to the eighteenth century.

Over the past two centuries of "categorical evolution," the first three categories have been simplified/consolidated into simply "White," while the latter, "slaves," are now referred to as Black or African American. However, the census remains a living document. In two centuries, it has undergone profound changes. Despite the well-meaning efforts of many individuals at the United States Census Bureau, the census itself remains rooted in our country's racial history. It has been a substantial indicator of not only where we've been but also where we are headed.

● ● ●

RACIAL HIERARCHY

While it should be stated that the census alone does not determine the "ethno-racial order" of the United States,[203] it has played an integral role in shaping the social hierarchies and political systems we have today. From chattel slavery and the Native American genocide of the 1700s and the 1800s to the eugenics movement and the one-drop rule of the Jim Crow era throughout the early 1900s (when Black Americans were granted "freedom from slavery" and then subsequently denied basic rights as fierce segregation laws became codified throughout the entire South and most of the Northern US), the Japanese internment camps in 1942, mass deportations of countless immigrants throughout the twentieth and twenty-first centuries, the 2017 "Muslim ban," and literally caging child migrants at the US–Mexico border in 2020, the census has been instrumental in tracking and determining not only who "becomes" American but *how* they become American.

Professor Hochschild explains how "for most of American history, a person's racial classification largely shaped his or her social status, civil rights, economic opportunities, political standing, and legal citizenship. [The census has] [t]he important task of deciding whether and where new populations fit into the American racial order."[204] This shaping of the social order continues today. However, despite the census's subjective categorization and fluidity of labels, two things have remained constant since its inception: White people remain on top, while an entire group once referred to only as "slaves" resides at the bottom.

Despite the best intentions and drastic makeovers of the US census in the twenty-first century, it continues to reinforce the status quo. Those in the middle of the color gradient simply wait in ten-year intervals to discover their fate in the reorganization of the racial order.

● ● ●

"FRACTIONED" IDENTITIES

The evolving racial categories on the US census are confusing and clearly demonstrate how abstract the definition of race is. Entirely new racial categories are created every ten years, while others disappear completely.

The only race that has remained constant since the inception of the US census in 1790 is White. For the first sixty years, White was the only color explicitly referenced. Conversely, during that same time period, any and all BIPOC Americans were accounted for simply as "the number of slaves and free colored persons" in a household.[205] Then, in 1850, drastic shifts set the stage for the current model of the census we use today. As described by Becky Little, a journalist for History.com, 1850 to 1930 was "a period of rapid change that saw both the end of slavery and the beginning of Jim Crow."[206] She goes on to describe how through most of the twentieth century, "many of the changes the census has gone through ha[d] to do with race and power in America. . . . [C]ensus information has been used to reinforce 'pure' White ancestry as the standard for full citizenship."

Beginning in 1850, the census was broken into specific columns that needed to be filled out about each person—one of which was "color."[207] This marked the very first time that the classification of "black" (lowercase) became an option on the US census. It also was the first year that "mulatto" was added to the census (designating someone with three-fourths or more of "African blood").[208] This was a direct result of slave owner and racial scientist Josiah Nott pressuring a Kentucky senator to include it on the census. Like Samuel Morton, Nott was a polygenist, believing that Black people and White people did not originate from the same species.[209] He wanted to study people of mixed-race ancestry to see if there were any adverse side effects, such as a shorter lifespan, for White people who had "African blood."[210]

However, not every category on the census was rooted in racial science; money was also a driving factor. In 1860, Indian ("Ind.") was added to the census strictly for taxation purposes; only Native Americans who were being taxed were to be accounted for. This made it easier for the US government to keep tabs on Native

American tribes and implement rigid taxation measures. But racial science was still the driving force when it came to designating who's who.

Whereas the instructions for the previous two censuses had simply stated, "The color of all slaves should be noted,"[211] the 1870 census instructions gave little room for ambiguity or scientific error when it came to "accurately" filling out this column: "[If] nothing is written in this column, 'White' is to be understood. . . . [Otherwise] the column is always to be filled [for non-Whites]. Be particularly careful in reporting the class Mulatto. The word is here generic, and includes quadroons [one-fourth African blood], octoroons [one-eighth African blood], and all persons having any perceptible trace of African blood. Important scientific results depend upon the correct determination."[212] At this point, the crude and imprecise work of race science had unapologetically become both a contributor to and beneficiary of the US census.

As barbaric as the terms "quadroons" and "octoroons" may sound, these racial "blood fractions" are still relevant in the twenty-first century, as we still often use terminology indicating that someone is half, a quarter, or an eighth Black—versus simply referring to them as multiracial. Miscegenation (the "scientific" term for racial intermixing, which was believed to have negative impacts on the White race) was not taken lightly in the United States during the nineteenth century (and arguably still is not by many Americans). White scientists, lawmakers, and statisticians became increasingly fixated on the notions of White purity. Consequently, "blood fractions" became more specific on each subsequent census, up through the turn of the twentieth century.

These racial designations made things more confusing and effectively created a racial hierarchy based on entirely false scientific pretenses. There is no actual way to measure blood fractions. These labels were completely subject to the biases of those who were supposed to visually determine who fit into which categories. Nonetheless, this is where concepts such as "biracial" and "mixed race" ultimately stem from.

Beginning in 1880, two different racial labels popped up on the census: "C" for Chinese and "I" for American Indian. The inclusion of Chinese was the direct result of the nearly 20,000 Chinese immigrants forced to do backbreaking labor on the transcontinental railroad throughout the 1860s and 1870s.[213] Chinese was used to racially categorize anyone from Asia or Southeast Asia for nearly a decade, until "Japanese" was added in 1890.

Meanwhile, the US census was forced to reckon with the classification of Indian as a race for one reason: racial "purity." An entirely new section was added to the census to make sure that all "full" as well as "part" Native Americans were "accurately" categorized. The bureau even stated that all "detached Whites and negroes" (i.e., defectors from society) were to be marked as "members of the Indian families in which they are found."[214] The same "blood fraction" rules applied to Indigenous peoples, only except for looking for signs of "black blood" in the White population, the census changed the point of reference, explicitly stating that the fraction of "white blood"[215] was to be documented in each Indian accounted for—ranging from measurements of zero to half-White blood.

In addition to "blood fractions," Native Americans were put under further scrutiny for financial purposes. Although the US government had brutally forced most Indigenous peoples onto reservations, the Census Bureau had the gall to instruct census marshals and assistants, "If the Indian has no occupation and is wholly dependent on the Government for support, write 'Ration Indian.'"[216] Making the Native Americans seem helpless allowed the United States government to further divide and conquer tribes. Moreover, this condescending myth of freeloading "ration Indians" ultimately set the basis for the (Black) "welfare queens" scorned by Ronald Reagan in the 1980s—yet another form of victim-shaming, even though both groups undeniably suffered from a chronic state of government-induced welfare.

While racial categories continued to expand on the US census, the most significant term on the US census today—"race"—did not appear until the twentieth century. For over fifty years, the category had simply been labeled "color." The newly adopted category "color or race" then remained on the census for over seventy years, after which the category was changed simply to "race"—as it remains to this day.

Beginning in 1930, terms that designated blood fractions were officially dropped from the census. As described by Becky Little, "by 1930, White statisticians acknowledged that deciding whether someone is 'black,' 'mulatto,' 'quadroon' or 'octoroon' on a census form is [too] subjective, and replaced all of these categories with 'Negro.'"[217] However, while the categories themselves disappeared, blood fractions remained the determining factor of who was who. The instructions that year explicitly stated that "a person of mixed White and Negro blood was to be returned as Negro, no matter how small the percentage of Negro blood; someone part Indian and part Negro also was to be listed as Negro unless the Indian blood predominated and the person was generally accepted as an Indian in the community."[218] "Black" was not capitalized on the census until 1970, when the choice became "Negro or Black." This was likely in response to the civil rights movement of the 1960s, when the use of "Black" with a capital "B" became a term of identity and empowerment.

As described by Barbara Kiviat, assistant professor in the Department of Sociology at Stanford University, beginning in the "the civil rights era of the twentieth century, Census data took on a whole new meaning. The antidiscrimination laws written in the

1960s and the affirmative-action policies that followed relied on Census data to determine if minorities were underrepresented in any number of realms, from home sales to small-business loans."[219] Yet despite these positive intentions, this racial data could be used to uphold the very discrimination it was supposed to help mitigate. While no longer legal, redlining—in which banks and mortgage lenders literally drew red lines around parts of the map (i.e., historically Black neighborhoods) where they intended not to issue any loans[220]—remained an ongoing issue, as Black Americans were continuously denied housing and home loans in most of the United States.

The year 1970 also marked the first time that the census switched from a fill-in column to predesignated bubbles for Americans to report their race, including a space to fill in "other"—leading to an explosion in the number of options over the following decades. In 1980, there were fourteen races to choose from.

The year 2000 unveiled perhaps one of the biggest turning points in the US census data collection process. "For the first time, respondents were allowed to check more than one race box," Kiviat says. "The change was celebrated by those hoping to usher in an era of post-racial America."[221] However, this also introduced a whole new layer of confusion when it comes to defining one's race.

• • •

"HISPANIC ORIGIN" STORY

Here's a fun fact: a person from Mexico living in the United States in 1930 would have witnessed the first and only time in US history that their ethnicity was listed as a race. Strangely, a mere decade later, this race disappeared from the form, and instead, they were counted as White.[222] And it gets even more convoluted.

Up until the 1970s, Mexicans living in the United States remained classified as White each time the census data was compiled. This is undoubtedly a modern-day White nationalist's worst nightmare: "You mean to tell me that Mexicans were considered White for over fifty years in America?!" In fact, the Census Bureau explicitly stated that "'Chicano,' 'LaRaza,' 'Mexican American,' 'Moslem,' or 'Brown' were to be changed to White."[223] That finally shifted when, beginning in 1980, the census created a brand-new category asking whether a person is "of Spanish/Hispanic origin or descent."[224] This brought about perhaps the most confusing "racial non-category" to date.

Now, if you're wondering what prompted this oddity, don't worry; the 2020 Census Bureau website had a "perfectly logical" explanation written in bold letters: "The concept of race is separate from the concept of Hispanic origin."[225] As if that's not confusing enough, the website explicitly stated that this is because "people who identify their origin as Hispanic, Latino, or Spanish may be of any race."

The US Census Bureau attempted to "clarify" this anomaly by stating that the "percentages for the various race categories [already] add to 100 percent, and should not be combined with the percent Hispanic,"[226] but then went on to say that "people of Hispanic origin [are] the nation's largest ethnic or racial minority. Hispanics constituted 18.1 percent of the nation's total population."[227] Yes, you read that right. Even though people of Latino ancestry made up nearly a fifth of the entire US population in 2017, the other predefined racial categories already added up to 100 percent—so racially speaking, they literally don't count. Sorry, "Hispanic, Latino, or Spanish origin" folks, but it looks like this decade's racial categories are all filled up. Maybe try again in 2030?

The racial identity debacle that occurs every ten years is what happens when scientists, statisticians, and politicians play tug-of-war with socially constructed categories. As a result of the current juncture in our racial framework (not to mention our fear of creating even more unwanted and offensive racial categories), we have determined that "Hispanic, Latino, or Spanish origin" (i.e., Latinx or Latine)* is an ethnicity rather than a race. It appears that there is simply too broad a variety of people ("Mexican, Mexican American, Cuban, Puerto Rican, Salvadoran, Dominican, Colombian, Guatemalan, Spaniard, Ecuadorian, etc.")[228] that fall within this category to be considered a single race—so the easiest approach was to label it an ethnicity instead (i.e., a group with shared traditions, beliefs, language, common ancestry).

Despite the Census Bureau's refusal to create a new race because it would be "too broad," the census does not appear to take issue with continuing to lump together equally large swaths of incredibly diverse people with complex ethnic origins—namely Black and White.

While the Census Bureau has historically succumbed to the insanity of racial science and "blood fractions" and ineffectively tried to delineate between race and ethnicity, this is not entirely the Census Bureau's fault. They are forced to operate in the same ever-evolving racial framework as every other American. Many of the changes over the last few decades have been made to be more inclusive and culturally sensitive. However, this only further highlighted the difficulty of trying to fuse socially constructed categories with ethnicity and nationality, as well as how subjective the definition of race really is. Consequently, while they did their best to be more accommodating on the 2020 census, things became even more confusing.

* * *

---

* As of 2023, the term "Latine" remains in use as a gender-neutral way to describe Latino or Latina people. However, the term continues to be received with mixed feelings by many within the community, as is the term "Latinx."

SO WHICH BOX DO I CHECK?

On the most recent 2020 census, the US Census Bureau provided a staggering number of options to choose from, designating fifteen categories and allowing people to check multiple boxes.

One of the primary ways the 2020 census tried to mitigate this confusion was by also giving the option of writing in a more detailed description of one's identity within three of fifteen categories available: "White," "Black or African American," and "American Indian or Alaska Native." This means that someone could identify as White but also write in a nationality such as Italian in the boxes provided underneath. While this left room for a more diverse spectrum of self-identification, it did not account for the other twelve categories, which are not races at all but rather ethnicities.

Despite the fact that race and ethnicity are not the same thing, the 2020 census listed the following twelve categories under a question that explicitly asked, "What is _____'s race?": "Chinese, Filipino, Asian Indian, Vietnamese, Korean, Japanese, Other Asian, Native Hawaiian, Samoan, Chamorro, Other Pacific Islander, or Some other race."[229]

While the intent here was clearly to broaden the racial framework, this is a blatant example of equating race to ethnicity and further reinforces the false idea that certain cultural characteristics, values, and beliefs are inherent to people because of their race. Having the ability to define one person as White and another person as, say, Korean in the very same question on the census implies that these are two equally valid ways of describing one's race. To make matters even more convoluted, the data from the person who checks the box for Korean will still be fed back into the broader category of Asian.[230]

This is because when it comes down to it, politicians, healthcare providers, scientists, banks, employers, etc., are likely not going to base their important decisions on someone being Korean versus

Vietnamese; they are going to (unwittingly) apply the broader category of Asian Pacific Islander (a catch-all replacement for its less politically correct predecessor, "Oriental")[231] that they have already been socially conditioned to believe exists.

American society and our institutions cannot simply "unsee" the broader category of Asian for the same reason we cannot "unsee" our preconceived belief in Blackness; when it comes to census data, people from Korea and Vietnam are still considered Asian in the same way that people from Zimbabwe and Ethiopia are still considered Black.

Similarly, while terms such as "red" and "yellow" will likely never show up again, any White American born in the twentieth century would know exactly which groups these centuries-old labels invoke. Why? Because labels don't go away; they are merely retired once they no longer serve their defining function or no longer fit within the spectrum of political correctness.

● ● ●

"DISASSEMBLING" ASIAN

While Asian Pacific Islander (API) and American Asian Pacific Islander (AAPI) have been the go-to politically correct terms for quite some time, they may be the next racial labels to go.

The term "Asian American" originated in the 1960s. Inspired by the Black Power movement's consolidated power against White supremacy,[232] the term was amplified by the pan-Asian student movement in order to help unify and acknowledge a shared identity, create more political power, and reject the geographically limiting term "Oriental"—which was a subjective term used primarily to describe all people from East Asia. Not surprisingly, the category was re-expanded over the next two decades and became Asian American and Pacific Islander/Asian Pacific Islander. However, once it was adopted by mainstream US institutions and White Americans, this broadening of the category—presumably to try and be more inclusive—ended up creating a new set of problems, effectively reinstating the overly generic and problematic category of Oriental, as well as reinforcing broad stereotypes and prejudices.

Many Asian community leaders advocate disaggregating Asian and Pacific Islander to ensure that Pacific Islander populations are not being further marginalized. A *Seattle Times* article explains, "Joseph Seia, the founder and executive director of the Pacific Islander Community Association (PICA) of Washington, said merging Asian American and NHPI [Native Hawaiian and Pacific Islander] together makes the specific needs of NHPI people invisible."[233] Seia compared the experience of many Native Hawaiian and Pacific Islander people "to the experience of urban Native American people, as the majority of NHPI are also indigenous to their original lands and suffered displacement, dislocation and subjugation due to colonization—including colonization and oppression by Asian countries."

By lumping so many groups together, economic and social disparities go unnoticed, particularly among refugees. Many who fall under the category of API suffer because of a tremendous economic, education, and healthcare gap, even within the Asian community itself. For example, "19 percent of Cambodians live in poverty in the US, compared to 12 percent of Asian people and 15 percent of all people,"[234] reports a 2015 Pew Research study. Moreover, because the overly broad term "AAPI" also includes South Asian Americans, these gaps become even more apparent.

Politics and policy reporter Li Zhou describes, "While Indian Americans have the highest median income [of all Asian Americans] of $100,000, for example, Burmese Americans have the lowest, at $36,000. Similarly, there are significant disparities among Asian Americans in educational attainment and health care outcomes: 94 percent of Japanese and Taiwanese Americans have graduated high school, compared to less than 66 percent of Laotian and Hmong Americans. And 22 percent of Nepalese Americans don't have health insurance compared to 6 percent of Japanese Americans."[235] These gaps rival those of Black and Indigenous communities in America, yet time and time again we are told that Asian Americans are part of the "success story."

Moreover, many "White writers pushed the idea of the 'model minority myth'—a racist trope that suggests that all Asian Americans are well off and pits them against other groups," which further adds to "the perception that all Asian Americans are broadly successful," thereby "camouflaging the struggles and diversity of many community members."[236] Consequently, many Pacific Islanders find themselves experiencing cultural erasure as well as societal oppression in a country that simply assumes that most Asians are doing just fine.

Ultimately, "the term AAPI is . . . meant to be inclusive, but its usage—by government agencies in particular—has had the opposite effect,"[237] according to Zhou. "The label aspires to unify a wide range of communities with common cause and shared experiences. But many feel it flattens and erases entire cultures."

Indiana University sociology professor Dina Okamoto sums it up best. When it comes down to it, "the [only] thing that these Asian American communities [have in common] is the experience of perhaps being viewed as outsiders"[238]—that and the heartbreaking fact that since the Covid-19 pandemic, there has been a dramatic surge in Asian hate crimes, meaning that one of the most uniting factors of the API community is currently fear of being attacked by nationalistic and racist Americans. The 2021 rise of the "#StopAsianHate" movement was a testament to this depressing reality.

According to a 2021 Pew Research report, the Asian population is currently considered the fastest-growing population in America.[239] However, this statistic is actually misleading when we take into account that this "growing population" includes at least twenty ethnicities and lumps together well over twenty-two million Americans who have almost nothing in common, other than a broad label that was assigned to them by the United States census. While the expanding and contracting categories on the most recent census were undoubtedly designed to make people feel more included, this $6.3 billion data will inevitably be lumped back into narrow racialized parameters to make social and political decisions.

During the all-encompassing fifteen-box census saga, one category remains missing altogether. Didn't catch it? I don't blame you—and I promise, the Census Bureau's explanation is even more baffling. Here's the million-dollar question: where does someone who identifies as North African or Middle Eastern place themselves on the 2020 identity spectrum? "Some other race"?[240] Not quite.

• • •

WHITE (ONLY) ON PAPER

On the 2020 United States census, people of North African and Middle Eastern descent are *still* considered White.[241] While this may seem like a fluke, this has been the case since the early 1900s. Somehow the bureau expects that a group the US has unjustly declared war on for well over two decades—both abroad as well as in our own country—should simply suck it up and call themselves White.

Most people of Middle Eastern and North African ancestry perceive themselves as anything but White. They not only miss out on the benefits or privileges of being considered White, but they also often face blatant discrimination and violent hatred from many proud White Americans.

It is insulting to expect someone from the Middle East to check a box claiming that they "belong" to the category of people by whom they feel most vehemently oppressed. Moreover, even within the most liberal and progressive communities, one would be hard-pressed to find a single White person who would identify a close friend from Saudi Arabia, Iran, Egypt, or Yemen as being White. This has led to the peculiar phenomenon in which many people of Middle Eastern descent refer to themselves as "White on paper" (i.e., white *only* according to the census).[242]

This still begs the question: why count them as White, and who came up with this idea in the first place? Strange as it may seem, this parameter of Whiteness isn't new at all. Designating specific people of Middle Eastern ancestry as White aligns with a term that goes back almost three centuries: "Caucasian." Both the term itself and the concept are attributed to the founder of modern anthropology, Johan Friedrich Blumenbach—a devoted White supremacist.

• • •

A SUPERIOR FORM OF ASIAN

During the 1700s, Blumenbach devised the term "Caucasian" for those who lived west of the Caucasus mountain range spanning the border of Europe and Asia.[243] Fast-forward to the twentieth century, and the millions of people of Middle Eastern descent suddenly categorized as White (i.e., Caucasian) happen to fit precisely within the designated geographical range devised by Blumenbach. A modern political map of the Middle East can confirm this "inadvertent" connection. Case in point, while American immigrants from Iran and Afghanistan can now technically call themselves White, Pakistani immigrants are still expected to designate themselves as "other Asian." Pakistan doesn't quite fall within the specified geographical range, whereas the other two countries are safely nestled within the "Caucasus zone."

The problem here is not merely the geographical alignment of Blumenbach's racial designation on the US census but also that his motives for creating the Caucasian race were firmly rooted in racism. As an unapologetic supporter of racial superiority, Blumenbach surmised that one's place of origin, skull shape (forehead, nose structure, cheekbones, jawline, etc.), and physical beauty (as defined by him) were instrumental in determining whether someone was considered Caucasian.[244] Because many people of Middle Eastern ancestry share similar facial features to those of European ancestry, Blumenbach considered their skulls of equal worth.

Blumenbach didn't stop there. As described by Professor Charles Loring Brace in his book *"Race" Is a Four-Letter Word*, Blumenbach firmly believed the Caucasian race represented "the closest approximation of God's intent for human form, and [that] other human populations . . . departed from that manifestation of the ideal."[245] Blumenbach's entire premise for the creation of this category was to elevate what he believed was the most superior form of the human race. Blumenbach genuinely thought that God *him*self intended for people to look like him—and this premise was at the heart of his "anthropological" studies.[246]

So what? Just because the term "Caucasian" is rooted in racist ideology doesn't mean that we believe any of this, right? Well, we can't simply detach the term (nor the science) from its original intent. This is a powerful example of how racial designations still hold tremendous sway even centuries after their inception in the public mind. White supremacy was baked into the foundation of anthropology itself; it was exclusively intended for "us" to study "them"—not the other way around. The term and category of Caucasian set us apart as the ones who were superior and divinely crafted, giving us permission to study our "inferior" counterparts.

While the term "Caucasian" did not explicitly appear on the 2020 census, unintentionally perpetuating this specific variation of White invokes a category built entirely upon racial supremacy. There was likely no conscious intent in upholding Blumenbach's version of Whiteness, yet this remains a powerful example of how racist ideology (often unintentionally) lingers for centuries.

Moreover, the ramifications of this socially and politically charged misclassification will likely have a profound impact on the statistical makeup of this country in the coming decades, as more and more immigrants from North Africa and the Middle East arrive. The Migration Policy Institute reported that "between 2000 and 2019, the immigrant population from the MENA [Middle Eastern and North African] region doubled from 596,000 to 1.2 million."[247]

Considering the desires, demands, and power of the "White population" as well as the "White vote," the effects of being able to bolster our numbers on paper remain to be seen. Like every census prior, the 2020 census results were quickly converted into hard data that in turn affects how our society will operate over the next decade, including policy decisions around immigration, law enforcement, education, healthcare, and electoral districts, to name a few.

Even though for decades, many Americans from the Middle East and North Africa have been expected to legally declare themselves White, the 2017 Muslim ban indicates that our social and political structures are simply not willing to acknowledge this categorical anomaly. One thing is for sure: despite their ongoing census designation as White, the supposed "White folks" hailing from North Africa and the Middle East are not being given the same rights or respect as their European-descended counterparts. While my race will still be guaranteed in ten years' time, the racial designation of people of North African and Middle Eastern ancestry on the US census will likely be called into question as their numbers continue to increase.

• • •

NONINTERCHANGEABLE TERMS

The Census Bureau openly states that "the [current] race categories generally reflect social definitions in the US and are not an attempt to define race biologically, anthropologically, or genetically";248 however, this confusion of categories on paper leads to equally confusing categorization of people in the real world. Consequently, the words "ethnicity," "race," and "nationality" are often used interchangeably to account for discrepancies or outliers.

For example, while Black is still clearly delineated, by also offering the term "African American" to encapsulate this particular racial category, the census implies that Black Americans can be defined either by a color gradient or their ancestral heritage. This leaves a lot of ambiguity in regard to people of African Ancestry who don't live in America (in the same way that "European American" doesn't account for those living outside of America or Europe who are identified as White). This very ambiguity proves not only that the concept of race was created by us but also that who exactly "belongs" within any category is noticeably obscure.

These categories become a compounding problem; the more categories one tries to create, broaden, or redefine, the more difficult it becomes to include everyone—as demonstrated by the increasing complexity of the census. As a result, countless Americans feel not only left out but also boxed in.

Despite White America's propensity to assign labels to other people, we are by no means the only arbiter of how people choose to self-identify.

• • •

BLACK IS BACK

While "black" (lowercase) first officially appeared on the US census in 1850 as a designation of skin color (indicated simply by the letter "B"),249 only in the last fifty years has "Black" (uppercase) become a signifier of identity—and more importantly, power.

As described by Afro-American studies scholar Zenobia Desha Jaye Bell in her 2013 dissertation, "for a good portion of history, African-Americans have decided for themselves what they would like to be called and how the government and media should refer to them."[250] Many names were proposed by various groups throughout the 1800s, including African, free African, Afro-American, Anglo-African, Aframerican, Hamite, and Tan American.[251] While many of these simply didn't catch on, others became problematic and fell out of favor for a different reason altogether: the subsequent appropriation and negative use of these labels by White Americans. This led to the ongoing need to reinvent, reclaim, and rename the "Black identity" in America.

Take, for example, the labels "colored" and "Negro." Both were reclaimed in the 1830s by Black Americans during a time of contentious debate between societal integration and African nationalism. Some Black Americans believed that holding firm to their African identity was the key to their freedom and enfranchisement. Others felt that it was paramount that they carve out a self-defined, unique identity that was not Afrocentric to be given a place and status within American society. Consequently, "Negro" and "colored" became "acceptable terms for African Americans during the 1830s and beyond because they signified a domestic rather than a completely foreign placement,"[252] describes Bell. Both terms were adopted for the same purpose: "to accomplish freedom and enfranchisement."

However, as with countless other terms of self-empowerment, White Americans continued to use these terms *against* Black Americans to further signify their inferiority. The term "colored" became a catch-all used by White Americans for *anyone* who did not identify as White. This left many Black Americans feeling that the term no longer represented them, and it fell out of favor among many Black communities throughout the mid-1900s, even though White Americans continued to use it for decades afterward.

Similarly, when "blood fractions" were finally dropped from the US census in 1930, the term "Negro" became a nationally agreed-upon identifier of anyone with even a minuscule amount of African ancestry. However, by this point, many Black Americans felt that this self-identifier had lost its purpose as a reclaimed signifier of freedom and empowerment. Moreover, some remained troubled that this term had previously been used exclusively in a derogatory context.

As described by scholars and history professors Bettye Collier-Thomas and James Turner in a 1994 research paper titled "Race, Class and Color: The African American Discourse on Identity," the term "Negro," which was originally used by the Portuguese as a descriptor (negro means "black" in Portuguese) during the height of slave trade, "fused not only humanity, nationality and place of origin but also certain white judgments about the irredeemable inferiority of the persons so designated."[253] Many Black Americans felt that they were self-identifying with a term of oppression. Not to mention the word's close connection to its even more pejorative cousin, n*gger—derived from the Latin word for the color black, "niger"—which had already become a powerful insult by the early nineteenth century.[254]

Despite this ambiguity, the term "Negro" remained in use well into the twenty-first century, within both White and Black communities. According to an NPR report, during the 2000 census, nearly 56,000 people chose to write out the word "Negro" under the "some other race" category.[255] Consequently, in an attempt to be *more* inclusive, the word "Negro" reappeared on the 2010 census, leading to some confusion over the next decade among a few (White-led) institutions that were trying to adapt to the modern political climate, the United States military being one of them.

While trying to mirror the "inclusivity" of the census, the US Army got itself into an embarrassing situation in 2014. In an updated version of its discrimination policies, the US Army unilaterally decreed, "Terms such as 'Haitian' or 'Negro' can be used in addition to 'Black' or 'African American.'"[256] Unfortunately, they did not include the crucial caveat that use of this terminology did not apply to White people. As expected, this misguided attempt to be more inclusive backfired, leading to a major backlash by mainstream media, including a *First On CNN* headline titled "Army says word 'Negro' OK to use."[257] This is just another example of a "self-inflicted land mine" that resulted from creating a completely subjective categorization system built on a social construct.

So, is it okay for us to use the term "Black"? It depends on who you ask, and in which decade.

● ● ●

BLACK (GAINS) POWER

During the civil rights movement of the 1960s, many Black Americans felt that it was time to reclaim their identities, signify their power, and "rebrand" once again. Fueled in large part by Black Panther members and outspoken racial activists Stokely Carmichael and Willie Ricks, the resurgence of the terms "Black" and "Black Power" signified the repurposing and rebirthing of a term that was initially used against the people it described. Part of the intention behind using "Black" was that it served as a deliberate and effective counterweight to its direct counterpart: White. The term "Black" positioned Blackness as a source of pride and identity, becoming a unifying label under which to build a stronger alliance against oppression.[258] It sent a clear message of resistance against Whiteness and a demand for racial equality.

Yet despite its positive intent of empowerment, many African Americans felt that the term "Black," just like "colored" and "Negro," did not properly encapsulate the complexity and richness of their diverse collective or individual identities. Many also felt that the term further signified racial divisiveness and did not serve the purpose of achieving unity or equality. As a result, in 1988, Reverend Jesse Jackson held a historic press conference to try to convince the entirety of America's Black population to adopt the term "African American." Not surprisingly, politically correct White people were some of the first to make the switch.

While the term "African American" has been around for well over three decades at this point, there is still no consensus among Black Americans as to whether they identify with or want to be identified by this label—and there will likely never be one. Now the Black Lives Matter movement that spread across the nation after the murder of George Floyd in 2020 has propelled the term "Black" back into the common (White) vernacular. Prior to this movement, many White people had dropped the racial term from their vocabulary altogether, deeming it politically incorrect and offensive.

Despite this marked political shift, there is still confusion in the White community as to whether it is now okay to call someone Black, and often it comes down to preference or context. This has become a point of contention, even within the African American community itself. While many people with African ancestry openly refer to themselves as Black, many are still not comfortable being described this way by someone who is not of their race.

It may be tempting to play it safe and continue to only use the term African American, but as described by Gary Younge, a sociology professor at the University of Manchester, "all African-Americans are black; but not all black Americans are African Americans."[259] This point becomes all the more salient when taking into consideration that Younge himself is a British professor and journalist whose family—of African ancestry—arrived from Barbados, located in the Caribbean; and that he lived in the United

States for a short period. As more immigrants from both Africa and the Caribbean (with African ancestry) arrive in the US, these catch-all labels come under further scrutiny by folks who do not want to be confined within predetermined Amero-centric racial categories.

• • •

"SAFE" LABELS

Up until 2020, there appeared to be one "safe" all-encompassing term to describe non-White people: POC (people of color). Surprisingly, this term dates back at least two centuries, first cited in 1796 in the *Oxford English Dictionary*.[260] However, in 2020, a more recently coined acronym quickly became the most politically correct term to call all non-White people: BIPOC (Black, Indigenous, and people of color). While this acronym appears to have begun trending after a 2013 tweet by Grind Toronto—a queer, sex-positive space for Black, Indigenous, and people of color—it didn't catch on in mainstream dialogue until Black Lives Matter protests took center stage in 2020.[261]

But what is deemed politically correct often changes with each passing generation. Another contender, BBIA (Black, brown, Indigenous, and Asian), also entered mainstream dialogue in 2021, although some have argued that it initially meant "being Black in America" before it was unwittingly repurposed.[262]

When it comes to all these acronyms, there is an unfortunate downside: their inherent vagueness. They become tricky to navigate when we want to know which group is explicitly being referred to (particularly when context is important). Like the term "Black," the nebulousness of the terms "POC," "BIPOC," and "BBIA" means that we end up lumping together different groups in conversations where ethnicity and nationality may be necessary distinctions. For example, simply saying, "BIPOC Americans are still being disproportionately targeted by police officers" does not necessarily give enough information when it comes to addressing the problem of Black Americans facing police brutality.

Another potential issue with these acronyms is that they inherently perpetuate and reinforce an "us" and "them" mentality. By default, we are still the only people that do *not* have color—meaning that White people are still the only group differentiated from all the other races being lumped under one acronym. So, while well intentioned, these acronyms often still uphold a racial hierarchy that allows White people to feel unique.

Ultimately, there are no easy answers when it comes to the ongoing, complex use of racial categories or politically correct labels. There will likely never come a point of total clarity or consensus on what the "best" racial terms are to call anyone. Both the labels and categories themselves will likely evolve throughout our lifetime, as they have for the past four centuries. As to what the census decides we can or *should* call others, only (another ten years') time will tell.

One thing is for certain: Whiteness isn't going anywhere—and White "owning-class" men are still the ones census data serves the most.

CHAPTER 9

A World Made "Just" for Me

EVERY TIME I am called White, it is a reminder of my status within society. This label conferring power and privilege was undeservedly placed upon me by those who came before me, to ensure that I would retain and never forget my status in "our" society. Add in the fact that I am also a male and American, and I have been designated a member of the highest-ranking group on a global level. To be described as a White American male denotes a status that few in this world will ever hold.

• • •

THE TOP TIER OF WHITENESS

Making up barely 30 percent of the total US population, White American men account for about 1 percent of the global population. Yet in 2020, we accounted for nearly 40 percent of the world's millionaires and collectively owned almost 30 percent of the entire world's wealth, close to double that of all European wealth leaders combined.[263] Beyond our material wealth, we maintain a global empire with over 800 active military bases spanning the globe—more than most other developed nations combined, and more than any other nation or empire in recorded history.[264]

In terms of the actual scope of our political and military power, the entire European Union pales in comparison to the world dominance collectively held by White American men. Political scientist and former CIA consultant Chalmers Johnson describes it best in a 2004 article: "Most Americans do not recognize—or do not want to recognize—that the United States dominates the world through its military power.... This vast network of American bases on every continent except Antarctica actually constitutes a new form of empire.... Without grasping the dimensions of this globe-girdling Baseworld, one can't begin to understand the size and nature of our imperial aspirations."[265]

While roughly 43 percent of active-duty officers are people of color, "the people making crucial decisions ... [remain] almost entirely White and male,"[266] describes *New York Times* Pentagon correspondent Helene Cooper in a 2020 article. "The military's upper echelons remain the domain of White men." As such, one could easily argue that the United States military is the physical embodiment of the power that we hold over not just the United States but also the rest of the world.

Even beyond our military might, our dominant status (whether revered or detested) is acknowledged on a global level—which brings us to a more important part of the shared White American male identity.

Whether we are aware of it or not, every single one of us possesses the protection of White (male) privilege. This is a fundamental cornerstone of White American male culture. While we tend to assume that we are uniquely self-empowered individuals with inalienable rights, this entitled belief is part of our shared identity. Those of us with the least amount of wealth and power still benefit from trickle-down privilege by virtue of simply being a White American man in a country that was designed by us and for us.

We often understand privilege as something exceptional beyond what we individually possess (i.e., the domain of those with more property, wealth, connections, and/or opportunities/ access than us). Because of this, many White American men who are not making a six-figure salary tend to have "privilege blinders."

We assume that privilege is only something that "those other guys" have.

Consequently, *all* White American men—regardless of our wealth, power, or status—would like to believe that we have worked for and earned everything we have. Yet we will quickly point the finger at another White man who has more wealth, status, or power than us and attribute those qualities to *his* unmerited privilege. We desperately want to believe in the myth of a meritocracy, but we can't even agree among ourselves what each of us deserve. Many White men feel that they have either not benefited from or been left out of the privilege pot altogether.

• • •

WHAT EXACTLY IS WHITE PRIVILEGE?

As I was writing this book, a White male friend asked me, "Are you at least going to talk about how some White people are treated like Black people?" In other words, he wanted me to address his belief that impoverished White people deal with many of the same struggles and disadvantages as Black Americans—a belief that is shared by many White folks.

First off, there is a fundamental flaw in this argument that needs to be addressed. This belief automatically implies that an equal comparison can be made between the treatment of *some* White Americans experiencing poverty with *all* Black Americans regardless of their socioeconomic status. Aside from the inherent racism of this comparison, the idea that some White people are exempt from White privilege *almost* seems logical when we consider that there are plenty of White Americans who experience homelessness, live paycheck to paycheck, and/or struggle simply to put food on the table.

The larger implication of this false belief is that if *some* White people are deprived of the tangible material benefits of privilege,

White privilege doesn't universally hold true. Not to mention that telling any White person in a desperate financial situation that they have any degree of privilege gets lost in translation. In addition to rubbing salt on a wound, the argument simply doesn't compute because of a contextual misunderstanding of the word "privilege."

For starters, White privilege is not about how much power or wealth we have; it's about having the luxury of living in a world that was designed by and for people who look like us. White privilege does not mean that we have had everything handed to us on a silver platter; nor does it mean that we have not struggled, worked hard, or experienced bias, prejudice, or hatred directed toward us.

Let's unpack this fundamental misunderstanding of what privilege means in the context of race and gender. DEI consulting firm Full Diversity Partners Global (FDP Global) describes privilege as a form of systemic advantage. Yet rather than simply defining privilege as "having more," FDP Global clarifies that "systemic advantage/privilege is not so much about what [someone] has, but what they don't need to think about and/or negotiate on a daily basis."[267] In other words, White (male) privilege isn't about having anything exceptional; it's mainly about being able to move through the world with a level of imperceptible comfort and safety.

Why is it imperceptible to us but so obvious to others? Just as fish are not aware of the water around them until they have been pulled from it, we don't notice it because we've been swimming in it all our lives. *Merriam-Webster's Dictionary* defines privilege as "a right or immunity granted as a peculiar benefit [or] advantage."[268] As White men, we must consistently make the effort to ask ourselves, what are we immune from? What are these supposed advantages and benefits that we all apparently share? It's easiest to see them when we acknowledge the things that others *do not* have—i.e., when we look outside of the "water" we've become accustomed to.

• • •

(UN)EARNED AND (UN)DESERVED

White men largely don't go through every waking moment of our lives wondering if something happened because of our skin color or gender (e.g., an odd comment, a strange look, or someone not holding the elevator door for us). We probably don't think about questioning whether a job opportunity was granted to us because of our skin color (although a lost job opportunity is a different matter). While many White men have likely assumed that a person of color or a woman was given an opportunity because of their race or gender, if someone were to claim that our achievements came as a result of our race and/or gender or that they were deprived of an opportunity that they deserved because of us,[269] we could simply default to the myth of meritocracy and convince ourselves that we are unique and qualified individuals—having earned our place with zero consideration of our skin color or gender.

Moreover, White men don't have to deal with the disheartening internal dialogue that people of color and women so often do: "Did I really earn this, or was I just part of a diversity quota?" "Am I being selected because someone sees me as a token minority?" "Are others going to think I got this job simply because I'm ____." In other words, every group but ours is regularly forced to question their own qualifications when they receive something that they *actually* earned. Given the advantages and privileges that White men have always experienced in our society, *we* are the ones who should be asking ourselves that question.

Furthermore, White men never have to worry that others will doubt our intellect or competency because of the color of our skin. Quite the opposite—our skin color and gender give us an automatic, unmerited appearance of being qualified in most subject areas, despite the fact that we often overestimate our own capabilities. One Harvard study found that women tend to apply for jobs that they are either overqualified for or 100 percent certain they are qualified for, whereas men, White men in particular, frequently apply for and receive jobs they are underqualified for.[270]

Ironically, despite the fact that we consistently receive undeserved opportunities and unmerited accolades, we continue to allege that others are taking *our* spots. White American men built our entire empire on the assumption that we are the most competent, most qualified, and most deserving people in our society—if not in all of human history. While many people have received the same message from society to "know your place," the meaning of this statement based on who it is directed toward could not be more divergent. White men certainly have known our place since this country was founded.

This is highlighted by the persistent wage gap (for men of color, roughly 87 cents to the dollar)[271] as well as the profoundly unequal distribution of land (White Americans still own over 97 percent of agricultural land in the United States),[272] property, and business ownership (White men still own nearly 60 percent of all employer businesses).[273] The gap becomes further underscored when taking into account that "it will take African-American families 228 years for their household wealth to reach that of White families,"[274] according to a 2016 report from the Corporation for Enterprise Development (CFED) and the Institute for Policy Studies. While there are countless people who identify as White and also live well below the poverty line, the net benefits of Whiteness still apply to every White person, albeit to a varying degree. Financial success might not always be one of those benefits, but our privilege presents itself in other ways. One of the most significant is safety.

• • •

MY SKIN COLOR KEEPS ME SAFE

Another benefit of privilege that applies to all White folks, regardless of gender or socioeconomic status, is that we have never had to wonder whether it is "safe" to be White. In the United States, we rarely, if ever, encounter instances when others harass, threaten, or even physically hurt us exclusively because of our race.

Case in point, there is a negligible probability that a policeman would automatically assume that I am driving a nice car because I stole it—despite the fact that White Americans were responsible for nearly 75 percent of car thefts in 2019.[275] If I were pulled over for speeding, the chances of getting my car searched or ending up outside of the vehicle with my hands above my head are exceptionally low. In fact, one study determined that in North Carolina, Black Americans were 115 percent more likely to be searched in a traffic stop than White Americans—despite the fact that *more* contraband was found in the disproportionately low searches of White drivers.[276] This is one of the many unfair reasons that most White children and teens are rarely subjected to "the (police safety) talk" by their guardians, unlike almost all of their peers of color.

Up until recently, "the talk" was something that only Black families in America knew about—or rather, *had* to know about. Only in the last decade or so has it popped onto the radar of progressive White folks, even receiving mention during the 2020 presidential debate between former vice president Joseph Biden and then incumbent president Donald Trump. When explicitly asked whether they understood why Black parents must give "the talk" to their children about what to do when they encounter law enforcement, Biden openly acknowledged the problem of institutional racism in America. He even called out the fact that "the talk" is necessary for Black Americans regardless of socioeconomic status.

His counterpart simply replied, "Yes I do" before going on to say, minutes later, "I'm the least racist person in this room."[277] Keep in mind that during a 2020 White House press briefing, Trump proudly declared, "I have done more for Black Americans than anybody—with the possible exception of Abraham Lincoln. . . . Nobody has even been close."[278]

Whether or not "the talk" has been on White America's radar, some form of this heartbreaking conversation has been a matter of life or death for many Black Americans since their forced arrival.

When giving the "the talk," a Black guardian has to explain to their children that if they get stopped by the police or pulled over for any reason, strict protocol must be adhered to. "The talk" involves painstaking detail about what to say and not say, when to move and not move, where to place one's hands and where not to put them, as well as how to handle the situation if one is asked to get out of the car or, even worse, arrested.

Not wanting to frighten their children, many Black families struggle with when to have this conversation. It used to be primarily a discussion with teenagers. However, given the current danger and volatility of simply being Black in America, a large number of Black adults are now teaching their children this painful lesson as early as elementary school. In a 2019 NPR report, adolescent psychiatrist Dr. Adrienne Clark recommended that Black parents start having these conversations by age six, as soon as their children enter school—though she does carefully advise that the discussion remain age appropriate with more necessary details only given as the child gets older.

"The talk" is not limited to traffic-stop etiquette. In many cases, it is effectively a guide on "how to survive as a Black person in America" that necessitates an ongoing conversation.

In a heartbreaking recollection written for a 2021 Boston University publication, financial aid administrator David W. Janey describes,

> "The Talk" was not a singular event, but a series of lectures that began when I was about 10. The content of those talks surely impacted me, but never more than when I saw the hint of a tear or fear in my dad's eye. To me, his fear signified that beyond this point he could not protect me. . . . That was when I recall becoming aware that the world was not as safe for me as it was for my White friends. Taking safety for granted was beginning to slip between my fingers.[279]

His commentary astutely highlights that safety from the police is a privilege that goes completely unnoticed by most White Americans.

The infuriating part is that so many of us White people who now know about "the talk" just dismiss these lessons as common sense, suggesting that if all Black folks simply complied with these "unstated rules," they would be perfectly safe. Yet as we have seen over and over, playing by the rules often does not work out—as was the case with Philando Castile in 2017, who explicitly told the police officer who murdered him that he was reaching for his wallet. But that still misses the bigger point: why should people of color have to adhere to such demeaning standards of conduct in the presence of a police officer that us White folks don't have to?

Whereas many BIPOC folks experience their skin color as a potential liability, my skin color keeps me safe in countless situations, especially when getting pulled over. When I was pulled over for a busted taillight and expired tags, it didn't even cross my mind to fear for my life. If I got pulled over tomorrow, I could cuss at the cops and likely get away with a ticket. Just ask former New Jersey Port Authority ethics chairwoman Caren Turner, who resigned in 2018 after being caught on video berating police officers during a traffic stop for an expired registration—in which she wasn't even the one driving the vehicle.[280]

Turner, a middle-aged White woman wearing sunglasses, was filmed pointing a finger directly into the officers' faces while scolding them like small children. "I'm very disappointed in the way the two of you are acting. You can't put together a sentence, and that's pathetic!" Turner sneers to the lead officer. She then turns to the other officer. "And you are just following him, so you are also a disappointment!" When the lead officer tries to verbally intervene, Turner jabs a finger at him and barks, "You *may* shut the f*ck up!" As Turner pivots to get back into her car, she hotly declares that she will be talking to the chief of police and the mayor about how she was treated by the two officers. Rather than lose his temper, the lead police officer coolly replies with his badge number.

This brazen double standard of conduct is unfortunately not at all surprising to many BIPOC Americans. In response to the 2018 *BET News* article that provided the above details, one commenter said, "A black man would have been wrestled to the ground after the first sentence. After that, pray for his life."[281] Another commenter highlighted the glaring disparity in the police treatment of George Floyd in 2020, stating, "Compare how police treated a black man in handcuffs begging for mercy to this White woman who curses at cops, insults their intelligence, [and] repeatedly disobeys their commands—and tell me there's no such thing as White privilege."

While the publicity of the incident ultimately led to her resignation, Turner even flexed her privilege during her departure, taking it upon herself to get one final jab in on Twitter: "I encourage the Tenafly Police Department to review best practices with respect to tone and de-escalation so that incidences like this don't happen again."[282] Needless to say, almost *any* Black American attempting the same traffic-stop stunt, regardless of their title or socioeconomic status, would likely end up with a very different outcome.

While Turner's political status was undoubtedly one of the factors giving her "immunity," this same luxury does not extend to BIPOC political figures.

State Representative John Thompson, an African American male serving in the Minnesota House for the 67A district, was pulled over for not having a front license plate in July 2021.[283] Sitting in the driver's seat with a flashlight shining into his eyes, Johnson informs the officer, "I'm actually a current state representative in this district. I'm State Representative John Thompson." At that point, the officer begins skeptically quizzing him about his driver's license before spending over fifteen minutes printing out a ticket.

Understandably annoyed, Representative Johnson tells the officer that he believes he was pulled over because of racial profiling: "You pulled me over because you saw a Black face in this car, brother. You looked in this car and busted a U-turn and got behind this car." The officer immediately denies the accusation, to which Johnson, now frustrated, replies, "Stop racially profiling Black men in their cars, sir." While the situation thankfully ended without violence, the officer was outraged by the accusation.

Unlike the expired registration incident involving Carmen Turner, who literally cussed out the officers, threatened their jobs, and walked away without a ticket before blasting the Tenafly Police Department on social media, St. Paul Police chief Todd Axtell went on Facebook and demanded a public apology from Representative Thompson for his unfounded accusation of racial profiling. Not only did the Minnesota state representative receive discriminatory treatment, but had he stepped out of the car and done what the New Jersey chairwoman did, the situation almost certainly would have turned deadly.

A similar incident took place in April 2021 with a Black Latino Army lieutenant in full uniform, Caron Nazario, who respectfully tried to navigate a traffic stop. Despite calmly holding his hands in front of him while asking the officers why he was being asked to exit the vehicle, the body cam on the commanding officer shows Nazario with two guns pointed directly at his head.

As the officers approach the vehicle, demanding that Nazario step out, Nazario, hands still out of the window, calmly states, "I am actively serving this country, and this is how you are going to treat me?" The officer does not respond and instead repeatedly pepper sprays him directly in his eyes from less than two feet away. After receiving four consecutive blasts to the face, Nazario is told once again to exit the vehicle. Eyes watering and coughing, Nazario sputters, "I don't even want to reach for my seat belt."

Even *if* this were simply a case of Nazario refusing to cooperate, the officers' actions were completely unmerited—especially given Nazario's completely justified questions and calm demeanor. However, this was *not* a case of Nazario merely refusing to follow orders; he literally feared for his life. Shortly before Nazario is pepper sprayed, the commanding officer is heard screaming at Nazario, "You received an order! Obey it!" Nazario replies, "I'm . . . I'm honestly afraid to get out," to which the officer coldly responds, "You should be!"

Unlike Representative Thompson, Lieutenant Nazario, and millions of other Americans of color, ethics chairwoman Caren Turner and I don't have to be afraid of the police. We have the luxury of knowing that there is a three-digit number we can call anytime, day or night, and likely within minutes, we will hear the sounds of safety on its way.

Growing up, I, like most of my White friends, was taught that police were the "good guys" and that they were there to protect us and keep our communities safe. What I didn't learn until much later is that "us" and "our community" had a less-than-subtle implication.

Similarly, it never crossed my mind until I started smoking marijuana as a teenager that the police would have any reason to mess with me. During those careless and cavalier years of my teenage life, it was a "luxury" for me to be "afraid" of the police because I was choosing to do something illegal that put me at risk. Also, "being afraid of the police" never meant fearing for my life or safety. I simply feared getting in trouble with my parents.

Not to mention that when I got busted for marijuana by the police on more than one occasion as a teenager, I got off with little more than an appeal letter to a juvenile court and writing a not-so-sincere apology letter saying that I had learned my lesson. I was also instructed to remind the court that I was a promising young teen with a bright future ahead of me. It was not until I became an adult that I recognized this as special treatment. As a teenager, I hated the cops for "needlessly" making my life more difficult.

The notion that the police are the good guys and our protectors is a very disconcerting and even unfair message for people of color, especially Black Americans—many of whom fear for their lives every time they hear sirens or see the red-and-blue lights flashing. That should come as no surprise when considering that early police forces in the South were designed for the sole purpose of keeping Black people oppressed and enslaved, a practice that has effectively continued for close to three centuries through the prison industrial complex.[284]

According to historian Gary Potter, early law enforcement in the South served three primary functions: "(1) to chase down, apprehend, and return to their owners, runaway slaves; (2) to provide a form of organized terror to deter slave revolts; and, (3) to maintain a form of discipline for slave-workers who were subject to summary justice, outside the law."[285] This means that a significant ratio of our country's early police officers were sworn to serve and protect White folks *from* Black folks, as well as to maintain their status as *our* property. Not until the late twentieth century were police even expected to help, much less be the guardians of, any people of color.

To be clear, the point in all this is not that the police are the "bad guys." The point is that as White folks, we have always had the privilege of knowing that the police have our backs and are here to serve and protect us. While a lot has changed in American policing over the past few decades, including an increasingly diverse police force, people of color—especially Black, Latino, and Indigenous peoples—still have very little reason to trust the police. They have every right to fear an institution that was literally designed to terrorize them and keep them in their place.

For those of us who still insist that they should just "get over it," it will take more than a few decades to undo centuries of deliberate oppression, intergenerational trauma, and the ongoing PTSD caused by the never-ending onslaught of Black Americans being murdered by the police. Moreover, it will take radical reform (or potentially a complete overhaul) in the criminal justice system to ensure that our police, judicial systems, and prisons are genuinely able to serve the people they were originally sworn *not* to protect.

While safety is one of the most significant and consequential unearned privileges that White Americans possess, another, more insidious form of privilege allows White men to move through the world completely oblivious to the inconveniences that others face on a daily basis: convenience.

• • •

WHITE CONVENIENCE

As a White man, I can go almost wherever I want, whenever I want—even with a hood over my head, sunglasses on, a mask over my face, and my hands in my pockets. I have been allowed into grocery stores, convenience stores, drug stores, restaurants, malls, and banks wearing a backpack, and into fancy restaurants wearing pajama pants and a frumpy T-shirt. When I go to large events, parties, and celebrations, I have the luxury of knowing that it will likely be full of people who look like me and will not be wondering whether I am supposed to be there.

In most situations I encounter, I can wear what I want, say what I want, and act how I want. White American men get to move through this country as "unique" individuals without having to worry about making a bad impression on behalf of our entire race or gender. However, it isn't simply convenience that sets us apart. We have effectively immersed ourselves in a world made in our own image.

• • •

A WORLD THAT LOOKS LIKE ME

Whether consciously or unconsciously, White men have *always* known our place in America—because we made this country for ourselves. Consequently, the vast majority of our role models, heroes, and leaders look like us. Lori Lakin Hutcherson, writer and creator of *Good Black News*, explains, "The canon of literature studied in the United States, as well as the majority of television and movies, have focused primarily on the works or achievements of white men. . . . If you have never experienced or considered how damaging it is, was, [or] could be to grow up without myriad role models and images in school that reflect you in your required reading material or in the mainstream media—that is White privilege."[286] In other words, what I perceive to be a normal textbook is really a distorted version of history full of people who look like me, written by people who look like me.

The money in my wallet and the coins in my pocket tell the same story, as do the images in most churches and temples. Until the twenty-first century, almost every doll, action figure, and television show depicted a world very familiar to me. According to one study by the UCLA Department of Social Sciences, up until 1986, almost 90 percent of the TV population was White.[287] While the ratio has shifted—with one recent study placing it at roughly 60 percent[288]—boomers, Gen Xers, millennials (like me), and many Gen Zers grew up in a world dominated by white film and television.

Beyond the world of film and television, even the monotonous nasal tone of many news anchors across the country has a familiar sound to it—including news anchors of color. This is no accident. The major news network NBC confirmed that every single anchor on all major news networks "share speech patterns [because] they are *all* taught to use standard broadcasting English, a form of pronunciation in which no letters are dropped."[289] Now, whose standard of English might they be referring to?

Former journalist and author Diana Page Jordan recounts how she was explicitly "taught in journalism school, that the 'perfect' anchor intonation was Midwest America."[290] These multimillion-dollar networks are well aware that folks like me inherently feel more comfortable receiving important information from people who "sound" like authority figures—in other words, White people. Proper vernacular and crisp speech patterns convey a sense of authority and intelligence that White culture values and expects. If this seems like exaggeration, this will make more sense later when we explore the roots of Academic English.

Similarly, reading books or watching movie series such as *Lord of the Rings* or *Harry Potter*, with almost all White characters, ensures that I will both visually and audibly relate to the characters and cultural norms. While *Harry Potter* does have people of color in it, consider that in in the movie version of *Harry Potter and the Sorcerer's Stone*, people of color spoke a cumulative total of approximately ninety seconds.[291] However, the *Lord of the Rings* movies definitely win the "silent minority" competition, with a cumulative total of forty-six seconds for the entire trilogy combined. Not to mention that the primary cast member of color speaking for those precious few seconds is disguised in thick makeup as a hideous and terrifying, evil, black-skinned orc.

As some of the most iconic books and movies of our time, both *Harry Potter* and the *Lord of the Rings* are expected to be in one's "mainstream cultural" arsenal. Not to mention constant references to some of the most successful sitcoms of all time, *Seinfeld* and *Friends*. But the problem starts much younger. In 2018, close to 50 percent of characters depicted in thousands of children's books submitted to a University of Wisconsin-Madison study on diversity within literature were White. While that may sound proportionately accurate, consider that the second largest group—animals—accounted for 27 percent of the remaining characters, more than all of the other racial and ethnic groups combined.[292] When it comes to setting and upholding cultural standards and norms, the importance of representation in media cannot be overstated.

Yet we can't blame media for our homogenized lenses; the media parallels our self-defined reality. We are seeing what we *want* to see, whether we are willing to acknowledge it or not. One area where this can't be ignored is Westernized versions of history.

• • •

COLORING IN TEXTBOOKS

While many of us are now aware that US history has disproportionately displayed the chorology and "questionable" triumphs of primarily White men, we have also instilled our superiority in a more dubious way. In order to make our current reality align with our "slightly embellished" version of the past, Western culture has gone through and impregnated almost all of modern history with a very whitewashed version of our nation. "Colonizers rewrite the history of places and people they colonize. Part of keeping total control is staking claim on the past,"[293] writes author, social activist, and philanthropist Edgar Villanueva in his book *Decolonizing Wealth: Indigenous Wisdom to Heal Divides and Restore Balance*.

Despite the fact that America was populated by millions of people prior to the arrival of Europeans, a 2015 research study conducted at Pennsylvania State University about K–12 curriculum "found that 87 percent of content taught about Native Americans includes only pre-1900 context . . . [and] 27 states did not [even] name an individual Native American in their history standards."[294] Similarly, many American textbooks inadvertently teach children that Black history starts here in the United States. There is hardly any mention that these human beings who were forced onto ships bound for America came from thousands of years of self-governance, broad cultures, expansive religions, and even conquering empires—including the Moors, a Black Muslim empire that ruled Spain for nearly 800 years beginning in 711 AD.[295]

Maddeningly, in 2023, a number of states including Florida, under the inspiration of presidential candidate Ron DeSantis, began removing African American studies altogether. DeSantis disturbingly shared his belief that we should instead teach young children that "slaves developed skills which, in some instances, could be applied for their personal benefit."[296] While this drew sharp criticism from many scholars, educational leaders, and politicians alike, DeSantis doubled down on his statement. Yet Ron DeSantis's horrific comparison of chattel slavery to trade school is merely the tip of the iceberg.

By chopping out these integral pieces of their identity, history, and culture, we damage the psyche of Black children, cutting them off from their roots while also unconsciously teaching them that their ancestors started out in chains until one noble White president finally decided to set them all free. This same savior myth furthers the superiority complex in many White children.

Yet it is not just the curriculum that is problematic; the heroes of our textbooks all look like us and have names that sound familiar—so familiar that we decided to "bump" these names a little further back in history, inserting White people into a fictionalized narrative of world history, including religion.

● ● ●

MADE IN *OUR* IMAGE

One of the most powerful elements of colonialism was the spread of modern Christianity. It can be argued that religion is not history; yet religion was the driving force behind most of Western history, even serving as the basis for the founding of America (with the arrival of the first European settlers claiming to flee religious persecution). Even though most biblical stories take place in the Middle East, the text that governs Christianity was filtered through a European lens and authorized by one man who wanted to "fix" Christianity in England.

When King James came to power in 1603, he inherited a religiously fractured country. The disagreement between different Christian factions threatened the stability of the empire itself. With the supremacy of the Anglican Church in question, King James's authorization of what became the King James Bible was intended to help settle some of the religious disputes and solidify his power and legacy.[297] King James was actually a religious scholar, having retranslated some of the psalms himself, and he was persuaded at a conference of European scholars that a universally accepted text was needed to help reunite England. The seven-year undertaking that followed led to one of the most printed texts in history, helping transform the English language and leading to many new phrases, such as "the root of all evil"[298]—now ubiquitous in modern culture and literature.

Yet calling it a "translation" is an understatement, especially considering that almost all Western depictions of historical Christian figures are now White. Moreover, the man who (according to his followers) claimed to be the son of God is boldly depicted around the world with blond hair and blue eyes. While many of us have already come to understand this caricature of Jesus—likely emerging sometime in the early fourth century[299]—as far from historically accurate, often overlooked is that many characters in the Bible have recognizably "European-sounding" names.

Matthew, Mark, Luke, John, Peter, Paul, Mary. Do these names sound familiar? While it may seem that these names have simply "evolved" over the course of their historical translations, most of these names and their current pronunciations simply did not exist among first-century Jews living in what is now Israel and Palestine.

However, while Jesus's image was outright changed to match the desired association of Whiteness, many of these names were not so much altered as they were adopted and modified by European culture/tongues—appropriated into Whiteness. While that may seem like an inevitable byproduct of the way in which Christianity evolved, one must also consider the centuries of European influence, dominance, and religious persecution that allowed Christianity to spread in its most current form. Christian names have now become popular even among BIPOC communities, but this didn't happen by accident. Some have adopted these names to blend in and avoid persecution, but countless others were forced to take on these names after being stripped of their roots (namely Black and Indigenous Americans).

Mentioning this is not about faulting Christians or even Christianity; it is simply about recognizing that we have put ourselves and the Western world at the epicenter of arguably the world's most powerful religion and have spread that religion to every continent. Think for a moment how differently many White Americans might feel about reading the Bible if the characters appeared Middle Eastern or even Black, or simply had names such as Shimon, Abimelech, Abihu, Yosef, Shelamzion, Akbar, or Mohammed.

Christianity is certainly not the only religion that has whitewashed its own history. Judaism has created a similar mirage as far as image is concerned. While many of the names have remained slightly more intact, if not downright difficult to pronounce, Judaism has become enveloped in Whiteness.

Most of its major iconic characters, all of whom lived in the Middle East (e.g., King Solomon, Moses, King David, etc.), now resemble the American Jews of today. Despite the fact that globally there have been and still are millions of Jews of color, pale skin has become almost ubiquitous with Judaism in America. A combined Stanford and University of San Francisco study determined that "Jews of color are chronically undercounted . . . and underrepresented in communal organizations."[300] The study also estimated that despite this misrepresentation, as many as 12 to 15 percent of Jews living in the United States are people of color—a much higher figure than most Americans realize.

Our unconscious assumptions of what Jews look like is heavily influenced by living in a Judeo-Christian framework that centers Whiteness as the norm. In an interview with the Jewish Telegraphic Agency, Ari Kelman, the leader of the above study and an associate professor of education and Jewish studies at Stanford, explained that "for most of the late 20th century and into the 21st century, the default assumption is that Jews were white or that [there was] such a preponderance of Jews identifying as white that any percentage of Jews of color was so small that they didn't matter."[301] Consequently, just as is the case with Christianity, Judaism in America has become entrenched in Whiteness—despite a significant number of its adherents not identifying as White.

Ultimately, whether Christian or Jewish, many of us who believed in God while growing up pictured an old White dude with a big beard wearing long white robes, a vision that many still can't shake. What makes this concerning is that this is the same way many children of color picture God. A set of seven separate studies conducted at Stanford University—published in early 2021 in the Journal of Personality and Social Psychology—concluded that people's, especially children's, perception of God has a direct effect on their beliefs about who is best suited for leadership roles in American society.

In one paper, the researchers state, "Collectively, our data provide robust support for a profound conclusion: Beliefs about who rules in heaven predict beliefs about who rules on Earth."[302] Steven O. Roberts, the lead researcher and assistant professor of psychology in the Stanford School of Humanities and Sciences, goes one step further, stating, "If you believe that a White man rules the heavens, you are more likely to believe that White men should rule on Earth." Considering that Western religion tells us that God made man in his image, it stands to reason that God prefers "certain" people to others.

One of the studies also analyzed a Google search of the word "God," finding that "of the images that depict God in a human form, 72 percent were of a White man."[303] It should be noted that of the remaining 28 percent, an astounding 6 percent were of a single man: actor Morgan Freeman, who played God in the 2003 film *Bruce Almighty*. Understandably, Google's current search algorithms replicate the religious beliefs of the Western world—including our odd obsession with and deification of Morgan Freeman.

Those Americans who do not believe in a traditional Christian or Jewish God or who consider themselves atheists, agnostics, spiritual, Buddhist, etc., are still detaching from a Judeo-Christian framework and understanding of Western society. As a result, it effectively doesn't matter *whether* nonreligious people believe in something—instead what matters is *what* they don't believe in. Evidently, if I were a White atheist or even a Buddhist, because of my social conditioning, the primary god I'd be renouncing would still be *the* God that looked familiar to me.

Equally important, choosing not to believe in a "standard"

version of a Western, monotheistic God does not automatically make me immune to the societal conditioning described in Roberts's studies about "who is best suited for leadership roles in American society."[304] Consequently, the association of Whiteness and God himself primarily with American Christianity allows White American Christians to feel much closer to the "source of power" than BIPOC Americans. The same applies to White American Jews—only our God has slightly curlier hair. Moreover, the depiction of God as *the* (White) father also unconsciously sends a clear message to everyone, including BIPOC Americans: White men are "supposed" to be the ones in control.

While the tides of religion as the heart of American society are slowly changing as more young Americans consider themselves nonbelievers or simply spiritual, we are still a Christian nation by numbers. Nearly 64 percent of American adults identify as Christian, according to a 2021 Pew Research survey.[305]

Unfortunately, whether Christian or Jewish, the familiarity, comfort, and trust that many religious White Americans have in either the King James Bible or the Torah—not to mention in Christianity or Judaism—are yet another extension of White privilege. These whitewashed versions of Western religion further alienate many people of color from both the texts as well as the religions themselves, which ironically were likely created by people who looked anything but White.

However, religion is not the only thing that received a whitewashing in America; our very thoughts, the words that come out of our mouths, and the words we put down on a page are also unconsciously filtered through our White lens. These words hold much more power than we recognize.

PART 3

A Whitewashed World: Extract and Assimilate

CHAPTER 10

The Power of White Language

PARDON ME, but might I indulge in a somewhat lengthy diatribe on what is considered Academic English—or should I say White language?

There are many layers to the "language of Whiteness." In our society, many White Americans, especially those in Northern states, have been taught that the way we speak is not only normal but also desirable. This goes back to the earlier points about news anchor accents and particularly overseas customer service agents painstakingly learning to speak "like us" so we feel more comfortable speaking to them on the phone—but also, more importantly, to make us feel that they are competent enough to help us.

"Customer service skills" on a job application is often a euphemism for knowing how to speak and engage with White Americans to make us feel comfortable and assured that someone is capable of helping us. Yet creating this globally homogeneous customer service culture is no small feat. Entire sectors of the customer service industry offer online courses and even apps designed to teach "call-center English" to better serve Western clientele. FluentU.com, for example, hosts a Business English Blog for nonnative English speakers that provides explicit coaching on what to say and what not to say to make the customer feel understood.[306] While these types of services are undoubtedly trying to help, the implication is simple: the customer is always "White."

The concept of "properly" answering the phone at a call center provides only a glimpse of the value placed on being able to speak fluent English. It does not convey the degree to which both literacy and language itself have been directly correlated with power throughout Western history.

• • •

LITERACY = POWER

Only in the last century has the Western world become the "altruistic" purveyor of global literacy. Throughout most of its history, literacy has been wielded as an indispensable tool of power.

Our modern school systems essentially tote literacy as a birthright, providing access to limitless books, magazines, newspapers, and online reading materials. The National Council of Teachers of English (NCTE) describes literacy as "the global metric we use to assess the health and competence of communities."[307] Yet prior to twentieth century, most societies carefully ensured that the well-educated and ruling classes were able to communicate among themselves in ways that the masses could not understand.

According to NCTE member Amber Peterson, the director of program innovation at LitWorld, a large number of scholars and historians "propose that written language [itself] emerged at least in part as a tool for maintaining power.... [O]ften those without power were prohibited from learning to read and write at all."[308] By withholding literacy, Western governing and religious bodies maintained the ability to set rules and laws, create and define scripture, and ultimately govern based on an encrypted form of power that those below them were unable to challenge or even grasp.

Taking into account the ongoing "colonialism, imperialism, and the sprawl of anglo-european, male-centered ideology from the fifteenth century onward," Peterson highlights that this is also the primary reason that "women [still] make up two thirds of the world's illiterate population, and that sub-Saharan Africa, the region arguably hit hardest by many of those inequitable power structures, has some of the lowest literacy levels in the world."[309] Yet this is not simply a matter of reading and writing; as a "global metric," it determines global success, including economic prosperity, environmental health, and access to healthcare.

Many scholars have recently begun to acknowledge that when taken in its broader and more accurate context, literacy requires essential components besides the ability to read and write. The United Nations Educational, Scientific, and Cultural Organization (UNESCO) went so far as to say that "literacy is now understood as a means of identification, understanding, interpretation, creation, and communication."[310] Literacy now includes critical societal and cultural elements that make developing the skills of reading and writing entirely dependent on context—particularly pertaining to societal values and norms.[311] For anyone to master literacy within a given culture, they must have a fundamental grasp of the historical, cultural, and political context in which they are immersed.

This does not mean that it is impossible for someone to learn how to read or write without knowing everything about a particular society. However, for them to progress to the level of mastery required to, say, complete a dissertation, publish in a peer-reviewed journal, write a government document, or even fill out a high-level job application takes a tremendous amount of not only "academic savvy" but also contextual social intellect. Because of this, there is a built-in selectivity element to Western literacy that disproportionately privileges those who can "properly" speak the language. In American society, this has led to the adoption of a consolidated language of power brought from Europe that we typically refer to as academic language.

It can be hard to understand something (e.g., White language) if we are imbued with it, so let's start by looking at another language:

the "language of the oppressed." In this instance, I am referring to the stereotyped language of Black Americans as perceived by White society.

• • •

"BLACK ENGLISH"

Most of us would be lying to ourselves if we said that we didn't know what it means when a White person calls out another White person for "trying to sound Black." Heck, even *Merriam-Webster's Dictionary* used "trying to sound black" as a sentence example for describing Black culture,[312] though this example was removed shortly after the Black Lives Matter protests in 2020.

But what does "sounding Black" mean? Well, this is a cultural phenomenon that stems from a distinct and traceable dialect with origins as far back as the transatlantic slave trade. According to Stanford University professor of education and linguistics John Baugh, its origins are most likely linked to the plight of enslaved Africans trying to learn the English language out of necessity.[313]

Most recently referred to as African American Vernacular English or Black English Vernacular, the concept of "Ebonics" has spurred debates among historians and linguistic scholars alike, leading to multiple and competing—as well as offensive— definitions of the speech patterns of many Black Americans.[314] John Baugh says, "Depending upon which definition of Ebonics one chooses, ensuing policy and economic decisions can have a profound social, education, legal and political consequences."[315] When the term is based on a deficit mindset, as it most often is, it automatically relegates the way that many Black Americans speak to a substandard version of English.

In the 1960s, this manner of speaking was commonly referred to as "Nonstandard Negro English"—the implication being that it was outside the standard for how English should be spoken. It later became referred to simply as "Black English." Understandably displeased with this pejorative term, African American social psychologist Dr. Robert Williams first coined the term "Ebonics" in 1973 at a conference sponsored by the National Institute of Health while discussing the psychological development of Black children.

Derived from the root words "ebony" and "phonics," Dr. Williams wanted to create a term that more scientifically characterized a "Black language." In 1975, he published *Ebonics: The True Language of Black Folks*. In it, he described Ebonics as existing on "a concentric continuum represent[ing] the communicative competence of the West African, Caribbean, and United States slave descendant of African origin."[316]

Williams's intent was to highlight the linguistic roots of this particular way of speaking. However, its meaning became misconstrued; many White people quickly glommed onto the idea that Ebonics was *the* official Black way of speaking, furthering yet another mass stereotype about all Black Americans. Instead of recognizing it as a unique dialect influenced by historical and cultural context, many White people mistook Ebonics as a speech defect, with some taking it even further by calling it a language entirely different than English and espousing that most Black Americans were incapable of speaking in any other manner.

Ironically, this misunderstanding and the contentious political debates that followed were never intended to be about whether Black Americans had an alleged language deficit. Quite the opposite, the concern about Ebonics stemmed from a significant educational deficit brought forth in a landmark lawsuit in 1979.

In a groundbreaking court case for equal education, a group of African American mothers in Ann Arbor, Michigan, sued their local school board in federal court for denying their children an equal education by refusing to accommodate their children's unique language style. The federal court ruled in the mothers' favor but did not provide specific guidance on how the schools should remedy the inequitable and insufficient education.

Consequently, rather than address the catastrophic failure of the education system, the lens was instead turned toward the "failure" of Black Americans, particularly Black children, to speak what was commonly referred to as "Standard English." In other words, the intent shifted away from fixing education to "fixing" children—something that the US education system had already attempted with the abhorrent Native American boarding schools throughout the nineteenth and twentieth centuries. More on this later.

• • •

EBONICS: A PRIMARY LANGUAGE?

In 1979, the California State Board of Education's adoption of a policy titled "Black Language: Proficiency in Standard English for Speakers of Black Language" set the stage for a firestorm of ill-informed school policy decisions fueled by gross misinterpretations of the term "Black language." In 1981, the California Department of Education mandated that districts provide learning skills in Standard English to address the needs of all "Black language" speakers. This ultimately led to the creation of the extensive Standard English Program (SEP), specifically designed to "improve proficiency in standard English for speakers of Black Language."[317] Far from resolving the issue, this only furthered the belief that Black children were deficient and needed to be helped.

As the learning gap between White and African American students grew, the problem only got worse. In the early 1990s, a number of struggling Oakland educators came forward claiming that their Black students—who made up nearly 53 percent of the city's enrollment—were "linguistically akin" to the nonnative English speakers in their classrooms, believing them to be at a severe disadvantage and that Ebonics should be treated as a second language altogether.[318] These educators assumed that without "proper" language skills, their Black students were ill equipped to thrive in American society. To make matters worse, by this point, countless Black children throughout America were being put into special education services as well as speech therapy as a remedy for what was perceived as a learning deficit.

This came to a head in 1997, when the contentious debate entered the national spotlight. Journalist Helen Ubiñas published an article in January 1997 exposing the depths of the language controversy that had spread across the nation. She describes how in December 1996, the Oakland school board passed a resolution that "recognize[d] Ebonics as a distinct language that is 'genetically based,' that is [considered] black students' 'primary language' and that ought to be used by teachers to teach students standard English."[319] This controversial move quickly shoved the Oakland school officials into the hot seat.

The scrambling school district quickly backtracked some of its problematic rhetoric (i.e., referring to Ebonics as a "genetically based" language). District administrators unsuccessfully tried to emphasize that the phrase was never intended to be rooted in biology but was rather meant to highlight the language's origin. This explanation did not appease many outraged Black parents and only bolstered the belief held by many White Americans that race was, in fact, genetic—and that Ebonics was proof of this.

The district also tried to quell the misunderstanding that children were going to start learning Ebonics in the classroom—a fear spread by some vocal White parents who had misconstrued one of the board's rejected ideas. This misunderstanding had come from a rejected proposal to train (White) educators to speak

Ebonics in order to more effectively teach Black students how to speak Standard English (similar to a foreign-language program). While that suggestion had not gained any traction, the fear of spreading "nonstandard English" among White children and educators certainly did.

In 1997, the debate eventually landed on the floor of the US Senate, which had become concerned about this growing issue on another front: federal funding. If Ebonics were officially recognized as a separate language, it would technically qualify for the Bilingual Education Program Title VII funding, which was distributed annually to schools with limited English-proficient students. This would mean that as part of the Standard English Program (SEP), millions of Black students across the United States would begin receiving explicit language instruction funded by 156.7 million in taxpayer dollars.

The Senate hearing put an end to the debate about whether to treat Ebonics as its own language. In his opening remarks, then Pennsylvania senator Arlen Specter referenced a statement made by secretary of education Richard Riley on December 24, 1996: "Elevating black English to the status of a language is not our way to raise standards of achievement in our schools for our students. It has been determined by the United States Department of Education and the Clinton administration that the use of Federal bilingual educational funds for what has been called black English for ebonics is not permitted. The administration's policy is that ebonics is a nonstandard form of English and not a formal language."[320]

To quash any additional misunderstandings by the American public, the committee included a detailed section in the appendix of the transcript titled "Standard English Program—A Brief Description." The document explicitly specifies that "this effort to improve proficiency in standard English for speakers of Black Language is not (1) a program for students to be taught to speak Black Language; (2) a program for teachers to learn to speak Black

Language; or (3) a program requiring materials in textbooks to be written in Black Language."[321] Though the intent was to correct any and all misunderstandings, the document reads more like a moratorium on Black language altogether.

While the Senate effectively shut down the debate about Ebonics as a language, the Standard English Program was still presented as the way to "solve" the "problem" of how Black children speak—versus acknowledging that the real problem was (and continues to be) racial prejudice, discrimination, and forced assimilation.

Someone did try to bring this issue to the table during the Senate hearing; however, it was relegated to a brief pre-prepared closing statement by the Center for Applied Linguistics:

> Much of the national discussion . . . suggests a lack of public awareness of how language works. Under-informed about what dialects are, how they relate to each other, and what functions they fulfill, people have voiced their biases about language in society. Ebonics, or African-American Vernacular English (AAVE), has been erroneously called "slang," "broken English," "poor grammar," or "improper usage," instead of the fully-fledged dialect that it is. This conversation is not just another harmless case of the lay audience having less technical information than the scientist. It is a matter of perpetuating the myth that there is one correct English. When this myth goes unchallenged . . . [any] dialect instruction is unlikely to succeed.[322]

Whether in education or the public, the current associations that most White people have toward this particular dialect cannot be divorced from the racist implication that Black language, and therefore Black people, are inherently inferior.

INFERIOR LANGUAGE, INFERIOR INTELLECT

The problem is obviously not the dialect itself. The problem is the unfair and harmful stereotypes and assumptions that Ebonics conjures up among us White folks—namely our unmerited belief in our superior intellect. One of the most damaging underlying implicit (and often explicit) biases that most White people hold is that anyone who speaks African American Vernacular English is simply not as intelligent as we are, even including White people who "try to sound Black." However, because we have stereotyped and categorized people of African ancestry into one large category (i.e., Black or African American), this prejudice continues to harm *all* Black Americans.

For most of US history, speakers of the dialect now contemptuously known as Ebonics were deemed intellectually inferior. Computational linguist and NLP researcher Chi Luu describes in a 2020 *JSTOR Daily* article how "grammatical features like double negatives, along with other marked grammatical differences to standard American English, such as use of habitual be, as in 'he be walkin',' or perfective, as in 'he done did it,' have stigmatized the speakers of Black English as linguistically backward, uneducated, or unintelligent."[323] Yet beyond the blatantly unfair stereotypes, this belief is completely unfounded.

A Merriam-Webster blog article indicated that while "the double negative might be near the top of the list of English grammatical crimes,"[324] many languages throughout history considered to be prestigious—including classical Greek, Latin, French, and Italian—employed these very same speech patterns. Shakespeare himself was no stranger to the double negative: "And that no woman has; nor never none shall be mistress of it."[325]

While the double negative is one of the most rebuked forms

of African American English Vernacular (AAEV), there is another contender for the top spot: the pronunciation of the word "ask."

As described by Shereen Marisol Meraji, the cohost and senior producer of NPR's *Code Switch* podcast, "'Ax' has gotten a bad rap for years. Pronounce 'ask' as 'ax' and immediately many will assume that you're poor, black, and uneducated."[326] This is such a common sentiment that in 1988, "New York City's first African-American schools chancellor, Dr. Richard R. Green, put it on his list of 'speech demons' . . . insist[ing] that 'ax' be eradicated from the vocabulary of students."[327] Simply referencing something as a "speech demon" worth eradicating is a clear and painful reminder of the colonial-style education that our public school system was founded upon. Eradication of "undesirable" native language was par for the course. Moreover, the fact that Dr. Green himself was an African American man further demonstrates how entrenched these harmful stereotypes and beliefs have become among the people most oppressed by them.

While many assume that this unique pronunciation is a mistake or at best a fluke, "ax" is as old as English itself, dating back nearly a thousand years. During another interview on *Code Switch*, Jesse Sheidlower, president of the American Dialect Society, described how "ax is a regular feature of the English language that . . . trace[s] back to the eighth century. The pronunciation derives from the Old English verb 'acsian,' meaning 'to ask.'"[328] Not only was it used by Geoffrey Chaucer—often referred to as the father of English literature—in *The Canterbury Tales*, but also it was incorporated into the very first English translation of the Bible, known as the Cloverdale Bible: "Ax and it shall be given."[329]

Centuries later, the term "ax" was inherited across the globe by enslaved Africans in the newly forming colonies (as well as by Black Caribbean and Indian South Africans), who continued to pass it down for generations. In a 2013 NPR interview, Stanford linguist

John Rickford explained that "over time it became a marker of identity," equating it to "taking language that has been imposed and making it your own." Moreover, Rickford explains that while it may be true that code-switching away from elements of AAVE such as "ax" can help in some academic and professional settings, the same does not apply within many social and family settings when it comes to "asserting [one's] own identity."

"You got to remember," Rickford firmly stated, "a lot of these language varieties are learned in people's homes. It's how people's mothers spoke, their fathers spoke, their friends spoke. I don't think any linguist is recommending that you get rid of your vernacular, because you need it—in a sense—for your soul."[330] While it may be true that well-informed linguists or historians would not suggest getting rid of the term "ax," the same does not hold true in most other contexts. The vast majority of White Americans still assume that this iconic piece of the English language is nothing more than an obnoxious speech defect.

So, between double negatives and seemingly unique pronunciations, Black English vernacular used in a different context or place would be considered the norm. However, because of the oppressive social and political context of White American culture, "Black English" has instead been deliberately pigeonholed into the realm of "slang," "broken English," and criminality. Professor Baugh explains, "Even after slavery was abolished in the US, a recurrent combination of racial segregation and inferior educational opportunities prevented many African Americans from adopting speech patterns associated with [more modern] Americans of European ancestry. As a result, generations of White citizens maligned or mocked speakers of AAVE, casting doubt on their intelligence and making their distinctive speaking patterns the object of racist ridicule."[331]

Unfortunately, despite context and knowledge, it is nearly

impossible for us to overcome these negative stereotypes and biases that have been forged over centuries. It is equally difficult to view ourselves as equal to someone who speaks in such a manner because we have set the unfair basic precedent that how White people communicate is inherently superior. Saying that someone is speaking Ebonics automatically implies that they are either incapable of speaking in the manner White society considers the gold standard of intelligence or are *choosing* not to do so.

In order for Black folks in America to have opportunities and be respected in academia, the corporate world, or the political arena, many of them have to pass a severely unfair and biased litmus test. As described by computational linguist Chi Luu, "getting job interviews, renting an apartment, raising kids to have better options and advantages, even getting through an unexpected, fraught interaction with the police—all these things can be made much harder simply because of a particular accent or dialect."[332] This is not only a Black-and-White issue. When it comes to success in America, *all* people of color are constantly evaluated by how "well" they speak "our" language. Their very success or failure often depends on it.

・ ・ ・

THE LITMUS TEST

The "oral litmus test" so many people of color must undergo to become successful in America goes beyond simply being able to speak "Standard English"; it is based on a person of color's ability to speak and act in a way that most closely mirrors their White counterparts.

To be clear, this is not merely a social phenomenon. There is an entire industry built around it, including online courses, classes, and even one-on-one coaching sessions. Known as accent reduction, accent modification, or accent neutralization, this process is designed to "help" people learn how to erase their accents in order to blend in and be more successful.[333] Using catchy taglines such as "Is your accent holding you back in your career or life goals?"[334] or "We help people speak with an American accent,"[335] these companies and coaches promise to help people overcome one of the ultimate barriers to advancing in American society.

Many of the teachers and coaches at these companies are people of color, many of whom had accents themselves and have committed to empowering others to overcome unfair odds. While it is a noble endeavor, it is important to understand why those odds exist in the first place.

Albeit subconsciously, most White folks are on the lookout for slight variations and incongruences in the speech patterns of our peers, acquaintances, and colleagues of color. When we detect a slight accent or dialect, we begin playing a sort of mental guessing game: *Where is he from? Does she understand what I'm saying? Should I speak slower so they can understand me?* These bias-driven questions distort our ability to be fully present in conversation and to see the other person as an equal.

Many of us also default to even more derogatory questions around competency, intellect, and even trustworthiness. Known as "accent prestige theory," the driving assumption is that those with an accent closest to Standard English (i.e., American English) or a British accent are more valued. A 2007 article published in the *Brigham Young University Undergraduate Journal of Psychology* examines a number of different studies conducted throughout the early 2000s that examined how American English and British accents are associated with not only higher intelligence but also attractiveness, friendliness, socioeconomic success, and trustworthiness.[336]

The researchers in one of the studies found that many White American participants were judging others not based on *what* was being said, but rather *how* it was being said. White Americans were particularly susceptible to their "past associations between accented speech and ethnicity,"[337] judging the speaker before taking the words into consideration.

Highlighted by another study was the fact that those experiencing accent discrimination often subscribe to the same biases because of their own internalized racism (oppression turned inward, leading to negative beliefs about one's own race). One of the studies had both Mexican American and White Americans rate individuals with Hispanic accents. The study concluded that "as the level of accentedness increased from speaker to speaker, the raters gave significantly lower status ratings . . . [which] suggests that [even those with] the same accent as the speaker will rate [others with the same accent] lower" based solely on how thick of an accent the speaker possesses.[338]

Each of these studies highlights the countless barriers to success that an accent can present. However, the accents are not the problem; the problem is the system and the people who devalue them. This is just one of the many ways that White Americans continue to restrict access to power.

The oral litmus test is just the first step. Those who pass are still often at a disadvantage compared to their White peers as they enter an environment that is far from welcoming or inclusive. They are accepted if, and only if, they abide by the cultural norms, standards, and speech patterns already in place.

For this to change we need to shift the focus off "other" accents and languages and turn the lens inward. After all, if there is a term for "Black speak," there must surely be a term for "White speak" other than Standard English. Maybe Albonics ("*albus*" being the Latin word for "white")? As it turns out, there is such a term, and it is much more subtle and coded than that—not to mention dripping with power and authority: Academic English.

WHITE ENGLISH

English for Academic Purposes (EAP), more commonly referred to as Academic English, is the most valued form of language in the Western world. The name inherently communicates an elitist/authoritative slant, as academia is arguably the most respected institution in Western society. Whereas "social English"[339] comes in many different varieties and dialects and is used in everyday communication among peers and family, "Academic English is the language necessary for success in school,"[340] according to Colorín Colorado, a bilingual site for educators and families of English-language learners.

Not surprisingly, access to Academic English has, until the implementation of public education in the twentieth century, been restricted almost exclusively to elite and wealthy White Europeans and Americans who had access to private tutors and higher education—hence the term "academic." But what exactly is "academic language"? As defined in the Glossary of Education Reform, academic language specifically "refers to the oral, written, auditory, and visual language proficiency required to learn effectively in schools and academic programs—i.e., it's the language used in classroom lessons, books, tests, and assignments, and it's the language that students are expected to learn and achieve fluency in."[341] Consequently, academic language is often still considered one of the primary indicators of class, status, and even intelligence.

It is no secret that many teachers now coach their students from a young age to use academic language on all their school assignments and while talking to adults. Eventually, this skill is expected to transfer from term papers and college entrance exams to writing résumés, cover letters, and company reports. Language proficiency tests, especially in public schools, are still considered a metric of academic rigor. Yet these tests are only designed to measure proficiency in English for Academic Purposes (EAP), a version of our language that is often ill suited for everyday conversational use. This disproportionately harms BIPOC Americans and immigrants who are trying to navigate an unfamiliar, inconsistent, and often contradictory hierarchical language system and culture.

While there is clearly positive intent behind most of these aptitude tests, the implication is unmistakable, even to our youngest children, that one must master Academic English to gain status, access opportunities and power, and to be valued in this country. Not to mention that telling students not to speak in the way they most comfortably communicate at home sends the message that there is something wrong with the way they (and their families) speak.

There is something deeply flawed in an education system that teaches one "correct" way for kids to communicate. Moreover, it seems contradictory and unfair for the education system to view nonnative English speakers as being at a deficit. While many of these children fluently speak and understand three or more languages at home and have a much wider range of vocabulary than their monolinguistic peers, they are often considered to be lagging "behind" simply for failing to master this one particular type of speech.

Perhaps even more frustrating is how illogical and inconsistent this supposed "esteemed" language is. As described by the Glossary of Education Reform, "learning academic English can be challenging, particularly for non-native speakers (for example, why do English speakers say embarrassment, shyness, and likelihood, instead of embarrassness, embarrasshood, shyment, shyhood, or likeliment?)."[342] The simple answer? There isn't one; nor do most teachers have a clue about how to explain these strange and seemingly arbitrary language rules.

But I want to be clear: I'm not blaming teachers. The devastating reality is that without mastering the "language of the oppressor," the way that many children of color speak will close doors and limit their opportunities. Using AAVE can be an automatic sentence to speech therapy and special education, as was the case for former athlete Rob Lane, now a gym owner and fitness trainer (as well as a close friend of mine). When transferring into a wealthier school district for better opportunities, Lane's difficulty pronouncing the word "ask" was considered a speech defect. This had a profound impact on his learning over the next few years. In addition to receiving speech services, he was placed into special education, making him ineligible to attend higher-level classes alongside his more "[af]fluent" and White peers.

While it may seem like speaking academic language is a choice, it's not that simple. This is not a matter of desire for status or conformity through sheer will. The proper use of Academic English is difficult to master and often requires immersion—inherently making it much more prevalent in White communities. According to the Glossary of Education Reform, "intentional English-language modeling is more common in wealthier, higher-educated, English-speaking households, [whereas] it is often irregular or absent in disadvantaged and non-English-speaking home environments."[343] Therefore many BIPOC Americans and immigrants are automatically at a disadvantage when it comes to Academic English (through no fault of their own).

In a 2004 research article published in the *Journal of Linguistics*, John Baugh, then president-elect of the Linguistic Society of America and also known for developing the theory of linguistic profiling (the auditory equivalent of racial profiling), argues that "in order to advance the teaching of Academic English, Standard English, and Workplace English . . . educators should address stereotypes associated with specific varieties [of English], students' goals, the potential benefits of gaining communicative competence in particular varieties, and the potential consequences of not gaining that competence."[344] While Baugh is firmly against the discriminatory aspects of "linguistic profiling," he also acknowledges that in order for BIPOC Americans to have a better chance at success, American educators should explicitly acknowledge and mitigate the disadvantages of not learning to speak in Academic English.

Whether or not American educators choose to acknowledge this unfair reality within the education system, most multilingual countries outside of the United States are well aware of this barrier and have been overcoming it for decades. In many developing nations, those who intend to go to English-medium universities are expected to go through at least one or two years of preparatory schools to improve their English for Academic Purposes proficiency level.

But how did this standard evolve in the first place? And perhaps more importantly, where did Academic English come from? The language of academia is rooted in the evolution of English itself, which first appeared in Europe and was often forcefully thrust upon others.

● ● ●

HOW ENGLISH EVOLVED

The English language originated during the fifth century when three Germanic tribes (the Jutes, Saxons, and Angles) invaded modern-day Britain—hence the term "Anglo-Saxon." Prior to that point, most of the population in that area spoke variations of the Celtic language. According to the Oxford International English School, "the word England and English originated from the Old English word *Engla-land*, literally meaning 'The land of the Angles' where they spoke *Englisc*."[345]

Over the next few centuries, English spread to different regions, evolving into various dialects that were influenced by other languages prevalent at that time, including one derived from

French and Norman (from the descendants of the earlier Vikings). This variant remained the most widely used until the fourteenth century. However, during that time, the nascent British government and its wealthy citizens also began to Anglicize (i.e., conform to Anglo-Saxon British culture) the English language.[346]

During the fourteenth century, a specific dialect now referred to as East Midlands or Chancery English began to develop near modern-day London. With his seminal *The Canterbury Tales* written between 1387 and 1400, Geoffrey Chaucer unknowingly laid the foundation for the spread of English in its modern form. Up until that point, many of the clerks who prepared official documents for wealthy Britons, royalty, and the church used Latin and French. However, Chaucer effectively elevated the English language to reside among previously more-revered linguistic counterparts. The adoption of this new form of language after the mid-fifteenth century instigated a progression of the English language in vocabulary, grammar, and pronunciation that in many ways heralded the onset of the English Renaissance.

An era defined by political strife, ruthless monarchies, and broiling tensions between the Catholic and Protestant churches, this roughly 200-year period—lasting from the fifteenth into the early seventeenth century—"drastically shaped what being English meant, at home and abroad. As literacy increased and printing accelerated [due to the advent of the printing press], the English language rose to a place of international prestige,"[347] describes the Chicago Poetry Foundation. "As a nation and a fledgling empire, England emerged as an indomitable economic and military force, sending explorers, merchants, and colonists as far as Africa, Asia, and the so-called New World"—including the establishment of Jamestown, Virginia, in 1607.

However, as English spread, the evolution of new variations, dialects, and slang—including Shakespeare's crude sexual innuendos, cuss words, and "colorful" wordplay—presented the antithesis of the more elitist forms of English language maintained by the church, royalty, and the aristocracy.[348] Similarly, colonialism itself "backfired" on the "purity" of the English language as many foreign words were quickly adopted into the mainstream (including "shampoo" and "candy" from India).[349]

As English took off in America over the next few centuries, the ensuing dialectical schisms further contributed to the refinement of the English language within religious institutions and elite society, leading to class distinctions based on pronunciation, grammar, and vocabulary. As was the case in Europe, one of the primary signifiers of wealth, class, intellect, and education became one's fluency in one specific type of English: Academic English. Moreover, it became a shared identifier with the elite educational and political institutions of Europe. Consequently, until the desegregation of public education toward the end of the twentieth century, the primary group that had access to Academic English was White Americans.

The way in which Americans speak remains a clear (and deliberate) indication of status within society. Moreover, as mentioned before, the mastery of not just literacy but also Academic English required extensive amounts of practice and exposure. With a "proliferation of linguistic irregularities, symbols, idiomatic expressions . . . [and] grammatical rules, academic language also demands that students acquire proficiency in different linguistic systems . . . contextual language . . . and complex, abstract meanings,"[350] describes the Glossary of Education Reform. Or in plainer English, for one to learn Academic English, one has to be exposed to the environment and context in which the language is maintained—namely higher education, an opportunity that is still limited for many BIPOC Americans because of ongoing social and systemic barriers.

While speech as a form of societal stratification is not limited to Western culture, the way it has become directly embedded into a racial context is unique. In a 2004 article about Academic English in the African diaspora, linguistics professor John Baugh describes how in many Western countries, including the United States and South Africa, "the common denominator of racial segregation has had clear... linguistic and educational consequences that have been, and might continue to be, detrimental to the welfare of historically subordinated racial populations."[351] As such, an intentional and ongoing divide has been created as generations of people of color in America, Europe, South Africa, and countless other nations are deprived of education and outright segregated from the society in which academic language exists.

This may seem like an unintended consequence versus a deliberate and calculated effort, but that is not the case. Just ask Carl Brigham, the avowed eugenicist who created the Scholastic Aptitude Test (SAT) in 1926. Yes, the one and only SAT—the test that, for many of us, determined our future college options, or lack thereof.

• • •

WHITE ENOUGH TO GO TO COLLEGE?

In his widely circulated *A Study of American Intelligence*, Brigham expressed his concerns that the because of "defective strains in the present population" (i.e., non-White, non-Anglo-Saxon Americans), the decline of America's education system "will proceed with an accelerating rate as the racial mixture becomes more and more extensive."[352] He specifically draws attention to the "infiltration of White blood into the Negro."

Brigham was just one of many outspoken advocates of the racial superiority and intellect of White people. He believed that the SAT would effectively prove this belief and neutralize the threat of *any* non-White Americans entering into upper academia.

What's even more devastating is that nearly a hundred years

later, the majority of Black Americans who continue to depend on this grueling aptitude test for gaining entry into college remain completely unaware of its designated purpose—to keep them from getting there.

The landmark decision in 2023 to overturn affirmative action in higher education shows how much our education system needs to acknowledge and reform the numerous barriers that are present to this day. Maybe we can at least start by eliminating this century-old test created by a proudly racist White man who intended to do everything in his power to stop Black people from going to college.

One thing is for sure. Like the elite aristocracies of Europe, White people within the United States created stratification, then ensured that those oppressed were robbed of access to literacy, "proper language," and academia itself. Those folks of color who manage to overcome the odds and make it through to this restricted realm are the exception to the intentionally imposed hierarchy. This gives much more weight to the Frederick Douglass quote plastered up in classrooms across the United States: "Once you learn to read you will be forever free." If only it were that simple, Mr. Douglass. The fine print on those posters should read: "Terms and conditions apply to *some*."

• • •

THE TOLL OF CONFORMITY

While code-switching, also referred to as style-switching, is often thought to mean simply changing the way one speaks, a more accurate description "involves adjusting one's style of speech, appearance, behavior, and expression in ways that will optimize the comfort of others in exchange for fair treatment, quality service, and employment opportunities."[353] As described in a 2019 *Harvard Business Review* article titled "The Costs of Code-Switching," "the behavior is necessary for advancement—but it takes a great psychological toll." The article highlights that "this kind of behavioral adjustment . . . has long been a strategy for [people of color] to successfully navigate interracial interactions and has large implications for their well-being, economic advancement, and even physical survival."[354] While this behavior is carefully deployed to make White people feel more comfortable and keep BIPOC people safe, it comes at a heavy price for those forced to abide by "the dominant code."

The article outlines the significant mental health costs associated with feeling forced to fit in. In addition to always maintaining a high level of vigilance and professionalism, many BIPOC Americans (particularly Black Americans) feel compelled to downplay their own race while disproportionately valuing shared interests with the dominant group. According to a 2009 study published in the *Journal of Applied Psychology*, "feigning commonality with coworkers also reduce[d] authentic self-expression,"[355] often leading to a sense of isolation and dissonance for many BIPOC Americans. Many simply sum up this unfair burden as having to work "twice as hard" just to fit in.

However, it's not only a matter of mental health. Code-switching also directly impacts work performance. One 2015 study published in the *Annual Review of Psychology and Organizational Behavior* determined that the burden of having to constantly fit into the dominant culture negatively impacts work performance and undermines motivation as a result of depleted cognitive resources, further contributing to exhaustion and fatigue.[356] Consequently, while many BIPOC Americans who conformed genuinely perceived "more career success than those who did not[,] . . . they also were [much] more likely to burn out,"[357] according to the *Harvard Business Review* study. Having to speak, act, and carry themselves in a manner inconsistent with their authentic selves in order to advance cost them the very thing they aspired to hold on to: their career.

Even more disheartening is that many BIPOC Americans who engage in this code-switching behavior face hostility and rejection from members of their own group, who often perceive them as "acting White."[358] This is exacerbated by the fact that among the White community, these conforming individuals are considered exceptions to "the norm" of their culture—the ones who rose above. This is especially unfair when one takes into consideration that many White folks are often impressed, if not shocked, when a person of color sounds like us, acts like us, or shares the same interests.

Even former president Barack Obama was no stranger to this double standard. His own vice president, Joe Biden, demonstrated it best when describing his counterpart as a "storybook" success: "I mean . . . you got the first mainstream African-American who is articulate and bright and clean and a nice-looking guy. I mean, that's a storybook, man."[359] While Vice President Biden undoubtedly meant this as a compliment and would deny any malice or nuance in his statement, the impact overshadows the intent. In the bigger context of how people of color are still expected to prove themselves and conform to our standards to be successful, this statement is not only condescending and patronizing but also a backhanded slap to Black Americans who don't "live up" to Obama's example.

Equally troubling were Biden's use of the terms "articulate," "bright," "clean," and "nice-looking." While these descriptors are undeniably flattering out of context, the implication that this "storybook" president defies the expectation of others who look like him reveals underlying assumptions about their "typical" appearance and behavior.

This cringeworthy "dubious compliment" didn't go unnoticed. *TIME* magazine mentioned it on their 2007 list of "Top 10 Joe Biden Gaffes," referring to it as a case of "foot in mouth disease."[360]

But this is not about Biden; it is about the millions of well-meaning White folks—especially those in power—who say things that reveal just how out of touch many of us are with our own unconscious biases and baked-in racist beliefs. Biden, who openly stated that he "doesn't have a racist bone in his body"[361] during his 2020 presidential run, is one of the millions of White Americans who fail to grasp that being racist isn't limited to disliking someone because of the color of their skin.

The longer we hold on to that constricting and shortsighted definition, which overlooks the systemic oppression backing up the power and intentionality of what systemic racism in America is and whom it serves, the more harm we will continue to perpetuate when we applaud people of color who sound like us and present themselves in a "familiar manner." Moreover, when White folks who deny their own biases and prejudices oversee schools, boardrooms, businesses, or elected to public office, the policies they create and uphold ultimately mirror that same colorblindness—hence the need for critical race theory, which examines structural and institutional racism, especially within the legal system and laws themselves.

Black folks in the US know all too well that the world typically portrays them as anything but "bright, clean, and nice-looking." All one has to do is go back to the definition of "black" in *Merriam-Webster's Dictionary* to see those descriptors: "dark," "dirty," and "grotesque."[362] Similar to the dichotomous definitions of the words "black" and "white" themselves, our perception of how we speak and act compared to how others speak and act is subject to the same biases.

Yet there are further consequences for everyone when White Americans stifle some types of speech and behavior while overvaluing our own.

● ● ●

WHEN ONLY WE SPEAK, EVERYONE MISSES OUT

The expectation of Academic English proficiency is one of the many reasons that the US education is falling behind. We waste inordinate amounts of time, energy, and resources simply trying to "fix" the way that children talk rather than using diverse language as a learning tool and empowering children to use multilingual, cross-cultural critical thinking and social skills.

Similarly, our entire nation's collective critical thinking skills are suppressed simply because we all too often fail to hear, listen to, or understand information when it comes to us from an "unfamiliar" voice. This is especially the case in situations that involve some form of public speaking—whether in school, the boardroom, or even political office.

White people, particularly White men, are often the first ones to speak and voice our opinions (over others) in public settings. We typically don't have to think about how our speech will be perceived by those in the room. We simply gauge our audience and speak accordingly—often with confidence and authority that comes from merely being the first to speak in so many situations. While individuals of color in that same setting might be more knowledgeable, better informed, and more qualified to speak insightfully on the matter, many are afraid to speak up because they feel insecure about their ability to communicate in a setting that values one type of speech over another. Not to mention the all-too-common phenomenon of a person of color saying something that goes unacknowledged, only for a White person to repeat the same words and be rewarded for their insight.

Additionally, White people don't have a great track record when it comes to "borrowing" the wisdom of those outside our sphere and then translating into "our language" for our own gain; from algebra to many forms of modern medicine, we frequently strip wisdom from people and then discredit those from whom it originated. Consequently, many folks of color might choose not to speak or share ideas for fear that it will be used for the benefit of someone else in the room.

But there is perhaps an even higher cost than what is stolen from others: the lost potential that is stolen from the world. Because of the importance placed on academic language, our entire society has missed out on a wealth of knowledge, ideas, and wisdom that could improve our quality of life. Doctors, lawyers, scientists, philosophers, professors, historians, authors, religious leaders, and artists alike have had their contributions either ignored, erased, or stolen—simply because they don't fit the desired mold of speech. More importantly, countless individuals will never be able to assume these coveted roles because they haven't mastered "proper" English.

A scientist who can't publish a paper that meets the standards of "academic rigor" may never receive funding for a new drug that could cure cancer. A would-be doctor who could otherwise become one of the world's top neurosurgeons might never get to hold a scalpel simply because she doesn't speak English "well enough" to get into medical school. A one-of-a-kind artist with a beautiful vision of how to restore fading classical portraits may never get the chance, because the elitist art world refuses to try to understand her thick accent.

As a language that was created and designed to consolidate power within a small minority, Academic English automatically casts doubt on those who either can't or choose not to communicate in such a manner. Countless individuals currently living in the world have ideas and knowledge that could fundamentally reshape our society but cannot, because they don't have the necessary credentials of White skin and proficiency in Academic English. Imagine if Isaac Newton, Nikola Tesla, or Albert Einstein were not considered White or were unable to speak "proper" Academic English.

WHITE CODE-SWITCHING

Mastering academic language isn't the be-all and end-all of overcoming White superiority. Academic language operates on a sliding scale, and knowing how to code-switch within that spectrum allows for additional access to social circles, as well as opportunities. We must be able to easily transition between casual and formal in direct response to which social circle we are speaking with.[363] For example, among my peers, if I used "I concur" instead of simply "Yup" or "I agree," I might be seen as bougie or elitist—and it would likely cost me social capital within these groups.

Conversely, for many people of color, particularly immigrants, overusing Academic English makes them stand out and appear inexperienced with White American social customs and cultural norms. The formal pronunciation and versions of many words and phrases are often not the most universal, and the proper or improper use of them indicate one's ability to "read a crowd." For example, an English-language learner will likely be taught to enunciate, "Hello. How are you doing today?" as a basic greeting. Yet in many situations they will encounter in the real world, the phrase "What's up? How's it going?" would be a much more acceptable greeting. Paradoxically, this makes our language system all the more separatist and elitist. Most White people typically know how and with whom to communicate in a manner that gives them access and opens the right doors.

A cover letter that I send to a potential employer might be steeped in formalities and high-level vocabulary. However, once I get the job, I can easily determine where on the sliding scale of academic language I want to be in order to speak to my coworkers and bosses—even having the luxury of venturing into "slang" with some colleagues. As is often the case, there are paradoxes and double standards when it comes to *who* is navigating these norms and how much power they possess.

Despite being president of the United States, Barack Obama scrupulously held to these restricting "social literacy" norms in order to be seen as competent for the role. During his eight years in office, President Obama was closely observed for any breaks from the status quo—particularly when operating within the political arena. If you have ever seen the viral clip of the former president formally shaking hands with a line of White NBA officials before giving an endearing pull-in-style handshake and hug to Kevin Durant, then you know what I mean. Sadly, according to many trolling White Americans who watched this clip on YouTube—as well as some additional clips of him fist-bumping only "certain" people—President Obama reveals his "true identity" when greeting his "own kind."

The amount of racist backlash to this single video clip demonstrates that many White people in our country still don't feel that a person of color holding arguably the most powerful position in the world has the right to display mannerisms or say anything outside of the (White) cultural norm.

In comparison, his immediate successor was given carte blanche to speak his mind, spouting nonstop lies, insults, conspiracy theories, racist and misogynistic remarks, as well as deliberately divisive rhetoric. If President Obama had voiced even one of Trump's more "colorful" lines, especially the one about shooting people in the middle of Fifth Avenue, he almost certainly would have been removed from office via a unanimous vote of incompetency. Yet it was not merely what Trump said that was tolerated but also how he said it. A 2016 CNBC article literally described him as "a transcriptionist's worst nightmare" describing how "his unscripted speaking style, with its spasmodic, self-interrupting sentence structure, has increasingly come to overwhelm the human brains and tape recorders attempting to quote him."[364] Former President

Obama was afforded no such privilege when it came to his rhetoric. His speeches and appearances were carefully scripted. Had he spoken in Trump's "severely unintelligible" style, he would not have been able to enter politics, much less become president of the United States.

This double-standard-ridden auditory hierarchy hardly stops at the way we speak and interact with one another. There is one more "secret weapon" that White society uses to withhold power from communities of color: our names.

● ● ●

WHAT'S IN A NAME? ACCESS, PRIVILEGE, AND POWER.

In the last few years, several prominent studies have shown what many BIPOC Americans have known all along: their names are often a barrier to success in America. Simply put, names are profoundly important when it comes to power and status in American society. These studies, including two notable ones conducted by the National Bureau of Economic Research and Harvard University, have concluded that people with White-sounding names—particularly men—have close to a 40 percent better chance of landing a job, including jobs with employers who claim to be pro-diversity.[365]

When it comes to social rank, Greg and Jamal simply are not the same thing. In the National Bureau of Economic Research study, researchers Marianne Bertrand and Sendhil Mullainathan scrupulously examined the statistical likelihood of discriminatory hiring practices based on one's name. They submitted nearly 5,000 copies of the exact same résumé to over 1,300 employment ads for various positions. The only thing changed was the name—one sounded White, and one sounded potentially African American (Emily and Greg vs. Lakisha and Jamal). They determined that for traditionally White-sounding names, they sent out "about 10 resumes to get one callback," whereas "those with African-American names needed to send around 15 resumes to get one callback."[366]

Even more discouraging, the study also concluded that one's credentials are often less significant than one's name when it comes to getting a callback. Bertrand and Mullainathan explain, "While one may have expected that improved credentials may alleviate employers' fear that African-American applicants are deficient in some unobservable skills, this is not the case in our data. . . . [It is] harder not only for African-Americans to find a job but also to improve their employability."[367] This effectively means that regardless of what qualifications or degrees an African American candidate has, their name will be a bigger indicator of whether they end up getting hired for a role.

The researchers found that "this discriminatory practice is just as strong for businesses that claim to value diversity as those that don't."[368] Even the jobs that use catch phrases such as "equal opportunity employer" or "minorities strongly encouraged to apply" frequently end up mirroring the same dismal statistics in terms of hiring practices and company demographics.

These barriers do not only apply to African American candidates. Similar studies have concluded the same results with Asian and Latino names. So, while it may seem on the surface that simply providing equitable education and robust job-training programs helps level the playing field, research has shown otherwise.

As if name bias weren't enough of a barrier, when it comes to corporate culture, White men often seek their own kind. In a 2021 article, writer and editor of *Harvard Magazine* Dina Gerdeman explains how "when a company's talent arbiters are White men, research shows, they tend to recognize the talents of other White men more easily. And so, the cycle continues: These employees get challenging assignments that help them learn new skills. With more opportunities to shine, they rise through the ranks faster, preserving the status quo."[369]

Consequently, the Johns, Mikes, Toms, and Jeffs of the world find themselves in an echo chamber of homogenous talent and ideas, assuming that merit alone got them to the big boss's chair. Meanwhile, "employees who don't make the 'talent' cut early on [i.e., women and people of color—even those recruited from the same competitive MBA programs] are left to find their own way; they flounder and eventually leave, reinforcing the judgment that they weren't worth investing in,"[370] explains Robin Ely, researcher and professor of business administration at Harvard University.

Ultimately, between the formidable gatekeeping forces of name discrimination, credential dismissal, and the incessant old-boy network, these systemically embedded biases are simply too entrenched for most people to rise above the odds, forcing many people of color to take matters into their own hands.

• • •

"WHITENED" CREDENTIALS

"Résumé whitening" has become a common phenomenon in our society. This typically involves changing not only one's name but also one's hobbies on a résumé simply to get a callback. A 2017 article published by the Harvard Business School reveals that a number of Asian applicants have painstakingly revised and edited their résumés and cover letters in order to hide references to their race, including changing hobbies. According to the research, "Asian applicants often change foreign-sounding names to something American-sounding—like substituting 'Luke' for 'Lei'—and they also 'Americanize' their interests by adding outdoorsy activities like hiking, snowboarding, and kayaking that are common in White western culture."[371]

These "erasure efforts" have had astonishing results in their chances at employment. The article determines that companies are twice as likely to call a candidate for an interview who submitted a "whitened résumé." Apparently, when it comes to hiring, even our hobbies and interests are presumed indicators of our race—and therefore indicative of our "primary qualification" (i.e., being White).

As a result, White identity components have become coded language on all résumés. Combined with place of study, degrees, and previous jobs, employers unconsciously create a racial profile of the ideal candidate for a position or company. Simply put, White culture is highly valued in the workplace.

I guess that means that an interest in stand-up paddleboarding or wine tasting might pay off after all. But anyone with the name Mohamed is going to have to think carefully about putting down his real name, much less including his years of community service at a local mosque. He might instead consider putting his name down as Matthew and substitute "church" for "mosque"; the research shows this simple change will make him twice as likely to get a callback.

Without a doubt, the way that Americans speak, act, and even what we like to do can directly affect our odds of success. Whether a consequence or the cause itself, this continues to provide White Americans with disproportionate advantages and opportunities. However, there is yet another, more deliberate way in which Whiteness has risen to the top of the racial hierarchy over centuries and continues to hold that unmerited standing: by stealing things that do not belong to us.

CHAPTER 11

The World Is Our Oyster: Taking What Doesn't Belong to Us

"What does it mean when White colonizers practice aspects of our culture while that privilege is still denied to us? . . . [They] come with a sense of entitlement. They consider themselves cultural ambassadors and under the guise of creating peace between all peoples, they believe it is righteous to exploit our most sacred teachings."[372]

—Waziyatawin, *Dakota Professor, Author, and Activist*

WHAT DO NUMERALS, mathematics, astronomy, irrigation systems, guns, compasses, calculators, futures exchanges (trading stocks), and Christianity all have in common? A better question might be what do all these things *not* have in common but are often inaccurately believed to share?

The answer: These are just a few examples of inventions that are frequently attributed to Western civilization. Yet every single one of these globally transformative elements were in some way, shape, or form taken from another civilization and used primarily for the benefit of White people—all too often to oppress others, including the very people from which they originated.

As the ones indisputably at the top of the pecking order, we now have a collective tendency to believe that certain things are ours for the taking. We frequently "stumble" upon something that we really like (e.g., resources, ideas, knowledge, wealth) and decide to make it our own.

THE PURVEYORS OF WESTERN CIVILIZATION

For nearly two millennia, White people, particularly White men, have exploited almost every people and culture imaginable, "acquiring" knowledge and resources as we colonized (and arguably destroyed) hundreds of nations. Yet by some combination of falsified history and self-induced amnesia, many powerful White leaders have become convinced that we single-handedly introduced Western civilization to the "outside world."

This has led to a persistent and destructive belief that Western civilization is the primary contributor and civilizer of the developing world. This sentiment was epitomized on a 2014 MSNBC panel when Iowa Republican senator Steven King challenged political journalist and author Charlie S. Pierce on his accurate assertion that White men still dominate the Republican political party.

King fired back, "This whole 'old White people' business does get a little tired, Charlie. I'd ask you to go back through history and figure out where are these contributions that have been made by these 'other' categories of people that you are talking about? Where did *any* other subgroup of people contribute more to civilization?"[373] Doubling down on his point, King boldly stated, "Western civilization itself [is] rooted in Western Europe, Eastern Europe, and the United States of America. . . . [E]very place where the footprint of Christianity settled the world—that's all of Western civilization."

While this challenge received backlash from many viewers, Senator King is not alone in his beliefs—especially considering that this comment was made two years before unapologetic nationalist Donald Trump was elected president. Even in the twenty-first century, this falsified chicken–egg conundrum remains the foundation of American exceptionalism and serves as the basis for belief in Western superiority.

For centuries, Europe has pilfered the world's material goods and ideas for its own gain; and from the moment the *Mayflower* landed at Plymouth Rock, the soon-to-be United States got in on the action. Many of our ancestors used to have to set sail to find these "untapped" sources of wealth and power, but our latest approach focuses on exploiting those right here on American soil. Cultural appropriation is one of the primary ways in which Western civilization maintains power over the rest of the world—especially here in America.

• • •

CONTEXT IS KEY

As defined by Dr. Akeem Marsh, a psychiatrist dedicated to working with medically underserved communities, cultural appropriation "refers to the use of objects or elements of a non-dominant culture in a way that doesn't respect their original meaning, give credit to their source, or reinforces stereotypes or contributes to oppression."[374]

To fully grasp cultural appropriation and what makes it so damaging, it needs to be differentiated from cultural exchange. Cultural exchange has happened throughout human history as people mutually share elements of their culture with one another. The key phrase here is "mutually share." Unfortunately, mutual exchange and benefit simply do not, and cannot, exist between a dominant culture and those they oppress.

On an individual level, cultural appropriation often occurs because of innocent curiosity or fascination (i.e., learning a new style of dance, admiring a style of clothing, or trying a new food). However, our larger, oppressive system has demonstrated time and again that it is only a matter of time before Whiteness collectively figures out ways to exploit (and often monetize) these pieces of others' identities for our own gain. We repeatedly fail to recognize that our perceived "cultural flattery" is often at the expense of the people and culture that we are ogling.

Simply put, any form of a dominant group "borrowing culture" must be acknowledged within an imperialist context. White folks casually deciding to adopt iconic components of cultures we have historically oppressed (and often still do) further undermines and strips the identity of the people these elements have been taken from. It also becomes an extension of the "ours for the taking" mindset that permeates ongoing Western colonization.

Colonialism has a "take what you want and leave the rest" attitude. When it comes to "taking" people's culture, "the rest" ends up being the part that provides context, significance, and meaning. What we take is usually the part that can most easily be monetized—and we rarely have any intention of sharing the profit with the people who unwittingly made us profitable. Once we (White America) have taken it from them, we promptly "water it down" and sell it back to them at a markup (e.g., Taco Bell, Chili's Mexican Grill, Magic Dragon, Chang's Mongolian Grill, coconut oil, turmeric). Or, worse, we claim it was ours all along.

While White culture can pick and choose the tokenized parts of a culture that we find fascinating, that privilege does not work the other way around. It might be tempting to argue that this is a two-way street. After all, if we are appropriating from others, then surely others must be appropriating from us. This can't always be about who's in charge, right? What about the countless things that have been adopted from White American culture? What makes it okay for others to take our stuff, play our music, wear our clothes, eat our food, or to act like us? Isn't that just "reverse cultural appropriation"—especially if the people are benefiting from or even making money off it?

While many BIPOC folks now willingly adopt elements of White American culture and lifestyle, this is not cultural appropriation for one simple reason: the power distribution is not equal.

• • •

CULTURAL APPROPRIATION: ONE-WAY STREET

It is tempting to believe the persistent myth that America is the great melting pot. However, America is more like a fishing net. White Americans no longer have to travel to faraway places to steal other people's stuff. Instead, White America simply waits, trawling the ocean of immigrants for "new" and exotic things that can be cheaply modified and commodified.

The argument that cultural appropriation is a two-way street is akin to the erroneous notion of reverse racism—both issues come down to the relative power of the two parties involved. As described by author and social activist Maisha Z. Johnson, an in-depth explanation of cultural appropriation must "address the particular *power dynamic* in which members of a dominant culture take elements from a culture of people who have been systematically oppressed *by that dominant group*. . . . [C]ultural exchange lacks that systemic power dynamic" (emphasis added).[375] Moreover, cultural appropriation must be addressed within its appropriate historical context.

Western culture has historically and systematically forced millions of people of color to assimilate. Countless societies were expected to unilaterally adopt our religion, lifestyles, beliefs, and practices—or potentially face genocide. For Westerners to now accuse these very people of copying us or benefiting from our culture adds insult to injury. One Native American blogger who chose to remain anonymous describes how "it is important to understand the history of colonialism and to understand that what you [White people] see as a parallel act of 'cultural appropriation,' is really the product of colonialism. To equate those things is to deny the historical and continued violence produced by colonialism, and it is also a huge reflection of privilege."[376] This privilege is why we still so often view blatant cultural appropriation as mere "cultural exchange." It feels easier to justify.

When viewed in this broader context, it is unfair to equate our incessant pillaging of other groups with elements of our culture being copied, emulated, or monetarily benefited from. The fact that some BIPOC folks *now choose* to adopt elements of our culture does not justify our desire to "adopt" more elements of theirs—especially without their explicit permission. When we choose to take parts of their identity, we are not only further stripping BIPOC Americans and immigrants of their identities but also flaunting and profiting from what we stole. We are essentially saying that once an item, belief, or practice has been thoroughly whitewashed and molded to our liking, then and only then does it have *real* value.

• • •

"BORROWING" OTHER PEOPLE'S STUFF

Obvious examples such as music, hairstyles, and clothes are just the tip of the cultural appropriation iceberg. Food, artwork, religious symbols, dances—many of these elements often become commercialized and "absorbed" into White society. The number of salt lamps, Buddha statues, incenses, and oil diffusers that now reside in therapists' offices, massage parlors, spas, coffee shops, upscale alternative medicine stores, swanky downtown apartments, college dorm rooms, and admittedly the shelf in front of me as I type this in my living room are constant reminders of the ongoing "exotification" and commodification of things that White America decides are trendworthy.

That the plastic Buddha statues on my bookshelf were purchased at a ninety-nine-cent store should be a clue as to how popular these sacred religious emblems have become. Similarly, Tibetan prayer flags and tapestries depicting Shiva, Krishna, Ganesha, and countless other Hindu gods and goddesses adorn many a "stoner den." I'm not saying that everyone who owns a

Buddha statue or tapestry needs to convert or else get rid of their decorations, but we should be cognizant that our chosen forms of décor are powerful and revered religious emblems that have been around for thousands of years.

To put it in perspective, let's say that the tables were turned. Many Christian Americans would probably find it rather odd, if not offensive, if a predominantly Asian country began putting up cheap plastic statues and posters of a crucifix simply because they liked the way it looked and the "chill ambience" it created in their homes and offices. (Of course, for a more accurate comparison to be made, Christians would have to be the oppressed minority, not be making any profit from the sale of these crucifixes, and have numerous other parts of their identity also taken from them.)

Similarly, most Jews would be put off if other people started wearing the iconic Star of David as a "cool alternative" to the typical five-point star. (Oddly enough, Lucky Charms sported the six-point star until 1991.[377] I'm sure that many Jews eating Lucky Charms back then had some questions about why their most sacred symbol was floating in their cereal bowl. Soggy Star of David, anyone?) It is worth noting that the Star of David wasn't used for religious purposes within Judaism until around the nineteenth century, when European Jews began integrating into Christian communities.[378] It has also been used by countless other cultures and religions (including Hinduism and Japanese Shrines), some dating back as far as the Bronze Age.[379] So who exactly does it belong to, anyway? But I digress.

Another iconic religious symbol that has been popularized is the bindi, the red dot placed on the middle of the forehead in many religious cultures of the Indian subcontinent. Countless White women and American celebrities have chosen to sport a trendy "third eye," particularly at music festivals. This seemingly harmless wardrobe decision undercuts the sanctity and ancient symbolism that the bindi represents in Indian culture. While White folks continue to butcher the word "namaste" at music festivals, yoga studios, and meditation retreats across the US, many Indian American schoolgirls are still being picked on by their White classmates for the "exotic" dots on their foreheads, along with their coconut-oiled hair and henna tattoos[380]—all of which have now become overpriced, popular trends and commodities within liberal White culture. Americanized "Eastern medicine" stores are notorious for this exploitative practice, with one major online Ayurveda company claiming that its fifty-dollar jar of coconut oil will "bestow intelligence upon its user and . . . subtly promote awareness and mental function"[381]—while not so subtly draining one's wallet.

Many Indian women have become fed up with their culture being idolized and tokenized by White Americans. Indian writer and journalist Yashica Dutt says, "For many South Asian women, the bindi is a significant cultural symbol. For teens at Coachella, it's a shiny thing to stick on your forehead."[382] This pervasive casual trend among White people led to a movement referred to as "#ReclaimTheBindi" before the 2015 Coachella Music Festival. A similar backlash occurred when White folks became obsessed with henna tattoos at "spiritual festivals," including Burning Man. As one anonymous Indian woman wrote on Tumblr, "They [White people] want the flavor but not the smell [in reference to curry]. They want the culture but not you."[383]

These cultural "accoutrements" only begin to highlight the true amount of wealth and culture that has been stolen from East Asia. While it is ultimately not helpful to compare levels of oppression and exploitation (i.e., who has it the worst), there is, perhaps one nation that exemplifies how exploitation, appropriation, and commercialization have shaped Western history: India—the land that countless White people visit to find ourselves and yet know almost nothing about.

• • •

WE LOVE THEIR THINGS . . . BUT NOT THEM

Liberal White folks are captivated by India. Even before *Eat Pray Love* flew off the bookshelves, White people flocked to this "exotic" and "mystical" oasis. We love yoga, their beautiful artwork, their gorgeous clothing, their colorful festivals and holidays, their nifty-looking gods, their wise sages, gurus, and who could forget their delicious food!

Untold numbers of White liberal millennials have pilgrimaged throughout India, wearing sandals, elephant-adorned poofy pants, incorrectly wrapped saris, and bindis on their foreheads. Yet before White people's obsessive love affair and subsequent appropriation of "everything Indian" began, we didn't exactly arrive there as welcome guests. Rather, we didn't so much as arrive as invade. And while it may seem like the days of Western imperialism in India are long gone, this context is crucial when we talk about how much we seemingly "love and admire" stuff from Indian culture. So, let's take a step back and look at how Western culture became so obsessed with India in the first place.

Long before we began appropriating elements of their culture, the West was plundering their wealth, subduing their power, and erasing their history. Beginning with the spice trade through the British Empire and up through present day, India has been pilfered beyond what many other developing countries combined have experienced. By one estimate, if adjusted for inflation, India is owed approximately $44.6 trillion for stolen wealth and resources[384]—nearly twice the combined GDP of the United Kingdom and the United States, and half of the entire 2021 global GDP.[385] Yet material wealth only tells part of the story.

DESECRATING AN ICON

When the British first "arrived" in India, they quickly began stripping India of its physical wealth, desecrating hundreds of sacred temples, statues, palaces, and tombs. This was certainly not the first nor the last time that the British stole from conquered lands, but it is one of the most blatant examples of unwarranted thievery. Gold and precious jewels were ripped right out of the stonework of palaces, temples, and arguably the most famous mausoleum in the world: the Taj Mahal.

Built during the seventeenth century by Emperor Shah Jahan as a shrine for his favorite deceased wife, Begum Mumtaz Mahal, the Taj Mahal is believed to have been decorated with as many as forty types of precious stones and rare metals.[386] However, by the end of the nineteenth century, British soldiers had stripped the entire structure down to its pale stone skeleton. Most of these valuable metals, jewels, and precious stones were then incorporated into the jewelry and coffers of British royalty.

Adding insult to injury, the British decided that the acres of lush gardens teeming with exotic plants and animals surrounding the tomb did not fit the British image of beauty. As the British settled in (i.e., trespassed) for the long haul, the entire garden was ripped out and sculpted into a traditional, tidy, British-style garden with neat rows, cobbled pathways, and manicured hedges. This form and structure fit the British standard of what a proper garden should look like, and is a style that still adorns many homes and arboretums today.

As part of this mutilation, an enormous grass lawn with uniform pathways replaced the original garden. While this may outwardly seem like a trivial detail, grass lawns are a direct legacy of colonialism. They originated in the seventeenth century and spread throughout Europe as a symbol of status, power, wealth, and of the triumph of man over nature. Because maintaining them took a tremendous amount of water, effort, and labor (i.e., people), the bigger and neater the lawn, the wealthier the owner.[387] Consequently, immaculate lawns remain an iconic symbol of Western dominance and colonialism.

Today, despite annual water shortages and rising temperatures, many residents in the Hamptons, New Jersey, spend as much as half a million dollars a year on their lawns, trucking in water, fertilizing, and paying landscapers thousands of dollars to spray-paint dead patches and wash bird poop from their lawns. "All the boys talk about in the Hamptons is the grass,"[388] says Hamptonian Sara Adams in a 2023 interview with *Vanity Fair* magazine. "I listen to it all the time. It's like a macho-testosterone-penis thing. . . . They sit down to dinner and the first thing they say is 'How's your grass looking?' I swear." Unknowingly, these Hamptonian men are upholding a petty legacy of testosterone-fueled "lawn envy" that stems directly from colonization.

Whereas $500,000 Hampton lawns merely encapsulate a "macho" evolution of the owning class, the Taj Mahal's new, immaculate lawn stood as a testament to the British claim, ownership, and "taming" of wild India. Putting a grass lawn in front of the Taj Mahal and then forcing Indian workers to painstakingly maintain it was a way for the British to further claim ownership over the mausoleum itself and incorporate it as yet another "trinket" on Britain's overflowing shelf of stolen wealth and power. This also calls into question the fact that many of us grossly underpay undocumented laborers to keep our lawns looking immaculate, while residing on land that was stolen from its original inhabitants.

Sadly, the Taj Mahal's sprawling grass lawn is now primarily used for Western tourists to take cheesy jumping selfies with the pillaged shrine of a dead woman's final resting place in the background. It is one of the most visited places on the planet, yet hardly any visitors stop to think about the unimaginable beauty that once radiated from the Taj Mahal's walls and its sprawling grounds before the Western world desecrated it.

While the Taj Mahal serves as an example of material wealth being physically plundered, the British were not simply after wealth or land. Their "foray" into India had a much larger goal: power. In order to achieve that desired power, nothing short of the world's most iconic and valuable diamond would do.

• • •

THE (STOLEN) CROWN JEWEL

To show the true power (i.e., brashness and ego) of the British Empire, upon their unwelcomed arrival, the British set their sights on what was and still is the most famous and expensive diamond in the world, the Koh-i-Noor—more commonly known as *the* crown jewel.

Weighing 105.6 carats, the Koh-i-Noor was likely unearthed thousands of years ago and passed down among countless rulers and religious groups, not to mention incorporated into the stories of Hinduism itself as a coveted item of the god Krishna himself. When the British arrived in India, they immediately sought this legendary diamond as a means to both increase their wealth and, more importantly, signify absolute British rule. As described by an article in *Smithsonian* magazine chronicling the theft of the diamond, "that symbol of prestige and power was irresistible. If they [the British] could own *the* jewel of India as well as the country itself, it would symbolize their power and colonial superiority. It was a diamond worth fighting and killing for."[389] This quest had nothing to do with appropriation; the colonizers wanted to possess the literal heart of India itself.

The British finally got their chance to steal the diamond in the nineteenth century when a series of chaotic and violent overthrows occurred, in large part due to the British occupancy. After the dust had settled, only two people were left in the familial line to inherit the throne of India: a ten-year-old boy, Duleep Singh, and his mother, Jindan. In 1849, the British ruthlessly imprisoned the boy's mother and forced him to sign a treaty that, among other ludicrous terms, required the boy to unconditionally surrender the Koh-i-Noor.[390]

Once the diamond was "acquired" from India and brought back to England, it was promptly put on display in the 1851 Great Exposition in London. Ironically, to the dismay of its proud captors, the public was less than impressed by the simplicity of this rough uncut diamond, likening it to a large piece of glass.[391] Taking matters into his own hands, Queen Victoria's husband, Prince Albert, decided to have the stone recut and polished as a gift for his wife. This shaved the diamond down to half of its original size (which had been nearly an astonishing one-tenth of a pound!). This mutilated diamond was then cast into a brooch and presented to Queen Victoria to add to her (stolen) jewelry collection. In 1937, the Koh-i-Noor eventually transferred to the (literal and symbolic) "head" of the Western world—upon the late Queen Elizabeth's crown. "For now, it remains locked in the Tower of London, advertised as a 'symbol of conquest'—firmly on British soil,"[392] describes NPR's international London correspondent in a 2023 article. "Meanwhile, the British sell tickets (currently, about $37 for adults) to see the Kohinoor—and have done so since 1851, when the diamond was the star attraction at the World Exhibition at the Crystal Palace in London." Talk about a (stolen) "gift" that keeps on giving! With roughly three million visitors a year, adjusting for inflation, that amounts to nearly one billion in revenue in the past decade alone.

The plundering of the Koh-i-Noor is much more than a financial loss for India. While its wealth remains incalculable, this diamond is an emblem of mythical proportions that previously represented India's position and status within the world. "To Indians, it's actually a perfect, perfect metaphor for what India went through: It was reshaped and re-cut and diminished into something that suited a British palate and British needs,"[393] describes historian Anita Anand, the coauthor of *Kohinoor: The History of the World's Most Infamous Diamond*. This was a pilfering of power and a theft of identity and is perhaps the starkest example of forceful appropriation. Like the diamond itself, India was chiseled, shined, polished, and eventually recast as the quintessential symbol of British rule.

Despite ongoing demands for the Koh-i-Noor's rightful return to India, "what tends to happen with these [requests] is that if you say yes to one, you suddenly find the British Museum would be emptied!"[394] said former prime minister David Cameron in 2010 on New Delhi Television. "It is going to have to stay put." Cameron's response was more than a cheeky comment; it was a literal admission that the Tower of London is nothing more than a heavily guarded safe house for stolen wealth—containing 23,000 gemstones, precious metals, and over a hundred valuable artifacts. Or as the Historic Royal Palace curators describe it, they are merely "continuing a long tradition of storing (stolen) precious objects here."[395] Precious indeed! The International Gem Society values the Imperial State Crown alone at nearly six billion.[396] At this point, the British have amassed so much that beginning as far back as the mid-nineteenth century, the term "English funds" became a euphemism for describing their stolen wealth.[397]

So what does the destruction of the Taj Mahal, the loss of a diamond, or a glorified safe house in London have to do with some random White festivalgoers adorned with bindis or putting up Ganesha tapestries in their dorm rooms? This is where the connection must be made to the less-than-subtle examples of stolen power, culture, and identity. When it comes to financial gain and cultural theft of things that don't belong to us, there is another current top contender unwittingly provided by India: Yoga—or rather, the entire American yoga wercase) culture.

• • •

IMPOSTER YOGA

For the vast majority of White Americans, yoga is merely a fun way to become stronger, more flexible, work on our breathing, relieve stress, and feel better about our bodies. While there is absolutely nothing wrong with White people—or anyone else, for that matter—practicing yoga to better our lives, the problem occurs when it is stripped of its intended meaning and the culture to which it belongs. This is further compounded by the fact that yoga has become a multibillion-dollar industry that almost exclusively benefits the Western economy.

Let's try to put this phenomenon in perspective: Imagine for a moment that the majority of Chinese restaurants are owned and run by White people and that many Chinese people are not able to open up Chinese restaurants because the demand for Americanized Chinese food has far surpassed the desire for the real thing. Now imagine that in order to even open a Chinese restaurant, one has to go through a certification process and pay money to primarily White facilitators to learn the art of cooking "authentic" Chinese food. This is where we are with yoga.

The trendy yoga studios that most White folks frequent are typically devoid of not only the spiritual context but also the entire purpose behind this ancient and sacred practice. "Many aspects of yoga have been misunderstood and more importantly misrepresented and commercialized over the past decades by people in power,"[398] explains yoga studio owner and podcaster Arundhati Baitmangalkar. Consequently, yoga in its current form would be almost unrecognizable to the people who created it.

• • •

YOGA HEADS WEST

Yoga originated close to 5,000 years ago as a philosophical pillar within an orthodox sect of ancient Indian philosophy, deeply connected to religious and spiritual practice.[399] In its original form, it had very little to do with body movement and flexibility; rather, it was a form of spiritual practice steeped in mantras, rituals, and core values. Despite the popular misconception, not everyone who practices yoga is a Yogi. A true Yogi is someone who has dedicated their entire life to understand, embody, and live all parts of Yoga. The physical aspect (i.e., asanas) only started becoming more prominent in the last two centuries.[400] Once the West got a taste of this "exotic form of stretching," we were hooked; however, for many White Americans, it wasn't love at first sight.

Yoga first publicly arrived in the United States in 1893, introduced by a man named Swami Vivekananda at an international conference in Chicago that was attempting to create a global dialogue of faiths.[401] However, because of its perceived connection to Eastern mysticism and sexuality—not to mention its primary proponent, Ida Craddock, being an outspoken women's-rights and sex advocate who wrote extensively on human sexuality and the occult[402]—Yoga quickly came under attack and was demonized by many Christian Americans.

Consequently, it did not gain significant traction until about 1919, when a more mainstream form was brought over by Yogendra, a man now referred to by some (White) people as "the Father of the Modern Yoga Renaissance."[403] This so-called renaissance led to the development of dozens of yoga retreat centers around the United States. This also spurred the development of multiple styles of yoga, yoga celebrities and gurus, as well as multiple publications.

Over the next century, true to form, America managed to take a deeply spiritual practice and strip it of any original context or meaning. By the late 1990s, yoga had overtaken aerobics as the most dominant exercise trend and become a burgeoning fad in wealthy neighborhoods, "especially urban neighborhoods with high concentrations of well-educated stay-at-home post-feminist mothers,"[404] describes professor and historian Jared Farmer in a 2012 paper, "Americanasana." By this time, as many as 85 percent of American yoga practitioners were White.[405] As celebrities, athletic brands, sporting goods companies, and influencers got in on the action, new and novel forms of yoga quickly dominated the Western market. Moreover, the vast majority of yoga studios in the US became White-owned, led by White instructors, and full of primarily White practitioners.

• • •

HOT YOGA, GOAT YOGA, WINE YOGA, WHITE YOGA

Despite not even being able to correctly pronounce the names of the traditional asanas (yoga poses), White folks have further popularized and reinvented the practice of yoga by adding soothing music, heated floors, wine, goats, and countless other novel components that further dissociate yoga from its original Hinduism-derived forms. Consequently, "yoga now belongs to . . . a postcolonial realm of religious cosmopolitanism,"[406] which includes "yoga with dogs, aqua yoga, disco yoga, naked yoga, and laughter yoga," according to Jared Farmer. This Americanized yoga is heavily influenced by "commercialism and narcissism . . . functioning without formal gurus [and using] instead . . . a rotating lineup of novel yet interchangeable Hatha 'rock stars' . . . [who] compete for audience share." Furthermore, hard-abbed Instagram yoga trendsetters continue to drive the mistaken notion that Yoga (capitalized) is all about enhancing the body.

Many self-proclaimed yogis have also created their own trademarked brands (which often include unique studios, products, and clothing) such as Yoga Booty Ballet™, Slim Calm Sexy™, Yoga for Golfers™, Taxi Yoga™ (for frequent drivers), Revista-Yoga™ (for wrinkles), and, of course, who could forget AntiGravity Yoga™. This is not to say that yoga as an exercise should be completely sterile of *any* outside influence, but when Western novelties become the expectation, their influence further minimizes the purpose of Yoga and creates collateral consequences. It is not merely the loss of its traditional culture or intended meaning that makes Yoga (capitalized) appropriation unjust; there are also harmful effects on the people from which it was taken.

• • •

REAL PRACTITIONERS GET PUSHED OUT

The Westernization and novelization of yoga has pushed many genuine South Asian practitioners and instructors to the fringes of, if not completely out of, this growing multibillion-dollar industry. Most White folks now have a distinctly Westernized palate for what yoga should look like, sound like, and feel like, and that expectation has overshadowed the practice itself as well as marginalized the people to whom it belongs.

Understandably, most of those who teach real Yoga are unwilling to conform to the whitewashed expectations of a practice they have devoted their lives to. This means that they often have difficulty starting their own studios or even getting hired at Western-style studios—despite being more qualified than most of the instructors. Arundhati Baitmangalkar describes her personal experience with this whitewashing of her spiritual practice in a 2021 article that she wrote for *Yoga International* magazine: "As a yoga teacher and Indian immigrant living in the United States, there has been no escaping it [the appropriation]. For many years, I didn't say much about what it feels like to have one's heritage stolen and misused in yoga spaces."[407]

In addition to calling out the offensive use of sacred symbols and deities as décor, Baitmangalkar highlights how most White-owned yoga studios try to mimic the "feel of the East" by placing deities or idols in random places, including on the ground, which is extremely taboo in Hindu culture. Even the simple act of sitting "with the soles of your feet facing an idol . . . is considered not only disrespectful but also shameful," Baitmangalkar explains.

The desire by White yoga studio owners and teachers to increase patronage by creating a pseudo-authentic and exotic feel has led to a complete disregard of the individuals who have watched their culture become selectively dismembered and desiccated. Ultimately, capitalism rather than spiritualism has become the driving force behind the evolution of Western yoga.

• • •

THE "RICHES" OF YOGA

Outside of the studio, Westernized yoga has blossomed into a swanky health-and-beauty industry riddled with White-owned magazines touting exaggerated benefits and health claims. "Perhaps the most characteristic feature of American yoga is its syncretism [i.e., amalgamation] with other popular forms of therapeutics like massage, chiropractic, aromatherapy, and music therapy,"[408] describes Jared Farmer. In the eyes of many Westerners, these other therapeutic practices have become synonymous with yoga. In addition to the misrepresentation and dilution of the practice, yoga magazines and websites further solicit and commodify Indian health foods, remedies, and traditional medicines.

The vast majority of yoga magazines and websites typically depict White women on their covers, alongside kitschy articles like "Om in 30 seconds," "Harness Your Inner Ganesha Power," "Hidden Treasures of the East," "7 Yoga Career Hacks," and, of course, "How to Use Yoga to Improve Your Skiing."[409] My personal favorite is an exposé piece on an "authentic radical yogi" named Stewart who is (apparently) "made for these times" with his "radical punky reggae yoga philosophy."[410] Because as we all know, punk and reggae are the heart and soul of true yoga. To be fair, considering the frequent misuse of the term "yogi," Stewart may be one of the few White yoga instructors who has gone above and beyond to embody both yoga practice and philosophy—but the way he is portrayed by *Om Yoga Magazine* is the problem.

These magazines elicit further cultural appropriation by sporting brands and ads for hipster apparel such as "Buddha pants."[411] Not to mention *LA Yoga Weekly*'s "Subscribe to our Newsletter" banner ad from 2021—which for some odd reason featured a muscular, blond, White dude standing against the backside of White woman wearing a shirt that says "Rebel" who is awkwardly carrying a skateboard while thrusting her buttocks against the man's waist and looking back at him seductively. Clearly that's what yoga is all about.

Besides its cultural desecration, the sheer commercial value of Westernized yoga is what makes it a contender for the "cultural appropriation Olympics." Stripped of its roots and given a Western makeover, yoga has become an engorged cash cow for White America. A 2016 Forbes survey "found that Americans spent $16 billion on [yoga] classes, gear and accessories"[412]—an almost $10 billion increase from just three years earlier. This number continues to increase as yoga studios and yoga certification programs pop up all over the United States. Some research indicates that the current yoga industry is worth over $84 billion worldwide, with the average practitioner spending nearly $65,000 over their lifetime on workshops, classes, and yoga accessories.[413]

In our monetization of a spiritual practice, has America's yoga obsession bolstered India in any way? Has the fact that almost one out of ten Americans have tried yoga strengthened Hinduism or Indian culture in the United States?

The simple answer to both of these rhetorical questions is a firm "no." As is the case with almost every instance of blatant cultural appropriation, those billions in profit inevitably go straight into the pockets of the people who appropriated yoga, while hardly a cent has benefited the people from which it was taken—besides the paltry incomes of overseas factory workers forced to work grueling hours using noxious chemicals to create yoga mats, garments, and accessories for export. Yoga has been stripped of its identity and appropriated as a mainstream form of exercise in America, becoming yet another opportunity for American capitalism to commodify something that does not belong to us.

As described by author Anjali Joshi, when appropriation leaves Indian culture "void of the significance that it was supposed to have—it strips the religious, historical and cultural context . . . and makes it mass-marketable."[414] In other words, White people don't actually love Yoga (capitalized); we love the appropriated version that we have created for ourselves—and so does our economy.

Am I saying that White people should stop doing yoga or should not teach yoga? No. It's not that simple, nor is that a practical solution. There is nothing wrong with people (White or otherwise) trying to improve their physical and mental health. But it is worth honoring the old saying "Give credit where credit is due." If you decide to practice yoga, at least study its history, research its spiritual elements, or find ways to give back to the people from which it was taken (monetarily or otherwise). Equally as important: avoid at all costs further perpetuating the stereotyped and contrived images of Hindu culture. If your yoga apparel or (White-owned) yoga studio is covered with images of the chakras, "om" symbols, Hindu gods and goddesses, incense, etc., and you do not see a person of color working there, it might be time to find another place to practice yoga—preferably one that is either owned or led by a South Asian practitioner or somehow gives back to the culture it emulates.

While yoga provides a solid example of what it looks like to pilfer someone else's culture for our own gain, countless other foods, styles of dress, décor, religious icons and practices, discoveries, as well as medicinal herbs and remedies have led to billions, if not trillions, in profit. Perhaps another contender for the gold medal in the appropriation Olympics would be the American music industry.

■ ■ ■

MUSICAL APPROPRIATION: ADJUSTING THE "DIAL" OF WHITENESS

In the past century, it has become perfectly acceptable for White musicians and vocalists to emulate lyrics, rhythms, and even vocal styles that do not belong to their culture. It is equally normalized for White producers, White-owned record labels, and White-owned stadiums and concert halls to make *insane* amounts of money from these appropriated elements.

For centuries, classical music dominated Europe. Once imported to America, classical music, alongside the traditional folk music of various immigrants, served as the foundation for many of the distinct blends that Americans listens to today. As described by film critic and *New York Times* columnist Wesley Morris, "'White,' 'Western,' 'classical' music [was] the overarching basis for lots of

American pop songs. Chromatic-chord harmony, clean timbre of voice and instrument: These are the ingredients for some of the hugely singable harmonies of the Beatles, the Eagles, Simon and Fleetwood Mac, something choral, 'pure,' largely ungrained."[415]

But the range of American music would not be what it is today had it not undergone a dramatic hybridization, incorporating (i.e., taking) the sounds and styles of countless other cultures. Many genres of what we now call Western music would be completely unrecognizable to our "classically attuned" Western ancestors. Western-style compositions with strict pattern and order gave way to multiple genres infused with soul, improvisation, and powerful rhythm. This was especially the case with the "adoption" of historically Black American music (i.e., soul, gospel, blues, jazz, etc.) by White musicians throughout the nineteenth and twentieth centuries.

Many elements encapsulated in Black American music had never before been used within the constraints of traditional Western music. Wesley Morris elaborates,

> Black music is a completely different story [than its Western counterpart]. It brims with call and response, layers of syncopation and this rougher element called "noise," unique sounds that arise from the particular hue and timbre of an instrument—Little Richard's woos and knuckled keyboard zooms. The dusky heat of Miles Davis's trumpeting. Patti LaBelle's emotional police siren. DMX's scorched-earth bark. The visceral stank of Etta James, Aretha Franklin, live-in-concert Whitney Houston and Prince on electric guitar.[416]

The fusion of blues and soul into the emerging popish rock and roll music of the '40s and '50s laid the foundation for most of the rock music that millions of White people know and love today.

Classic rock, indie, metal, punk, and even grunge genres—although typically considered White music—would simply not exist had they not been built upon the music of Black culture.

One of the primary reasons why musicians such as Elvis Presley, the Rolling Stones, Led Zeppelin, and even the Beatles initially faced visceral resistance and pushback from White America was that they were pulling inspiration directly from Black music. These appropriated sounds were unrecognizable and even abrasive to the ear of many White listeners. Prominent leaders of the evangelical church in the '50s and '60s, including musician and popular radio DJ Bob Larson and David A. Noebel (who made it his spiritual mission to take down the Beatles),[417] campaigned vehemently against what they considered to be "a black invasion of white America,"[418] describes American poet and essayist John Haines in a 2011 article for a *Black Music Research Journal*. Noebel referred to rock and roll as "a designed reversion to savagery," while Larson once proclaimed, "All one needs to do is make a trip to the places where rock 'n roll has its roots . . . and observe the ceremonies which often go along with this kind of music . . . to know the direction in which we as a nation are headed."[419]

However, outside of the church, millions of White Americans and Europeans quickly became accustomed to these "new" and "exotic" sounds—eventually claiming many as our own. Since then, countless White musicians who heavily "borrowed" from Black musicians have become immortalized in the Rock and Roll Hall of Fame.

One of my favorite bands of all time, Led Zeppelin, was notorious for copying riffs as well as entire songs from African American blues musicians and not giving them any credit. To add insult to injury, their lead guitarist, Jimmy Page, spent his formative years frequenting clubs featuring Black musicians and amassing a collection of blues vinyl records from the Deep South. Page went on to use this style of music (as well as entire songs) to sell out stadiums and make ungodly amounts of money during a time when Black musicians were not even allowed to perform in most public spaces.[420]

Not to be outdone, the Rolling Stones most famous line, "I can't get no satisfaction," is a blatant example of musical thievery. Guitarist and songwriter Keith Richards "borrowed" this phrase from African American Vernacular English. Beyond the appropriated dialect, the infamous lyric itself was also likely "borrowed" from one of Keith Richard and Mick Jagger's rock idols, African American rock and roll pioneer Chuck Berry. Ten years before the debut of the Rolling Stones' smash hit "Satisfaction," Chuck Berry released a song containing the lyrics "I don't get no satisfaction."[421] After Berry's passing in 2017, Jagger sang his praises and thanked him "for all the inspirational music he gave to us."[422]

Jagger's use of the word "gave" should be taken with a grain of salt. Unfortunately, like so many other Black musicians of his time, Chuck Berry "can't get no" credit for one of the most iconic phrases and songs in rock and roll history. At least the Rolling Stones finally had the decency to "ax" another one of their most iconic (as well as disturbing) songs, "Brown Sugar," from their 2021 US tour set list, as it literally references raping enslaved Black women:[423] "Gold Coast slave ship bound for cotton fields . . . slaver know he's doin' all right, hear him whip the women, just around midnight . . . Brown Sugar, how come you taste so good? . . . Brown Sugar, just like a Black girl should."[424] Beyond a glaring example of dialectal appropriation, this song epitomizes the racial fetishization touched on earlier.

Not to be ignored, the "King of Rock and Roll," Elvis Presley, arguably built his entire sound, image, and many of his most famous hits, including "Hound Dog" (originally performed by Willie Mae "Big Mama" Thornton in 1952), upon the style, talent, and creativity of countless Black musicians and Black culture.[425]

However, blues and rock are just a drop in the ocean of our conquest of music.

WHITEWASHING HIP-HOP

It does not take a genius to see how cultural appropriation has become rampant in the modern music industry. It goes unspoken in White culture that sounding (and acting) Black is cool—but *being* Black is not. African American comedy legend Paul Mooney described it best: "The Black man in America is the most-copied man on this planet, bar none. Everybody wanna be a n*gga, but nobody wanna be a n*gga."[426] Mooney was alluding to the fact that many White people have a complex, complicated, and condescending relationship with what we consider Black culture versus Black people themselves.

There is a reason *besides* talent for why artists like Eminem and Post Malone have become so popular. Imagine if a White dude who was trying to make it as a rapper went onstage and spoke the way they would on a college entrance exam. In fact, let's try just that with a popular song by Post Malone—a tatted, cornrowed, gold-grill-sporting White rapper who claims that he is hated "because [he's] White and [he's] different."[427] Not to mention his claims that he has been the victim of reverse racism.

Original lyrics by Post Malone:

> My momma called, see you on TV, son
> Said shit done changed ever since we was on
> I dreamed it all ever since I was young.

Academic English translation:

> My mother phoned me recently and exclaimed, "I saw you on television, son!"

> Many things have changed since I've become successful.
> I've dreamed about this fantasy since I was young.

Just doesn't have the same ring to it, does it? This is not to say that the musicians themselves are always the problem; but the style and manner of rap and hip-hop were created by the Black American community. These genres were born out of struggle, oppression, and the rhythm and stories of their ancestors. This means that when White people try to emulate hip-hop culture, we are unwittingly stripping the music, the style, and the culture of its original meaning and intent. To be clear, there are plenty of White people who are eager to outright build wealth off of Black culture and willfully exploit it for themselves, but those are not the people I am referring to here.

Let's consider the implications of Post Malone and many other White rappers' "adopted identities." From his style, swagger, appearance, voice, and even the content of his music, Post Malone exudes an identity that, simply put, is not his own. This takes us into the realm of a controversial term: "wigger."

The Post Malones of the world are often referred to as "wiggas" or "wiggers." This derogatory term was made popular in the '90s and used by primarily by White people to describe other White people who emulated Black culture. Case in point, back in the 1992 when the brand FUBU (For Us By Us)—a brand made for those within hip-hop culture (as the name would imply)—became popular in the United States, many suburban White kids and teens around the country began proudly sporting the gear because it was cool, it was urban, it was risky, and it was subversive. Countless White parents were furious when their teens came home in loose-fitting jeans, Air Jordans, and a FUBU logo plastered across their chests. These FUBU-sporting youth perfectly fit into *Merriam-Webster* definition of a wigger as "a usually young white person whose clothing, language, and mannerisms are regarded as imitative of those stereotypically associated with African-Americans: a white person who admires and seeks to emulate black culture."[428] The terms "admiration" and "emulation" fall far short of the mark when it comes to describing this well-known identity-stealing phenomenon.

Black American writer and rapper Michael Penn II gives a much better definition of a comparable term, "white n*gga": "a person of Caucasian/ European descent who selectively commandeers traits and characteristics associated with Blackness and Black identity in the context of the United States of America, mostly rooted in the contrived and stereotypical. Traits include, but aren't limited to: hairstyle, clothing, choice of vernacular, accent, body movement, political alignment, etc."[429] Whereas *Merriam-Webster*'s version presents this as innocent flattery, Penn's definition highlights the element of White folks *taking* something that isn't theirs and creating a manufactured stereotype.

Penn emphasizes another critical element of this particular form of cultural appropriation in a critique specifically of Post Malone: "I liked Post Malone's music until I realized it was just the musings of another white n*gga who sports all the customizable chocolate parts without the trappings of being a whole Black person."[430] Penn explicitly calls out how Post Malone—a.k.a. Austin Post—gets to pick and choose the aesthetic and superficial parts of an identity he thinks is cool, and he gets to do so without having to experience or truly understand the oppression, struggle, and suffering as well as the ancestry, pride, resilience, and resistance that went into forging the identity and culture he claims to embody.

Like so many other White hip-hop artists, Austin Post ultimately gets to move through the world with the privileges of a White man while sporting the external appearance of an exploited culture. Any resistance he faces is by his own volition—as he is choosing to copy a stereotype that he helps to perpetuate. Black Americans don't get to choose whether they are perceived as Black or not. "[S]ociety designated him that privilege. His success epitomizes the functionality of a post-racial America. . . . [He] is popular simply because he mirrors the trends of today in a digestible skin tone,"[431] elaborates Penn.

Despite how it may appear, Austin Post is not the problem; he is a symptom of the much larger phenomenon of cultural appropriation. He is one of countless White people who gets to emulate parts of a culture they find themselves drawn toward. While his rock and roll predecessors took selective pieces of Black culture, Austin Post has done all but self-identify as Black, selling out stadiums, posing on the covers of magazines, and making millions of dollars in the process.

Meanwhile, many Black musicians, particularly hip-hop artists, still struggle to overcome the endless racial barriers of trying to make it as an artist in a White-run music industry. This becomes even more significant when we look at what happened to jazz and blues music in America. These forms of music were shamelessly pilfered from the Black community at a time when racial oppression and exploitation were par for the course. As a result, not only were these styles of music copied, but also many of the songs themselves were stolen outright by White musicians who made millions off of them.

Perhaps the biggest irony is that since the founding of our country, White America has always been about private property, patents, and copyrights when it comes to *our* stuff.[432] Yet we tend to view objects and ideas that belong to other people as ours for the taking. It's no wonder that we hardly think twice about stealing music from Black culture. Since we first got our hands on it, we've been watering it down, repackaging it, and redistributing it to a mass audience of White people as our own brand.

This brings us to one more crucial part of cultural appropriation: White justification.

• • •

BUT WHAT IF IT DOESN'T OFFEND THEM?

The reality is there are always going to be some aspects of cultural appropriation that are not going to offend every person of color. Plenty of BIPOC Americans couldn't care less about what White folks choose to do when it comes to style, food, music, etc. Some just don't feel that it affects them personally, and that's okay. But finding a few people of color that don't mind *certain* elements of appropriation does not give us carte blanche to justify our actions and claim that everyone else shouldn't care either. As author and social activist Maisha Z. Johnson points out, there are "too many White people [who] use this tactic to tell us that we're wrong about racism—citing the [one] Native friend who doesn't mind cultural appropriation, or the Black celebrity who disagrees with Black Lives Matter protesters. . . . For one thing, Black people are not a monolith. We're allowed to disagree. And your Whiteness doesn't grant you the authority to determine which one of us is right."[433]

It's easy to see how absurd it would be to explain to a person of color that it's okay for me to use an offensive slur because I have another friend who looks like them and doesn't seem to mind. Yet when it comes to cultural appropriation, many of us default to this logic. On the opposite end of the spectrum, many progressive White Americans go to painstaking lengths to explain to a person of color who is not offended precisely why they *should* be offended by a form of cultural appropriation. The fact that they don't care does not indicate ignorance, indifference, nor apathy on their part. Whether someone else is offended is in many ways irrelevant; we need to be reflecting on our own complicity, not telling them how to feel about other White people's actions.

At the end of the day, cultural appropriation only tells part of the story of colonialism. While White culture has taken more than its fair share from others, there is another way by which it has more insidiously asserted, as well as inserted, itself throughout the world: forced assimilation.

CHAPTER 12

Our Society, Our Rules: Making "Them" More Like "Us"

THE "AMERICAN DREAM" has become a synonym for success in many places well beyond our borders. American styles, brands, food, music, media, and culture can be found on almost every continent. Yet this "voluntary" assimilation has only become voluntary in the last century. Forced assimilation has probably been the single most effective tool of colonialism, especially right here at home. In the United States, the persistent "melting pot" analogy holds true in a more sobering way than was originally intended—with the ongoing erasure of many BIPOC Americans' cultures and identities.

As colonialism formed the backbone of Western society, it became essential to devise methods by which to force others to conform to *our* culture, *our* standards, *our* practices, and *our* beliefs. In order to do this, a void had to be created into which we could "insert" our culture. Understandably, most BIPOC folks have actively resist being "Whitened." Centuries of oppression and "identity theft" have left many marginalized communities at odds with what it means to "be American." In many cases, especially with Black and Indigenous Americans, we've left them with no other option but to adopt pieces of our culture in order to survive and not face further persecution, violence, and in some cases outright genocide.

Consequently, while it may outwardly appear that many people from other cultures and countries have voluntarily, willingly, and even eagerly adopted certain parts of White culture, this completely ignores the extent to which Whiteness has fought to ensure that ours is the indisputable dominant culture. In order to see how this was done, one need look no further than the Native American boarding schools throughout the United States and Canada during the nineteenth and twentieth centuries.

While enslaved Africans and African Americans were subject to centuries of exploitation, there was very little intention for them to become more like us; the opposite was more often true. Conversely, the Native Americans presented a unique challenge to the European settlers in America. Determining that it was too difficult to enslave them on their own land, and unwilling to concede to cohabitation, White America embarked on a brutal two-century campaign to solve the so-called "Indian problem."[434] The plan was simple: either they would be assimilated or they would be eradicated.

• • •

FORCED ASSIMILATION

The idea of using education as a tool for assimilating Native Americans goes back as far as the early colonies. A bill was passed by the Continental Congress in 1775—a year before the Declaration of Independence was even signed—that allocated $500 for Native American youth "education." While warfare and genocide were certainly not off the table, "schools were seen as both a cheaper and a more expedient way of dealing with the 'Indian problem,'"[435] writes *New York Times* correspondent Rukmini Callimachi in a 2021 article titled "Lost Lives, Lost Culture: The Forgotten History of Indigenous Boarding Schools."

Beginning in the mid-1820s, the Office of Indian Affairs (now the Bureau of Indian Affairs) began carving out Indian reservations across the United States. Many Indigenous children had already been forced to attend Christian day schools near their homes. As reservations became more prevalent, many of these schools were built on the reservations themselves. However, when it became apparent that the Indigenous children—who had daily contact with their families—were not assimilating into Christianity and Western culture as quickly as hoped, the "solution" the Office of Indian Affairs came up with was to start sending them to faraway boarding schools, where they would be deliberately cut off from their roots.

Starting with the opening of the Carlisle Indian school in 1879, more than 350 "Indian residential schools" were constructed across thirty states over the next century—with Oklahoma, Arizona, Alaska, New Mexico, and South Dakota containing nearly 60 percent of them.[436] These abhorrent institutions were modeled after traditional British boarding schools and built around a policy known as "aggressive civilization."[437] Native American children were literally kidnapped from their families and subjected to premeditated cultural genocide.

The actual number of children taken during this brutal campaign remains unknown; the Bureau of Indian Affairs did not keep track of enrollment numbers. However, some scholars estimate that by 1926, as many as 61,000 (or 83 percent of the total population of Indigenous children at that time) had attended boarding school.[438] It is likely that altogether, the United States attempted to assimilate hundreds of thousands of Native Americans through this compulsory process.

These children were completely cut off and deprived of their beliefs, customs, religions, language, and even their own names,[439] often facing severe punishment for trying to hold on to these parts of their culture and identity. Moreover, upon their arrival at these schools, countless Native children died from exposure, starvation, and Western illnesses, including the flu and tuberculosis. Many were buried in unmarked or mass graves and never returned to their families; numerous graves are just now being unearthed in the twenty-first century.[440] Those who survived the brutal transition promptly had all of their possessions stripped from them, including their clothes. Their hair, sacred to many tribes, was chopped off, and they were bathed and forced into school uniforms.

"You became an orphan on that day,"[441] described Dzabahe, a Navajo woman, in a 2021 interview on Colorado Public Radio. In 1953, Dzabahe was taken at age eleven to a government boarding school in Arizona. "My life was a shamble because everything that I was, everything that I believed in, my language, everything, I learned I was doing it all wrong." Sadly, Dzabahe's experience is far from unique. Once conformed to a Westernized appearance, these abducted children were subjected to years of intensive Christian education. Moreover, they were deliberately deprived of foundational learning skills and critical thinking opportunities that would have allowed them to gain power beyond what their captors intended them to possess. Instead, they were taught subservience in order to assimilate into a subordinate version of White Christian culture.

While many of our White parents and grandparents were busy learning algebra and skipping rope at recess, entire generations of Native children were being starved of their childhood and heritage. As described by the educational institution Facing History and Ourselves, those who administered and taught at these boarding schools were complicit in a "willfully neglectful system where thousands of students perished from malnutrition, poor medical care, and diseases . . . where child labor was a norm and where academic achievements were severely compromised."[442] Even more disturbing, the severe lack of accountability and oversight allowed for rampant physical and sexual abuse.

In an NPR podcast interview, David Anderson—Choctaw Nation member and former assistant secretary of the interior for Indian affairs in the George W. Bush administration—painfully recalled how his father arrived at one of these schools unable to speak a single word of English. After receiving regular beatings and having his mouth washed out with soap, his father ultimately left the school proficient in English but had forgotten his own language entirely.[443] David's father was one of countless children to face indescribable cruelty.

The Carlisle Indian school, founded in 1879 by Captain Richard H. Pratt, was the model and exemplar for these institutions throughout the US and Canada. Pratt's practices and beliefs can be succinctly summarized by two sentences he wrote in 1892: "All the Indian there is in the race should be dead. Kill the Indian in him and save the man."[444] For Pratt and many other White Americans, this wasn't simply a matter of wiping out the Indigenous culture; it was done under the guise of salvation.

By this time, the allocated budget for Indian assimilation was nearly $2.6 million[445]—roughly $80 to $90 million today when accounting for inflation. The number of Indigenous boarding schools significantly increased after the compulsory-attendance law passed in 1891 enabled and legalized the above-mentioned kidnapping. Congress even authorized the secretary of interior to withhold sustenance, including rations and money, from any Native American family that refused to send their child to school.[446] Canada followed suit in 1920 with the same compulsory-attendance amendment, which became known as the Indian Act.

Both United States and Canadian officials were unapologetic in their desire to open as many schools as possible. They boasted about their intentions to "absorb" the Indian population. Duncan Campbell Scott, an outspoken member of the Department of Indian Affairs and the man responsible for the compulsory amendment in Canada, said, "I want to get rid of the Indian problem. . . . Our objective is to continue until there is not a single Indian in Canada that has not been absorbed into the body politic and there is no Indian question, and no Indian Department, that is the whole object of this Bill."[447] Simply put, Scott was determined to exterminate any Indigenous roots that lingered in North America—a sentiment many White people shared at that time. In their supposed "noble cause of Christian salvation," the White authorities allowed a cultural genocide to continue unabated well into the twentieth century.

Shockingly, not until almost a century later, in 1978, did the United States Congress officially repeal this compulsory-attendance measure under the Indian Child Welfare Act. However, the damage had been done, and countless Native Americans were left marooned in a culture and society that neither belonged to them nor felt like something they belonged to. Many were unable to connect to their ancestry yet were also rejected by the society that had forcibly "civilized" them. Adding insult to injury, many of them were then forced onto small patches of land rife with unregulated gambling, alcohol, and tobacco—and then we simply expect them to forgive us and move on.

While this may seem like the trauma of generations past, the last boarding school in the United States, located in Washington state, did not close until 1980, while another in Canada remained open until 1996.[448] As described by Russell Box Sr. of the Southern Ute tribe in a 2021 *New York Times* interview while recounting his heartbreaking experience of being sent to boarding school at age six in southwestern Colorado, "We couldn't speak our language, we couldn't sing our prayer song. . . . To this day, maybe that's why I can't sing."[449]

Anthony Craig, an Indigenous educator and scholar, sums it up with a quote from his mother, who was forced to attend a boarding school in Washington during the 1900s: "Boarding school was there to teach me how to be a good White woman."[450] Like Russell and like Anthony's mother, thousands of Native Americans are still processing the intergenerational trauma, abuse, and brainwashing. The problem of this cultural genocidal era lingers among newer generations.

While the deliberate assimilation model is no longer in practice, as of 2020, the Bureau of Indian Education (BIE) still funded roughly 183 schools "located on 64 reservations in 23 states, serv[ing] approximately 42,000 Indian students. Of these, 58 [were] BIE-operated.... The Bureau also fund[ed] or operat[ed] off-reservation boarding schools and peripheral dormitories near reservations for students attending public schools."[451] Moreover, not until March 2020 did they formalize a decision to create standards, assessments, and accountability systems (SAAS) for all of these schools.[452] One can only wonder by whose standards these 42,000 children are being assessed—or what the accountability for learning looked like up until that point.

Over the course of the past two centuries, cultural extermination has proved much harder than politicians and school officials had anticipated. In an ironic twist, many of the targeted and banned elements of Indigenous populations, including their beliefs, spirituality, and sacred items, became fascinating to White Americans.

Despite over 400 years of genocide, some White folks now feel that it is okay to put Indigenous culture on display in homes and offices. Many of us have trendy, Native American–inspired artwork, mugs, refrigerator magnets, and even bumper stickers. Still others choose to hang dream catchers over beds or from rearview mirrors, completely oblivious to their true meaning or even from which tribe they originated. Moreover, the multibillion-dollar sports industry plasters jerseys, helmets, key chains, and entire stadiums with offensive, stereotyped Native American images, names, and stylized logos.

Our appropriation of Native American culture isn't merely an example of colonialism's attitude of "take what you want and leave the rest." This takes it one step further: take what you want ... and destroy the rest. And if the "the rest" cannot be destroyed, at least make them play by your rules.

These days it no longer takes compulsory boarding schools to conform Indigenous peoples to our standards of "American" culture.

Elements such as college entrance exams, Academic English, and corporate culture successfully uphold an assimilation model that requires dexterity, compromise, and sacrifice on everyone else's part but ours.

• • •

DRESSING THE PART

While there are countless examples of blatant forced assimilation in America, many subtle and insidious forms go unnoticed (by most White people). White Americans are so used to living in a country that caters to us that most of us are fundamentally incapable of recognizing when things that we deem "normal" or "standard practice" are anything but. We expect others to adhere to these standards because, in our minds, that is just the way things are. Once we have placed value on something being done a certain way, the expectation is that in order for *anyone else* to succeed, they must play by these rules.

In the United States, despite our progressive claims of valuing diversity and inclusion in the workforce, many companies can't get beyond the clothes people are expected to wear. Take for example the expectation that successful and powerful men should wear a formal suit and tie—even in the middle of summer. Not to mention the absurdly oppressive and uncomfortable outfits women are expected to wear in the corporate world. Because we are the dominant culture, our expectation by default becomes the standard set for everyone else living in "our" society. In order for people of color to be taken seriously in the business world, they are expected to wear *our* Western clothes.

This is undeniably a form of forced assimilation. Furthermore, this sends the message that other cultures' traditional forms of dress have less value and are not appropriate by our societal standards.[453]

Even more unfair is the hypocrisy of the fact that some of the most financially successful White men in America—including Jeff Bezos, Mark Zuckerberg, and Elon Musk—choose not to wear business suits at all. Why? Because White men don't have to once we've "made it." Not only do most people already see us as powerful, but also our choice *not* to wear a suit once we are in a position of power further indicates how successful we (think we) are.

That same luxury of shirking the expected attire and breaking (our) mold does not apply to BIPOC folks in the business world. For example, a Black corporate leader wearing Mark Zuckerberg's signature blue jeans, gray T-shirt, and tennis shoes would likely be stopped by security and asked which department he works in—which is exactly what happened in September 2021 to Angel Onuoha, a graduate of Harvard University, hedge fund cofounder, and associate product manager at Google, who was stopped while riding his bike around the Google campus and escorted by two security guards to verify his ID badge.[454]

Perhaps the most frustrating part about all of this is that—similar to my freedom as a White person to speak more informally in a business setting—I get to wear what I want, no matter how strange, and have it be a reflection of me as an individual. My choice to wear something odd, mismatched, or even worn and tattered without having it reflect poorly on my entire race or community is a privilege that does not extend to BIPOC folks.

However, the "dress to impress" model does not begin and end in corporate America. Here we turn to our public education system, which brings us to another example of "White etiquette" (i.e., forced assimilation): the seemingly well-meaning school rule to take your hats off indoors.

• • •

NO HATS IN THE BUILDING

In most schools in the United States, children are still asked to remove their hats in school. Furthermore, schools are legally allowed to require that children remove their hats upon entering the building.[455] This may seem like harmless etiquette to most of us, considering that the practice of removing one's hat out of respect has been a part of Western culture for over half a millennium. However, removing one's hat has additionally been associated with acknowledging the presence of one's superior.[456] Consequently, as Western culture marched across much of the globe, we required others to follow this particular custom, especially those we colonized.

Given our country's track record with public schools designed to assimilate non-White communities, it is only to be expected that this particular school rule disproportionately impacts students of color. Dr. Chris Emdin, author of *For White Folks Who Teach in the Hood . . . and the Rest of Y'all Too: Reality Pedagogy and Urban Education*, describes how for many BIPOC students, hats remain one of their few remaining forms of self-expression. Demanding that they remove their hats is one more way in which Western culture gets to determine how *everyone* should dress and act while in our presence. Similar to the banishment of Indigenous attire during the nineteenth and twentieth centuries, for many BIPOC students, being asked to remove their hats and put them away—or even worse, having their hats confiscated by an adult—is like having an authority figure tell them that a part of their identity is not valued or even allowed at school.[457] The message conveyed is simple: "Either play by our rules, or there will be consequences."

One only has to step foot into an "urban" public school to watch assimilation in action.

● ● ●

SIT UP STRAIGHT!

Our attempts to fix our education system are not going to be successful if we cannot grasp one fundamental fact: our current system is built upon an assimilation model rather than an empowerment model.

While outwardly the basic rules in schools (e.g., walk in a straight line, raise your hand to speak, use your inside voice) may seem like necessary, time-honored traditions, practices, and even values, they are still "our" rules, being enforced upon others. This becomes all the more troubling when considering that much of our current public education system was conceived during the late 1830s by Horace Mann, secretary of the nascent Massachusetts Board of Education.[458] While Mann did believe in the potential for public education to be an equalizer, this era was fraught with forced compliance, strict discipline, corporal punishment, as well as outright and deliberate discrimination.

As described Pam Caito in an article written for the Johnson County Public Library in Indiana, "around 1837, state law required teachers to be examined for certification. When it came to [a] teacher's curriculums, there was no prevailing teaching philosophy, except for one thing, 'Spare the rod and [you will] spoil the child' [i.e., don't hold back on hitting them, or they will become brats]. Teachers soliciting work would often include methods of discipline in their advertisements. A teacher's ability was often measured by their ability to govern a classroom."[459] Educators were typically judged by their skills as authoritarians and disciplinarians over their qualifications as educators. Caito goes on to describe how "laws were strict at the time for adults [and] it was believed by the pioneers that schoolmasters needed to instill self-discipline in children early, so they would meet the standards of the community." There is no question whose "standards" are being referred to here. However, these rules and standards did not universally apply.

Certain people (i.e., young White males from privileged backgrounds) were mostly exempt—as many of them had tutors and received what would now be considered a private education.[460] Initially, wealthy White people who expected their children to remain in power would not have dared put their children in "inferior" public institutions.

Moreover, it was commonly known that not everyone was *supposed* to benefit from this education system. Half a century before Horace Mann began his social experiment, in 1779, Thomas Jefferson himself proposed a two-track education system in order to sort "the mass of our citizens . . . into two classes—the laboring and the learned"—or, as he more bluntly described it, "raking a few geniuses from the rubbish."[461] Outside of those "few geniuses," public schools were primarily designed to help prepare children to become functioning, productive, and assimilated members of our society.

Our public education system remains rife with White cultural norms that go beyond the expectations of dress, mannerisms, and etiquette. Dr. Chris Emdin elaborates on this idea, describing how our current school system measures the success of people of color based on how well they assimilate into White society.[462] For decades, we have forced young children to sit in uncomfortable desk chairs, raise their hands to speak, and walk in a quiet, single-file line to get from one place to the next. This doesn't even take into account the White-centric teachings, lessons, and ideologies that every student is indoctrinated into as part of their "assimilation education."

Again, while most individual teachers are doing their best to support and empower students of color, even working to dismantle oppressive structures from within the education system, as an institution our school system is still steeped in supremacy culture. We foster a perfectionist mindset that values competitiveness, a sense of urgency, right-way thinking, and a worship of the written word over oral communication.[463]

As described by the Centre for Community Organizations, a nonprofit focused on DEI efforts and strengthening the impact and voices of grassroots organizations, we uphold a system that places teachers and administrators in "positions of authority [that restrict] the freedom and responsibilities of those subordinate to them in the subordinates' supposed best interest."[464] These values and practices then translate directly into the workplace, further reinforcing the cycle of oppression, as educators are forced to prepare students for the unforgiving corporate world that Whiteness created.

Despite the valiant efforts of countless educators, we are currently reinforcing a conformity model rather than an empowerment model. Steve Denning, a senior contributor to *Forbes* magazine, explains in a 2020 article that while many teachers are making heroic efforts in "the current rigid system[,] . . . [i]n effect, many teachers are [also] prisoners of the existing system. They can even be seen as suffering from the Stockholm syndrome in which they develop a psychological alliance with their captors during their 'captivity.' . . . One can only wonder what they could accomplish if they were working within a system that was not only properly resourced but also flexible and responsive to the real needs of the kids."[465] Until we shift our priorities, our school system will remain a way for White culture to both preserve itself and exert itself upon others. Indigenous scholar Derek Rasmussen describes, "If you put people in a cement building away from their families, in age divided cohorts, under fluorescent lights, and feed them hydroponic learning, you are creating a soilless culture. . . . These forms of education uproot us from the land, from our place, and from our bonds with each other."[466]

In a sense, we are still ideologically "kidnapping" children of color and indoctrinating them into a Eurocentric system of norms and expectations. As such, many of our efforts to fix the current education system are merely attempts to retrofit a system to do things that it was never intended to do. Efforts to embolden students of color and prepare them to access higher levels of education go against what the system was designed for. Without first acknowledging that we are using an outdated platform geared specifically for assimilation, we will not be successful in our attempts at reform.

• • •

APPROPRIATION AND ASSIMILATION: TWO SIDES OF THE SAME COIN

> "Western knowledge and science are 'beneficiaries' of the colonization of indigenous peoples. The knowledge gained through our colonization has been used, in turn, to colonize us in what Ngugi Wa Thiong calls the colonization 'of the mind.'"
> —Linda Tuhiwai Smith

Understandably, many White folks have a hard time making the connection between cultural appropriation and forced assimilation. But they are inseparably linked. While on the one hand we adopt, display, and even revere elements of others' cultures, we simultaneously demand that members of those cultures give up their identities to be "welcomed" into our society. If they play by our rules and uphold our ideals, values, and even mannerisms, we continue to admire, display, and monetize the parts of them we find novel and exotic. We take what we want and then assimilate the rest, and the assimilation is one-sided for the same reason that appropriation is one-sided: the lopsided power dynamic.

Many BIPOC folks feel frustrated, angry, and at times scared of the collective power of White America.[467] The bulk of us still expect them to respect us and "our" country while we do everything in our power to remind them that they are not a part of us.

While many White progressive liberals try to embody ideals of cultural diversity and racial tolerance, in reality we support these concepts because of the inherent belief that they are on our turf, and that we—"the good White people"—allow and want them here. When it comes to our day-to-day lived experiences, many of us likely prefer homogeneity and consistency in how America looks and feels to us.

Our living situations frequently tell the true story, especially in liberal havens such as Seattle, Portland, and San Francisco. In fact, many of "America's most progressive, forward-thinking, open-minded, and social-justice-focused cities . . . have the worst racial disparities in the nation and some of the worst racial segregation,"[468] describes *Madison365* editor in chief David Dahmer in a 2015 article. "[Many] Black and brown people of all socioeconomic backgrounds feel uncomfortable and unwanted in progressive cities that are often segregated as bad as Jim Crow Deep South. In the end, there is very little 'Coexisting' in the land of 'Coexist' bumper stickers." (These very bumper stickers could be seen as an act of cultural appropriation in that we are taking others' sacred religious symbols and cleverly combining them into a trite cliché, before haphazardly sticking them on the backs of our cars where they get splattered in mud, oil, bird poop, and brake pad residue. But, hey, they make me look inclusive *and* cool, right?)

When it comes to cultural appropriation and assimilation, the expectation that other people give us what's theirs and then conform to our society upholds the unfair power dynamic between White people and BIPOC communities. Moreover, once we've stripped them of their riches (both cultural and literal), we often fail to see them as full human beings. We stereotype them and assign them to large groups in a way that fits our understanding—just like the "Coexist" bumper sticker.

Of course, there are White people who don't want them here at all. These White nationalists boldly and unapologetically tell them to "go back to where they came from" and make it painfully clear that they are not welcome in certain neighborhoods. Yet some of the most racist and xenophobic Americans still love Taco Tuesdays. If Americans liked Mexicans half as much as we like Mexican food, speaking Spanish would be a prerequisite for higher education.

This begs a pressing question. If most of "American" culture has been built upon a Frankenstein's monster of different beliefs, ideas, and values, then what exactly are we? Perhaps more importantly, *who* are we?

PART 4

Who Are We?

CHAPTER 13

White "Culture"

TWO FISH are swimming in the ocean. One fish says to the other, "How's the water?" The other fish looks at him, perplexed. "What's water?"

So, what exactly is White culture? How can we begin to define something that most of us have been "swimming" in all our lives? It is easy for us to see the "other": the things we clearly define as "non-White." But how do we define what it means to be us—to be White? How do we define "White culture?" Microbreweries, fondue dinner parties, and NPR? Or Bud Light, guns, Trump rallies, and NASCAR? Both, maybe? Is there even such a thing as "White culture," or is it simply too broad to define?

For the sake of clarity, let's narrow down the focus to my area of expertise: what it means to be a White American male.

It is easiest to start with the low-hanging fruit of stereotypes.

• • •

FROM NASCAR TO NPR: THE SPECTRUM OF THE WHITE MALE PERSONA

We often default to stereotypes to make sense of the world. Even if we don't outwardly believe them, they still hold space in our minds and influence how we think about ourselves and those around us. So, before we address the "White" piece of the equation, let's look at some stereotypes about men in general:

- Men are messy.

- Men are obsessed with getting laid.

- Men are more aggressive and prone to violence.

- Men are not in touch with their emotions.

- Men love sports.

Obviously, these stereotypes are far from universal—hence, they are stereotypes. Sure, plenty of men are messy, and sure, many of us think about sex *a lot* (on average about nineteen times a day, according to one study published in the *Journal of Sex Research*).[469] But does that define who we are as a collective?

Let's narrow it down to just White men. Here are a few more stereotypes that are more specific to White men to help us pinpoint just what makes us who we are—or rather, separates us from the rest:

- We like to drink beer and watch football.

- We love guns and hunting.

- We love big trucks and off-road vehicles..

Or how about these:

- We love good wine and National Public Radio.

- We are into wearing socks with cool patterns on them.

- We enjoy driving Teslas and reading the *New York Times*.

Something is clearly not working here. These stereotypes don't seem to encapsulate all, or even most of us White men—not to mention that some flat-out contradict themselves. While some of these stereotypes hold true for some individuals or groups of White men, they still don't capture the essence of our "culture."

More importantly, they don't help us understand what we have in common that ultimately defines us as White American men.

The infamous coffee-table book *Stuff White People Like* does a fantastic job summarizing "the unique taste of millions,"[470] playfully highlighting the fact that many White Americans see themselves as pioneers of individualism yet fall prey to the most cliché and predictable trends of our culture. However, in writing his book, author Christian Lander, a White male, was primarily describing a specific demographic of White Americans, and one of my personal favorites to poke fun at: progressive White Americans.

Part of what made Lander's book so fascinating is that while it addresses stereotypes in a laughable way, it also points out an uncomfortable truth about our understanding of ourselves: we are not the unique, special snowflakes that most of us think we are. While we seem to have no problem making blanket stereotypes about other cultures, we have consistently failed to come to a consensus about who we are in terms of a shared identity, or even what we stand for.

● ● ●

RUGGED INDIVIDUALISM

The main paradox is that one of the main things that makes White American men unique is our persistent belief in our own uniqueness. We see ourselves—and often only ourselves—as individuals. As such, many White American men get to identify and act however we want without it reflecting on all of us (though many women and BIPOC folks would beg to differ). For me to exist as a White man in America, I hardly have to shift anything about myself. I can just be me.

This belief is no accident; our predecessors were deeply invested in creating the self-distinguishing qualities that made us who we are as White men, and they primarily based those qualities on intelligence and a superiority complex rooted in wealth and power.

One of the only parts of White male culture that we can each see—even if we as individuals don't necessary feel a part of it—is our shared collective power and status at the top of the "societal food chain."

• • •

WHAT WHITE AMERICAN MEN HAVE IN COMMON

There are a few shared threads that hold us together regardless of what music we listen to, whether we prefer beer or wine, or how we politically identify. Let's steer away from stereotypes and look at some distinct shared pieces of our White American male identity. We must have something in common, right? How else could we have risen to the top of the social order to rule the entire country and arguably the world, collectively owning nearly 30 percent of global wealth[471]—even though we only account for roughly 1 percent of the world's entire population?

A few facts about White American men:

BUSINESS

- White American men own and lead almost all the Fortune 500 companies.

- White American men own most of the entertainment industry in America.

- White American men make up the majority of the academic, tech, and scientific sector.

- White American men own, as well as coach, almost all the major and minor league sports teams in America.

PRIVILEGES

- White American men have always been allowed in places that others historically weren't—e.g., banks, restaurants, bars, public restrooms, etc.

- White American men can speak in a room without having to wonder if people are thinking of them as an ambassador of their entire group.

POWER AND WEALTH

- White American men collectively own most of the wealth in the United States.
- White American men collectively own most of property in the United States.
- White American men have held all but one seat in the homogenous lineup of presidents since our country's founding.
- White American men are the only group that has been allowed (entitled) to vote throughout the entirety of the country's history.
- White American men still collectively hold the majority of seats in both Congress and the Senate—nationally and at a state level.
- White American men make up the vast majority of roles in the judicial system in our country.
- White American men make up the vast amount of leadership roles in education.
- White American men own and run most colleges and universities in the United States.
- White American men own and run most of the industrial and agriculture sectors.
- White American men make up the majority of the police and military force in this country, especially in leadership roles.
- White American men collectively decide when our country goes to war, who we go to war with, and who is going to fight on the front lines.

- White American men chose the name of this country, as well as the names of almost all the states, capitals, and cities.
- White American men wrote the Articles of Confederation, the Declaration of Independence, and the Constitution.
- White American men still decide who we consider White in our country.

Need me to keep going, or are you noticing a pattern? These are all examples of how White American men have consolidated power among ourselves. If we were to narrow down these examples to some specific norms, values, or assumptions about the collective culture of White American men, they would be as follows:

- It values the individual over the collective.
- It defines what is considered normal.
- It creates the standards for success.
- It creates and judges values, beliefs, and behaviors.
- It asserts power, superiority, and control over others.
- It reflects White cultural assumptions about and upon others.
- It values certain ways of knowing (e.g. Academic English) over others.[472]

All of these elements reflect an attribute in which we are uniquely complicit: power and privilege. But can privilege really be called culture? Are power and culture synonymous in our case?

While we individually may not agree on whether to watch football and drink beer on a rainy Sunday or take our electric vehicles into the woods to forage for mushrooms, that doesn't change the fact that almost everyone outside of our demographic can attest that White American men are the ones in charge of *our* country. Moreover, according to our predecessors, God "himself" intended that this would always be the case in America.

• • •

A DIVINE PERMISSION SLIP

It is no secret that throughout most of modern history, White men have unflinchingly assumed that we were the apex of the entire species, not to mention every other species on earth. Our ability to dehumanize others as well as ourselves was and unfortunately still is a big part of our psyche. It is even enshrined in our most sacred tome: the Bible.

The Bible, which remains the predominant source of religious wisdom in White American culture, is in many ways directly responsible for White America's view of itself. The scriptures often served as the basis on which White colonizers justified their violent spread across America.

Many of America's early settlers subscribed to Manifest Destiny, a phrase coined in 1845 by American columnist, editor, and diplomat John L. O'Sullivan.[473] Like O'Sullivan, they believed that they possessed a "God-given, sanctioned right to conquer the land and displace the 'uncivilized,' non-Christian peoples who, it was believed, did not take full advantage of the land which had been given to them,"[474] describes a 2014 article on the Smithsonian American Art Museum website.

One Bible quote in particular became the cornerstone of Manifest Destiny and was referenced by a multitude of early-American leaders: "Let Us make man in Our image, according to Our likeness; and let them rule . . . over all the earth. . . . Be fruitful and multiply, and fill the earth, and subdue it; and rule over the fish of the sea and over the birds of the sky and over every living thing that moves on the earth."[475] This statement, supposedly uttered by God *himself*, was frequently taken out of context to justify White male settlers' exploitation of resources and other human beings.

Another quote frequently referenced during this time was Matthew 28:18–20: "All power is given unto me in heaven and in earth. Go ye therefore, and teach all nations, baptizing them in the name of the Father, and of the Son, and of the Holy Ghost: Teaching them to observe all things whatsoever I have commanded you."[476] Yet perhaps the most iconic phrase used by leaders and religious authorities to describe the supposed role of their colonies was the "city upon a hill" described in Jesus's Sermon on the Mount. This phrase was first used in America by John Winthrop, a founder of the Massachusetts Bay Colony, to remind his people to be on their best behavior, as the eyes of whole world—and God—were upon them.[477]

Beginning in the nineteenth century, that phrase (and its skewed, moral-purist implications) metastasized into a collective self-centered belief that America was *the* "city" Jesus had referenced nearly two millennia prior. Nineteenth-century Americans further expanded "upon Winthrop's notion of 'a city upon a hill' to encompass the idea that all other countries should look to the United States as a model nation. Just as the . . . Puritans had seen it as their divine right to 'tame and cultivate' the frontier, so too did nineteenth-century capitalists and politicians see the expansion of the frontier as providential, their personal and professional profit in harmony with the nation's economic development,"[478] according to the same Smithsonian article. As such, this phrase became the very basis for current American exceptionalism.

In a 2019 article for *Bible Study Magazine*, writer Eli T. Evans explained that "the idea that 'We the People' are God's chosen people has been the organizing mythos of American politics from the beginning."[479] Evans goes on to say that "what started as a picture of America as moral example morphed into the idea of America as moral compass." Many nineteenth-century capitalists and politicians simply did not see their actions as selfish. Evans writes,

> Slavery? War? Injustice? Native American genocide? All have been carried out as the will of Providence. . . . In the nineteenth century, it was widely held that the nation had a "manifest destiny"—a mandate from on high to sweep over the continent, no matter what or who might get in the way. . . . Today we know a similar (if less pernicious) idea by a different name: American exceptionalism. What was once a call to morality before the eyes of the world has become a license to define morality as coinciding with our national interests.[480]

White Americans have always been able to fall back on the excuse that our actions are God's will. This has given us a "divine permission slip" to oppress and exploit other human beings to gain access to wealth and extract resources. As America rose to become a global power in the twentieth century, "city on a hill" became the go-to phrase for a number of modern United States politicians and leaders, including John F. Kennedy and Ronald Reagan.[481] Whereas before it was relegated to national expansion within North America, this nationalistic sentiment became used to justify building a militarized, capitalism-driven global empire to uphold our "shining" example of liberty and justice.

Many Americans still believe that our country is *the* undisputed beacon of freedom and democracy and that it remains our God-given duty to maintain our status as the most powerful country in the world. Any challenge to that status is seen as an infraction of God's will. This belief is especially common among powerful White Christian politicians.

American exceptionalism is most clearly summed up by a WWI political phrase: "God bless America," re-popularized by Ronald

Reagan when he went off script during his 1980 Republican party presidential nomination acceptance speech.[482] This statement, now a mainstay in the American political arena on both sides of the party line, has Manifest Destiny at its core.

Reagan's use of the phrase was far from inadvertent. Before uttering his politically transformative sound bite that would shape the political arena for decades to come, Regan proudly declared to his "congregation" of Republican followers in Detroit, "Can we doubt that only a Divine Providence placed this land, this island of freedom, here as a refuge for all . . . who yearn to breathe freely?"[483] He went on to ask the audience and the nation watching on television, "Can we begin our crusade, joined together, in a moment of silent prayer?" With God's blessing, Reagan set out on a "crusade" that would leave permanent scars on the American economy, military, criminal justice system, and livelihood of millions of people of color.

We continue to justify wars, drone strikes, resource extraction, heavily weaponized military bases, and outsourced labor as part of our moral duty to maintain order and peace. There have always been those who believe it is our unalienable right to subdue, subjugate, and exploit all that we deem to be beneath us, other humans included. Moreover, regardless of our individual religious beliefs, only through sheer denial could one refute that our country was founded as a Christian nation—and in essence remains one today. Countless atrocities have been committed in the name of God and justified by cherry-picked scripture (i.e., God made us in "his" image and then commanded us to rule over everyone and everything as he saw fit).

Despite our self-proclaimed Manifest Destiny, there are some significant divides among White folks that are worth examining when it comes to understanding how our collective power is distributed, as well as how it shapes our culture. Our political beliefs have a significant impact on how we demonstrate our sense of entitlement, privilege, and power over others. However, to unpack the role of politics in White American male culture, we first need to step back and examine the political spectrum of White America as a whole.

CHAPTER 14

The "White Spectrum"

WHEN IT COMES to most modern White people, there is a familiar political spectrum that reflects—or in many cases defines—our beliefs, hobbies, interests, and even religious affiliations. From ultraliberals to ultraconservatives, White political culture exists on a continuum that seems implausible. Let's start by looking at the two extremes.

On the far-left end of the spectrum are the ultraliberals, or the progressive socialist "crusaders." On the other end, we have the evangelical, neoconservative White nationalists. If we were to color-code the distribution of political ideologies, White America exists on a political spectrum from ultraviolet to infrared.

Why not just blue (Democrat) to red (Republican), you might ask? These additional color bands account for the extremes that lie beyond the "visible spectrum" within the mainstream political arena (i.e., they don't hold an actual seat in the Senate or in the House, but they certainly hold sway over politics in America—although the infrared have begun to infiltrate the highest offices in America, a fact that probably merits its own chapter).

To be more specific, the ultraviolet accounts for the "kumbaya bunch"—the "trees have feelings" too, orthodox vegan, "Coexist" bumper stickers (plural), communal-living evangelicals of meditation and yoga poses they can't pronounce properly. (I guarantee that someone just got offended reading that last sentence. Yes, I'm picking on you, liberals.) On the other side of the map, the infrared includes Q-Anon Holocaust deniers who vehemently wish the South had won the Civil War and believe that the earth is flat as a board.

The main problem with trying to pinpoint White American culture is that beyond our shared identity around privilege and power, there simply isn't such a thing. Rather than trying to conceptualize Whiteness as *a* culture, it is easier to think of it as a socially constructed identity. "Whiteness is a racial perspective or a worldview . . . supported by material practices and institutions. . . . Whiteness is not a culture but a social concept,"[484] explains Professor Zeus Leonardo of the Berkley Graduate School of Education in a 2009 article. Whiteness connects us through a shared identity built on systems of oppression, whereas White people as individuals often grant ourselves the autonomy to operate as independent from that framework. This is in large part because we don't identify with folks on other parts of the continuum.

Despite all sharing a manufactured identity based loosely on shared ancestry and melanin, we still very much exist within pockets that don't exactly mix. Many of us came from conservative nationalistic upbringings, while others came from households that preached equality and unconditional tolerance toward everyone (except, of course, for people who are intolerant; I'll let you ruminate on that one for a moment). Many of us also came from working-class or struggling families, while others came from summer vacation homes and trust funds dripping with Ivy-league lineage.

Regardless of how we politically or socially identify, as long as we can "play nice *enough*" with each other, we can band together where it counts—under a fictitious, cobblestone identity that upholds power over others. More importantly, we don't have to "play nice" with anyone outside of Whiteness unless we choose to or it serves our own interests—or unless we are absolutely forced to, as is the case with many White politicians in America, who are still ultimately serving their own interests by doing so.

However, these social, political, and cultural differences come at a price: the differences that have shaped America have also eroded its stability from the beginning. From the minute colonists stepped foot on American soil, tension between different European settlers became one of the defining features of our blossoming "American culture."

• • •

THE (DIS)UNITED STATES OF AMERICA

While we like to call our country the *United* States of America, this country has always been an amalgamation of clashing desires, ideals, and beliefs that pretend to get along under the roof of one government. Author Richard Kreitner writes in *Break It Up: Secession, Division and the Secret History of America's Imperfect Union*, "There was no golden age in America." From its onset, "the United States split into hostile camps. . . . [B]itter disputes arose[,] . . . threatening to rip them [the early colonies] apart."[485] This was the case long before America officially declared itself a country.

Over two centuries ago, after traveling throughout the early colonies in the mid-1700s, British minister Andrew Burnaby made the declaration that "fire and water are not more heterogeneous [dissimilar] than the different colonies in North America."[486] He went on to make a *very* accurate prediction, stating, "Such is the difference of character, of manners, of religion, of interest . . . [that] were they left to themselves [i.e., detached from Britain], there would soon be a civil war from one end of the continent to the other." Burnaby was right—and it took less than a century for his ominous prediction to come true in 1861 with one of the bloodiest wars in modern history.

Barnaby even went so far as to say that the schisms between

White Americans were so vast and violent that the early colonists would potentially wipe themselves out, allowing Indigenous and African Americans to have the continent for themselves. "The Indians and Negroes," Barnaby claimed, "would, with better reason, impatiently watch the opportunity of exterminating them all together."[487] Essentially, non-White Americans could just wait while White folks duke it out and kill each other over their differences.

While this genocidal suggestion may sound farcical, consider that the American Civil War left nearly 750,000 people dead in just four years—approximately 504 people per day, or 2.5 percent of the entire US total population. In today's numbers, this would be the equivalent of 7,000,000 deaths, or nearly 5,000 deaths per day.[488] In comparison, Covid-19 averaged about 1,100 deaths per day in 2020 and 2021.[489]

However, Barnaby was not alone in his prediction that the United States was headed toward an inevitable "downfall over differences." Most of the Founding Fathers, as well as prominent US presidents and politicians, were equally concerned about the inevitability of a civil war due to the vast differences among the desires, beliefs, and attitudes of early Americans (i.e., White people). George Washington, John Adams, James Madison, Thomas Jefferson, as well as Alexander Hamilton and Benjamin Franklin were just a few of these outspoken leaders who often shared their concerns.[490]

Even after the Constitution was ratified, White Americans within the various colonies continued to sabotage, commit subterfuge against, and even kill one another. Many were convinced that the new nation would crumble once George Washington left office. Perhaps most concerned was Thomas Jefferson, who would go on to become the third US president. When George Washington was preparing to step down from office, Jefferson played a crucial role in convincing him to remain for a few more years, hoping it would stave off the almost certain demise of the United States.[491]

Jefferson was likely correct, as the elections that took place after Washington's departure in 1797 almost led to an all-out civil war—with John Adams, his immediate successor, struggling to stave off mutiny. John Adam's son (John Quincy Adams), who himself became president two decades later, feared that the United States might "soon divide into a parcel of petty tribes at perpetual war with one another."[492]

Despite their extremely divergent political and personal beliefs, all of these leaders had one thing in common: they recognized the instability, volatility, and hostility of the US population toward one another, and most believed that a civil war was inevitable. Considering this universal belief of our early leaders, the January 6 insurrection may be an omen of things to come.

This brings us to another strange paradox about White America. Ironically, one thing that most White Americans have in common is a dislike for other "types" of White Americans. The political spectrum is rife with, if not driven by, hatred toward the other side. As historian James Roger Sharp describes, in the 1790s, "[White] Americans survey the political landscape as if looking though hideously distorted spectacles, seeing grotesque and distorted shapes and figures that were products of intense and deeply felt fears."[493] To overcome these fears, White America turned those distorted lenses outward.

Our early leaders recognized that war and hatred against a common enemy was one of the only things holding White people and the United States together. As better described by Pennsylvania representative Benjamin Rush in 1776, "the [United] States of America cannot be a Nation without war."[494] Whether against the Native Americans, the British, the Spanish, the French (or currently the Middle East, BIPOC Americans, and immigrants), White Americans on different ends of the spectrum only come together when our nation is under threat. The 9/11 attacks on the World Trade Center in 2001 proved this beyond a doubt—as did the Cold War beginning in 1947, the bombing of Pearl Harbor in 1941, the Mexican–American War in 1846, the War of 1812, the American Indian "Wars" from 1775 to 1918, and, of course, the American Revolution in 1776.

Arguably the primary thing that unites White Americans is our fear of everybody else. Yet once a threat has passed, ultraviolet and infrared become sworn enemies once again.

While the American Constitution might be seen as the saving grace in all this, some scholars argue that this cherished document may have caused the divisions to escalate. Author Richard Kreitner explains, "The Constitution [merely] changed the government without altering the fundamental nature of American politics. People from different states and regions remained hostile toward each other as ever, as divided by geography as they were by interests, ideas, and identity. . . . [F]orcing Americans to settle their differences under a single roof, the new Constitution, meant to stave off dissolution, may actually have made things worse."[495] Although history books tell us the Constitution was created to immortalize democracy and set the United States on a glorious path, it was more a desperate means of trying to keep the United States from imploding. One issue in particular stood at the forefront of these disagreements: slavery.

The South was not the only side that wanted to secede; countless Northerners, particularly abolitionist disunionists, petitioned for dismantling the union decades before the Civil War began. According to Kreitner, many believed that breaking the union apart might be the only way to "rouse [Northern] White Americans from their addiction to the narcotic of compromise."[496] This wasn't a mere difference of opinion. Many abolitionists and disunionists adamantly believed "that the Constitution wouldn't have been possible without morally indefensible compromises . . . [and] that the country was held together by the blood of the enslaved."[497] Consequently, some abolitionists in the North were more disgusted with fellow Northerners they believed were allowing this heinous blood pact to continue than with the South.

To these abolitionists, the Constitution was a deal with the devil in its unequivocal declaration that the North would help capture runaway slaves, profit from slavery, and "valiantly" come to the South's aid in the event of a slave revolt. Referring to *all* people as one race, outspoken newspaper editor William Garrison accused his fellow Northerners of "treading upon the necks, spilling the blood and destroying the souls of millions of your race," arguing that the union should "crumble to dust" rather than uphold a document "dripping as it is with human blood."[498] In 1861, as the country prepared for war, many Northerners were more than eager to let the South go—but their leaders felt it their sworn duty to protect the sanctity of the union at all costs (or rather, to preserve the union in order to preserve their status, wealth, and power).

Over two centuries later, many of these fault lines remain as salient as ever, yet we seem hopelessly ensnared by a distorted belief in American exceptionalism and self-preservation at all costs. Essentially, when it comes to the stark divisions among White Americans, getting along may be the exception to the norm. The same thing could be said about Whiteness itself.

● ● ●

WHITENESS ACROSS AMERICA

Anyone arriving for the first time in twenty-first-century America would likely be confused about why we bother to call ourselves united in the first place. Depending on where they arrive, an outsider might not recognize that they are visiting the same country.

What do liberal folks from Humboldt, California, conservatives from Granville, North Dakota, the Ivy-league Hamptonians in New York, or cowboys in Dallas, Texas, really have in common besides a shared White identity?

In many ways, White culture in our society is akin to the variations in White folks across Europe—although Europe had the common sense not to fool themselves into thinking they were all somehow united. While White people from, say, Spain might visibly resemble White people from Italy, they certainly do not profess to be of the same mindset or culture. Similarly, trying to lump Swedes and Serbians under one culture and government would prove difficult.

America, on the other hand, has chosen to huddle under a shared blanket of Whiteness. Yet despite having the same skin color, most White people in America identify very differently from one another, often taking more pride in region of birth than our country as a whole.

Even more telling, many White people in America choose to move from their hometowns specifically because they don't feel like they fit in or belong with the group of White people they were born into. Countless are the stories of White people who have moved from a small, conservative town to a big, liberal city. Take Austin, Texas, for example. Austin goes out of its way to distinguish itself as being more progressive and forward thinking than all of its surrounding territory. The same could be said about Seattle, Washington, a small blue dot in a sea of red. Head twenty minutes outside of the city, and the Confederate flag isn't hard to find.

However, while we remain very divided when it comes to how we see the world, we can agree on one thing: we are White.

● ● ●

WHAT THE HELL ARE WE?

One prevalent form of hypocrisy on all sides of the cultural and political spectrum is that we often *only* agree that we are White when it strengthens our connection to others who share our same outlook and beliefs. We are quick to separate from our White counterparts we don't like or those who clash with how we view ourselves or the world around us. We unite or divide when it benefits us individually or collectively.

Many White liberals are particularly guilty of this; we seek to disavow and disown the parts of Whiteness that we see as bad while claiming to tolerate others and embrace diversity—all the while living in a neighborhood of 98 percent White people, shopping at Whole Foods, and hanging out in trendy microbreweries on the weekends.

Who the hell are we, then? That is difficult to answer. White folks are a confused group indeed, having intentionally relinquished our ancestry and heritage before cramming ourselves into a world of clashing identities on the basis that we all supposedly shared a common vision: the American Dream. Author and activist Tim Wise does a fantastic job summarizing why this is such a challenging question in his book *White Like Me*.

An oversimplification of Wise's point would be that most of our ancestors went out of their way to become American because that decision was in their best interests in terms of fitting in, building a "safe" community, and succeeding financially.[499] This meant letting go of their home languages, styles of dress, holidays, foods, customs, traditions, rituals, etc. Whereas many BIPOC Americans had these things forcefully stripped from them *by* White people, many of our European ancestors willingly gave up their European identities in hopes of making a new life.

Most of us only have fragments of our ethnic ancestry, idealized or tokenized at best. My own Polish, Ukrainian, Swedish, Italian,

Scottish, and English ancestors would undoubtedly see me as an American. My love of pizza and perogies doesn't make me Italian or Polish; it just means I like some of the same food that my folks brought over here with them.

Given that I am making such a strong case that a homogenous White cultural identity does not exist, one could easily make the argument that other racial groups such as Black Americans should also not be lumped together under an umbrella term such as "Black culture." However, there is a notable difference.

Most people of African ancestry living in the United States were stripped of their land, families, roots, culture, heritage, and even their names. As a result, it became imperative to carve out and define a culture for themselves—to rename and reinvent an identity in which they could take pride and use as a connecting thread among themselves. What some now define as "Black culture" creates a system of ideas and beliefs that allows them to unite against shared forms of oppression. More importantly, Black culture was created by Black Americans—not by the White people subjugating them.

It should also go without saying that just as is the case with us White folks, not every Black American is compelled to adopt all elements of Black culture. Moreover, Black culture continues to evolve and develop and allows Black Americans to define their own individual as well as collective identity.

Ultimately, while some White people in this country realize that we are living in our own cultural creation, others don't. Many White Americans don't realize that the iconic images of Norman Rockwell paintings, cheerful Fourth of July celebrations, and apple pie do not resonate with a large portion the people living in this country. They also fail to realize that the infamous patriotic sentiment of "land of the free and the home of the brave" is a romanticized historical fallacy that significantly undermines the very real pain and suffering that so many Americans still endure to become and remain a part of this shared dream. This is for one simple reason: White America still gets to determine who is and who is not free.

One of the primary groups that can attest to a distinct lack of freedom is non-White immigrants seeking asylum in America. From separating children and parents to locking people in cages, the United States has made it very clear that not all immigrants are welcome here. More importantly, we continue to send a very clear message that some immigrants are more welcome: those who look like us.

• • •

RECENT ARRIVALS

So, what about those of us White folks who have arrived more recently? Unlike during the twentieth century, many immigrants to America now choose to retain their cultures and identities, bringing heirlooms, customs, religions, communities, languages, lifestyles, beliefs, and cuisine with them. However, there remains a prejudicial and unfair double standard that exists for *all* immigrants of color compared to European immigrants.

Despite the historical pushback against certain types of European immigrants throughout most of our country's history, White America has become adept at learning to "absorb" other White Europeans to further bolster our numbers and solidify our hold over the country—especially as more immigrants of color arrive. Whereas most people from Europe are now warmly welcomed, no questions asked, a tremendous amount of fear, prejudice, and lambasting is directed toward non-White arrivals, especially those who choose to embrace their homeland and their language.

But don't take my word for it. Former president Donald Trump (who managed to get his Slovenian wife into the country via some questionable paperwork) put it best: "Why do we want all these people from shithole countries coming here?"[500] As if that statement weren't racist enough, he doubled down when he promptly followed it up by saying that we should have more immigrants coming in from countries like Norway.

While it would be easy to point the finger at Trump, he echoes the sentiment of many White Americans. One only has to listen to the coded statement that countless White Americans have echoed: "Trump says what I'm thinking!"

Let's face it, many White Americans are proud of their racism and openly express it. Moreover, they want others to bear witness to their beliefs. There are plenty of visual reminders designed to let immigrants and people of color know that they are still not welcome in many parts of America. One such example was a large, letter-board sign outside Casa D'Ice Restaurant & Lounge in North Versailles, Pennsylvania, which read:

> US Constitution in English
> Bill of Rights in English
> If you don't want to speak English
> Please feel free to return to the shithole
> of a country you left behind.[501]

• • •

"WE ~~HOLD~~ PRETEND THESE TRUTHS TO BE SELF-EVIDENT"

Those of us who have a hard time considering ourselves racist often go in the opposite direction. We have experienced glimpses of these same prejudices, but we suppress them and overcompensate by putting up big lawn signs that say, "I support immigrants!" and "Refuges welcome here!" I'd be curious to see how many of us would open our homes to even one of the thousands of refugees who arrive in America every year—or the thousands who end up on the street.

We often like to fall back on another, equally naive sentiment to point to a brighter future ahead: "All men are created equal." This is a cornerstone of our principles and values, and many of us like to inspire one another with this feel-good sentiment. But our country has always been deliberately structured in a way that does not mirror this principle in any shape or form. While the pride in this guiding principle is genuine, we need to remove it from a supposedly "self-evident truth" and shift it into the realm of aspiration, at best. We could make it true by inserting a neon caveat at the end of this declaration—"and therefore should be treated as such"—but we cannot continue to fall back on the "good intentions" of our Founding Fathers.

Moreover, contrary to popular belief, this butchered line doesn't mean what most of us think it does, having been taken completely out of context by modern Americans. Not only did this iconic statement apply solely to land-owning male citizens of pure European ancestry, but also it served a two-fold purpose that had nothing to do with the warm and fuzzy sentiment about equality as we think of it today; the first purpose simply had to do with self-governance, whereas the second was a calculated jab at the British monarchy.

• • •

ALL (WHITE) MEN ARE CAPABLE OF SELF-GOVERNANCE

There is a critically overlooked phrase directly before Jefferson's proclamation of equality: "We hold these truths to be self-evident." This statement puts Jefferson's meaning of equality into its proper context. Jefferson firmly believed that White men had an undeniable right to independence from the British and to self-governance—a fact that he and many of the other Founding Fathers presumed to be "self-evident." As described by scholar, historian, and Stanford professor Jack Rakove in a 2020 interview, "when Jefferson wrote 'all men are created equal' in the preamble to the Declaration, he was not talking about individual equality. What he really meant was that the American colonists, as a people, had the same rights of self-government as other peoples, and hence could declare independence, create new governments and assume their 'separate and equal station' among other nations."[502] This wasn't so much about treating people equally as individuals as it was about receiving recognition as a free and independent people, no less than the British or any other European populace.

However, this was not the only reason Jefferson used the phrase "All men are created equal." Rakove reveals that its second and perhaps more important meaning was a not-so-subtle "F you" to King George III and the British monarchy.[503]

• • •

DOES *OUR* GOD PICK FAVORITES?

Rather than simply stating, "All men are equal," Jefferson's use of the word "created" in this phrase is where its true meaning lies. He was deliberately invoking the belief that God is responsible for creating all (White) men, while cleverly stating that God did not give any (White) man power or control over another. But why is that such a big deal?

Jefferson's more rebellious motive can be seen in the carefully chosen words immediately following his misconstrued declaration of equality, which state that "[White men] are endowed, by their Creator, with certain unalienable Rights, that among these are Life, Liberty, and the pursuit of Happiness."[504] In order to understand why this line makes the preceding "All men are created equal" rebellious, it is important to understand the political and religious climate in which it was conceived.

When America was founded, England was still under a form of

governance known as the "Divine Right of Kings,"[505] which Jefferson and the other fifty-six signers of the Declaration of Independence firmly believed was—to put it nicely—a bunch of rubbish.

The divine right of kings dates back to medieval Europe. Like in Ancient Egypt, Rome, and Greece, many people in early Europe took for granted that God bestowed power upon all ruling monarchs. "Although it is now considered to be absurd, this divine theory instituted a political hierarchy that prospered during its time period,"[506] describes European historian and royal commentator Tiffany Foresi in a 2014 article titled "'The absolute right to rule' – The Divine Right of Kings." She says, "As a whole, this concept states that only God can judge a monarch, because only he has the authority. It believes that a form of monarchical government is the most appropriate, and allegiance should only be sworn to the legitimate heir to the crown."

This belief solidified when King Henry VIII came to power in 1509, thereafter using it to justify breaking away from the Roman Catholic Church. This became the source from which all subsequent royalty drew their (false) power—and they reinforced this belief through elaborate dress, religious ceremonies, customs, and ritual. This is why the spectacle surrounding the coronation became such a big deal in England; it was a ceremony to appoint God's chosen ruler. Moreover, the monarchy upheld the notion that subjects were there to serve the divinely appointed ruler, not the other way around.

Abuse of power was rampant under this system. Foresi explains how "the driving force behind the success of the divine right of kings was the idea of punishment to enforce obedience. . . . [Monarchs] would hold public executions"[507] and torture anyone who challenged their reign. These tyrannical rulers used constant fear and propaganda to create a genuine belief in divine retribution should subjects ever revolt against the ruler—and therefore God himself.

By the time King George III came to power in 1760, the concept of divine rule was being challenged, especially by those who were carving out leadership roles for themselves in the American colonies. Jefferson wanted to make sure that King George III knew that America had no intention of following in British royalty's egomaniacal footsteps—and more importantly, that America unapologetically believed he was no better than them, and God certainly believed the same.

Ultimately, a more accurate interpretation of the "All men are created equal" principle is that our Founding Fathers believed themselves to be fully capable of self-governance without the oversight and restrictions of the self-proclaimed divinely appointed Crown.[508] This simple truth was "self-evident" to all those on the left side of the Atlantic who were unilaterally breaking away from the centuries-old "divine ruse."

So here we are in the twenty-first century, trying to retrofit the Declaration of Independence to serve our modern progressive agenda. After all, I'm sure our Founding Fathers would be absolutely fine with us tweaking it "ever so slightly" to include women, immigrants, the LGBTQ+ community, and BIPOC folks, right?

As long as White progressives default to this line of our Constitution ("All men are created equal"), we will continue to fool ourselves into thinking that our country was founded on good intentions—as if reciting this virtuous creed trumps the fact that we have created a society that not only misunderstands the actual meaning but also directly contradicts it.

Another, more insidious issue arises in trying to inaccurately repurpose this statement. Even with its well-intended interpretation, many White folks try to use it as panacea to the woes of racial discrimination. It's our way of trying to gloss over the fact that the majority of our country's founding charter was created to enshrine racial disparity within American democracy. Even in early America, many prominent leaders struggled to swallow this bitter pill.

Senator Tallmadge, angry that his fellow Northern senators were allowing slavery to continue, decided to call a spade a spade. During a historic debate over the Missouri Compromise in 1819, he boldly declared, "Let us at least be consistent, and declare that our Constitution was made to impose slavery, and not to establish liberty."[509]

CHAPTER 15

Fight for What's ~~Right~~ White

OUTSIDE OF A (debatably ongoing) cold war with Russia, America has been fighting wars almost exclusively against countries with non-White populaces for nearly half a century. Whether Vietnam, Korea, Iraq, Afghanistan, or Iran—not to mention the countless "unofficial wars" and coups that the US has instigated in South America, Central America, the Middle East, and Africa—we have become more united by perceived threats from foreign nations whose populaces don't look like us. As a result, the current wave of immigration, particularly coming from the Middle East, Central and South America, as well as Asia, has left many conservative White Americans feeling as if a literal invasion were taking place.

There is, however, one situation in which America actively encourages people of color to fight and even provides them with ample guns and ammunition: when we send them overseas to fight in wars on our behalf—especially when the fight is against other non-White people. Serving our country is often leveraged as the "pathway out of poverty" for many communities of color.[510] Yet the reality tells a different story.

• • •

"TARGETING" PEOPLE OF COLOR

No one can argue the fact that our military disproportionately recruits marginalized populations experiencing poverty, especially Black and Latino Americans.[511] In addition to sending an inordinate number of recruiters into low-income communities and high schools, the military further incentivizes enlistment through guaranteed college tuition as well as room and board. Targeted recruitment has become such a pervasive issue that several politicians have tried to enact legislation to ban military recruiters from schools altogether.

But the military has other means to get through to their desired recruitment pool. Besides simply going into schools, the military also uses targeted advertising through specific media channels that are more likely to connect with BIPOC communities.[512] Among other tactics, the Army created a recruitment music video in 2019 that included the line "Uniform: paid for. Electric bill: paid for. Water bill: paid for."[513] This lyric is targeting struggling, working-class Americans—containing zero racial overtones. But when combined with the not-so-subtle genre of hip-hop, it becomes obvious who this video is geared toward.

Undeterred by their first hip-hop flop, in 2023 the Army held *American Idol*–style job interviews to select two full-time rappers to join the Army band. In a 2023 NPR interview, Master Sergeant Lauren Urquhart, the senior producer of the US Army Field Band, explained how "the two [rappers] were hired specifically for their talents and also to expand the Army's outreach."[514] The caveat being outreach to *certain* communities.

For many BIPOC folks who do get recruited, the novelty tends to wear off quickly.

■ ■ ■

CAMOUFLAGED COLORS

Within the military, there is a substantial deficit of leaders of color, often leading to minimization and outright denial of any discrimination reported by BIPOC military personnel. According to a Reuters Special Report conducted in 2019, racial discrimination within the military often goes unreported because many service members of color feel that their complaints will either not be taken seriously or potentially make matters worse. This is because the military has a closed-loop investigation policy when it comes to these types of allegations. All investigations are conducted from within (i.e., the military investigates itself), and often only if an overt act of racism occurs.

The report determines that the current equal-opportunity process of reporting racial bias or discrimination "is often a dead end, resulting in little action, or worse, backfiring on the complainant. That's because filing an EO [equal opportunity] complaint is often viewed as an act of defiance in the military."[515] The expectation of conformity and loyalty work directly against the defendant. This is in large part because the military is still inundated with a colorblindness mentality.

Many military leaders pride themselves on how progressive they believe the United States military is. In a 2021 Fox News interview with Tucker Carlson, Representative Michael Waltz, R-Fla., a former Green Beret and veteran of the War in Afghanistan, demonstrated this when he spoke out against current military efforts to mandate racial-bias training:

> One of the things that has me so disturbed as a member of the armed services committee and a combat veteran is when you come into the United States Army, is from day one, you are all the same.... You are told the only skin color you should worry about is camouflage.... The enemy's bullets don't care about Black, White, or Brown, or political party or race or religion or any of that. And we shouldn't care about it either as we are teaching the future leaders of the United States Army.[516]

Representative Waltz didn't stop there. He, along with other conservative military leaders, claimed that racial-bias training within the military, especially discussing White privilege, puts soldiers' lives at risk because it hinders their ability to act quickly.

> As a Green Beret, I can't imagine being in a situation in combat where I am ordering a soldier to charge a machine gun and he now has the seed planted in his mind—am I sending him because he is African-American? Should I feel guilty because of White privilege? . . . That is absolutely destructive to morale, to unity, to everything that I know from a military that, by the way, integrated way before the rest of the country, in 1948.

This belief that the military is the "great equalizer" blinds its leaders to how people of color are often disproportionately harmed during military service.

• • •

WOUNDED WARRIORS

In addition to facing outright racial discrimination during basic training and active duty, many BIPOC soldiers who are lucky enough to return home alive are mentally and emotionally scarred, facing outcomes considerably worse than the circumstances they were trying to escape by joining the military in the first place.

In 2017, the National Alliance to End Homelessness reported that "43.2 percent of veterans experiencing homelessness [were] people of color [33.1 percent of which were Black], compared with 18.4 percent of the general veteran population."[517] White Americans, on the other hand, accounted for only 56.8 percent of all veterans experiencing homelessness, despite accounting for more than 81.6 percent of the general veteran population.

Equally concerning, in 2015, the National Institute of Health cited research that showed that "nearly half [of all veterans experiencing homelessness] experience significant mental illness and 70% report substance use problems."[518] These data points combined mean that BIPOC veterans are much more likely to not only become homeless at some point but also grapple with severe mental health and substance abuse issues. Yet these issues are just the tip of the iceberg when it comes to the experience of returning soldiers.

Homeless veterans of color are also at higher risk for a number of adverse issues that already disproportionally impact their communities, including chronic physical health problems like diabetes, hepatitis C, and HIV, as well as significantly increased overall levels of violence and incarceration. To make matters worse, the lack of resources, basic services, housing, and employment opportunities available to homeless veterans leaves many in an inescapable cycle of poverty, mental illness, and substance abuse, often leading to incarceration, early death, or suicide.[519] These returning soldiers of color may have literally dodged a bullet, but for many, the real battle starts when they return home to a system effectively set up to fail them.

The heartbreaking reality is that countless people of color who have bravely chosen to serve in the US military—many with the explicit hope of finally being accepted and embraced by their country—have returned home only to face the same hatred, mistreatment, discrimination, and violence they experienced before they left.[520]

• • •

FIGHTING FOR EQUALITY

War and race have been inseparably entwined since our country's founding. Black veterans in particular have faced the brunt of racial backlash after every major US conflict since our country was founded for one reason: White folks believe that military training makes them a threat.[521] The Equal Justice Initiative describes how many "Black veterans died at the hands of mobs and persons acting under the color of official authority; many survived near-lynchings; and thousands suffered severe assaults and social humiliation."[522] Ironically, one of the primary reasons they faced such brutal treatment was because they now had military experience and were therefore considered even more dangerous. White America essentially trained them to fight for our country, then decided to dispose of them for our own safety afterward.

The truth is, many returning Black soldiers did feel more empowered to speak up and to challenge America's racist system upon their return. As described in a 2017 report published by the Equal Justice Initiative entitled "Lynching in America: Targeting Black Veterans," "the experience of military service for African Americans often inflamed an attitude of defiant resistance to the status quo that could prove deadly in a society where racial subordination was violently enforced." As a result, "no one was more at risk of experiencing targeted violence than Black veterans who had proven their valor and courage as soldiers."[523] This merited "defiant resistance" is a clear testament to the fact that many Black veterans were bravely willing to push back on America's inability to acknowledge their service and sacrifice—even if it meant risking their lives (again).

Yet this deplorable brutality toward Black Americans who had served their country was a reflection of one of White America's most pervasive fears during the nineteenth and twentieth centuries—that Black America would rise up and demand justice. Hardly anything scared White American men more than an educated or combat-trained Black man who didn't know "his place."

While White Americans may no longer be assaulting and killing Black veterans to send a message, marginalization and mistreatment of military personnel of color is still rampant in the

United States, as shown by the Caron Nazario incident mentioned earlier. Ultimately, these episodes serve as a reminder to folks of color that even donning a United States military uniform and risking their lives for America's freedom is not a guarantee of their own safety—or even their basic rights and dignity.

Understandably, some BIPOC individuals historically chose a different approach to fight for equality or freedom: fighting alongside the enemies of America. This phenomenon is enshrined in the original lyrics of "The Star-Spangled Banner"—an anthem celebrating America's victory against the British during the War of 1812. In the final verse of the original song, there was a cryptic message indicating the fate of many slaves who attempted to escape or, worse, side with the British (in hopes of gaining their freedom) against America during the war.

> No refuge could save the hireling and slave
> From the terror of flight or the gloom of the grave,
> And the star-spangled banner in triumph doth wave
> O'er the land of the free and the home of the brave.[524]

Simple translation:

> There was nowhere for escaped slaves to hide—especially ones who chose to hire themselves out to the British as mercenaries. They would experience sheer terror followed by swift justice as we chased them down and slaughtered them for their unthinkable act of treason.
> Meanwhile the flag flew triumphantly over our free and brave nation.

In an article published by the American Battlefield Trust, historian and author James A. Percoco explains how Black slaves and other people of color "were faced with several choices during the War of 1812. They could either fight for the United States, a nation that professed equality and freedom but lacked delivery, watch from the sidelines, or take a chance to secure freedom by joining the British forces."[525] Despite the likely outcome of death, countless Black and Indigenous people chose to fight against America during both the American Revolution and the War of 1812. At that time, the British encouraged slaves to escape, then trained and armed them to fight. Several regiments consisted entirely of former enslaved people fighting on behalf of the British navy.

While external-facing wars such as the American Revolution and the War of 1812 posed a threat to the future of the United States as a White-centric nation, our internal divisions have been the driving force in shaping race in America.

• • •

THE WAR FOR WHITE POWER

Our country may currently seem to be at a political crossroads larger than any we have faced. Yet this extreme divide is nothing new. And although it looks like things are coming to a head and that we are at the climax of this division, history shows otherwise.

Despite what most of us were taught in school, the Civil War was not about preserving states' rights. It was a war to decide the fate of slavery in the United States. Period.

The Confederate vice president, Alexander H. Stephens, gave a rousingly racist speech in Savannah, Georgia, on March 21, 1861, a few weeks before Confederate forces fired upon Fort Sumter in Charleston Harbor. Stephens did not mince words in describing his disgust with many Northern politicians' sympathies toward African Americans:

> Fanaticism [in the North] springs from an aberration of the mind from a defect in reasoning. It is a species of insanity. . . . They assume that the negro is equal, and hence conclude that he is entitled to equal privileges and rights with the White man. If their premises were correct, their conclusions would be logical and just, but their premise being wrong, their whole argument fails. . . . Our new government is founded upon exactly the opposite idea; its foundations are laid, its cornerstone rests, upon the great truth that the negro is not equal to the White man; that slavery subordination to the superior race is his natural and normal condition. This, our new government, is the first, in the history of the world, based upon this great physical, philosophical, and moral truth.[526]

Stephens believed that the North would inevitably lose the war because "they were attempting to make things equal which the Creator had made unequal," and such an effort was doomed to fail. Stephens's prediction of a Southern victory was obviously wrong, but his unapologetic stance on White supremacy was unscathed.

After the four-year bloodbath of the Civil War, while the institution of slavery itself was finally outlawed, the country was as split as ever. The fight to maintain slavery and White dominance did not stop in 1865. Yet many of us are still indoctrinated with the falsified "decisive victory" version of the Civil War in which the good guys won, and all the slaves were set free by noble Abraham Lincoln.

Today, America continues to reel from this deep wound that nearly brought our nation to its knees. The impetus behind the Civil War is a living part of US history.

Southern "heritage" and Southern pride remain staples of large swaths of White American culture, as demonstrated by ongoing White-supremacy protests, frequent displays of Confederate flags, bronze statues of men who adamantly defended racial supremacy, and revised Civil War reenactments in which the Confederacy triumphs. If anything, the brutality that followed the Civil War, including the Jim Crow era, public torture and lynching, eugenics, mass incarceration, and exploitative labor practices via the thirteenth amendment are the primary legacies of the Civil War.

White supremacy cannot and will not be stopped simply through fighting and brutal slaughter, nor by the diplomatic swipe of a pen declaring the end of slavery. In the end, fighting a bloody physical war over deeply held racist beliefs led to the magnification of the conflict on a psychological level—further entrenching the belief of racial supremacy for many Southern White Americans while making countless Northerners completely oblivious to their own complicit racism because their ancestors were the "good guys" who fought against slavery.

The Civil War arguably remains the most overt example of a division in political and ideological Whiteness in the history of our country. Yet despite this fundamental disagreement among White Americans around the issues of slavery itself, as well as the status of Black Americans in our society, the power that Whiteness holds was left untarnished. The Civil War only further embedded the terms of Whiteness in America. The subsequent policies, and laws, as well as racial science and the eugenics movement, ensured that White power became more sanctified and protected and that "racial ambiguity" would never occur again.

The marginalization and exploitation of people of color (namely Black Americans) continued uninhibited, giving way to the industrialization of the prison system as a never-ending supply of cheap labor. More importantly, many of the systems currently in place continue to uphold the willful oppression of Black Americans in order to guarantee that power remains consolidated within the confines of Whiteness. The Civil War may have ended the practice of chattel slavery, but it left the concept of White supremacy unscathed, giving way to another century of White dominance in America.

PART 5

The Fall of Whiteness?

CHAPTER 16

The War on Whiteness

> "The America that we know and love doesn't exist anymore. . . . This is a national emergency, and we must demand that Congress act now."
> —Laura Ingraham, Fox News

OUR WHITE RACIAL IDENTITY allows us to live in a socially constructed frame of mind that we make up as we go along, with each passing generation.

This relatively new racial category, conceived in the seventeenth century, has left a lot of room for ambiguity and confusion. What it means to be White in America has been constantly changing since the seventeenth century. As things stand now, White supremacists are right about one thing: American Whiteness, in its most current form, is in fact disappearing.

As has been shown throughout this book, this fear is not a new phenomenon. From early immigration of "less desirable" Europeans (e.g., Irish, Italian, etc.) onward, racial scientists and those on the far end of "Anglo-Saxon spectrum" have been spouting fears of White adulteration since our country was first founded. However, Whiteness itself is still nowhere near disappearing. How can this be? How can our current concept of Whiteness be continually dissolving while Whiteness itself is thriving?

As it turns out, the vagueness around the concept of Whiteness may paradoxically be its saving grace, as well as what allows it to continually increase its power and influence on a global scale. Whiteness is based entirely on subjective, irrational, and shifting societal beliefs; its nebulous foundation and its kaleidoscopic, shifting nature make it outwardly appear to be under perpetual threat and on the cusp of disappearing altogether. However, the difficulty in pinning down what Whiteness is, actually serves as an advantage in that it forces Whiteness to constantly adapt in order to sustain itself.

What we are witnessing is not an existential threat to Whiteness but rather a small slice of an ongoing process of evolution. Whiteness is not disappearing; Whiteness is merely experiencing growing pains as it once again reinvents and redefines itself.

● ● ●

STRANGERS TO OUR OWN RACE

Whiteness as we know it today would be almost unrecognizable to our predecessors from as recently as the twentieth century.

While it may appear that the definition of Whiteness has remained fairly stable throughout the past few generations, this is based on a shortsighted understanding of our racial identity. Our failure to grasp the fluidity of Whiteness beyond the scope of our own lifetimes (versus across multiple generations) creates a Groundhog Day effect; each successive generation of White people become fearful and reactive to changes in the status quo. The futile desire to pin down Whiteness once and for all, coupled with a persistent false belief in its biological basis, leads to generation after generation of xenophobia and a feeling that Whiteness is constantly under siege—a misconception compounded by the fact that each generation of xenophobic White Americans creates frustration and anxiety in the next generation of nationalists by regaling them, often from a very early age, about "the way things used to be and ought to remain."

Whiteness has undergone immense shifts in its identity even within the last century. Today many White Americans enjoy sharing where their European ancestors are originally from, but openly stating one's ancestry or place of origin was a serious liability throughout most of American history.

● ● ●

"HYPHENATED AMERICANS"

From 1890 to 1920, the term "hyphenated American" was commonly used as an epitaph "to disparage [European] Americans who were of foreign birth or origin, and who displayed an allegiance to a foreign country through the use of the hyphen,"[527] describes Hyphenated America, a short-lived organization created by two Columbia University students in 2020 that was committed to helping newcomers navigate the US immigration system. "The term 'the hyphen' was a metonymical reference to this kind of ethnicity descriptor [e.g., Irish-American, German-American], and 'dropping the hyphen' referred to full integration into the American identity." Many of those who willingly assimilated not only looked down upon but also distrusted and detested hyphenated Americans.

In a 1915 address to the Knights of Columbus, President Teddy Roosevelt unapologetically declared, "There is no room in this country for hyphenated Americanism. . . . [A] hyphenated American is not an American at all. Our allegiance must be purely to the United States. We must unsparingly condemn any man who holds any other allegiance."[528] Roosevelt went on to demand that those who retained their nationality go back to where they came from. "He has no place here; and the sooner he returns to the land to which he feels his real heart-allegiance, the better it will be for every good American." After Roosevelt's impassioned speech, the *New York Times* ran the headline "Roosevelt Bars the Hyphenated; No Room in This Country for Dual Nationality . . . Treason to Vote as Such."

Roosevelt was certainly not alone in his beliefs. This nationalist sentiment was shared by many assimilated White Americans, who urged newcomers to either fully embrace their new, White American identity or go back home. The alternative was to face ridicule, persecution, and even violence. As indicated in the last portion of the *New York Times* article, another common belief at that time was that anyone carrying a hyphen should not be allowed to vote in the United States, for fear that they had ulterior motives that were not in the best interests of America.

However, for many incoming European immigrants, it was not as simple as "dropping the hyphen." Until the turn of the twentieth century in the United States, millions of people of European ancestry existed on the "outskirts" of Whiteness. Two such groups, the Irish and the Jews, were excluded not just from White privilege and access but also from the very category of Whiteness.

Both groups are examples of a recent drastic evolution in Whiteness—one that many nationalists believed (and arguably still do) would be the end of Whiteness itself. Yet the story of how the Irish and Jews "became" White is critical to understanding the subjectivity and adaptability of Whiteness over the past three centuries.

• • •

"BECOMING" WHITE

When the Irish first began arriving in America, Anglo-Saxon Americans simply could not see the similarities, often viewing them as something abominable. In her book *How the Irish Became White*, Noel Ingatiev describes how some considered the Irish as "an intermediate race located socially between Black and White."[529] It is hard to believe that while millions of modern White Americans now get inebriated and pretend to be Irish every March 17, many of their great-grandparents used to refer to the Irish as "n*ggers turned inside out"[530] while also claiming that Black Americans were merely "smoked Irish." Yet the Irish had stiff competition when it came to being the most hated Europeans.

Jews were viewed with equal, if not even more, disdain, supposedly posing a danger to White America by threatening its racial purity. So entrenched was this view that many racial scientists tried to devise new categories to ensure that Whiteness retained its distinctiveness and first-class status. In his highly regarded book published in 1905, *The Effects of Tropical Light on White Men*, surgeon Charles Woodruff made the case that "the Semitic type is the link between the Negro and the Aryan."[531] This outlandish claim was directed at one group of Jews in particular—a group from which the contrived and stereotyped image of all Jews having big noses and curly dark hair comes from.

Hailing from Eastern Europe, Ashkenazi Jews have what many White Americans consider a distinctive appearance. (Emerging research does, in fact, show that the entire population of roughly 10 million Ashkenazi Jews in the world today can likely trace their ancestry to a small group of just over 300 individuals who lived between 600 to 800 years ago with both European and Middle Eastern ancestry.)[532] Most White Americans at the turn of the twentieth century held a strong sentiment that Jews were simply not the same race as them, and they likely didn't give the assumption a second thought.

The irony of this inflammatory debate is that many Jews immigrating from Europe at that time had little interest in how they themselves were racially categorized. While some possessed their own prejudiced understanding of status and class, the notion of racial superiority and racial categorization was unknown to many *until* they arrived in America.[533] Living in small, isolated, tight-knit communities, most were much more focused on attaining the status of "American" than being considered White—though they sought to receive the same associated privileges and rights that other White Americans held.

As more Jewish and Irish immigrants came to America, White inhabitants of twentieth-century America experienced an involuntary shift in their racial identity. Unwilling to acquiesce to the notion that these outsiders could be considered White like themselves, these "purer" White Americans feared contamination. This was merely another stage in Whiteness's ongoing evolution, but this shift fueled anxiety and hatred throughout White America, leading to public outcry, protest, violent hate crimes, and outright banishment of entire Irish and Jewish communities.

Nonetheless, Jewish and Irish immigrants were begrudgingly assimilated into the White race over the course of mere decades—and in some cases even less time. As second and third generations of these outsiders were born in the United States, attaining higher status and making their way into political office, they became tolerated and accepted. While the WASP (White Anglo-Saxon Protestant) community actively fought to keep the Irish and Jews from becoming a part of "normal" White society, other White Americans provided these outsiders with bona fide "Americanization" programs and support systems.

Many newcomers were aided in establishing themselves and building successful communities and businesses—especially during the New Deal under President Franklin Delano Roosevelt. As a part of the New Deal initiatives, Southern and Eastern European immigrants in particular were provided with social programs and financial support under the belief that they could be "turned American" in the second or even first generation.[534] This was not an act of goodwill by the United States government but rather a concerted effort to produce a strong and compliant workforce, build loyalty and allegiance to the United States, and forge a unified belief in a shared White identity.

In the first two decades alone of the twentieth century, as many as thirty million Southern and Eastern European immigrants were absorbed into American Whiteness through *compulsory* indoctrination programs.[535] Political writer and educator David Dean describes how over thirty states passed laws specifically "mandating their participation in 'Americanization programs' run by state and local governments, civic organizations, and corporations."[536]

While these programs undoubtedly contained helpful elements like financial literacy and English instruction, they also included multiple lessons geared specifically toward forced assimilation, Dean explains. Americanization programs heavily emphasized "American history, civics, and patriotism aimed explicitly to separate them [Southern and Eastern European immigrants] from their ethnic communities, create acceptance of female subjugation [in] the home and male exploitation in the workplace, label their traditional culture inferior, and replace their connection to their homelands and local histories with this same sanitized history of the White American elite that former generations of White settlers had already accepted as their own."[537] Ultimately, these compulsory programs were designed to erase one identity in order to instill a new one: White American.

Unlike their soon-to-be-White counterparts, most immigrants of color, Black Americans, and Indigenous people who had been here for millennia were denied access to Whiteness and citizenship. Mexican immigrants seeking basic assistance in the 1920s were given a prepaid one-way ticket back to Mexico. Similarly, Black Americans were still actively suppressed. White Southern landowners vehemently fought to ensure that absolutely zero support was given to Black Americans—especially Black farmers— for fear that they would cease to work as penniless sharecroppers.[538]

Meanwhile, the only thing incoming European immigrants had

to do to eventually be absorbed into Whiteness and gain American citizenship was effectively relinquish their ancestry and heritage. By adopting the language, customs, and culture of their new home country, many of them were likely to barely "make the cut," but only one generation later, their children were often welcomed as full-fledged members of White society.

Exactly as intended, the void left behind after being stripped of their heritage led many of these "newer" White folks to glom onto their White identities. They developed "especially powerful attachments to Whiteness because of the ways in which various Americanization programs forced them to assimilate by surrendering all aspects of their own ethnic organization and identification,"[539] writes author George Lipsitz in *The Possessive Investment in Whiteness*. With each passing generation, their descendants became further enmeshed in Whiteness, in many cases willfully letting their ancestry go altogether to become proud (White) Americans. Whether by necessity or out of a desire to assimilate, many of these people who relinquished their ethnicities were our great-grandparents, grandparents, parents, or, in some cases, us.

As described by revolutionary activist and writer James Baldwin, every European that arrived in the eighteenth through the twentieth century "paid the price of the ticket. The price was to become 'White.' No one was White before [they] came to America."[540] Just like every European before them, the more these newcomers shifted their allegiances and established themselves as American by adopting the language, customs, and cultures of that time, the more accepted they became by White society. They also worked to clearly delineate themselves from those at the bottom of the hierarchy. "To gain acceptance, each new infusion of immigrants had to enter into a silent, unspoken pact of separating and distancing themselves from the established lowest caste. Becoming white meant defining themselves as furthest from its opposite—black,"[541] describes

Isabel Wilkerson, journalist and author of *Caste: The Origins of Our Discontents*. Mere decades later, neither they nor other White Americans would consider them anything *but* White.

It should be acknowledged that despite over a century of assimilation, while almost every European American is now accepted unequivocally as White, many Jews still face heavy persecution both here and abroad. Yet while anti-Semitism exists throughout our country, to many White Americans, Jewish simply means a novel variant of White—and that's assuming someone chooses to reveal their religious/cultural heritage instead of hiding it.

● ● ●

WHITE ALL ALONG

This begs the question: were Jews and Irish people White all along, and other White people simply could not (or would not) see it, or did Whiteness itself have to evolve to accommodate a more diverse version of itself? Strangely, the answer is both.

In the case of both Jews and Irish immigrants, White Americans "broadened the net" to let others in while also slightly shifting their own views of themselves in relation to the newly assimilated. Once Jews and Irish Americans were finally allowed into the "Whiteness club," many of them became full-fledged members and staunch supporters of Whiteness—even leaders. According to professor of history Mark LeVine in a 2019 *Al Jazeera* article, "the majority of Jews embraced Whiteness as it became more readily available to them from the 1960s onwards, believing it offered unprecedented protection against any possible resurgent anti-Semitism."[542]

Despite originally being excluded and even persecuted, many Jews and Irish quickly began to benefit from White privilege, holding considerable amounts of wealth, power, and influence over American society. Many also adopted the customs of White hostility toward other races, including slavery.

• • •

THE JEWISH CONFEDERACY

One often overlooked fact about early Jewish American history is that Jews have been here since well before the United States became a nation. Several Jews who lived in the Southern states from colonial America up to the Civil War were not only wealthy slave owners but also actively involved in the slave trade.

Ansley Davis and David Wise were two of the most prominent Jews involved in the slave trade during the mid-1800s, frequently publishing ads in newspapers throughout the South for the sale and purchase of enslaved Black Americans. "Davis, whose family owned one of the largest Jewish-run slave-trading companies in the entire South, would tour the [New Orleans] region every summer seeking new slaves, which he later sold"[543] upon his return to Virginia, according to *Haaretz*, an Israeli newspaper. In a 2021 article titled "The Uncomfortable Truths of Jewish Life in the US South," journalist Ofer Aderet describes how "Jews in America today are distraught knowing that their brethren were among the slave owners and traders of the past." This is especially disconcerting to many modern Jews, considering that the entire holiday of Passover is a celebration acknowledging their ancestors escape from slavery in Egypt.

Additionally, prior to the rise of radical hate groups such as the Ku Klux Klan, many Jews had become well established in the South. Some became prominent leaders. There were as many as 200 Jewish mayors throughout Southern cities in the 1800s, including in Selma, Alabama; El Paso, Texas; and Georgetown, South Carolina. Many cities even had more than one Jewish mayor. Georgetown holds the record at seven.[544]

One of the most powerful Jewish Americans in the South at that time was Judah Benjamin. Benjamin became the United States senator for Louisiana before later being appointed to secretary of state and secretary of war in 1861 under Confederate president Jefferson Davies during the Civil War. Before his foray into Southern politics, Benjamin had gained national recognition for his law practice. Prominent Oregon lawyer Richard M. Botteri, who specializes in government relations and election law, writes that Judah Benjamin was "regarded as the best lawyer practicing in the South . . . and the most consequential southern American Jew of the nineteenth century."[545] Fourteenth president of the United States, Franklin Pierce (1853–1857), who was against the abolitionist movement, even offered Benjamin a seat on the Supreme Court.

Benjamin, a slave holder himself, believed that enslaving Africans was not so much a moral issue as a matter of property rights guaranteed by the Constitution—comparing the Northern interest in ending slavery to trying to steal someone's horse.[546] Many early-American Jews shared Benjamin's point of view, some even choosing to fight for the Confederacy.[547]

Ironically, many people in the North discriminated against Jews during that time. "In some instances, antisemitism emanated directly from the [Northern] government,"[548] describes journalist Ofer Aderet. "In 1862, during the Civil War, an order was issued by Ulysses S. Grant—who would become president nine years later—evicting all Jews from the general's military district, comprising parts of Tennessee." Only when Jews protested did Abraham Lincoln override Grant's directive.

After the Civil War, many prominent Jews attempted to escape the South. Union soldiers caught many of them, while others, including Benjamin, fled the country. The rise of anti-Semitism in the late 1800s—aided by extremist groups such as the Ku Klux Klan, which began targeting Jews alongside Black Americans—effectively eradicated Jewish power and prosperity in the South and all but erased this early chapter of Jewish history from our textbooks. Within mere decades, Jews were again reduced to a fringe status within Whiteness, a phenomenon that would continue into the twenty-first century—reminding them of their tenuous place within the subjective confines of Whiteness.

As an inflammatory side note, whereas some of my White Jewish counterparts still feel like they are not "fully White" and like to distinguish themselves by identifying with the struggles of people of color, there are some critical flaws to this argument. For one, people of color have never been accepted into the club. Moreover, *all* people within the category of White have benefited directly from the exploitation of those not considered White, regardless of how we personally identify. Not to mention that once European Jews were accepted into Whiteness, many became just as racist toward Black Americans as many of their Christian counterparts.[549] So, fellow Jewish White folks, please, I beg of you—stop trying to relate our struggle with the struggles experienced by people of color. It is *not* the same. While it does share parallels regarding discrimination and prejudice, and even genocide, anti-Semitism toward Jews and racism toward BIPOC Americans, while undeniably connected, are not the same thing.

As described by James Baldwin in 1967, "the American Jew's endeavor, whatever it is, has managed to purchase a relative safety for his children, and a relative future for them. . . . Furthermore, the Jew can be proud of his suffering, or at least not ashamed of it. His history and his suffering do not begin in America, where black men have been taught to be ashamed of everything, especially their suffering."[550] Whether or not we choose to take pride in our heritage and ancestral struggle, many Jewish folks of European descent have one final option that BIPOC Americans do not have: religion.

When it comes to Jews of European descent, our religion is ultimately a choice. If you or I really wanted to, we could simply change our last names, raise our children as Christians, and they (and likely we) would become full members of Whiteness within a single generation. People of color will never have the same ability to be seen as White by choosing to relinquish their religion. This is certainly not to say that we should abandon our roots; nor am I minimizing the unfair and painful implications of having to make such a decision. But the reality is that many Jews did choose this option during the twentieth century, and many still do.

While we face our own struggles in terms of acceptance and safety in this country, I, as a Jew of European descent, can still confidently walk down the street not fearing for my life when approached by a police officer. I can attend almost any elite and private university. I can even move freely among different groups, choosing to disclose my religion at will.

While the story of the Jews and Irish in the nineteenth and twentieth century is primarily one of assimilation, Whiteness is a not a one-way street, as the dismantling and erasure of Jewish power and wealth in the South after the Civil War clearly proves. Whiteness has historically made attempts to exclude those who once benefited from its umbrella, based on the social and political climate. Simply because a group is currently invited to join in the benefits of Whiteness does not automatically grant them indefinite privilege and immunity.

Although nineteenth-century Jews in the American South benefited from Whiteness, this does not mean that they were considered White by their Christian peers. Many in Europe and the United States refused to see them as such.

Southern Jews are not the only ones who have been banished from the benefits of Whiteness. Starting barely a century ago, American Whiteness made an even more concerted effort to erase from its ranks a group that had once been revered: Germans.

● ● ●

KICKED OUT OF THE CLUB

While it goes without saying that Barack Obama would have stood zero chance of becoming president a century ago, more surprising is that the same could be said about his successor, Donald Trump, for one simple reason: his German ancestry.

Initially, many colonists were wary of the increasing number of German immigrants in the 1700s. In a 1755 essay, Benjamin Franklin wrote about his concerns with the rapidly growing German population and their perceived reluctance to assimilate. Discussing how Germans had been allowed to "swarm into our Settlements," Franklin writes, "Why should Pennsylvania, founded by the English, become a Colony of Aliens, who will shortly be so numerous as to Germanize us instead of our Anglifying them, and will never adopt our Language or Customs, any more than they can acquire our Complexion?"[551] Franklin's reference to their complexion is not an offhand comment; he was deeply troubled by what he saw as a literal "darkening" of White American society.

Like many of his contemporaries, Franklin believed that only the Saxons and the English were "the principal Body of White People on the Face of the Earth. . . . I could wish their Numbers were increased."[552] In his essay, he expresses his worry about the degrading status of White America, writing that "the Number of purely White People in the World is proportionally very small. . . . [T]he Spaniards, Italians, French, Russians and Swedes, [are] generally of what we call a swarthy Complexion; as are the Germans also."

As he saw it, the White founders of America were doing a favor to the Western Hemisphere by "Scouring our Planet, by clearing America of Woods, and so making this Side of our Globe reflect a brighter Light." He felt particularly strongly that German immigrants, who he casually refers to in a letter to one of his peers as "generally of the most ignorant Stupid Sort,"[553] were compromising the Anglo-Saxon-based White identity in America.

Benjamin Franklin would not have been pleased with the turn of events, nor popular opinion, over the next century.

As more German immigrants made their way to America, the common view dramatically shifted in favor of German ancestry. By the turn of the twentieth century, Germans made up the largest non-English-speaking group in America.[554] This influx was not by accident. Germans were at that point considered to be one of the more respectable, even venerated, groups within the White race. Some judged them the backbone and "gold standard" of Whiteness, as well as White culture in America.[555]

However, during the outbreak of World War I, this once estimable group of White Americans became wholly demonized. Whiteness isn't exactly kind to its own when it feels betrayed. Anti-German hysteria swept through America, forcing many Germans to completely cut ties with their ancestry. Thousands began lying about their heritage, changing their names, and painstakingly teaching their children to speak without a trace of an accent. They became so distrusted and reviled that White politicians and citizens alike banded together to overthrow any power and influence held by German Americans.[556]

German Americans were harassed, attacked, and in some cases killed. In 1918, Robert Prager, a German immigrant in Collinsville, Illinois, was captured by a drunken mob, stripped naked, and wrapped in an American flag before being dragged through his own town and hung from a tree. Despite his brutal persecution, before his fellow countrymen murdered him, Prager did the most patriotic thing imaginable: he kissed the American flag he was wrapped in and declared his undying love for his new country.[557]

Given that Germans were unquestionably considered White even during the early twentieth century, it may seem like this "witch hunt" was simply a question of national loyalty unrelated to race or ethnicity—more comparable to the McCarthy-era blacklisting. However, that is not the case. German culture and all of its accoutrements were shucked from the White American identity. German-speaking schools were closed, German businesses and grocers were forced out, and German culture, including music, dance, folklore, dress, and food was erased.

While it was obviously not possible to entirely strip German immigrants of their Whiteness, by virtue of their physical appearance and cultural similarities to many of their non-German White counterparts, this was a powerful example of how Whiteness dictates who gets to be a full beneficiary of privilege and power—even within our own ranks.

However, in this case, the German "demotion" was fleeting. True to form, once the war ended and the political climate shifted, Whiteness reshaped and rearranged itself once again. German Americans quickly regained their place among White society—ironically in large part due to their compulsory assimilation during the war.

In an unexpected plot twist, the war may have bolstered the overall power and influence of German Americans by artificially speeding up the assimilation process of over eight million immigrants. As the war ended, most people of German ancestry had detached from their ancestry and blended in out of necessity, "infiltrating" almost every corner of America, completely undetected. Once German ancestry returned to favored status, they quickly regained the advantages of White privilege, access, wealth, and power.

Whether it relates to the absorption of Jews, Irish, Germans, or any other European group, one thing remains clear: the concept of Whiteness is constantly being reinvented in order for it to endure. Yet many Americans and politicians do not take solace in the fact that Whiteness itself can be altered. They believe that there is a far greater looming threat to Whiteness, one that extends beyond the scope of mere assimilation-induced growing pains.

As the population of America continues to shift rapidly in the twenty-first century, more conservative Americans now believe that we are witnessing an all-out racial assault on White America—that we are being overrun by people who look nothing like us. Perhaps even more disturbing to these folks is the possibility that if we don't do something to stop them from taking over America, *we* will slowly become *them*.

These fears were initially the battle cries of a fringe sect of conservative nationalists fueled by fanatical conspiracy theorists. However, this impending "crisis" has now surfaced at the forefront of the American political discussion in the last decade.

● ● ●

WHITENESS GETS A RUDE AWAKENING

In 2008, two major things happened in America that shook the foundation of "White security." The first was the election of our country's first president of color. The second was that in August of that year, the US Census Bureau released a momentous prediction that "by 2050, minorities would make up more than 50 percent of the population and become the majority."[558] These two occurrences fueled a resurgence of White nationalism, reclusiveness, and identity politics that had been lying just below the surface and in the realm of denial—even for many self-proclaimed progressive Americans.

Yale psychologist Jennifer Richeson has been studying this phenomenon since the initial US 2008 census report. She, along with multiple other researchers, replicated experiments that clearly demonstrated "that [even] people who think of themselves as not prejudiced (and liberal) demonstrate threat effects"[559] similar to those who are openly more conservative. Richeson's results also showed that many White Americans, including those who reported progressive ideology, have an underlying "sense of a zero-sum competition" when it comes to the impending possibility of a "minority majority" shift.

To many progressive White folks, President Obama's inauguration was a historical landmark moment—and a chance for us to pat ourselves on the back for how far our country has come. Yet what most of us failed to recognize was that while we were busy celebrating, the election of a Black president had stirred something deep within the White American psyche. Consequently, eight years later, many of us were caught completely off guard by the backlash that prompted the election of the subsequent president. We were not prepared for America to show it's "true colors."

While it may be hard to accept, one of the primary unintended consequences of Barack Obama's presidency was the election of Donald Trump. This is not to say that President Obama is at fault for his successor; rather, America's unpreparedness and unwillingness for such a radical challenge to the racial hierarchy led to an unfortunately predictable outcome. In her book White Identity Politics, Ashley E. Jardina highlights these recent social and political shifts:

> For a number of whites, these monumental social and political trends—including an erosion of whites' majority status and the election of America's first black president—have signaled a challenge to the absoluteness of whites' dominance. These threats, both real and perceived, have . . . brought to the fore, for many whites, a sense of commonality, attachment, and solidarity with their racial group. They have led a sizeable proportion of whites to believe that their racial group, and the benefits that group enjoys, are endangered. As a result, this racial solidarity now plays a central role in the way many whites orient themselves to the political and social world.[560]

For many progressive Americans, this is done unconsciously. We may view ourselves as welcoming and inclusive, but our hospitality often only extends to the point where we are still the ones maintaining the majority of political and social clout. When it feels as if another "minority" group is either rising to power or trying to "impose its will upon us," many of us default to our more tribalistic tendencies.

While White liberals would still like to believe that former president Obama stands as a symbol of hope and our country's growth and change, his legacy is grossly overshadowed by the polarization, discrimination, and outright racism broiling at the heart of our society. As soon as Trump took office, he set out to demolish his predecessor's legacy. Ta-Nehisi Coates explains in a 2017 story for The Atlantic, "The foundation of Donald Trump's presidency [was] the negation of Barack Obama's legacy."[561]

Long before Trump's presidential victory, when he first secured the Republican nomination, comedian D. L. Hughley aptly summed up the underlying sentiment of White America in an interview on The View. When asked if he was surprised that Trump had progressed so far in the presidential race, Hughley quickly retorted, "I'm not shocked . . . [b]ecause I think that ultimately America is aspirational. . . . Obama is what we would like to be. Donald Trump and his supporters are what we are."[562] To further his point, Hughley continued, "We want to be different. . . . We'll put Harriet Tubman on the front of a twenty-dollar bill, but leave Andrew Jackson on the back. So, we got a slave on the front, a slave owner on the back." White America can't make up its mind because we are not ready to let go of power. We are trapped between a desire for racial justice and maintaining the status quo of being in charge.

Individually, many White Americans are fighting for a more diverse and inclusive future, but our collective White identity holds tightly to the reins of power. As summed up by Michael Eric Dyson in *Tears We Cannot Stop: A Sermon to White America*, "whether he wished to be or not, Donald Trump [was] the epitome, not only of White innocence and White privilege, but of White power, White rage, and yes, even of White supremacy."[563] Despite the fact that Trump was not reelected in 2020, we cannot be fooled into thinking that the pendulum is back in balance. It has never been. White America is simply not willing to let go.

The ongoing pushback on immigration taking place in both America and Europe is rooted in one simple thing: fear. White America is terrified of losing power and control; conservatives continue to sound the alarm of an imminent overthrow instigated by the "invaders." Yet this false-flag hysteria has been used countless times throughout US history, whenever we witness an influx of another "uninvited" group—from the Naturalization Act of 1790 (when US citizenship became only available to White immigrants)[564] to the Chinese Exclusion Act of 1882 and the Immigration Act of 1924 (which ended immigration from Asia altogether and set strict quotas for Eastern and Southern European immigrants).[565] Although America has always been one big amalgamation of many unwelcome peoples, built entirely by immigrants, we continue to fall into the same woefully destructive cycle.

Moreover, we continue to reinforce a traumatizing assimilation ritual to ensure that those who have most recently joined us know where they stand in relation to other Americans.

● ● ●

WITH OR AGAINST US

One of the easiest ways to unite any group of people is to create a common enemy. WWI and WWII helped codify Whiteness by further assimilating countless European immigrants who fought alongside us, many of whom even fought against their country of origin. However, there is a much more insidious way in which Whiteness has remained entrenched: we encourage those most recently indoctrinated into Whiteness to join us in our longstanding ritual of antagonizing all subsequent "invaders."

Since the inception of the American hierarchy, "newcomers learned to vie for the good favor of the dominant caste [White],"[566] Isabel Wilkerson describes. "They [incoming Europeans] could establish their new status by observing how the lowest caste was regarded and imitating or one-upping the disdain and contempt, learning the epithets, joining in on violence against them to prove themselves worthy of admittance to the dominant caste."

This pattern remains prevalent today. Sadly, because of internalized racism and xenophobia, it has also taken root in many BIPOC communities toward many newer immigrants—even those coming from their own countries of origin. Frequent ridicule, including slurs and denigrating phrases such as "FOB" (fresh off the boat), is often directed at recent arrivals. While some argue that this is simply the process of initiation, or even a term of endearment,[567] when observed in the broader context, "FOB" is undeniably harmful toward people who are expected to relinquish their customs, language, and culture to fit into American society.

America is no different than a big playground run by cool kids or bullies. Once an outsider is finally allowed into the ranks, they are expected to turn around and be cruel to those who remain on the outside. This often includes giving the cold shoulder to people who were previously friends (i.e., breaking allegiance with previous kin). The primary difference here is that we are full-grown adults with legislation, judicial systems, border walls, and intercontinental ballistic missiles to back us up.

As we progress through the twenty-first century, we are experiencing another paradigm shift in our shared understanding of what it means to be White.

CULTURAL DEMISE

There is a simple and glaring oversight in the logic of the White supremacists vehemently fighting to "make America great again": White America has been redefining itself since day one. White culture is not disappearing—it is merely evolving. Recent cultural and power shifts are part of the process that has been ongoing since Whiteness was first created.

Some White Americans might still clamor for a Norman Rockwell, baseball, and apple-pie version of Whiteness, but most of us would not identify with our "past selves" as much as we might think. Other than our collective concentration of power and privilege, White culture has never been in a fixed state. It changes as the world shifts around us—often in spite of us. Whiteness has witnessed the rise and fall of farmsteading families at the turn of the century; fast-money speakeasy-goers of the 1920s; white-picket-fence homeowners of the '50s; the "tune in and drop out" hippies of the '60s and '70s; the hairspray and high-waisted-jean rockers of the '80s; the dot-com boomers of the '90s; and the social media and K-pop devotees of the early twenty-first century.

Undoubtedly, our current version of White culture will be nearly unrecognizable to what our great-grandchildren will experience. Decade by decade, White Americans assimilate beliefs, trends, and ideas into our own self-defined bubble of cultural norms. Only in hindsight do we see the drastic changes that have taken place both in ourselves and in our collective culture. It is almost like looking at a middle school yearbook and wondering what the hell we were thinking when we rocked that one hairstyle—you know the one I'm talking about.

A number of White Americans would prefer to go back a few decades to what they either remember or assume was a better version of America. Yet if we were to go back too far, White culture would likely be unappealing. And many of our ancestors might not recognize or accept us as their own kin—either visually or culturally. Our dialect, styles of dress, mannerisms, and culture would simply be too far removed from their sense of self, much in the same way that many White people are currently at odds with each other based on significant divisions of cultural, political, and spiritual beliefs.

These opposing and contradictory pieces of Whiteness are in many ways what make Whiteness so enduring in the first place. Again, this is where history shows us how Whiteness's ability to reinvent and redefine itself has allowed us to remain in power. By continuously figuring out how to blend the new with the old, we have rebuffed and suppressed all perceived threats to Whiteness.

Nearly every element of our culture, including our cuisine, art, music, dance, politics, science, medicine, and even spirituality, came from somewhere else. Whether it is the incorporation of "newly discovered" spices into our food, the footwork infused into our classical dance steps, or the soulful and bluesy sounds now commonplace in our rock music, what we currently define as White culture is an amalgamation of other cultures from Europe and around the globe. We have both strategically and unwittingly woven these outside elements into our own identity. Quintessential parts of White American culture are often a veneer designed to hide the fact that a large part of White America was built upon things that never belonged to us, not to mention the blood, sweat, and tears of those we oppressed and stole from.

As the United States becomes a more globalized society, all areas from science and technology to politics and religion have begun to accommodate our changing paradigm. What many White Americans fear is not so much a loss of White America but rather a loss of their specific understanding of Whiteness and White existence.

While it is human nature to fear change as well as romanticize the past, we must remind ourselves that as individuals, we are experiencing only a small sliver of White America as it continues to evolve over centuries. This seemingly stable illusion of Whiteness is all it takes to drive our fear and hatred toward outsiders. To those of us who are resistant to the ever-changing nature of Whiteness in America, a rather terse expression aptly sums up the solution to our woes: "Let go or be dragged." Ultimately, whether we want it to or not, Whiteness will continue its evolution—not only to accommodate others but, more importantly, to preserve itself.

The fluidity and elasticity of White culture defines it and provides its strength. This is why White America is so adept at rebranding and reshaping. As long as we can outwardly flaunt the unified front of a free society fueled by healthy capitalism and a robust democracy, we can continue to inwardly modify and tweak our own culture however we want.

Moreover, if Whiteness were a single definable cultural or political entity, it would be much easier to overthrow. Our divergence essentially makes us immune to the divide-and-conquer strategy that we ourselves have used to oppress so many groups. Similarly, despite our stark cultural differences and perhaps outright hatred of those on the other side of the political spectrum, we still agree on a racial label and the status/privilege that comes with it. When push comes to shove, we unite under this label against a shared "other." As long as we can easily identify us versus them, we feel more secure in our status.

So, is White culture on the brink of extinction? Far from it. We are like a snake shedding a layer of skin as it grows even larger, and we are just experiencing another round of growing pains.

While the fear of a cultural overhaul keeps many White folks up at night, another piece of our inheritance is also being called into question: our very purpose and role in a society that we attempted to create exclusively for ourselves.

● ● ●

LOSING OUR PURPOSE

There is a critical stage of extinction, known as "functional extinction," that perfectly encapsulates the existential fear many White Americans have of losing their status in America. Barring some catastrophic event, functional extinction is a predictable occurrence on the path to complete extinction. One of the defining characteristics is that the declining population ceases to perform a significant role in the ecosystem in which it evolved.[568]

The fear that White America is losing its place and its power is essentially a belief that a "functional extinction" is currently underway. In this case, the concern by many conservatives is that we are losing our role and our place within an "ecosystem" we created for ourselves rather than happened to evolve with.

Many White folks simply feel helpless amid the social and political shifts rapidly taking place in America. What some White Americans are most terrified of is becoming a marginalized group within "our own" country. Millions of Americans have fallen prey to the same shortsighted, xenophobic sentiments that have plagued our nation for over four centuries—and conservative media outlets, talk show hosts, and political pundits are more than happy to fan the flames.

● ● ●

NATIONALISM ON STEROIDS

The fear-based argument by conservative politicians has always gone something like this:

"My fellow White Americans, we are facing a crisis like none we have ever faced before. We've endured economic upheaval,

wars, terrorist attacks, and even a pandemic, but there is a more devious enemy that is now poised to tear apart our democracy from the inside out—and it is threatening our very survival as a White, Christian nation. We are currently in the midst of a national emergency that requires immediate action, or else we will lose the country we know and love. As more and more immigrants flood into our country, our America will cease to be—and we will become the oppressed minority, forced to the fringes of our once loved nation. We will be overrun by Chinese communists, black and brown socialists, or worst of all, Muslims and Sharia law."

While this may sound like the ravings of an eccentric White nationalist, this type of rhetoric has risen to the forefront of our political arena and the mainstream media. On her popular Fox News show, which first aired in 2017, American television host Laura Ingraham evangelizes many White Americans' frustration through frequent rants about her belief in our country's impending implosion. In one such tirade in 2018, she made sure to reinforce to her millions of viewers that the political Left is entirely to blame for this completely avoidable disaster: "Massive demographic changes have been foisted upon the American people, and they are changes that none of us [conservatives] ever voted for, and most of us don't like."[569] She goes on to spout her fears about a takeover by the Far Left and their "progressive love" agenda, arguing that rampant immigration and liberal ideals will prevail if Congress doesn't take action immediately.

Laura Ingraham is not merely a sideline political commentator. Trump's Make America Great Again Committee helped finance an episode of her podcast during the 2020 reelection campaign.[570] Perhaps more concerning, in 2016, Ingraham spoke at the Republican National Convention and even directly advised Trump before his upcoming fall debates. She was a serious contender for the White House press secretary position. In a 2016 *CNN Business* article, Ingram responded to an interview with Tucker Carlson, stating, "If my country needs me, and if I can do something to . . . advance the Trump agenda, which is stuff I have written about now for 15 years . . . then I obviously have to seriously consider that."[571] While she was not chosen, her backing by the White House and the size of her following demonstrate a painful truth: many Americans, including the forty-fifth president of the United States, still feel that White supremacy deserves a seat at the table when it comes to politics.

Yet Trump and media celebrities like Ingraham are merely the latest embodiment of a sentiment that has long broiled beneath the surface of American politics. Ingraham's use of one phrase in particular, "renewing America"—especially when one thinks about the sharp increase in White nationalism, anti-immigration laws, violent hate crimes, and the attempted insurrection at the Capitol in January 2021—is a chilling reminder of not only where our country has been but also where it may be headed.

While many conservatives are taking a stand against the supposed downfall of "American culture," a number of Americans and politicians have begun to fear something far greater. As globalization inevitably pushes us toward a more racially and ethnically diverse society, the fringe White-supremacist notion of an impending "racial extinction" has unfortunately captured the imaginations of the Far Right. Millions of White Americans believe that we are currently witnessing the demise of our "once great nation" and potentially the end of Whiteness itself.

This growing belief presents itself in three primary configurations of fear that often overlap within the spectrum of nationalism:

- Our cultural demise (i.e., losing "the America *we* know and love")

- The loss of *our* power/control over *our* American democracy

- The extinction of the White race itself (i.e., that people of "pure" European ancestry are slowly disappearing)

CHAPTER 17

The Loss of White Power

"There cannot be privilege without oppression.
Privilege is built upon oppression."
—Unknown

BOUNTIFUL INHERITANCE

Inheritance is probably one of the most critical foundations of social and political power in America. For nearly four centuries, Whiteness has collectively managed to pass down not only multiple generations of accumulated wealth but also stolen land, status, and power. Only in the last few decades has our (unearned) rank at the top of our civilization finally come under significant scrutiny—and with it, a reckoning of our ill-begotten wealth, influence, and power.

In the current political turmoil that erupted after the 2020 election, many White Americans are trying to grapple with an uncomfortable question: what might happen if we were no longer the ones calling the shots in "our own" country?

Much of the societal conflict in America today, particularly among White folks themselves, is rooted in a deep-seated fear that we may be on the verge of losing our "inheritance" and becoming "influentially bankrupt." Even moderate and progressive White Americans are waking to the realization that we may be losing our long-standing social and political power. Many are not quite sure how to reconcile that achieving true equity requires us to call our own status, wealth, and power into question—and to potentially relinquish some of our inheritance.

There is a direct correlation between our privilege/advantages and the oppression of those we claim to support. Privilege is built upon oppression—and many of us are fearful of ending up on the other side of that harmful scale we have built our entire society upon.

Many well-meaning progressive White folks want to keep what we have, while somehow ensuring that others have it as well. On the other end of the spectrum, many White Americans have zero interest in letting our pilfered inheritance be redistributed. To them, equity and equality are a zero-sum game. Only one group can "win." Seeing as we have established ourselves as the clear victor, many White folks feel we must hold on to our power, or others will try and take it (back) from us.

Consider for a moment the term "conservative," rooted in the term "conserve." To conserve simply means to "protect (something, especially an environmentally or culturally important place or thing) from harm or destruction."[572] *Merriam-Webster* threw me a bone here and decided to prove my point by providing a fitting example: "He conserved his inheritance."[573] White America continues to pass down a stolen inheritance. Some are merely fighting harder than others to "conserve" it.

Even if some amount of that wealth was earned "fair and square" by White folks who did not come from a background of wealth and privilege, it is worth considering whether non-White Americans had the opportunities that were essential for our ancestors to build that wealth in the first place. For those of us who did rise from the working class, or even from abject poverty, the word "privilege" is often received as an insult. Rather than argue semantics, it is more important to remember that privilege simply means that we were given certain access and advantages over others, over generations.

Case in point, my Jewish grandfather came from a working class home. However, he served in the military, which ultimately helped him to go to college, buy a home, and eventually make his way into the rapidly growing aerospace industry during a time when none of those options were available to most people of color (all of this in spite of him being Jewish). The challenge to my inheritance is therefore not a question of whether my grandfather worked hard or earned what he had; it is about acknowledging that he was both given a distinct advantage simply by being a White man in the mid-twentieth century—a significant head start that opened countless doors that were firmly held shut to others.

Ultimately, by quibbling about whether we deserve what we have, we distract ourselves from the larger issue. In America today, many people, most of whom are White, continue to benefit from both historical and ongoing oppression and exploitation of others. While it might seem obvious to say that we should simply redistribute or give back some of the wealth that was stolen, this would not address the systems and structures that created the unequal distribution of wealth in the first place. The "unnatural" order would quickly restore itself as a small share of wealthy White Americans siphoned back the redistributed wealth and, more importantly, took back their power.

For most of American history, outspoken racial supremacists and politicians have been some of the most influential leaders in America. While they may no longer directly hold as many political positions, the power of White nationalism still holds sway in American politics. Yet because many parts of America have become more progressive at the turn of the twenty-first century, the need to "rebrand" White supremacy became paramount to successful campaigning and policy implementation.

• • •

WHO'S IN CHARGE HERE?

In the wake of the 2016 election, White-supremacy tropes have become increasingly more frequent and tolerated in political discourse, with former president Trump openly stoking the flames.

While it has become more common, overt White supremacy still does not appeal to a large base of White American voters.

"In such a changing landscape, old-fashioned racist and xenophobic appeals [were] unlikely to be politically successful beyond a small fringe, so the propagandists of racism ... develop[ed] subtler approaches to stoking fear and hatred for political ends,"[574] describes author Simon Clark, a senior fellow in national security and international policy at the Center for American Progress. "To do so, they have repackaged racist traditions in language and forms that could more easily enter mainstream political discourse." This includes common phrases such as "tough on crime," "build the wall," "voter fraud," and "urban voters."

There are countless politicians who unconsciously or secretly hold racist beliefs and ideology yet continue to remain in power by carefully choosing their words. In a 2022 press conference, US Senate minority leader Mitch McConnell set off a firestorm when he left out the word "all" when referencing American voters. McConnell stated, "African-American voters are voting in just as high a percentage as American voters" (implying that White people are Americans while African Americans are not). While he claims that he misspoke, his actions say otherwise. The very thing he was being questioned about when he claimed to have "misspoken" was his role in upholding voter-suppression laws that disproportionately target communities of color. Additionally, his proof that he was not racist was that he had hired black staffers in the past.[575]

Like McConnell, most politicians still recognize "that being directly associated with White nationalism harms their reputation, so they use dog whistles, or euphemisms, to appeal to White nationalist supporters without alienating more moderate ones,"[576] Clark explains. This allows many racist leaders to remain in power without facing the wrath of their progressive constituents.

White supremacists are indirectly used by many politicians as a barometer of the current political climate. By understanding the extremes, politicians can be more equipped to make concessions and compromises to appease their more conservative constituents. When push comes to shove, many politicians—even some of those who consider themselves more progressive—are not willing to lose an election because they are perceived as too radical or, even worse, anti-White.

● ● ●

THE KKK STILL HOLDS SWAY

In recent decades, outspoken White supremacists, including Holocaust denier and former Ku Klux Klan leader David Duke, continue to have the ear of many politicians and influential Americans.[577] The Southern Poverty Law Center describes Duke as "the most recognizable figure of the American radical right, a neo-Nazi, longtime Klan leader and now international spokesman for Holocaust denial."[578] Yet Duke himself is no stranger to politics. He ran for Louisiana state senate in 1975 and 1979, was elected to Louisiana's House of Representatives in 1989, where he served until 1993, then nearly became governor of Louisiana in 1991. Duke also ran for the US House in 1990 and the US Senate in 1999, and even took a stab at the highest office in the land, attempting two different presidential runs in 1988 and 1992.[579] While he did not achieve his full political aspirations, Duke has nonetheless played a significant role in American politics.

Most politicians don't agree with Duke's extreme ideology, but many still recognize his clout in White America. In fact, in 2002, Duke used his influence to blackmail several Democratic and Republican legislators. He threatened that unless they stopped publicly criticizing one of his political allies, former House majority whip Steve Scalise (a man who voted twice against making MLK

Day a state holiday in Louisiana and spoke at a White-supremacist conference hosted by Duke himself in 2002),[580] Duke would release a list containing the name of every politician he had direct ties with—including those who attended his conferences and came to his children's birthday parties. Duke went as far as warning his dissenters to "be looking over their shoulders,"[581] all to ensure that he could continue to pull the strings.

Yet beyond the realm of blackmail and political manipulation, politicians take into consideration the political desires of people like David Duke for one simple reason: they recognize that many White Americans privately share similar views.

After refusing to condemn White supremacists on four separate occasions, former president Donald Trump played his usual denial card regarding a potential presidential endorsement from David Duke. When directly asked by Jake Tapper of CNN's *State of the Union* about Duke's support in the 2016 presidential election, Trump bumbled: "I don't know anything about David Duke. I don't know what you're even talking about with White supremacy or White supremacist. I don't know. I don't know, did he endorse me, or what's going on?"[582]

Trump's response in this situation is about as denial ridden as that of a teenage boy who just got caught watching porn. Especially considering that Trump had literally cited Duke's endorsement as one of the main reasons for ending his first exploratory presidential campaign with the Reform Party back in 2000. In a public statement explaining his decision not to run, Trump claimed that "the Reform Party now includes a Klansman, Mr. Duke, a neo-Nazi. . . . This is not company I wish to keep."[583] I guess Trump's caveat should have been ". . . unless the racist neo-Nazi in question might help me win the presidency sixteen years from now, in which case, I plead the fifth."

In 2016, Trump once again seemed to have a publicity-induced change of heart. Duke, who had openly supported Trump and rallied America's Far Right behind Trump's MAGA campaign, went after Trump when the president did an about-face and attempted to backtrack on some of his divisive rhetoric. After initially claiming that there were "very fine people" on both sides during the violent Unite the Right rally that took place in Charlottesville, Virginia, in 2017, Trump finally got around to condemning those whom he had just spoken so highly of, tweeting that we must "condemn all that hate stands for" while claiming that "there is no place for this kind of violence in America." One can only assume that his publicists either hacked his Twitter account or simply explained to him using a picture book that openly supporting neo-Nazis might hurt his chances in the 2020 election.

Duke, who had exuberantly referred to the neo-Nazi march as "a turning point," was not pleased by this betrayal from a powerful White man he had openly endorsed; Duke had even told his followers that voting against Trump would be "treason to your heritage."[584] After President Trump condemned the Unite the Right rally, Duke openly admonished him for going after the people who Duke firmly believed had put him "in the presidency" in the first place.[585] Despite Trump's double-crossing duplicity, Duke made it clear that he was going to continue pushing for the same agenda that Trump himself had run on: restoring America to its "former" glory. He stated that he and his followers were still "determined to take [their] country back.... We are going to fulfill the promises of Donald Trump. That's what we believed in. That's why we voted for Donald Trump."[586]

After Trump lost the 2020 election, many of the people who stormed the Capitol on January 6—encouraged by none other than the president himself—were the people Duke was referring to. However, David Duke is certainly not the only racial purist involved in American politics.

INFLUENCING THE "WHITE" HOUSE

> "We can't restore our civilization with
> somebody else's babies."
> —Former Iowa Representative Steve King (2017)

To say that Stephen Miller, former president Trump's chief political strategist and speechwriter, is a strong proponent of White supremacy would be an understatement. In a cache of over 900 emails that was dug up by the Southern Poverty Law Center, Miller spoke directly about race science and eugenics, as well as the "great replacement" theory, espousing his concerns about an immigration-induced White genocide.[587] While he was careful to publicly keep these views hush-hush amid his yearlong political prominence, Miller is widely viewed as one of the masterminds behind Trump's rise to power in 2016.[588] Rarely in the public spotlight himself, Miller remains a prominent figure in politics, continuing to endorse political candidates and working with congressional conservatives on anti-immigration policies.[589]

Miller may be pulling the strings in the background, but more prominent political leaders have figured out ways to express their supremacist beliefs more subtly. In 2019, former Iowa representative Steve King (2003–2021) expressed his concern that "certain" immigrants are "denigrating Western civilization."[590] At a town hall meeting, King stated that "if we presume that every culture is equal and has an equal amount to contribute to our civilization, then we're devaluing the contributions of the people that laid the foundation for America, and that's our founding fathers."[591] Of course, King also wanted to make sure that people understood that he was not being racist, following up with "It is not about race, it's never been about race. It is about culture." Uh, whose culture are we referring to exactly, Mr. King?

Like so many other conservative politicians, King has used Twitter as a blunt sounding board for his nationalistic beliefs, tweeting in 2017 that "culture and demographics are our destiny. We can't restore our civilization with somebody else's babies."[592] When someone who had the ability to create (as well as block) legislation for nearly two decades flippantly makes comments about "restoring our civilization" and "somebody else's babies" without rebuke, one has to wonder how many other White-supremacist beliefs are flying just below the radar—influencing both policy decisions and American minds. But it's not simply what's under the radar that's having an effect on American politics.

Nationalistic rhetoric has become a mainstay of the Republican Party and has only escalated since Donald Trump unwillingly left office in 2020. Emboldened by millions of steadfast Trump supporters, on April 16, 2021, ultraconservative House Republican representative Marjorie Taylor Greene attempted to launch the America First Caucus, a political group focused on protecting "Anglo-Saxon political traditions" and reestablishing America.[593]

Much of the rhetoric contained within the seven-page policy platform sounds as if it were pulled directly from Hitler's *Mein Kampf*. In addition to supporting architecture and infrastructure projects that "befit the progeny of European architecture," the America First Caucus policy platform unapologetically declares that "America is a nation with a border, and a culture, strengthened by a common respect for uniquely Anglo-Saxon political traditions."[594] The document also explicitly highlights the threat posed by immigration without proper assimilation: "Societal trust and political unity are threatened when foreign citizens are imported en masse into a country, particularly without institutional support for assimilation and an expansive welfare state to bail them out should they fail to contribute positively to the country."

Fortunately, this *"Mein Kampf* tribute" created enough of an uproar to force Greene to retract the proposal the very next day.

In many ways, though, the damage had already been done. Many Americans agreed with Greene's unapologetic Anglo-nationalism, and the media frenzy merely amplified her platform. Moreover, the manifesto itself had rapidly spread across the internet, where it was picked up by others willing to continue forward with or without Greene's explicit support.

Minnesota Democratic representative Dean Phillips tried to mitigate the destruction of her divisive platform by calling out the danger in the media's obsession with Marjorie Taylor Greene and her caucus agenda. "Don't say the names of the people joining the 'America First Caucus,'" Phillips wrote on Twitter. "Don't amplify their hate and ignorance. Don't share their propaganda and enhance their fundraising. They are as relevant or irrelevant as WE make them. Ignorance isn't bliss, but it's better than amplification."

While this is a noble sentiment, Marjorie Taylor Greene was merely one in a long line of political pundits willing to openly echo the nationalist sentiments they share with countless White Americans. The "America first" agenda was not born in the document created by Greene and her political allies; it is a deep longing that lives on in the hearts and minds of millions of White Americans.

Sarah Cupp, a CNN political commentator, sums it up best. Regarding the politicians such as Trump, King, and Greene who fuel the fires of nationalism, xenophobia, fear, hate, etc., "whether they're right or wrong is beside the point. It's a fear and loathing that many in politics . . . have happily fomented and stoked to win votes. . . . [Trump] is just the latest prophet of this religion, and unsurprisingly, he has plenty of devout followers."[595] One thing is for certain: no matter who is in office, the further our country strays from the "comfort zone" of a White Christian nation, the louder the cries of "Make America great again" will become.

While Trump's successor, President Joseph Biden, ran his campaign on a platform almost entirely designed to mitigate the harm done by his predecessor, millions are hell-bent on ensuring that the next person in office will be able to put *his* foot down and work toward restoring our country to its "former glory." The events on January 6, 2021—with the storming of the US Capitol in an attempt to overthrow Biden's election—were likely a preview of things to come. Our country's political divide is steadily growing, and a compromise between a "new America" and our "former glory" remains elusive at best, destructive and violent at worst.

Consequently, while the progressive side of White America outwardly strives to be an "Obama nation," our collective "Trumpness" remains at the heart of our social and political institutions. Despite the audacious (and incorrectly understood) claim that "all men are created equal," our political landscape continues to remind us that there are some significant caveats to this idealized conception of American democracy.

• • •

POLITICAL DOMINATION

Usually, telling someone that they are "free to leave" is a way of giving them autonomy over whether they choose to stay somewhere—unless it happens to be the most powerful person in America reprimanding four women of color in Congress by telling them that they are "free to leave" the country if they are unhappy with the United States, and that they can "go back to the totally broken and crime infested places from which they came."[596] Former president Donald Trump was making a statement about national allegiance and loyalty—but in a way that sent a clear racist message: either play by our rules, or go back to your inferior countries.

While many politicians ceremoniously rebuked President Trump for his comments, mostly by "bravely" speaking up on social media, his authority remained unchallenged. Trump's ability to maintain immunity even then was a telling indication of the level of permissible racism within our government. Yet there was more to Trump's statement than mere racism and rudeness. His comment was a reminder that America's power is still unquestionably consolidated within the confines of White male authority and influence—and that those in office who exist outside of this "old-White-boy network" are there on a tenuous lease.

All too often, BIPOC folks in politics are treated like the kids on the playground who have barely made it into the "in crowd" and therefore must continuously earn their place by proving their loyalty and showing their willingness to go with the flow. Nonetheless, Whiteness is experiencing some significant growing pains in its three-century-long "golden era" of White-held political dominance. As our country undergoes significant shifts in demographics over the coming decades, it would appear that our governing bodies are on the cusp of a major overhaul. Yet the numbers tell a different story.

• • •

"MINORITY" RULE

Our government has remained virtually homogenous since before our country was founded. While we are undoubtedly seeing a shift in political representation compared to just a decade ago, at the current trajectory, our country is still many decades away from seeing a genuine change in who holds power.

The current Congress, the 118th, remains heavily lopsided. In 2023, White men still account for nearly 54 percent of all members of Congress, compared with roughly 35 percent of the general population.[597]

While White folks may be on track to become a minority percentage of the overall US population by mid-century, Whiteness continues to hold the majority share of power. Not to mention that the other 25 percent of congressional seats are distributed among multiple races and ethnicities. Based on these numbers alone, it would be naive to assume that people of color will magically have political control of the United States by 2050. Undoing centuries of stolen and amassed power cannot happen simply because more people of color are entering America.

• • •

POWER BY RATIO

Minoritarianism (i.e., the consolidation of power by a small group—in this case, wealthy White men) will likely remain the prevailing form of government for decades to come. The idea that White political power will be overthrown as more non-Whites assume leadership positions presupposes that every other racial and ethnic demographic besides our own can and will consolidate into one aligned governing force. With the increasing number of BIPOC Americans in leadership scattered among various races and ethnicities, history tells us that political power will remain concentrated in the largest unified racial group.

To put this in perspective, this would be analogous to a boardroom with fifteen people, in which seven are White and the remaining eight are of multiple races. Even though White people technically would not be the majority by number, this boardroom would disproportionately empower them because of their collective identity and aligned agenda. The seven White folks would most likely operate on a similar agenda with similar goals, while the other eight members of the board would try to represent as well as serve their individual, diverse communities in addition to trying to accommodate the needs of whole—including the White investors.

This analogy would be more accurate if it used company shareholders instead of board members. A White minority shift in the general populous by 2050 does not automatically mean a White minority shift in our government. Given the current lopsided ratio of our government, such a shift is incredibly unlikely—meaning that the gap of disproportionate representation may grow even wider as the general White population dwindles below 50 percent.

In that case, in order for the ratios within our hypothetical boardroom to more accurately reflect our current government, roughly eleven out of the fifteen board members would have to be White in order to account for the close to 75 percent White representation in Congress in 2023.[598] This doesn't take into account that this hypothetical company's owner, CEO, CFO, directors, and head managers would likely also be White by the current model. There is currently no evidence to show that the racial dynamics of the "boardroom" will undergo a significant shift in representation over the next few decades.

Even if the White members do somehow become the minority group on the board and drop below eight, they will still have unified racial representation. Not to mention that White people were the ones that built the boardroom in the first place (or, rather, forced others to build it), created the rules, assigned the seats, and set the terms of engagement.

As will likely be the case in 2050, in our current population, White people still hold a collective majority in that we are united in the recognition of our racial status within American society, both among ourselves as well as in others' perceptions. The remaining races and ethnicities have to overcome their current lack of access, power, and wealth to simply catch up while simultaneously overcoming the deliberate separation, divides, and competition that White America historically and deliberately created among them when we first assigned them to their respective racial categories (i.e., the divide-and-conquer strategy). Unless everyone else bands together in a collective front, we will likely continue to hold the majority representation in our government, along with the resulting rights and privileges.

Another important paradox is at play here when it comes to BIPOC Americans holding positions of power: without a substantial number of White votes, few people of color would have a shot at gaining political office.

● ● ●

"ALLOWING" POLITICAL DIVERSITY

White people make up the vast majority of the voting body in the United States, accounting for most election outcomes—including elections of women and people of color.

One Pew research study determined that in the 2020 election, "non-Hispanic White Americans [made] up the largest share of registered voters in the US, at 69% of the total as of 2019." Not surprisingly, "Hispanic and Black registered voters each account for 11% of the total, while those from other racial or ethnic backgrounds account for the remainder (8%)."[599] Along party lines, those numbers become even starker, with White voters accounting for over 80% of Republican voters. However, these numbers only paint part of the whole picture. Presidential elections are not determined by popular votes in America; they are determined by gerrymandered zones carefully carved out to ensure certain votes hold more power.

Our antiquated electoral system continues to give disproportionate representation to "White voters in several key battle-ground states including Wisconsin (86% [White]), Ohio (82%), Pennsylvania (81%) and Michigan (79%)."[600] This effectively means that the United States government is able to ensure that White America still holds disproportionate power at the polls.

But if White people are such a dominant voting power in the

US, how have so many people of color managed to get elected at local, state, and national leadership positions? While a significant increase in the number of registered BIPOC voters over the past few decades accounts for part of this phenomenon, as does the fact that smaller elections are still determined by popular vote, the will of progressive White voters is largely responsible for the diversification of the United States government.

This diversification is a classic example of White people "allowing" others into our space. When it comes to the diversity of our political system, we are still in the infancy stage; any semblance of real inclusion and equity is light-years away. In this stance of performative allyship, we selectively choose to give away some of our power—the glaring caveat being that it is still our power to give away in the first place.

Just as it was exclusively in White men's power to "give" women and people of color the right to vote, the same currently applies to people of color assuming roles of leadership. While non-White voters and government leaders greatly impact our political landscape by electing representatives and pushing through legislation despite White resistance, progressive White voters play a crucial role in ensuring that this power is not taken back.

We (progressive White voters) feel comfortable with the decision to elect people of color because we agree with their political agenda. More importantly, *we* are the ones choosing to elect them. Simply put, because it feels like it is our choice to make, we support it. But when people of color become the voting majority in America and potentially begin to elect people we don't agree with or feel represented by, many progressive White voters will likely begin to sympathize with how many of our more conservative counterparts have been feeling about our changing political landscape.

The current dynamic of the progressive White political power structure is like a company giving shares away. Right now we are still the majority shareholders. Another way of thinking about it is that we are the wealthy kid in the sandbox who allows others to play with our toys as long as we know that we can snatch the toys back whenever we feel like it—not to mention that these other kids are playing in *our* sandbox to begin with. If we were expected to give up partial ownership of the toys and the sandbox itself, the inclusionary sentiment would likely change.

While many progressive White Americans are more than willing to support a diversified government, most of us are not in support of a more *equitable* government. Should we ever get to a stage where legislators of color begin openly advocating for policy reform that would create more equitable outcomes at the expense of existing White wealth and power, White American progressives would likely experience a reckoning of what true allyship means. If, say, a Black congressional member proposed a bill suggesting that as a form of reparations, all Black and Indigenous Americans should no longer have to pay federal taxes, an idea that has already gained some traction, this would undoubtedly be viewed by many as a form of radical identity politics.

On the off chance that people of color do become the majority within the US government in the next few decades, one can only wonder what would happen if they justifiably began to leverage their new power to appoint their own acquaintances to political offices—something that White politicians have been doing for centuries through a revolving door of nepotism. This would be especially uncomfortable for White America if the majority of elected representatives, Supreme Court justices, and the president and vice president were of a single racial demographic other than White. America is becoming used to seeing more female and BIPOC political representation; we are not, however, ready to see true political power shifted into the hands of another racial demographic—where White people are represented by a minority share.

No matter how progressive some of us may consider ourselves, this degree of "dethroning Whiteness" would not sit well for many White Americans. Many of us would likely end up feeling like outsiders in our own country—as many BIPOC communities have felt all along when staring at a sea of White men sitting in almost every political chamber. Conservatives may still proudly declare that we are "one nation, under God," but for the vast majority of White Americans, this creed only holds true if it is a God and a government that prioritize, and look like us.

• • •

"MAKE AMERICA ~~GREAT~~ WHITE AGAIN!"

Many White folks on either side of the political spectrum try to hold on to the idea that America was founded on the ideals of democracy and equality. Yet ask *any* person of color when America was great, and they will likely have a very difficult time answering. The phrase "great *again*" cannot be assessed in a vacuum; it needs to be scrutinized in relation to the entirety of American history. Only when the false narrative of "liberty and justice for all" is removed from the equation does the statement "Make America great again!" become logical.

Many conservative White Americans know exactly what they are saying with this outspoken demand. It has a less-than-subtle meaning for those who openly support building walls and upholding good old "law and order"—in which case, the statement is not at all illogical or naive but instead a blatant declaration of intention to restore the previous ethnoracial order. In these folks' minds, the goal is to reestablish a White-led Christian nation.

Those in the "Make America [White] Again" camp fundamentally view our country as a White-led Christian nation that *allows* other people to live here as long as they play by our rules. However, the key difference in comparing the United States with many other nations that are run by one primary ethnicity or nationality is that White folks are not the original inhabitants of America. Our ancestors brutally stole this land and established an empire built on racial oppression—while also forcing other people here against their will. In contrast, China's and Costa Rica's core populations, for example, have been there for tens of thousands of years. Many African countries such as Nigeria can claim ancestry dating back nearly 200,000 years. Outside of the countries that have been devastated by colonization in the past few centuries, many nations are still under the leadership and stewardship of people whose ancestry and roots exist almost entirely in their own land.

White people can only claim that this is a White Christian nation if we are willing to openly admit that we first stole it and then forcefully made it into one—and that we never had any intention of giving it back.

The fact of the matter is most White Americans are simply not ready to live in a nation run primarily by *other* people. While it may feel uncomfortable to face this truth, it is important not to fool ourselves into thinking that we have come further than we have. Most of us must also unnervingly admit that the current arrangement of "allowing" others to have some wealth and hold positions of power makes us much more comfortable than the notion of people of color rising to power of their own volition. Under these circumstances, even some of the more conservative White folks will tolerate a certain degree of "token diversity" within our government. Yet when BIPOC Americans take a "nondiplomatic" approach to achieving equality, White supremacy quickly shows its true colors.

• • •

THE RIGHT TO FIGHT

> "The government of [*our*] people, by [*our*] people, for [*our*] people, shall not perish from [*our*] earth."

Despite the horrific conditions that most BIPOC Americans in this country have endured for hundreds of years, the minute that something resembling a power other than White begins to amass, many White folks get anxious to find a peaceful solution (ideally one that is still in our best interests) to defuse the tension once our attempts to negate the situation no longer work.

In almost every single revolution in US history in which people of color attempted to *take* back some degree of power or wealth, rather than peacefully requesting to be granted access or basic rights, White supremacy quickly trounced them.

There is a reason that we now dutifully celebrate Dr. Martin Luther King Jr. (albeit a fictionalized, passivist version of him that erases all of his radical views and reduces him to four words: "I have a dream") while uncomfortably tiptoeing around Malcolm X and the Black Panthers' integral role in the civil rights movement. Many of us want to believe that Rosa Parks was simply a tired old woman who wanted to sit down, rather than an active member of a multifaceted, strategic, and coordinated movement designed to dismantle the existing power structure.

Going further back, names of Black revolutionary leaders such as Gabriel Prosser, Denmark Vesey, and Nat Turner rarely make it into US history books—and when they do, their valiant efforts throughout the nineteenth century to set their enslaved brethren free are merely referred to as "slave revolts," a term which dehumanizes their courageous efforts and ignores who (i.e., White people) and what (i.e., slavery) they were trying to free themselves from. While I am not condoning violence, it would be unfair not to try to empathize and recognize why such drastic actions were, and sometimes still are taken. For most, violence is still a last resort, but many people of color in America have been left with no other choice.

More importantly, there is a flagrant double standard here when it comes to who gets to fight for their freedom in America. James Baldwin described it best in a 1969 interview on the *Dick Cavett Show*: "If any White man in the world says give me liberty or give me death, the entire White world applauds. When a black man says exactly the same thing—word for word—he is judged a criminal and treated like one, and everything possible is done to make an example of this bad n*gger so there won't be any more like him."[601]

Historically, when White people have risen up against oppressive forces, including using lethal means to achieve a desired outcome, we immortalize them in our textbooks as courageous heroes and build statues. Countless examples abound: Bacon's Rebellion? Led by a pissed-off, selfish, aristocratic White man who was known for slaughtering Indigenous peoples any chance he got. The Boston Tea Party? Angry White men dressed as Native Americans expressing their disapproval of high taxes imposed upon them by the British. The Revolutionary War? White men shedding the reins of tyranny in large part by breaking the "rules of war" and setting up ambush attacks in the woods against the British (a tactic "borrowed" directly from Indigenous peoples who were looked down upon and chastised for using it against White men). The Civil War? Angry White men fighting among themselves about whether they should be able to enslave other human beings.

Notice a pattern? Our country is used to White men with weapons loudly voicing their opinions and using force and violence whenever "necessary." By now, most of us have been indoctrinated with the same rhetoric around American exceptionalism: "Freedom isn't free!" "Fight for your freedom!" and, of course, "Give me liberty or give me death!"

Yet there is perhaps no better indication of the double standard of who is allowed to fight for freedom than what took place on January 6, 2021—when a group of primarily White men stormed the United States Capitol, emboldened by the rally cries of the president himself.

After losing the 2020 election, Donald Trump brazenly egged on his despondent supporters and told them to fight back and take the election that was stolen from them. "You'll never take back our country with weakness.... You have to show strength.... Demand that Congress do the right thing ... [and] fight like hell," Trump announced on national television. A torrent of heavily armed, angry White people (mostly men) descended upon the United States Capitol, tearing through police barricades, breaking through scaffolding, shattering windows, throwing flash-bangs, hurling tear gas, and scaling walls with ropes.[602] Many of these individuals shouted death threats toward elected officials as they stormed the building. This group of self-appointed freedom fighters, many armed with tactical gear and carrying multiple firearms, occupied the Capitol for nearly six hours—some with the explicit intent of taking members of Congress hostage—before police were finally able to secure the area.

To put this in perspective, a measly ten police officers were deployed to guard the east gate as heavily armed rioters amassed at the steps of arguably the single most important government building in the United States. In comparison, Black Lives Matter protests that had occurred blocks away only months earlier were met with hundreds of police officers in full riot gear, SWAT teams, armored vehicles, and even the National Guard. It goes without saying, but a large group of Black Americans attempting to break into the Capitol Building would have ended in a bloodbath long before they got close to the front steps, even if not a single one of them were armed.

For those tempted to counter with the fact that a few people of color were also at the January 6 riots, consider that the only reason these folks were not stopped was because White men were leading the charge. Their presence was completely contingent on joining a bunch of White men. If this riot had been led or instigated by people of color, with white allies fighting alongside, the outcome would have been extremely different.

Ultimately, the rioters that descended upon Washington, DC, were not doing something out of character; they were doing what their country has always allowed (and even encouraged) them to do. Whereas non-White Americans must carefully choose their battles, assuming they choose to fight at all, these White men flaunted the First and Second Amendments, even if it meant terrorizing and vandalizing in their attempts to uproot the establishment. White American men have been taught that the right to fight for our freedom is our birthright, and even our duty.

People of color in America have never had the right to fight for their freedom. Conservative and progressive White Americans alike prefer them to march hand in hand while peacefully singing, "We shall overcome!" because that's what makes us feel safe, unthreatened. BIPOC folks in this country have learned the cruel lesson that the minute they decide to rise up and fight, bullets will all too often silence their voices.

This is why a potential shift in demographics presents a scary scenario. As more non-White immigrants enter the country, many conservative White Americans, alongside the wealthy elite and a large portion of our government, will likely do everything in their power to ensure that Whiteness maintains its place at the top—even if that means fighting for it. Meanwhile, most of White America still tightly holds to the infamous sentiment that "the government of the people, by the people, for the people, shall not perish from the earth."[603] In order for this quote to live up to its intended meaning, the word "the" needs to be supplanted with "our": "The government of *our* people, by *our* people, for *our* people, shall not perish from our earth."

Just as "All men are created equal" was never intended to include non-White Americans, in the minds of many Americans, Lincoln's infamous quote also presupposed that White Christians should always have full control of our government. Undoing centuries of engrained White supremacy will not occur simply because of the demands of well-meaning, progressive White people.

Politics, power, wealth, culture, and opinions aside, some questions linger when it comes to the fate of Whiteness on a global scale. We are currently witnessing a decline of the overall European population and a rapidly increasing multiracial population, especially in the United States. A nagging fear of an all-out extinction of Whiteness itself is making America feel like a much more hostile place to the beneficiaries of Manifest Destiny.

CHAPTER 18

White Extinction Theory

As THE EARTH'S POPULATION increases exponentially, the "ancestral ratios" of our entire species and the overall demographic makeup of our civilization has shifted dramatically. The United Nations Department of Economics predicts that by the year 2050, the world population will be close to ten billion.[604] However, the growth of our species during that time will be far from evenly distributed. Over the next quarter century, half will likely take place in Africa. India and Asia will also account for a significant percentage of the overall global population growth.

When comparing these increases to the declining population in Europe, people of strictly European ancestry are quickly becoming a minority of the overall population. As stated by the United Nations, "fertility in all European countries is now below the level required for full replacement of the population in the long run (around 2.1 children per woman), and in the majority of cases, fertility has been below the replacement level for several decades."[605] Consequently, one of the seemingly essential factors for determining Whiteness—European ancestry—appears to be unwittingly phasing itself out. Does this mean that Whiteness is on the way out? Not exactly.

• • •

THE GREAT REPLACEMENT

The most current iteration of "White extinction theory" was developed and popularized in 2012 by French novelist and nationalist Renaud Camus, in his book *Le Grand Remplacement* ("The Great Replacement"). "Camus postulated that black and brown immigrants were reverse-colonizing native 'white' Europeans,"[606] describes the Counter Extremism Project. Camus was certainly not alone in his development of this idea, nor the first; he was merely echoing countless xenophobic predecessors.

Now commonly referred to as "the Great Replacement" in conservative American politics, this enduring theory is built entirely upon the belief that Whiteness is a vanishing race. *New York Times* journalist Farhad Manjoo describes it as follows: "'The Great Replacement' is a racist and misogynistic conspiracy theory that holds that White people face existential decline, even extinction, because of rising immigration in the West and falling birthrates among White women (caused, of course, by feminism)."[607] Many conservative Americans effectively believe that immigrants and women are to blame for the decline of the White race. These folks are now stoking the fear that an all-out "racial extinction" is on the horizon if White people don't act fast and prioritize our "survival."

It would be tempting to dismiss this as a conspiracy theory and point the finger at White supremacists such as Camus and the fear-mongering, ultraconservative media. However, fears of White displacement, White extinction, and even White genocide have existed in America, Europe, and Australia for well over a century and are gaining more mainstream social and political traction in the twenty-first century.[608] These beliefs fuel protests, discrimination, racist policies, strategic segregation, voter suppression, immigration bans, as well as violence toward many non-Whites.

Journalist Jane Coaston writes in a 2018 *Vox* article, "The sentiment among white nationalists has little changed since the Civil War: Whiteness is a valuable commodity, essential to the very nature of American and European life. And it is under attack—not by violence but by immigration, and by sexual intercourse between whites and nonwhites [i.e., miscegenation]."[609] This belief took center stage as the American population rapidly expanded in the early 1900s. It was during this time that eugenics—championed by characters like Harvey Kellogg—made its way to the forefront of American society and identity politics.

Throughout the entire twentieth century, the "belief that the dilution of white bloodlines—bloodlines that offered political, economic, and social authority over nonwhites—would result in societal disaster led to states across the country banning interracial marriages and enforcing strict rules regarding exactly what it meant to be white," Coaston continues. In 1916, Madison Grant, an American lawyer and eugenicist, published *The Passing of the Great Race*. While it initially had little success, his fourth edition became a popular read in the 1920s, launching this theory into the public imagination.

Grant espoused that the "founding-stock" of the United States was being phased out by Black Americans and non-White immigrants, including Jews. In his book, he explained how "neither the black, nor the brown, nor the yellow, nor the red will conquer the White in battle. But if the valuable elements in the Nordic race mix with inferior strains or die out through race suicide, then the citadel of civilization will fall for mere lack of defenders."[610] Like many of his time, Grant believed that the White race was unwittingly killing itself off—and that without an active defense strategy, the trend would accelerate until Whiteness was wiped off the earth.

Unsurprisingly, immigration restriction acts were passed in both 1917 and 1924, and the term "White genocide" became a touchstone in White-supremacy groups shortly after WWII. By the 1960s and '70s, a growing number of neo-Nazi groups had formed throughout the United States. These groups took an even bolder stance, latching onto the belief that both contraception and abortions—which they believed were disproportionately available to and being used by White people—were directly contributing to a racial extinction.[611] This false assumption led to a 1972 publication by the National Socialist White People's Party titled "Over-Population Myth Is Cover for White Genocide." While a fringe theory at that time, it has since become one of the underlying motives behind the ongoing backlash against abortion in America.

Countless extremist groups in both Europe and America have also taken the "genocide theory" one step further, espousing that this is all part of a secret, concerted effort controlled by none other than the Jews to undermine and ultimately overthrow White Christian nations.[612] These neo-Nazi organizations suggest that rather than being the villains, black and brown immigrants are merely pawns in the Jews' greater takeover agenda.[613]

These far-fetched theories have bled into the more "refined" rhetoric of conventional media and politics. Moreover, these theories have become the basis for much of our increasingly contentious political environment in the twenty-first century, influencing countless policies on immigration, abortion, and social-welfare programs.

Along with White extremist groups, well-connected and powerful organizations such as the Kellogg's Race Betterment Foundation and the Pioneer Fund heavily influenced the political arena of the twentieth century. More recently, these organizations have given way to modern nationalist groups, including the National Policy Institute, the American Identity Movement, Generation Identity, and the New Century Foundation, which have taken a firm stance against immigration and even overseas humanitarian efforts.[614]

In 2017, the New Century Foundation's primary publication, *American Renaissance*, featured an article by author F. Roger Devlin, in which he writes,

> We cannot "cull" Africans as if they were deer, but we can eliminate the misguided humanitarian aid that is doing so much harm. . . . Obviously, we must be prepared to do what is necessary to defend our own living space, up to and

including shooting intruders. Whites are so used to seeing Africans as objects of humanitarian concern that many are unable to grasp that they may also be dangerous rivals. But in fact, fertility is a major advantage they possess over us. We should not attempt to compete with them directly, but we can and must prevent our living space from becoming a dumping ground for their excess fertility. If we fail, it will mean a darker future for all humanity.[615]

While Devlin's disturbing and extremist sentiment will likely never appear in mainstream media, it is an increasingly common belief, watered down and repackaged into a more politically correct version by which the conservative party continues to garner political support.

Yet the entire notion that Whiteness can and will go extinct is flawed for one simple reason—a point upon which so much of this book hinges: it assumes that the socially constructed category of race is scientifically, genetically, and mathematically quantifiable. In order for me to believe that something *can* be eliminated, I have to believe that there is something *to* be eliminated in the first place.

While some combination of European ancestry has remained a qualifying factor of Whiteness over the past four centuries, the presupposition that there are definable "traits" of Whiteness that will eventually no longer exist in the global population is inaccurate.

• • •

POPULATION OVERRUN

The same factor that invalidates the genetic theory of Whiteness also refutes the assumption that we are being overrun by "others": the subjectivity of Whiteness itself.

While the actual number of Anglo-Saxons may in fact be declining strictly from an ancestral/heritage standpoint, not only have Anglo-Saxons always been a small minority in the overall population of the United States, but also this one group of Europeans is no longer the baseline of Whiteness. Fair skin, blond hair, and blue eyes have only ever represented an incredibly small segment of the American population. This "superior version" of a White racial appearance (as it would be categorized by a twentieth-century race scientist) is effectively obsolete and has been for quite some time.

As discussed earlier, the category of Whiteness was vastly expanded during the twentieth century to incorporate countless European groups, mitigating the perceived population decline. By constantly updating our self-imposed standards of racial purity, the White population increases not through procreation (which assumes a genetic basis) but through assimilation. This means that within mere generations, the White population can rapidly expand. As already shown, throughout the twentieth century, the White population simply absorbed previously banned nationalities and ethnicities such as Jews, Irish, Poles, Italians, Greeks and other darker, olive-skinned Mediterranean populations, Eastern Europeans, and Spaniards, vastly increasing the amount of people considered White in America.

As the category continues to expand its boundaries, Whiteness will likely just morph into something beyond our current understanding of what it means to be White—a phenomenon that happens with almost every passing generation. Nonetheless, a dynamic change is taking place in the global population, driven by two primary elements: population growth and globalization.

• • •

PROCREATION + GLOBALIZATION = DESTABILIZATION

Let's examine the foundation of the misguided belief that globalization is the driving force behind the decline of Whiteness.

Whether for economic opportunities or because of climate change, political destabilization, or simply a desire to live elsewhere, humans of every color are crisscrossing the globe on an unprecedented level. Consider that prior to the transatlantic slave trade, mass transcontinental migrations had previously occurred over the course of millennia. Yet within centuries, more than ten million people were unwillingly "displaced" onto almost every continent—not to mention the tens of millions of Europeans who spread across the planet during the nineteenth and twentieth centuries.[616]

With the advent of modern air and sea transport, humans have over mere decades exponentially shifted the biological latitude-based color gradient that established itself over the course of eons due to climate variations and genetic mutations. Many humans are now biologically breaking ties with their homogenous ancestral populations by choosing to have children with others outside of their ethnicity.

According to *National Geographic*, "a 2010 Pew Research Study found that . . . one of out of every seven new marriages [in the United States] is among people of different racial backgrounds."[617] That number is steadily climbing. This increase in "racial intermixing" (as it is defined by race scientists) has led to the White American fear of what is ostensibly a quantifiable scientific phenomenon: that White skin is slowly being phased out. Echoing the sentiments of Benjamin Franklin, who was "partial to the complexion of [his] Country," many believe that rather than "making this Side of our Globe reflect a brighter Light," we are instead unwittingly "darken[ing] its People."[618]

A more modern description of this belief has a more scientific-sounding name: beige theory. However, this pseudoscientific theory stems directly from eugenics and is based on a complete misunderstanding of genetics.

● ● ●

RACE IS *NOT* A FRACTION

"Beige theory" assumes that as global populations continue to "mix together," the entire population will effectively homogenize into a singular shade that is neither black nor white but somewhere in the middle. This radical version of the White extinction/White genocide theory is based on scientific misunderstanding coupled with racism, xenophobia, and fear.

This theory is also directly rooted in the erroneous racial science used during the height of eugenics, in which the contamination of the White race was referred to as "miscegenation." According to this false genetic belief, once a White bloodline is mixed with another, it cannot ever "become" White again. In other words, Whiteness can literally be "bred" out of the global population. Many White supremacists assume this beige theory is unmistakable proof that "pure" Whiteness must actively be preserved. Besides the palpable racist underpinnings of such a belief, there are fundamental flaws and misunderstandings to this theory—both regarding the contamination theory of miscegenation as well as the overall premise of beige theory itself.

First off, beige theory does not apply to an individual so much as to global averages. While certain shades of tan will become more common as more people "mix," this theory more specifically accounts for an average of all skin tones found on earth. The increase of non-White people does not inherently imply a decrease of White people. The global average of skin tones will darken primarily because of disproportionate population growth in certain areas, *not* by a decrease in Europeans or "breeding Whiteness out of the population."

Another common misunderstanding concerns genetics when it comes to the "disappearance" of *any* race: fractions. Beige theory is inherently based on the notion that race can be quantified by fractions (i.e., half-White, quarter-Black, etc.) and is therefore an example of how blood fractions have unwittingly remained the foundation of scientific misunderstandings about race and ethnicity. The one-drop rule of the Jim Crow era persists in our minds today, distorting our modern perception of race.

Let's analyze this as an erroneous math problem—as was done frequently less than a century ago. If a White person has a baby with a Black person, their offspring will be half-Black and half-White, correct? What happens, then, if their offspring goes on to have a baby with a "fully" Black person? What fraction White will that baby be?

By this logic, if this pattern of reproduction continues, the fraction of Whiteness should become exponentially smaller with each generation. So let me ask you this: in which generation/at what racial fraction are the descendants of the initial interracial couple officially considered Black? In other words, when does Whiteness "disappear" from their family appearance? To make things even more confusing, what if I told you that the Black person in the first interracial couple had an unknown fraction of White ancestry? Where does that leave us?

Despite the fact that we often hear descriptions such as "half such-and-such," fractions simply do not work when it comes to race. People can be interracial from a purely subjective social lens, but there is no such thing as "half-Black," a "third-Asian," or "a quarter-White." Why? Because these categories are not based on math or biology, and the categories themselves constantly fluctuate among different generations. Moreover, people's skin tone and features vary dramatically even within nuclear families, despite the same combination of ancestors. This can be the case among siblings and even fraternal twins of interracial as well as monoracial families.[619] Ultimately, Whiteness cannot be "fractionally eliminated" from the global population because fractions don't exist when it comes to race.

RACIAL PLAY DOH?

Beige theory is built on an entirely false understanding that assumes we are all being racially "mixed" together like a big lump of "racial Play Doh." In truth the genes that define appearance cannot mix in the first place. Despite taking high school biology, most of us still have little grasp of how genes express themselves when it comes to race. Instead, we unwittingly default to the same understanding held by race scientists of the early twentieth century.

For example, when we see a multiracial person, we tend to assume that their physical characteristics and features are a "mixture" of their parents'. Rather than biology, we default to our understanding of color, by which we learn that mixing white and brown pigments together produces a lighter shade of brown. Any modern scientist can tell us that this is not what happens with our genes.

In an article published in *Areo Magazine*, geneticist Razib Khan describes the basis of this common misunderstanding: "The average human, using common sense philosophy, observes that the offspring of two parents are a *mix* of the characteristics of the parents . . . [and] many assume that characteristics are being *blended* together. This is not what is occurring. Rather, configurations of genes lead to the [expressed] characteristics."[620] In other words, the genes themselves do not mix together; some are merely expressed while others are not.

"Genes are discrete units of heredity," he continues. "They do not blend, but preserve a full range of potential variation from generation to generation. Variation does not disappear because the genes do not disappear. They rearrange." A recessive trait does not mean that a trait disappears or is blended when paired with a dominant trait. Rather, the recessive gene is simply not expressed in certain combinations when paired with dominant traits; that recessive gene remains completely intact, and can easily reemerge in a subsequent generation with the appropriate combinations of chromosomes. This is why red hair, blond hair, and blue eyes persist throughout populations around the globe—even in populations with much darker skin than ours.

There are two very important points here. First, the subjective features we have used to label ourselves as White do *not* disappear from our gene pool simply because we choose to procreate with someone who is not considered White by our subjective standards. Second, given the right conditions and right combination of genes, the features that lead to the appearance we consider White can and likely will "resurface."

Many early evolutionary biologists failed to grasp this notion, believing that traits of a species were being eliminated with each subsequent generation, leading to a more homogenized version of that species. That misunderstanding was then carried into the field of taxonomy, anthropology, and subsequently the race sciences of the twentieth century—leading to countless misrepresentations and false assumptions about how race is connected to genetics. This common misunderstanding is where the unscientific notions of White purity and racial contamination come from. Unfortunately, past errors still influence our modern-day perceptions of race, particularly in regard to Whiteness.

Khan explains that if we were to look "forward in time, the science of genetics tells us that the full range of human physical expression will still exist . . . because the underlying genetic variation will persist."[621] Simply put, "science tells that the beige future will never arrive, because there are no genes for *beigeness*. Beige is simply one expression of genetic variation among many." There will most certainly be some beige-skinned people, as there have been for countless millennia, but this does not mean that we are all slowly being mixed into one big ball of "racial Play Doh," never to return to the "naturally occurring" global gradient. Our genetics simply won't allow it.

Many people in the future will still fall under the current racial categories (although the categories and names themselves will likely have changed again and again). Yet it's worth pointing out that even now, countless individuals do not and never have fit within our contemporary categories of race. In trying to pin people as Black, White, Asian, etc., we forget that there are limitless unique combinations of appearances and genetic variations within the human population, and many folks fall somewhere between these entirely subjective categories.

Here's where things become even more confusing. Because of our current racial biases and partialities toward our own lived experiences, it is easy for us to assume that the current color spectrum of people, and the resulting racial categories that have been assigned, will remain the norm. But consider that most racially identifiable populations we now consider to be "stable" and easily distinguishable are actually a result of intermixing between nations and tribes that have long since disappeared. This even includes Northern Europeans, the archetype of Whiteness that many of our Anglo-Saxon ancestors considered to be the "purest strain" of our lineage. The Northern European appearance is the result of many different arrangements of genes from very different groups of people combining.[622]

While a White person procreating with someone not considered White will indeed likely produce an offspring with outwardly different features than their White parent, this does not mean that the "defining physical traits" of Whiteness are lost in the genetic makeup of that resulting lineage. Within mere generations, the subjective traits of Whiteness can resurface—or even be "restored."

• • •

WHITENESS "RESTORED"

While White-supremacy theory insists that racial intermixing permanently extinguishes the White lineage of any subsequent offspring, a trend toward darker skin can be reversed within a few generations. It is common knowledge that many African Americans carry European ancestry (either from consensual relationships or as a result of forced procreation with White men centuries prior), but there is also data showing the opposite to be true. A substantial number of White Americans have a detectable percentage of African ancestry.

An article published by the *Washington Post* explains that "a 2014 study of 23andMe customers found that around 5,200, or roughly 3.5 percent, of 148,789 self-identified European Americans had 1 percent or more African ancestry, meaning they had a probable Black ancestor going back about six generations or less."[623] This fact would horrify any paranoid racial purist. Yet in less than two centuries, by virtue of their ancestors choosing partners of European descent, the subsequent generations managed to turn their lineage White "again"—leaving countless White Americans completely oblivious to their non-White ancestry.

While some self-identified White Americans welcomed this new discovery, or were at least accepting of it, a survey conducted by West Chester University in Pennsylvania found that of 3,000 people surveyed who had newly discovered African ancestry, two-thirds of them were displeased with the revelation and saw it as an affront to their racial identity.[624] After all, according to the Jim Crow–era one-drop rule, they are technically not White. This just goes to show how asinine racial quantifiers can be.

While most of us are familiar with the term "passing" (in this context, a person of color being perceived as White), this reflects a different phenomenon altogether. These 23andMe participants are not merely passing as White; they are White. Society has granted them Whiteness strictly based on their appearance. More importantly, they themselves unquestioningly saw themselves as "fully White" until they received DNA test results telling them otherwise. They experienced the world as White people, receiving the benefits and privileges that come with that identity—never once having to question (or be questioned about) their societal status.

Undeniably, those who were upset by this data likely chose not to tell their peers, thereby hiding their "one drop" from the public eye. Yet despite how these folks feel about this identity upheaval, they have one thing in common: their Whiteness was quickly "restored" by virtue of the reproductive decisions their more recent ancestors made. One surprising example of this "restored to Whiteness" phenomenon is the mother of none other than former president Barack Obama.

In 2012, a team of four genealogists at Ancestry.com discovered that President Obama's mother, Stanley Ann Dunham, a self-identified White woman from Kansas, had at least one ancestor of African ancestry dating back four centuries.[625] Even more surprising, after nearly two years of painstakingly working backward through DNA analysis and combing through extensive marriage and property records, the scientists also discovered strong evidence that President Obama may be a descendant of the first legally documented slave in America: John Punch, the man who was sentenced to a life of servitude after he was caught running away with two European indentured servants.[626]

Sheryl Stolberg, a health policy expert for the *New York Times*, describes how the records they uncovered "suggested that Mr. Punch fathered children with a White woman, who passed her free status on to those children, giving rise to a family of a slightly different name, the Bunches, that ultimately spawned Mr. Obama's mother, Stanley Ann Dunham."[627] Yet the story gets even stranger. These same researchers also determined that "over time, as the Bunches continued to intermarry, they became prominent landowners in colonial Virginia and were known as White." They not only were considered White by their contemporaries but also themselves identified as White, with one family member even choosing to fight for the Confederacy during the Civil War.

While it may not be possible to prove beyond a doubt that President Obama is the eleventh great-grandson of John Punch himself, this is not the point. What is more important is that genealogists have determined that his mother, a White-identifying woman, as well as countless other White-identifying Americans are the direct descendants of mixed-race families that for all intents and purposes "became White" again.

While this example proves that it is possible to "resurrect" a White lineage after a few generations of "selective breeding," Whiteness might eventually disappear in a way that has nothing to do with willful procreation. We can self-select all we want, but at some point, we will be fighting a losing battle against evolution itself. If one thing remains constant, it is the inevitability of change, variation, and mutation.

• • •

FORCED EVOLUTION

Let's imagine that fearing "racial contamination," a large group of self-proclaimed White supremacists decided to completely isolate themselves on a deserted island and procreate exclusively within their own race. (I should probably point out that this scenario isn't that different from what has been happening in America for centuries. Also, for the purpose of this thought experiment, we are excluding the harmful effects of incest, something that many royal families in Europe are all too familiar with.)

These island escapees' attempts would be futile in the long run. Over the course of many generations, their descendants would likely begin to morph into something unrecognizable—for the exact same reason that many of our distant ancestors did not share our skin color and nor will our far-removed descendants. Unavoidable mutations eventually lead to dramatic physical changes, including skin color, even within completely isolated communities.

While it would be easy to assume that our skin color reaches a certain shade and then remains stable, evolution won't allow it. Dark and light skin naturally ebb and flow throughout populations. In an NPR interview, Professor Nina Jablonski, head of the Penn State Department of Anthropology and author of *Skin: A Natural History*, explained that "over the last 50,000 years, populations have gone from dark pigmented to lighter skin, and people have also gone the other way, from light skin back to darker skin. . . . [A] population can be one color (light or dark) and 100 generations later—with no intermarriage—be a very different color."[628] While 100 generations may seem like an eternity, especially considering that America is only a few centuries years old, drastic changes of our epidermis can occur within the blink of an eye from a genetic and biological standpoint. Skin color, hair texture, nose shape, and countless other features, even within an isolated group, are fleeting.

For all we know, our descendants may face persecution for having the "wrong" skin color—although I would like to believe that thousands of years from now, people will not hold the same primitive prejudices and beliefs about race. That said, given that these drastic biological changes often take hundreds or thousands of years, we can be certain that the features used to define the current subjective category of Whiteness are not going to be phased out any time soon. Moreover, Whiteness as a concept is likely going to evolve long before these intergenerational changes can occur.

While demographics continue to shift and evolve as they always have, many White Americans will desperately scramble to hold on to something that is inherently fleeting and subjective. With climate change intensifying and further destabilizing many developing countries, the stage is set for what are likely to be some of largest multination mass migrations in human history.[629] Consequently, whether Whiteness undergoes any drastic changes in the next century, the structures and systems that were deliberately set up by and for White Americans are going to be tested. Many White Americans have no intention of going down without a fight.

PART 6

Trauma, Self-Harm, and Healing

CHAPTER 19

What Does It *Really* Mean To Be White?

"Is there such a thing as 'Good Whiteness'?"
—Professor Chenjerai Kumanyika, Journalist and Scholar

MANY WHITE FOLKS have a hard time pinning down the characteristics or virtues of being White. For example, while I recognize that I am a privileged White American man, my desire for fierce independence and autonomy when it comes to how I define myself paradoxically makes me feel separated not only from my community and (ironically) my race but also from my very identity.

It would be dangerous to fool myself into thinking that Whiteness is simply a facet of my heritage. Quite the opposite; Whiteness is likely one of the factors that most inhibits my humanity, cutting me off from my history and heritage—especially as a White male. Being part of a "collective colonial identity" has reduced my ability to experience empathy, compassion, or kinship toward those my people have oppressed. It has created a similar barrier even against other White people. Whiteness attempts to strip each and every one of us of our humanity because its entire premise was created upon the basis of power and exploitation, not to establish a rooted identity. As mentioned before, rather than give us a clearer picture of who we are, Whiteness erased a large part of our European ancestry and ethnic identities.

RACE SUPERSEDES ETHNICITY

Many of us still do not understand what it means to be White—or rather, what our Whiteness means (to us or to others). During a diversity, equity, and inclusion workshop I attended with some colleagues a few years back, a White male faculty member stood up and *inadvertently* made this point very clear. In the midst of over fifty adults, of which about ten were people of color, this particular staff member felt it was necessary to serenade the whole room with a five-minute speech about how important our Whiteness is, and how it is nothing to be ashamed of. His reasoning was that our Whiteness is an integral part of our heritage, a part of who we are, and what defines us as people.

What this colleague was describing was not his race but rather his ethnicity. Yet even when someone explained the misunderstanding to him after his speech, he seemed confused. These concepts were clearly one and the same in his mind. He could not distinguish between a socially and politically constructed identity and the European ancestry that had mostly been erased from his family *because* of the very Whiteness he was trying to claim was virtuous.

Once again, race and ethnicity are not the same thing. Our heritage and ethnicity were not maliciously created, nor do they serve the same purpose as our Whiteness, which is to ensure that we have power over others. Our ethnic makeup comprises significant pieces of our identity and ancestry that were legitimately passed on to us to provide us with a sense of roots and belonging: culture, music, food, stories, religion, and shared ancestry, among others.

Unfortunately, those parts are often completely overshadowed by our Whiteness, which was *designed* only to give us status and privilege. "The effort to get people to come together under the banner of whiteness has . . . always been about power and exploitation,"[630] explains Professor Chenjerai Kumanyika, journalist, scholar, and collaborator on the 2017 NPR series *Seeing White*. Ultimately, the reason that Whiteness doesn't have a collective culture is because it has no inherent meaning other than conferring a status of unmerited superiority and control over others.

● ● ●

TEACHING (WHITE) KIDS THEIR PLACE

Whiteness isn't simply an identity; it is a collective mindset, and a sick and disturbed one at that. This socially constructed mindset comes at a heavy cost to all involved. Writer and DEI consultant Melissa Hillman explains, "[Whiteness] means nothing but accorded cultural superiority over people of color, especially Black people, and, as such, the only heritage, culture, and traditions of 'whiteness' are slavery, lynching, racism, oppression, . . . When [we] raise [our own] children to understand they are 'white,' that means literally nothing but which position they occupy within a deliberately created system of racial hierarchy."[631] Teaching our children that they are White is not about teaching them who they are so much as it is about teaching them what they are unfairly entitled to and where they stand in our society compared to those around them.

We also teach them what to say or not say, how to act or not act, and how to think of themselves and others. Our children learn a sense of entitlement, self-importance, and impunity that children of other races simply do not, and cannot, feel by virtue of the "lower status" categories America has forced them into. Just as our society intentionally as well as inadvertently teaches our young boys "what it means to be a man," we also teach our children "what it means to be White."

Does this mean that we should ignore the fact that we, or our children, are considered White (i.e., embrace colorblindness) or at least try to teach our children to see themselves as something other than White? Unfortunately, it's not that simple, nor can we make our Whiteness invisible to others, especially those we oppress. Telling someone where in Europe my ancestors are from does not change the fact that they will still perceive me as White. Try as I may, there is no way for me not to be White in the eyes of those around me.

Case in point—try as we might, we fail to shield our young children from the stigmas attached to their gender and sexuality; we will likewise be unable to shield our children from inevitable societal conditioning as they grow up in a world created for them. More importantly, we cannot protect them from our own unconscious biases, prejudices, and fears—many of which we can't detect in ourselves.

• • •

"WHAT DO YOU LIKE ABOUT BEING WHITE?"

Despite clearly knowing that we are White, we seem at a loss when defining our Whiteness and, more importantly, how our Whiteness defines us. A large part of the collective White identity comes from understanding the things that do *not* apply to us.

Tim Wise, racial activist and author of the book *White Like Me*, asks a pertinent question of White folks that many, including myself, have a hard time answering: "What do you like about being White?" In the many race and equity workshops he has led over the last few decades, he has asked countless folks this question about their race. Across the country, the answers have remained consistent within respective racial groups. Wise describes how BIPOC Americans are always able to come up with an impressive list, outlining the "strength of their families, the camaraderie, the music, the culture, the rhythms, the customs, their color, and . . . most prominently, the perseverance of their ancestors in the face of great odds."[632]

But White participants always struggle. In almost every training, they managed only to come up with some shared sentiments about the things they don't have to deal with: "We like not being followed around in stores on suspicion of being shoplifters. We like the fact that we're not presumed out of place on a college campus or in a high-ranking job. We like the fact that we don't have to constantly overcome negative stereotypes about intelligence, morality, honesty, or work ethic, the way people of color so often do."

Rather than describing what/who we are, White people "define ourselves by a negative, providing ourselves with an identity rooted in the relative oppression of others . . . . Inequality and privilege [are] the only real components of Whiteness. Without racial privilege there is no Whiteness, and without Whiteness, there is no racial privilege." Wise takes it one step further, declaring that "being White means to be advantaged relative to people of color, and pretty much only that."[633] So while privilege may seem like a mere component of Whiteness, it is arguably *the* defining trait.

Whiteness was designed to elevate us by establishing and strengthening our combined collective power. And while many of us try to circumvent this by linking our Whiteness to our specific European heritage (as my White male colleague attempted to do), our ethnicity or nationality does not define what makes us White; instead, these elements are eclipsed by Whiteness. Whiteness does not care whether we accept it, because the very creation of Whiteness (as well as Blackness) in this country was built upon an institutionalized form of exploitative racism—designed to ensure that folks who look like us always benefit from our color and status.

• • •

WHITENESS SPREADS THROUGHOUT AMERICA

White men created race in the seventeenth century and willfully spread White supremacy to subjugate and dominate other human beings. Far from an accident, upon its deliberate conception in the late 1600s, the belief in a collective form of Whiteness, as well as the label "White" itself, were intentionally spread among people of European ancestry because this newly formed identity stood to amass tremendous wealth and power.

Many incoming Europeans were eager to join this new, elite club in order to access its benefits and fought hard to be seen as White, even if that meant decades or even centuries of disapproval and ridicule. Not to mention that shunning the idea of Whiteness would have made one an outsider to those who embraced it, making it less likely that one could build a "supportive" community.

Journalist and *Caste* author Isabel Wilkerson explains, "Oppressed [Europeans] passed through Ellis Island, shed their old selves and often their old names to gain admittance to the powerful dominant majority. Somewhere in the journey, Europeans became something they had never been or needed to be before. They went from being Czech or Hungarians or Polish to white, a political designation that only has meaning when set against something not white. It was in becoming American that they became white."[634] In this way, Whiteness "spread" even to those who had no idea what it was.

However, Whiteness could not exist in a void. It required a counterpart to sustain itself. The category of "Black" was designed to fill that role. It wasn't so much the creation of Blackness that defined race in America but rather the creation of Blackness as the antithesis of Whiteness. Everything and everyone else fell somewhere on the spectrum between the two in this newly devised, one-of-a-kind, racial caste system. The crucial method for those in power to remain in power was to be very clear on who *was* and who *was not* White in early America.

As slavery and land-theft-motivated genocide became the driving economic forces within early America, racism rapidly spread throughout. It became the foundation of the newly created

White race. For Whiteness to collectively exist and retain control over others, it required perpetually stoking the flames of this primal tool of oppression.

Like a virus, racism infected many of its hosts through a mere exchange of beliefs. Once it infiltrated the mind of its new host, its strength burgeoned, drawing upon other deeply held prejudices, before rapidly spreading to others—especially within homogenous populations. Within less than a century, racism as a feature of White supremacy had spread into almost every major civilization on earth.

To this day, it continues to advance, becoming embedded in White people's minds and hearts, reprogramming them with fear, hatred, and a sense of entitlement. Many people are simply born into "previously infected" families and communities. Others who encounter it quickly begin exhibiting the symptoms. But unlike a naturally occurring virus, racism was created within White supremacy and spread intentionally through propaganda, lies, and fear mongering.

Racism is essentially a carefully crafted concoction of beliefs, teachings, and practices folded within the structural design of White supremacy. With the full support and financial backing of powerful White landowners, business owners, and government officials who stood to make vast profits during the seventeenth through twentieth centuries, race scientists effectively took a more primitive "virus" (i.e., prejudice and fear of the other) and inserted it into a codified system of beliefs, practices, structures, and systems that would define America.

Like Frankenstein's monster, White supremacy and racism were constructed in a lab by scientists like Johan Friedrich Blumenbach, the creator of the Caucasian race, and Samuel Morton, "the father of scientific racism."[635] They were further "perfected" by eugenicists during the early twentieth century, who performed gain-of-function research—experiments that aim to produce an increase of a desired function—and thereby created the oppressive monstrosity we live with today.

Historically, the more racist one was, the more easily one could retain power and status as well as justify horrific actions toward other human beings. Yet as it continues to (be) spread in the twenty-first century, it has morphed into a more insidious and sophisticated being, "infecting" even the most unsuspecting and well-meaning White folks. It bends the will of conservative and liberal hosts alike, many of whom continue to create, vote for, and uphold entire systems of governance that allow it to spread.

While White supremacy and racism easily spread through media, societal values and norms, and our peer groups, arguably the most effective form of transmission is through inheritance. Like our understanding of race itself, White supremacy and racism are often something we inherit from our predecessors. As children, we are indoctrinated into a society shaped by racial beliefs, biases, stereotypes, and prejudices. Without our ever having to be explicitly taught, the seeds of White supremacy and racism are planted in our developing minds long before we know they are there.

What makes matters worse is that so many White children from well-meaning families are still told that our society is a meritocracy where everyone can succeed regardless of their race or gender. This ideal is completely out of alignment with the unequal reality our children experience while growing up, leaving many of them to draw their own harmful conclusions.[636] This explains why so many White folks who grow up in racially homogenous communities often don't recognize their own racism (or their entire community's racism) until they either leave home or experience an unexpected population shift at home. The latter often leads to significant tension, animosity, and even violence in what may have otherwise seemed a warm and welcoming community. For many White folks, the more diverse our neighborhoods, towns, cities, and society become, the more symptoms of racism bubble to the surface.

• • •

INVOLUNTARY HOSTS: INTERNALIZED RACISM

Though several of the following points have been made in earlier sections, I'd like to delve more deeply into them here. Racism has spread well beyond the White population to infect many of the very people it was designed to oppress, further entrenching White-supremacy culture within the global community. When it spreads among communities of color, the "virus" mutates into the internalized oppression, or "internalized racism,"[637] as mentioned earlier. Put simply, internalized oppression is when marginalized folks consciously or unconsciously take on the mindset of those who exploit and oppress them.

In his book Decolonizing Wealth, social activist Edgar Villanueva refers to internalized oppression as "one of the darkest and most insidious results of the trauma of racism and colonization."[638] He further explains that "when you live inside of a system like this [White supremacy and colonialism], breathing the air, drinking the water, watching the television, it is . . . almost a given that you will absorb the myths and cultural stereotypes. You will be affected by it and infected by it." This is not simply a metaphor; in addition to potentially instilling a low sense of self-worth and beauty,[639] internalized racism has been linked to increased violence, including domestic abuse, within certain communities—namely Black and Native American populations. During a keynote address to the White Privilege Conference in 2017, American writer and activist Jacqueline Keeler, a woman of Dineh and Yankton Dakota heritage, explained, "Native people have the highest rates of suicide, poverty, rape and murder of any group within the United

States bar none. Young Native men have a suicide rate 9 times that over other young American men."⁶⁴⁰ Beyond a doubt, the beliefs and stereotypes that have long been perpetuated by White people about racial superiority have become internalized in many people of color, creating self-inflicted harm.

Through a brutal divide-and-conquer strategy (e.g., colonization, forced assimilation, and systemic oppression), White supremacy has instilled a strong desire in almost every population not to be at the bottom of the racial hierarchy, leading to hatred within, between, and among races—a phenomenon often referred to as horizontal oppression. That absolutely does not mean that people of color cannot also be prejudiced, biased, or downright hateful toward other groups of people; but racism is much bigger than just a negative feeling toward other people. Racism requires a distinct power differential backed by systematic oppression in order to thrive. In a 2021 interview with *Vox Magazine*, Scott Kurashige, professor and chair of comparative race and ethnic studies at Texas Christian University, reminded Americans, "What we need to realize is that there's this timeless structure, in which there's always one group on top and another at the bottom. . . . [T]his country has had a White supremacist ruling class structure since the beginning."⁶⁴¹ As a result of this "ruling class structure," oppressive attitudes toward and among other racial and ethnic groups often become a survival mechanism by which many immigrants hope to avoid being relegated further down the hierarchy (by White Americans).

Many immigrants, especially those arriving from Africa, feel pitted against multigenerational Black Americans, for fear of being labeled sympathetic, or even worse, cast among those at the bottom. Significant "conflict and tension between both [of these] groups result directly from the dominant White racial framing,"⁶⁴² describes sociologist and researcher Benjamin Aigbe Okonofua. "Groups unable to effectively challenge the forces that oppress them [often] attack themselves or people like themselves." Okonofua refers to this divisive hierarchy tactic of White supremacy as "manipulative deflection . . . [and] deprivation diminishes the construction of a holistic Black identity and produces confusion and conflict among Blacks in the United States."

Racism within and among communities of color is merely a symptom of the structures and beliefs that have defined America since day one, allowing racism to spread rampantly and proliferate in the White American psyche.

• • •

MASKING THE SYMPTOMS (I.E., COPING WITH WHITENESS)

Many well-meaning White folks undeniably want to put an end to White supremacy. Yet like so many other problems in Western society, rather than treat the actual cause, we end up trying to mask or manage the symptoms—in this case racism. Far too many passionate, progressive Americans attempt to merely fix any and all instances of racism they observe around them. Other, more moderate folks simply ignore it and hope that it will go away. A still growing portion of the population believes that "White supremacy culture"[643]—as described by writer, consultant, and activist Tema Okun—is a liberal hoax being foisted upon the American public by critical race theory–espousing socialists who want to destroy America for their own liberal agenda.

These three primary coping strategies are completely rooted in denial and cognitive dissonance and manifest as three distinct personas: radical patriots, radical liberals, and radical deniers.

• • •

RADICAL PATRIOTS

Radical patriots are perhaps the easiest to spot. Rather than hide, they make their presence and opinions known. They typically downplay while also blatantly denying and ignoring the negative parts of our country's history—or rudely suggest that we all just move on. They double down on their nationalism, worshipping the Constitution and singling out our nation as the bedrock of freedom and democracy.

Radical patriots glorify the Founding Fathers and their achievements. They pompously wave the American flag as a symbol of the greatest nation on earth, placing their hands over their hearts during the Pledge of Allegiance or standing self-importantly during the national anthem. Moreover, they expect others to do so as well and take it as a personal affront and insult to our "great" country when anyone chooses not to. Former San Francisco Forty-Niner's quarterback Colin Kaepernick—now a civil rights activist—unfortunately learned that the hard way.

Radical patriots not only suppress their own feelings that don't align with an inflated story of triumph and victory but also ignore and deny the feelings of others who feel that America has caused harm. Radical patriots tend to expect those who have been most oppressed by America to "get over it" and "pick themselves up by the bootstraps." Moreover, radical patriots expect that once these "defectors" and "troublemakers" see the error of their ways, they will do an about-face and come to love, respect, and join the American revelry.

Yet what so many radical patriots fail to recognize is that many of the people they consider disloyal have spent their entire lives wishing they could love America the way these radical patriots do—and that some of them have even learned to love America in spite of its innumerable flaws.

Ultimately, most radical patriots cannot, and likely will not, ever come to fully understand the erroneous nature of the binary beliefs that govern their understanding of themselves and the world they live in. Furthermore, if they were to try to see it from a different point of view, the reality would be too immense and painful to face—forcing them to question not only the world they live in but also their values and their fundamental sense of America itself. It would also call into question their racial identity and understanding of Whiteness. That is something that most radical patriots are not yet capable of facing and why they remain radical patriots despite the limitless truths in front of their eyes.

Even further along this end of the spectrum are those who proudly spout their White-supremacy beliefs. We know these people; many of them fill our history books, are celebrated with giant bronze statues, and, unfortunately, sometimes sit at our dinner tables. "Don't tread on me!" "Build the wall!" "Blood and soil!" "Go back home!" These folks are not merely racist but also openly so and proud of it. Or in the words of two-time former governor of New York and presidential candidate Horatio Seymour, in 1868, "This is a white man's country: Let white men rule."[644]

For the most part, this unapologetic version of racism was forced underground after the civil rights movement and suppressed to the outer fringes of conservative politics prior to the 2016–2020 Trump administration. Many of these folks met in secret, hid behind keyboards, and, every so often, were caught on a video that went viral. However, during the Trump era, the lines between radical patriotism and radical racism became more blurred, and they remain dangerously intertwined. While many steadfast radical patriots would not consider themselves at all racist, nor condone the actions of those who are, they certainly share a common form of delusional thinking.

Radical patriots avoid all feelings of self-hate by blaming "other" people for all of their problems. American psychiatrist and best-selling author M. Scott Peck commonly used a term in the 1970s that aptly explains those who fall into the radical patriot category:

"character disordered." In *The Road Less Traveled*, Peck explains how "those with character disorders are in conflict with the world and they automatically assume that the world is at fault. . . . [They] are much more difficult, if not impossible, to work with [in therapy] because . . . they see the world rather than themselves as being in need of change and therefore fail to recognize the necessity for self-examination."[645] Consequently, while these radical patriots outwardly appear bold and proud, many live in fear, distrust, and hatred. Some even fall into the conspiratorial realm, losing touch with reality altogether and getting pulled into the likes of Q-Anon and "Pizzagate."

These types of White Americans fail to recognize that they are the primary cause of their own psychological distress. They try to soothe fears that *their* America is slipping away by holding fast to prejudices and biases, believing that the problem is "out there" and can and should be dealt with. They vehemently defend their turf from those they assume to be the cause of their suffering. But this psychological distress is attached to the inherent neurosis caused in large part by Whiteness itself.

True White supremacists incorrectly assume that reestablishing America as a White Christian nation would alleviate the fear, distrust, and hatred they are "forced" to experience. The irony is that if this nightmare scenario were to happen, the people causing the fear, distrust, and hatred would likely be the only ones left.

● ● ●

RADICAL LIBERALS

Also known as bleeding-heart liberals, radical liberals typically go in the opposite direction of radical patriots, trying to assuage their guilt by rejecting America and often their own Whiteness. They want to rebuild American democracy to include everyone and give a voice to all. They want America to fully own its part in the suffering of other people, both past and present, while working toward living out what they assume to be the "true meaning of its creed" that "all [people] are created equal." While on the surface, this may seem valiant and selfless, beneath it lie motives fueled primarily by denial and guilt.

Ironically, just like radical patriots, radical liberals are quick to see the problem "out there" but often fail to recognize the problem within. They consider themselves crusaders of social justice and an ally to all, remaining blind to their complicity as well as direct responsibility for the hierarchical way America remains structured. In a 2009 paper titled "Toward a Radical White Identity," Susan Goldberg and Cameron Levin, members of Los Angeles–based anti-racism organization AWARE-LA, describe how these folks typically view "racism as the problem itself rather than a tool of a greater system. . . . [R]acism is seen as the source of racial oppression" rather than as a tool.[646]

Because of this overly simplistic point of view, radical liberals tend to focus too much on undoing individual racial prejudices, without addressing the deliberate structural and systemic barriers that uphold racism (often to their own economic benefit). "This means that in the liberal model there are [only] two roles: oppressor and oppressed," describe Goldberg and Levin. It becomes common for radical liberals in America to assume that they are part of the solution (that they are the "good guys" in the fight against racism) and therefore it is their duty to help "fix" others to fix the system.

Many of these self-proclaimed social justice warriors become completely consumed by "call-out" culture, taking it upon themselves to point out every single instance of prejudice that occurs around them, unable to see that constantly pointing out the symptoms does not solve the bigger problem. In many cases, this leads to overly politically correct, censored spaces that mask the underlying biases and prejudices still residing in the minds of those now too afraid to speak. Not only can this lead to a "counterproductive culture in activist spaces," but it can also backfire by "reinforcing [underlying] fear-based right-wing and White nationalist messaging."[647]

While many radical liberals stand guard, eager to verbally attack a complete stranger for the slightest hint of prejudicial speech or behavior, many remain completely silent when confronted with a situation in which racism is being exhibited by a close friend or family member. In these instances, radical liberals often shut down and default to "White solidarity" (i.e., going along with the oppressive energy in order to not be outcast from the group or cause problems).[648] This stems from a hypocritical desire not to make things uncomfortable or awkward with those close to us.

Instead, radical liberals primarily channel their focus far outside of their own circle, in a broad, sweeping attempt to "fix" what they can't rectify within themselves or those closest to them. They immerse themselves in social causes, have lengthy discussions about racial equality—primarily with other White people—read dozens of books about race, and seek out opportunities to be seen in a "good light" by their peers as well as by people of color. Many try so hard to be politically correct in front of BIPOC folks that conversations end up feeling superficial and unnatural.

When these White folks do wake up to their complicit involvement and unconscious biases, things tend to get worse before they get better. In a 2021 op-ed titled "The Nightmare of the Newly Woke," Melissa DePino, author and founder of Privilege to Progress, a national movement to desegregate the public conversation about race, describes this phenomena in striking detail:

> There's this thing that happens when we white people first start to realize that racism is not just something outside of ourselves, but embedded in the way we see and move through the world, that it's both inside of us and all around us. First

we're shocked and overwhelmed, then we read our first book and decide we're experts. We "understand" the complexities of systemic oppression. We "get it." We quickly become arrogant, self-important. We spew our newfound knowledge to everyone we encounter. We are evangelists! We start antiracism Instagram accounts and make TikToks confessing to the world that we're racist. We speak for Black people in their spaces, defending them like they don't have the agency or capacity to do it themselves. We condescend like the white saviors we are. We put our performative fists in the air in what we think is solidarity. And we are judgmental, shaming, and self-righteous to other white people who are, in truth, no worse than we are.[649]

DePino's spot-on analysis of the "newly woke" gives credence to the fact that most White folks don't do ourselves any favors when it comes to earning the trust of our BIPOC peers. Many people of color have expressed feeling not only unheard and invalidated by radical liberals but also unsafe around this particular type of White person, primarily because that person either cannot see or simply denies their own privilege and racism. By assuming that they are an ally to all, radical liberals are much more likely to commit frequent microaggressions and unconsciously act in their own best interests. Salina Gray, a member of a cross-racial activism organization called the Racial Justice Alliance (RJA), describes her sentiments as a Black woman around these types of White people:

> I'm very uncomfortable when people walk on the proverbial pins and needles around me. . . . So, for me, I'd be more comfortable hanging out with an avowed racist than a bunch of mainstream whites who claim to be down, because claiming to be down often means to be culturally assimilated. Often, it's them using language that they feel will make me comfortable,

it's doing and having interests they feel will allow me to accept them as a black person instead of a white person.[650]

Beyond simply vying for acceptance, many radical liberals assume that deference is an automatic sign of solidarity. Performative measures often end up superseding self-awareness and the deep inner work of true anti-oppression. All too often, their words speak louder than their actions.

Many feel like they are doing their part by simply putting a rainbow sign in the front yard that reads: "In this house, we believe that Black Lives Matter, women's rights are human rights, no human is illegal, science is real, water is life, in religious freedom, love is love, kindness is everything."[651] Never mind the fact that 95 percent of those signs are in front of three-story homes in predominantly White neighborhoods that Black folks do not feel comfortable walking through.[652] Also problematic is the fact that a sign that sandwiches "Black Lives Matter" among other quintessential liberal beliefs (belief in science, religious freedom, etc.) diminishes the urgency and importance of the movement—effectively making it appear that Black Lives Matter can be taken for granted. While these are all noble beliefs, slapping them together on one sign and displaying them for the world to see is about as effective as saying, "I don't see color." For those who choose a sign that only says, "Black Lives Matter" and assume that they are off the hook, the old saying "Actions speak louder than words" still stands true.

To be fair, the original creators of the "rainbow belief" signs are donating all proceeds to the ACLU (American Civil Liberties Union). While this is undoubtedly a noble cause, it unfortunately furthers the notion that radical liberals have the luxury of simply stating our beliefs, donating money to charities and advocacy groups, voting, and maybe going to a few protests a year—at which point we feel like we have done our part in ending racism, discrimination, and oppression.

But for any of us to really start addressing the problem, we have to turn the lens inward. Trying to root out one's own racism is incredibly painful, bringing up untold amounts of shame, guilt, and self-hate that many of us are not prepared to handle (or, more often, refuse to acknowledge). Many White folks are unwilling to acknowledge our privilege and are afraid of what we might find within.

Instead, we are more comfortable with employing the most common coping strategy: radical denial.

• • •

RADICAL DENIERS

Radical deniers are those who claim they don't have a racist bone in their bodies. Folks who identify as liberal or moderate on the political spectrum often fall into this camp. They get to have their cake and eat it too. Not only do they get to deny their own complicity/role in upholding structural racism, but they also get to reap the benefits of White privilege, without the guilt—feeling like they've got no skin in the game (pun intended). They go about their lives, oblivious to how their comfort and privilege is directly tied to someone else's suffering and oppression.

Although there are some folks who are genuinely in denial even to the point of "ignorant bliss," many radical deniers are plagued by an underlying sense that something is off. They often suffer the same neuroses as the radical liberals who actively push back against their Whiteness and American exceptionalism.

Yet racist-avoidant White folks are not victims. In fact, both radical liberals and radical deniers are often some of the most insidious upholders of systemic racism. This is the type of racism that cannot be seen by those who wield it but can still be felt by those whom it effects and toward whom it is directed. Publisher and former journalist John Blake explains, "[These] progressive folks in Blue states, the kind who would have voted for Obama a third time if they could—are some of the most tenacious supporters of systemic racism . . . because their targets can't see their racism coming—and often, neither can they. These people are often motived by unconscious racism they are loathe to admit and disguise their racial hostility with innocuous-sounding terms like 'neighborhood schools' and 'property values.'"[653] This type of racism fuels misguided public policy and creates a lack of understanding, empathy, and compassion toward those whom radical liberals and radical deniers claim to see as equals.

Both radical deniers' and radical liberals' conversations and daily interactions are laden with mistaken beliefs, prejudices, and biases that slip by unnoticed by many other White folks. They support integration but live in homogenous neighborhoods. They appreciate diversity but only on their terms. Many vote progressively but don't want to sacrifice anything to ensure that such measures gain real political traction.

All too often, those who claim immunity to racism surround themselves with likeminded people and unwittingly spread and encourage "colorblindness." Many deniers go so far as to claim that we are living in a post-racial America where everyone can succeed if they just try hard enough (i.e., the "meritocracy myth").

This viewpoint is delusional, shortsighted, and effectively sabotages the chances for people of color to be granted equal access. Those who choose racism blinders will continue to unknowingly perpetuate the beliefs, systems, and ideas that uphold and strengthen White supremacy in America.

● ● ●

CAN WHITENESS EVER BECOME GOOD?

Is it possible to redefine or remold Whiteness in a way that detaches it from the inherent connotation of racial superiority it currently holds? Can we make a "cleaner" version than what it has historically proven about us?

Simple answer: no.

I would argue that trying to rebrand or recreate Whiteness into something good is about as futile as putting cotton balls on a porcupine to make it feel safer. The reality is that Whiteness is built upon privilege, power, and exploitation. To dismantle that definition and replace it with something positive is nearly impossible. It doesn't matter how many layers of cotton balls we add; the core of Whiteness remains sharp and dangerous.

This *does not* mean that White folks are incapable of doing exceptional amounts of good and making positive changes in the world when it comes to racial justice. However, those who choose to use our privilege for good are doing so despite our Whiteness. We are swimming upstream by using our Whiteness as leverage to open doors for others. Therefore, altruism exhibited by individual White people or groups of anti-racist White people is by no means a positive net gain for Whiteness, nor does it help redeem Whiteness as a whole. It instead further proves that there is something fundamentally wrong with Whiteness. Why else would people have to work so hard to dismantle it? These acts of altruism are subversive to the very power differential that Whiteness was designed to uphold.

In a sense, Whiteness demands to be treated as an entity in and of itself. Because of the nature of both how and why it was created in the first place, Whiteness does not like to be challenged. Moreover, it does not like to give away any of its control, authority, influence, or power. On the contrary, while many of its members are trying to dismantle it from within, Whiteness as a collective entity continues to siphon power back to itself—because that is what it was designed to do.

This is not about blaming individual White people or even White people in general. We did not, nor can we, choose to be white. Rather, Whiteness drafted many of our ancestors to help uphold a brutal caste system that benefits a small segment of the population under the guise of promising us protection, access, privilege, and a chance of gaining power and wealth ourselves.

The more we (White folks) support and empower those outside of our own race, the more we demonstrate precisely what Whiteness has unfairly taken from them. In essence, we are working against Whiteness to give back stolen power and wealth. Consequently, well-meaning White individuals or groups who commit selfless acts to restore power to those outside of our tribe are initiating a coup.

Whiteness is ultimately fragile at its core. Deep down, it knows that without a consistent source of stolen power, loyalty, and complacency, it will be exposed as the corrupt and narcissistic monarch it really is. More importantly, as is the case with any powerful sovereign with a fear-based reign, the fall from power is anything but graceful—and Whiteness will continuously lash out to maintain control over not only those it oppresses but also those within the monarchy whom it deems traitorous to our race.

While many of us are well versed on White privilege as a passive form of unfair advantage, this tyrannical version of our collective Whiteness (i.e., the core of White supremacy) is painful to accept. It challenges our unmerited status but also our sense of identity. So, the question remains: Is it even possible to remedy our oppressive throne? Is it possible not only to simply expose the corrupt core of Whiteness but also to consciously work toward dismantling its power altogether?

One way to do this might be for us to begin to refer to our Whiteness as what it really is.

• • •

RESTORING WHITE TO ITS "INTENDED" MEANING

What would it be like if the label "White" conveyed the full power of its meaning? What if every time someone referred to me as White, it automatically implied that I was a knowing participant in the systematic oppression of others for my own gain?

While this may seem unreasonable or even outlandish, consider that this is not actually changing the meaning of the word but rather resurrecting its original purpose and intent. To be called White simply means that we have (or at least have access to the possibility of achieving) status, wealth, power, and privilege above those who are not considered White—simply by being a member of a fictitious social category.

I am not necessarily advocating that we stop calling ourselves White, nor that the term "White" is evil, per se. I am, however, suggesting that we start owning what our title *really* means. It is time to acknowledge that the label itself embodies a racist connotation. This racial label should not be divorced from the cruelty and inhumanity it stems from. Otherwise, we will continue to ignore that Whiteness was founded entirely on racial subjugation.

● ● ●

A HYPOTHETICAL CONUNDRUM: LETTING OUR WHITENESS GO

This begs a hypothetical question in three parts: Would it even be possible for our society, or for the world, to fully let go of the label "White" itself? Would White people be willing to do so? And if the answer were yes, would it accomplish anything?

To let go of the term "White" obviously would not solve the current problems caused by Whiteness. However, going with this hypothetical for a moment, making the simple shift toward something different—such as European American—could at least be an acknowledgment that the label "White" holds an inherently racist connotation, therefore making it more of a slur than an innocuous term used to describe one's racial identity.

Hypothetically, "White" could be restored to highlight the cruelty and inhumanity that someone *can* possess when they choose to willingly enact their power and privilege. If this were to happen, "White" would no longer be just another racial category. It would be reinstated to its original intended meaning, with the correct supremacy connotations attached to it.

While this may seem like a matter of semantics, letting go of the word "White" doesn't mean simply replacing it with another politically correct term to try to restore balance, feel better, or relieve the burden we've put upon others. It could instead signal a conscious shift and acknowledgment of our inherently oppressive racial identity.

That said, there are some significant flaws in this hypothetical scenario. For one, this would not work if it only occurred on an individual level, like when White people misguidedly try to adopt the term "Caucasian" to be more politically correct. Making this shift would require a full acknowledgment not only by most of the world's White-identifying population but also, more importantly, by those in power.

Political and religious leaders would have to fully concede to the inherent racism built into the core of Whiteness. They would need to unanimously call it out for what it is, as well as take ownership of ongoing transgressions committed in its name. Otherwise, a different label would simply represent another way of letting ourselves off the hook and disassociating ourselves from the wrongdoings of Whiteness, thereby adding insult to injury.

Ultimately, this remains a problematic hypothetical. Whether or not we choose to someday relabel ourselves, which is entirely possible given the ever-evolving labels on the census, it is more important to ask ourselves how we unfairly benefit from Whiteness today.

In that case, what about just getting rid of race altogether? Not likely. To completely dismantle our understanding of ourselves as racial beings would require a fundamental shift in consciousness that is next to impossible. Redefining our sense of identity and letting go of our place in society—a place we have painstakingly created and defended for centuries—is not something that many White people are prepared, nor willing, to endure.

There is no guarantee that the White race is going to remain in power indefinitely. As our textbooks often remind us, it is difficult to gauge which side of history we are on until a major shift has occurred within a given civilization. Who knows? Thousands of years from now, a more developed civilization may look back on the entire White race as a barbaric primitive people, similar to the way many of us now view Columbus and his men as pillagers and plunderers. (I'm sure there are plenty of White historians who would still disagree with me on this last sentiment.)

Thus far, history has been written by the winners, and White people have declared ourselves as such. Yet as globalization moves *our* civilization forward (often begrudgingly), there will be inevitable consequences in how the world views us and how others respond to and treat us. White America exudes a false sense of normalcy. We are like the iconic neighbors with the big house, beautiful yard, three-car garage, and white picket fence that suffers immensely behind closed doors. What we display to the outside world does not scratch the surface of what's hiding underneath.

It may appear that Whiteness is serving its intended lucrative purpose while keeping White people immune from its harmful side effects, but our Whiteness leads to numerous collateral consequences to our mental and spiritual health.

Let me be clear: This is not about having pity on ourselves.

There is much more at stake. Without healing our own racial trauma, White people don't stand a chance of stopping the ongoing harm caused by Whiteness and racism in America.

CHAPTER 20

Tortured and Traumatized

THE INVENTION OF WHITENESS and its compulsory racism comes at a heavy cost. The fear, hatred, paranoia, biases, prejudices, nationalism, and xenophobia fueled by intergenerational trauma, neuroticism, self-hatred, guilt, and loss of identity are just a few of these unintended symptoms. In recounting one of his early memories in the 2013 book *Combined Destinies: Whites Sharing Grief about Racism*, an anonymous writer (a.k.a. Bob) describes his experiences growing up in a racist family in the South.

In trying to make sense of his father, a devout Christian minister, having a catastrophic nervous breakdown, Bob explains, "Dad's participation and membership in the Ku Klux Klan (KKK), was without a doubt the primary cause of his breakdown. You can't be a minister of the gospel and practice racial hatred without paying a significant psychological price."[654] Bob describes how the White South remains big on appearance and propriety as a way of compensating for the prevalence of significant mental illness throughout the population: "Southern families have always been famous for the bachelor uncle or maiden aunt locked away in the attic wearing Confederate gray or antebellum gowns.... Southern writers have mined this trove for decades." Mental illness remains scandalous and shameful in many parts of the South, keeping this side of Whiteness deliberately out of view.

However, this is not a Northern versus Southern debate. This is part of the White American psyche. Through years of stolen land, genocide, slavery, and ongoing exploitative labor practices, police brutality, and mass incarceration, many White Americans have remained willfully unconscious of the psychological price of oppressing entire populations of other people for our material benefit. Yet in the last decade, more White Americans have become plagued by guilt, self-hatred, and fear. The more we learn about our past, the more unsettled we often feel with our country, our beliefs, and our sense of self.

There is a common saying in the therapy world that speaks to the current state of White America: "Hurt people hurt people." In other words, the pain that we have internalized is being taken out on ourselves as well as those around us. This absolutely does not excuse our, or our ancestors', behavior. It is merely a call to awareness: we need to bring context to how our country has become so psychologically screwed up.

So, what do I mean by "hurt people"? To understand how America got to where it is socially, politically, etc., we must understand how we got here psychology. I am referring to the things that drove us to flee our homelands hundreds of years ago and the psychological damage we unknowingly brought with us.

Acknowledging the collective story of our ancestors' transition from Europe to America through the lens of Whiteness, racism, and oppression is the first step in understanding how to mitigate the harms of White supremacy and toward healing from the multigenerational trauma that has wreaked havoc on our civilization. The stakes have never been higher.

Racism, misogyny, capitalism, and America are inextricably interconnected—and until we understand how the parts overlap, we are becoming more and more likely to witness the downfall of a country rife with trauma, hatred, and delusion.

● ● ●

TORTURED SOULS

The history of Whiteness is overflowing with (almost) unbelievable acts of racist and misogynistic barbarity, subjugation, and oppression. Even before our European ancestors arrived in America, many of them had already witnessed and partaken in unspeakable acts while living in Europe.

In his groundbreaking book *My Grandmother's Hands: Racialized Trauma and the Path to Mending Our Hearts and Bodies*, Resmaa Menakem devotes an entire chapter to this very subject. He draws on the work of numerous authors and historians to describe Europe as a brutal and primitive world full of pain, suffering, fear, and trauma. This was especially the case in England, America's primary locale of "parental" lineage.

To say that England was a disturbing place to live during the sixteenth and seventeenth centuries would be an understatement. Public torture and execution were enthusiastically utilized by religious zealots and ruling tyrants as a common deterrent against crime, treason, and heresy. The iron maiden was only one of many hellish devices used for these purposes. Part of the Tower of London itself was used as a huge torture chamber.[655]

This type of treatment was par for the course throughout many parts of Europe. Besides providing a carnal form of entertainment (like the gruesome events staged in the Colosseum two millennia prior), blood spectacle served a purpose. There was a thriving transfer market for public executions in England, according to historian Sean McGylnn. Powerful men would bid to stage these events in front of their homes and subjects to instill fear and maintain law and order.[656]

Religious persecution also inflicted untold amounts of trauma, as Puritans and other "less than desirable" Christians were dragged behind carts, branded with hot irons on their tongues and foreheads, or had their noses split in half or their ears cut off.[657]

It wasn't only torture that made Europe such a hostile place. As overseas colonization became more prevalent, wealthy Europeans began to snatch up public lands previously worked by serfs, in hopes of building fortunes on the privatization of land use. From roughly 1550 to 1650, the wealthy began a forced exodus of peasants into already overcrowded cities—an ongoing global phenomenon as large corporations continue to "acquire" rural farmers' land and force them into cities.[658] Women were especially targeted. Within most of the small farming societies, women not only had been given more rights but also served integral roles, even as leaders. A concerted effort was carried out to ensure that these "pagan" women were stripped of all power.

In a 2021 article titled "Roots Deeper than Whiteness," David Dean describes,

> Witch-hunts [became] a tool of this cultural revolution and the movement to take away the commons. Hundreds of thousands, if not millions, of women were tortured and killed throughout Europe. . . . Particularly autonomous women were in the greatest danger of persecution. Herbalists and traditional healers, widows and the unmarried, and outspoken community leaders were regularly targeted. Mass government-run propaganda campaigns led peasants to fear one another, effectively dividing and weakening them against the threat of enclosure.[659]

This deliberate erasure of powerful women further ensured that patriarchy became a centralized form of leadership in Europe. It also served to erase the traditional beliefs, folklore, and customs that were often handed down by women in smaller societies. "During this time, the isolated nuclear family and women's inherent inferiority were also emphasized," and powerful women and healers became associated with the devil, describes Dean.

As more people were forced into cities, daily life became more horrific. It was considered normal for adults and children alike to see chained, bound, and flogged prisoners, mutilated hanging corpses, as well as severed heads and mangled body parts impaled on spikes around city walls.[660] These grotesque displays served as a daily reminder of what happened to people who disobeyed those in charge.

Poverty, starvation, sickness (including the Great Plague), suffering, war, and death molded our ancestors' lives. "Communities were traumatized and splintered," describes Dean. "The fortunate [so to speak] worked in urban textile mills under grueling conditions . . . . Most were not so lucky and lived on city streets as beggars at a time when loitering and petty theft were punished with physical mutilation, years of incarceration, or death."[661] Across multiple generations, many of our European ancestors witnessed and experienced things that left them mentally and physically scarred for the rest of their lives.

While millions were suffering throughout Europe, those who attempted to escape often didn't fare much better. Despite what we were told in school, many of them sought not religious freedom but rather a chance at economic success.

● ● ●

THE INDENTURED AND INDEBTED PILGRIMS

The fairy-tale version of the Pilgrims setting sail aboard the *Mayflower* in 1620 to escape religious persecution is not exactly accurate.

Most of the Pilgrims were seeking economic prosperity. They were fleeing the Thirty Years' War tearing through Europe, mass overcrowding, disease, and economic hardship. Many of the Pilgrims had already "enjoyed" religious freedom for over a decade in the Dutch city of Leiden before deciding to come to America.

After escaping England in 1608 in pursuit of religious freedom, they had been given full permission to worship however they wished in Leiden.[662]

Yet despite having achieved religious freedom, most of the soon-to-be *Mayflower* refugees lived in extreme poverty, working grueling hours making textiles with little pay. William Bradford, a Pilgrim leader living in Holland at that time, wrote that many of those still suffering religious persecution back in England "preferred and chose the prisons in England rather than this liberty in Holland with these afflictions."[663]

When the Pilgrims finally chose to leave for America, it was primarily with the intent of making money and owning their own land. But having accumulated no wealth after nearly twelve years of labor, they were forced to come up with a way to finance the expensive journey across the Atlantic. They had no supplies, no seafaring experience, and no boat—certainly a key requirement for traveling across an entire ocean.

But the Pilgrims were in luck, or so they thought. Wealthy investors across Europe were looking for ways to capitalize on the seemingly endless supply of resources being brought back from other lands. The English East India Company, founded in 1600, had become a lucrative source of stolen wealth from the East, and many wealthy Europeans were eager to establish the same in the West. In fact, by 1610, ten years before the Pilgrims began their fateful voyage, "Britain alone had about 200 vessels operating off Newfoundland and New England [while] hundreds more came from France, Spain, Portugal and Italy,"[664] estimates author and historian Horace Mann.

Those who attempted to set up trading posts did so with little success, as the land was already "thickly settled and well defended" by Indigenous peoples. That would soon change due to warfare and disease. Yet these failed attempts did not deter many investors, who still clamored to claim new land and capitalize on overseas wealth.

By deliberately maintaining deplorable living and working conditions in the slums, powerful merchants further incentivized displaced farmers to agree to oppressive terms of servitude overseas in exchange for the potential of owning land in the new colonies. Yet "even with this mixture of urban poverty, hyper-criminalization, and merchant campaigns to encourage the poor to go to overseas colonies as indentured servants, only some willingly left their home country,"[665] describes David Dean. Over the course of decades, tens of thousands of people were shipped to the new colonies against their will, beholden to overseas contracts that kept them in debt:

> The Virginia Company, a corporation with investors and executives intent on profiting from the theft of labor and foreign land, began collaborating with the English government to develop a solution to the problems of unemployment and vagrancy. Homeless and incarcerated women, men, and even children, began to be rounded up and put on ships headed to the plantation colony of Virginia to be bought and traded by wealthy British royalists. . . . [O]f the nearly 75,000 English indentured servants brought to British colonies in the seventeenth century[,] most were taken against their will.[666]

In the case of the Pilgrims, however, they saw a chance for mutual benefit and sought out one of these companies to finance their passage.

A wealthy joint-stock enterprise known as the Merchant Adventurers—an investing firm of over seventy London businessmen—decided to take a bet on this group of eager entrepreneurs. While the Pilgrims seized the opportunity, this would prove to be nearly catastrophic for the overly ambitious and ill-prepared group, who were now contractually bound to pay back their investors in full for not only the ship but also the crew and a whole year's worth of supplies.[667]

Moreover, the Pilgrims had to agree to work exclusively for the Merchant Adventures for seven years upon arrival, sending back ships full of resources, including fur, timber, and fish—only after which would each male colonist over the age of sixteen receive a share of the company itself and no longer be contractually bound. In order to make an even larger return on their investment, the Merchant Adventures forced the Pilgrims to take along with them a group of complete strangers who were also seeking to start a new life and make money. This created strife and disagreement during the voyage as some of these unwelcome newcomers on the ship attempted to weasel their way out of the contract.

When the Pilgrims and their tagalongs finally set sail in July 1620, they were forced to turn back twice because the first ship they were traveling on, the *Speedwell*, promptly began leaking. Author and historian Charles C. Mann says, in a 2005 piece published in the *Smithsonian* magazine, "The Pilgrims' lack of preparation was typical.... [While] expeditions from France and Spain were usually backed by the state, and generally staffed by soldiers accustomed to hard living, English voyages, by contrast, were almost always funded by venture capitalists who hoped for a quick cash-out."[668] I guess it should come as no surprise that the founding of America was funded by greedy venture capitalists who wrote up exploitative contracts and cut corners, hoping to make a quick buck; especially seeing as not much has changed.

The *Mayflower*, now an iconic American namesake, was simply a backup for the leaky *Speedwell*. But their leaky ship was an omen of things to come.

Charles Mann reveals that the Pilgrims made another critical error in judgment before setting sail: "The Pilgrims had refused to hire [none other than] the experienced John Smith [a.k.a. the Pocahontas kidnapper, whose real name was John Rolfe][669] as a guide, on the theory that they could simply use the maps in his book. In consequence, as Smith later crowed, the hapless *Mayflower* spent several frigid weeks scouting Cape Cod for a good place to land, during which time many colonists became sick and died."[670] When the Pilgrims finally found a suitable location after a grueling sixty-six-day journey, things quickly went from bad to worse.

By the time the freezing, sick, and starving Pilgrims finally set foot on land, many of them were desperate and afraid. They stumbled upon an abandoned Indigenous village, where they immediately "dug open burial sites and ransacked homes, looking for underground stashes of food. After two days of nervous work, the company hauled ten bushels of maize back to the *Mayflower*,"[671] where they hunkered down, hoping to survive the winter. Far from the fruits of a triumphant arrival or a Thanksgiving feast, the first sustenance for America's founders was excavated from sacred burial sites and abandoned villages.

Despite their best attempts at gathering food and staying warm aboard the ship, only half of the 106 people on the *Mayflower* survived their first winter in America, with 14 of the 19 women succumbing to disease and exposure.[672] There numbers were so few that nearly four centuries later, it has been estimated that as many as ten million Americans are descendants of the fifty-three survivors.[673]

Had it not been for a few Native Americans taking pity on the disease-ridden refugees, this group of helpless settlers would very likely have perished. If anything, the story of Thanksgiving, which *supposedly* took place the next fall in celebration of their first successful harvest (all thanks to the Native Americans), should really be a day of gratitude for those Indigenous people who took pity on our ancestors and paid the ultimate price.

Fatefully, the Indigenous village that the Pilgrims had stumbled upon was one of a multitude of abandoned villages along the New England coast. Beginning in the early 1600s, earlier explorers and traders, including John Rolfe, unknowingly brought multiple pathogens to the Natives, which spread rampantly. A single disease that arrived from Europe in 1616 had killed off close to 90 percent of the coastal inhabitants there.[674] This means that the primary reason the Pilgrims had a place to live and any available food was that earlier arrivals had unintentionally killed off tens of thousands of Indigenous peoples, most of the remainder of which had fled further along the coast or inland, unknowingly carrying these diseases with them and killing tens of thousands more.

Even more tragic was that the new arrivals simply assumed that the ongoing deaths of their Indigenous hosts was a sign that God himself favored their arrival. As described by Charles Mann, newly elected Plymouth colony governor "[William] Bradford is said to have attributed the plague to 'the good hand of God,' which 'favored our beginnings' . . . sweeping away great multitudes of the natives . . . that he might make room for us."[675] This so-called favoritism led to over fifty of the original colonial settlements being established directly upon abandoned Native villages.

This was a common assumption at that time. An earlier explorer, Ferdinando Gorges, who set out from Maine to Massachusetts in 1619, had independently concluded the same thing, decreeing that the land had been left "without any [people] to disturb or appease our free and peaceable possession thereof . . . we may justly conclude, that GOD made the way [to do] his work."[676] By 1633, somewhere between a third to half of all of New England's Indigenous peoples had been wiped out by European diseases. Nonetheless, even with the support of the early Natives who did not succumb to disease, "God's work" proved challenging for the Pilgrims.

Had they not "discovered" a bounty of beavers "readily available" to be slaughtered for pelts in this new land, they would not have been able to pay back their investors. "As a business enterprise . . . [t]he Plymouth Colony barely survived, let alone thrived, after a brutal first winter in America, and the *Mayflower* returned to England empty of commodities,"[677] describes author and historian Christopher Klein in a 2020 article in *History Magazine*. Several other ships that were sent to bring back resources were subsequently sunk or captured by pirates. This did not please the venture capitalists back in England, who had now invested significantly more money in hopes of a long-term return.

Rather than the initial seven-year contract, it took the Pilgrims nearly three decades to pay off their staggering debt to the Merchant Adventurers back in London—and they were only able to do so because of the help they received from the Indigenous populations and the soaring demand for pelts back in Europe. Moreover, by the time they finally managed to settle their debt, multiple other "investment voyages" with far more manpower, skills, and resources had also staked their claim in the booming fur trade, quickly overpowering the small Plymouth enterprise. The Plymouth colony itself was eventually swallowed up by a large corporate entity that became the Province of Massachusetts Bay in 1691. One need look no further than this to prove that America was founded on capitalism, not religious freedom.

Disease and a complete lack of basic survival skills is not all that these Pilgrims brought with them to early America. They brought their beliefs, their experiences, and their trauma. It didn't take long for many of the early "freedom-seeking" settlers to revert to the trauma-driven ways and lifestyles they had inherited back home. In addition to hostile actions against Native Americans, many began imposing familiar forms of abuse and punishment as their colonies grew. Just as it had been in Europe, public torture and execution became the primary means of exerting power and control as corporate entities gobbled up more and more "open land" to create large farming operations or extract raw materials—the very things early Americans were fleeing from.

Many early settlers were so disenchanted with their condition of corporate servitude that they ran away in droves. David Dean explains that in the early days in the Jamestown colony, roughly "one in seven Englishmen fled to live within the more egalitarian

Tsenacomoco or Powhatan Confederacy."[678] To stop this from occurring, the Virginia Company enacted a decree called Laws Divine, Moral, and Martial, "threatening execution for desertion in order 'to keep English settlers and Native Americans apart.'" Despite this, many were willing to risk death rather than be bound by the terms of servitude that were laying the foundations for what would later evolve into outright chattel slavery.

• • •

> Note: Trigger warning! The following section contains descriptions of extreme acts of racial violence.

TRAUMA TRAVELS, BLOODLUST ABOUNDS

These early settlers who came to North America hoping to find a better life ultimately brought their "baggage" with them. As the old saying goes, "Wherever you go, there you are" (which roughly translates in this context to "If you dislike yourself and/or have unresolved trauma, it follows you wherever you go until you are willing to deal with it"). Not surprisingly, the pain that many of the early settlers had both witnessed and experienced back in Europe was then taken out on others—especially those they enslaved.

While White Americans inflicted untold amounts of psychological harm upon our entire society during nearly three centuries of slavery, the bloodlust did not stop in 1865. Public torture and execution became a mainstay in many Southern towns and cities. Historian Leon F. Litwack estimates "that between 1882 and 1968, at least 4,742 African Americans were murdered"[679] by public lynching. To put that in perspective, that is one legally sanctioned murder every week for over eighty-five consecutive years. Black Americans were regularly lynched, riddled with bullets, burned alive, and dragged through the streets. These gruesome spectacles would draw crowds in the thousands—including young children, who quickly became desensitized to the gruesome sights. Victims had fingers and toes cut off one by one, skin peeled from their bodies and faces, or were repeatedly dipped into a bonfire.

"At their worst, lynching were episodes of sunlit municipal sadism,"[680] describes journalist Richard Lacayo in a 2000 *Time* magazine article. "Newspapers announced the time and place in advance. Excursion trains were organized to move crowds to the scene. At the wilder scenes, the crowd egged itself on into a frenzy beyond imagining."

In one such instance in Southeast Alabama, a Black peanut farmer named Claude Neal was accused of the murder of a young White woman. On October 26, 1936, a lynch mob broke him out of jail and drove him almost 200 miles to the town of the murder, where he was tortured for nearly twelve hours before his limp body was dragged behind a car to the front of the deceased victim's home. Southern railroad companies deployed multiple trains to transport people from eleven states to witness this blood spectacle.[681]

By the time Neal's body arrived at the victim's home, as many as 7,000 people were eagerly awaiting the brutal display. A woman ran out and plunged a butcher knife into Neal's heart as the crowd descended upon his remains, kicking, stomping, and even driving their cars over his body. Little children took part as well, using sharpened sticks to jab the mutilated corpse. The mob finally rejoiced as Neal's body was hoisted high in the middle of the town square, a trophy for all to see.[682]

Claude Neal is one of countless victims of White bloodlust in the American South after the Civil War. Others were repeatedly dipped into large bonfires, had their skin peeled off, or had corkscrews used to tear out chunks of flesh. During these grisly events, vigilante capturers, executioners, and spectators would gather pieces of the victims' remains as morbid souvenirs to take home with them.[683]

Even more disturbing is that photographers often fought to be the first on the scene, receiving tips ahead of time. Hundreds of White families insisted on having their pictures taken with the mangled remains. Eventually, these photographers began installing portable on-site printing stations to make souvenir postcards for families to send to their relatives. Execution scenes became an entire category of the postcard industry. Journalist Isabel Wilkerson explains, "By 1908, the trade had grown so large, and the practice of sending postcards featuring the victims of mob murders had become so repugnant, that the US postmasters general banned the cards from the mail."[684] This did little to stop the burgeoning industry, however, as envelopes became an easy workaround.

Whether they were on the receiving or instigating end, untold amounts of trauma became embedded into the collective psyche of White Americans. Yet that trauma did not start here; it began centuries earlier, nearly 3,300 miles away. As described by Menakem, the trauma that all of America is currently grappling with "can be traced back much further [than slavery and Jim Crowe] through generation upon generation of White [people], to Medieval Europe."[685] Most of us now openly condemn the acts of our ancestors, but that trauma remains unmetabolized in most Americans and negatively impacts our society today. We are still in various stages of denial, revulsion, anger, and grief as we come to terms with the horrors that Whiteness has inflicted upon all of us.

> End trigger warning.

SELF-INFLICTED SUFFERING

When it comes to White people in America, most of us remain stuck in that "soilless culture" Indigenous scholar Derek Rasmussen refers to.[686] In addition to having limited knowledge of our ancestry, many of us also tend to detach from our immediate families and move away as soon as we can. We define independence as a prerequisite to being successful in America. Rather than having rites of passage that root us in our communities and ultimately establish our position as leaders and elders, White America's obsession with independence has severed us from these important traditions and communal pathways.

What we might call rites of passage in America are all about breaking away, often in an attempt to redefine ourselves. Milestones such as getting a driver's license, graduating high school, starting college, and buying our first homes ultimately all have one thing in common: they are about finding or forging our own paths to establish ourselves as self-reliant adults. However, this quest for self-reliance comes at an exceptionally high price.

As we get older, many Americans—including BIPOC Americans now unwittingly living on a similar path toward independence—begin feeling lost and deprived of meaningful close connections. A Harvard report published in 2021 found that "36% of all Americans—including 61% of young adults and 51% of mothers with young children—feel 'serious loneliness.'"[687] This was exacerbated by the 2020 pandemic, which made it painfully clear just how detached many of us have become from the people we rely on most.

Our culture of fierce independence affects our mental health and takes a staggering toll on our bodies. A 2021 report published by the CDC described a litany of significant health consequences linked to loneliness and isolation. Conducted in 2020 by the

National Academies of Sciences, Engineering, and Medicine, the study found that loneliness and isolation "was associated with about a 50% percent increased risk of dementia . . . a 29% increased risk of heart disease and a 32% increased risk of stroke . . . a 68% increased risk of hospitalization, and 57% increased risk of emergency department visits."[688] By sheer numbers, this means that our desire for independence comes with a risk of premature death that potentially "rival[s] those of smoking, obesity, and physical inactivity." Americans are literally dying from loneliness and isolation—and this can be traced directly to the Western cultural norm of striving for independence and individualism.

Perhaps the saddest part is that by the time most White Americans decide we want to begin reconnecting with or giving back to our families or communities on a deeper level, it is often too late. Our tradition of sending our elders into assisted living is one of the most telling indicators of how detached we have become. Up to a quarter of the Americans aged sixty-five and above are experiencing significant social isolation.[689] This isn't to say that anyone should be shamed or blamed for this painful and often necessary decision. Rather, it is a critique on a much larger, heartless system that often won't allow us any other choice if we want to succeed in the "traditional way" (i.e., amassing a nuclear family, house, yard, well-paying job, benefits, etc.).

When coupled with willful denial and systemic repression of a shared heritage filled with traumatic memories, it only makes sense that there would be some significant long-term, intergenerational side effects for most Americans. For White Americans, that combination often manifests in severe depression, neurosis, deep distrust, and aggressive, sometimes lethal outbursts.

White American men seem to have a hard time acclimating to the world we have created for ourselves, and our "civilized" society has had many unintended side effects. Tim Wise points out, "There must be a reason that the United States has so much higher a rate of drug and alcohol abuse than other nations, including other wealthy and industrialized nations. And there must be a reason that, according to the available research, White Americans have such a disproportionate rate of binge drinking and substance abuse [as well as self-injury and eating disorders] relative to persons of color—contrary to popular [White] perception."[690]

Moreover, the rates of suicide are also disproportionately high among White Americans men. According to the American Foundation for Suicide prevention, in 2018, "white males accounted for 69.67% of suicide deaths . . . [and] the rate of suicide is highest in middle-age white men in particular."[691] It could be argued that we White men are literally killing ourselves to escape the pain we have both inherited and continue to create—and perhaps worse, killing others.

● ● ●

TRAUMATIZED AND TRIGGER HAPPY

Let's consider one more fact about White American men that should not be ignored: even though White males only account for about 35 percent of the US population, over 52 percent of the 142 mass shootings recorded between 1982 and April 2023 were carried out by White men.[692]

Unsurprisingly, of any demographic in America, White men are by far the most vehement defenders of the Second Amendment—not to mention the ones who created our current gun laws. Collectively, we are also very prone to gun violence, and one type in particular: mass shootings.

A Department of Justice study concluded that across the mass shootings carried out since 1966, the (over 97 percent) male shooters had either experienced trauma, had a specific grievance, or had a "script" of justifications for their actions.[693] Many of these specific grievances and "scripts" have increasingly become linked to religious hatred, White supremacy, nationalism, and xenophobia.

Most of the recent shootings—particularly those in synagogues, temples, and mosques—have been carried out by White men,[694] many of whom believe they are carrying out the will of White America. In 2022, Peyton Gendron wrote a 180-page document referencing the "the Great Replacement," equating it to genocide, shortly before opening fire and murdering ten people in Buffalo, New York.[695] Patrick Crusius, who murdered twenty-one people in 2019 at a Walmart in El Paso, Texas, was one yet another example of countless White men who subscribe to the idea that America is being overrun by non-White immigrants and that it is *our* duty to stop this from happening.[696]

The same study also noted that there has been a dramatic increase in the number of mass shootings over the past decade, often motivated by racism, religious hatred, and misogyny.[697] This is not a coincidence. The recent surge in White nationalism, xenophobia, and misogyny in our country coincides directly with a marked increase in immigration.[698]

Perhaps even more concerning, White males almost single-handedly account for the dozens of K–12 school shootings.[699] In 2021 alone, there were thirty-four documented school shootings in the United States.[700] To put that in perspective, there are only about 180 days in the average school year, which means at least one shooting every week.

Yet despite this glaring disproportionality, most of America still fails to recognize that a handgun or combat rifle in the hands of a disenchanted White male is a far bigger domestic danger than a Cold War–era Kalashnikov rifle in the hands of a radicalized Islamic militant. The fact of the matter is most terrorism in the United States comes from within and is carried out by White men.[701]

Privilege built upon the oppression and subjugation of others comes with serious collateral damage to our collective culture as well as our individual psyches. This is particularly relevant to those of us who feel like we haven't been given the privileges we are "entitled" to or haven't been able to live up to our role/status as White men. The racism and misogyny built into White male culture leads to a sense of pressure to "man up" and *seize* our "rightful" place on top. Failing to live up to our self-ordained dominant status can unconsciously feel like a loss of our very identity and understanding of ourselves as White men. All too often, when this happens we look for something or someone else to blame for our shortcomings—most often immigrants, women, and BIPOC Americans.

Like our European ancestors from the Dark Ages onward, we live in a world filled with fear, hatred, and disillusionment. Until we are willing to face the real enemy within, in the form of collectively self-induced trauma, our country will remain stuck in denial of our chauvinistic, xenophobic, misogynistic, and trauma- and fear-driven beliefs and motives.

• • •

SELF-INDUCED PTSD

The time has come to face our intergenerational trauma. This is not only about empowering communities of color; it's also about focusing on how our Whiteness comes at the cost of our humanity. Until we look within and address the nightmares of our past, we will repeat patterns of abuse. We will witness more murders of innocent Black Americans; we will see new surges in White nationalism; and we will remain in a world steeped in fear and denial—a world we created for ourselves.

One could call this trauma an expanded form of White guilt, but it is ultimately much more than that. Unfortunately, we don't fully recognize or understand the symptoms we are experiencing—

nor do we realize that what we experience as individuals is linked to a common thread in our country's history. Brutality, oppression, subjugation, and cultural and literal genocide are the bedrock of our White heritage.

As a collective and as individuals, White America exhibits many of the most common symptoms of PTSD listed on the Mayo Clinic website, including "negative thoughts about [ourselves], other people or the world, hopelessness about the future, self-destructive behavior, irritability—angry outbursts or aggressive behavior, and overwhelming guilt or shame."[702] But we are also suffering from another, often more destructive symptom of PTSD: denial. Instead of confronting the trauma, we repress, deny, or "tough it out." Like unresolved abuse or alcoholism, trauma is then passed down to the next generation.

Our collective PTSD stems from a racialized nightmare that began long before most of our ancestors even stepped foot on American soil. White people—White men in particular—have spent the ensuing centuries fighting to maintain control and remain in power. While countless individual White people have tried to stand up against the cruelty and tyranny carried out by our own race, they were the exception rather than the norm.

The whitewashed version of American history, in which we dub ourselves the brave founders of a "new" world and the crusaders of justice and democracy, perpetuates our denial. We have to face reality: *"our"* version of American history is a fabrication—one built almost entirely on a foundation of Christian Manifest Destiny. We must acknowledge that White men collectively have been one of the most brutal forces in shaping world history. Our colonization of America was no glorious rise to power; it was an invasion and, in its subsequent tyranny, more akin to the likes of Genghis Khan, Attila the Hun, or even Adolf Hitler.

More difficult to swallow is that many of us are the direct descendants of these villains, and we still reap the ill-begotten spoils.

As a result, we are haunted by the means by which we achieved our status and success. Even those who may have only recently immigrated to America from Europe often come from countries with similar histories of hostility and colonialism.

Regardless of how long our ancestors have been here, every single one of us has benefited from the plunders of White tyranny. We cannot pass on our individual ancestral stories without considering their role in the much larger story of colonization. When taken from this broader perspective, many of our ancestors were collectively the "bad guys" that vanquished the real heroes. Each and every White American lives on stolen land. Each and every White American receives certain advantages as a result of a system that was created solely for our benefit, whether or not we asked for it.

In many cases, our collective history of brutality, which now allows so many of us to live in relative comfort and privilege, is too much for us to face. Yet for many White Americans who currently do not own property or have any significant wealth, there are compounding layers to this unpleasant version of American history.

Millions of disenfranchised, working-class White Americans have little to show for their ancestors' complicity in creating and upholding a racial caste system. For these folks, there is another mental barrier to cross in recognizing that they are still at a distinct advantage over those in a similar social or economic position who are not White when it comes to jobs, access, and safety. And despite the fact that Whiteness has not worked as much in their favor, many are among the most vehement defenders of Whiteness.

As was the case directly after Bacon's Rebellion, in which the rich and powerful strategically pitted lower-class White Americans and indentured servants against their Black counterparts, our current system is designed to retain the illusion that embracing Whiteness will ultimately work in our favor—no matter what our current socioeconomic status. This is why so many White Americans who experience poverty still support right-wing nationalist policies that suppress voting rights and cut taxes for the richest (White) Americans.[703] They are repeatedly told that immigrants and BIPOC Americans are to blame for their current situation while simultaneously being placated with the myth of trickle-down economics and the hope that they too may someday achieve the wealth and riches experienced by the top 1 percent.

Meanwhile, many struggling White Americans continue to lambaste and sabotage the hopes of BIPOC Americans who experience the exact same economic hardship, unfairly viewing them as a threat to their job safety or as lazing, freeloading, and undeserving.[704] This persuades them to vote against policies that would likely be in their own best interests, thus further harming the communities they blame for their hardships and allowing the cycle of harm to continue.

It should be explicitly acknowledged that the trauma and PTSD experienced by other communities in this country far outweighs our own—especially Native Americans and Black Americans whose lineage goes back to the days of chattel slavery. Even though they are the true victims, many have taken it upon themselves to try to heal the damage inflicted upon their ancestors. Many don't have a choice but to confront their trauma; they are still living in its shadow and facing ongoing oppression. Despite this, our society tries to seduce these marginalized communities into a perverse form of Stockholm syndrome, expecting them to fall in love with, respect, and pledge loyalty to a country that was created not *for* them but *by* many of their ancestors' forced labor.

● ● ●

UPROOTED

> "One of the things that most afflicts this country is that White people don't know who they are or where they come from."
> —James Baldwin

French philosopher and activist Simone Weil once described how "the disease of uprootedness" plagues the entire Western world.[705] As has been made apparent throughout this book, most people living in the Western world are no longer attached to ethnicities, cultures, traditions, or ancestors. Instead, we live in Rasmussen's aforementioned "soilless culture," hydroponically feasting upon a toxic sludge of self-made "culture" defined primarily by colonialism and capitalism.

Our heritage and ethnicities have effectively been swapped out for a false sense of unity and superiority based on similar skin color, loosely connected phenotypes (i.e., physical traits), and a false collective narrative. In exchange for our ancestral roots and regional histories, we receive a ceaseless epic of valor, conquest, and supremacy fueled by the inherent belief that White people were destined to "settle" and "civilize" the entire world.

"Our" story of triumph and determination has been a waking nightmare for those on the receiving end of this brutal Manifest(ed) Destiny. Rather than "civilizing" those we encounter, "the White man carries this disease [of uprootedness] with him wherever he goes,"[706] describes Rasmussen. We subject outside cultures to the same neurotic values, beliefs, and systems that define and govern Whiteness. We strip them of their connections to the land, their ways of knowing, and their stories, forcefully inserting our culture and our beliefs alongside a (false) promise of democracy and economic prosperity. Moreover, we convince ourselves that this extractive system is not only sustainable but also in everyone's best interests.

Unlimited economic growth entrenched in an insistent belief that it is our duty to spread freedom, democracy, and capitalism has become the model by which we define ourselves as a culture. Those who choose not to participate in this "race to success" are typically viewed as lazy, deficient, naive, rebellious, or ungrateful. American Whiteness is inherently nothing more than a model of competition driven by hierarchical capitalism. Author Edgar Villanueva writes, "We [Western Civilization] are all infected with the colonizer virus which urges us to divide, to control, and to exploit."[707] Whiteness is based on doing more, making more, being more, and having more, automatically implying that others will and *should* have less.

Putting our roots down in this culture is toxic and corrosive. It has taken a huge toll and will continue to do so until we choose something different—until we choose a path of healing.

In an article titled "Roots Deeper than Whiteness," David Dean describes how once we finally "understand this story, we can more easily divest ourselves of the dysfunctional role we have been groomed to play, and join with people of color in the creation of a life sustaining society."[708]

CHAPTER 21

Healing From Whiteness

> "It is no measure of health to be well adjusted
> to a profoundly sick society."
> —Jiddu Krishnamurti

WHITENESS INHIBITS our ability to experience compassion, empathy, and kinship toward those we have oppressed, as well as toward each other. Perhaps more importantly, Whiteness has disconnected us from ourselves. In many ways, Whiteness itself could (and probably should) be considered a form of mental illness.

We created a racial category based on a set of beliefs about others and ourselves that inevitably leads to inner turmoil and mental anguish. We became victims of the unavoidable mental, spiritual, and even physical toll this dehumanizing identity has taken on our entire society and us as individuals.

Therapist and healer Resmaa Menakem addresses this issue head-on. In *My Grandmother's Hands*, he highlights how racialized trauma is passed through generations of family abuse, unsafe structures and institutions, damaging cultural norms, and even through our epigenetics.[709] While we often try to address these issues on an intellectual, psychological, and philosophical level, the real damage is stored in what Menakem refers to as our "soul brain." Fear, prejudice, dissociation, and cognitive dissonance are built into the very understanding of our racial identity.

Overcoming denial and attempting to remedy centuries of systemic oppression carried out unwittingly on our behalf is a tremendous undertaking. The burden can feel unfair. We might think, *I didn't ask for any of this. Why is it my job to clean it up?!* But when we understand the magnitude of the suffering created internally and externally by our Whiteness, it becomes painfully clear that ignoring it will only make it worse.

•   •   •

FACING OUR DEMONS

> "Try to realize it's all within yourself. . . .
> No one else can make you change."
> —George Harrison

The fact of the matter is that many of us are not ready to do what it takes to address our own racism head-on. We continue to view these issues as purely systemic (i.e., as something that is out there) or simply as a moral issue (i.e., we just need to stop treating other people badly because of the color of their skin).

Rather than face the collective brainwashing that made us see ourselves as White in the first place, many would like to believe that we can stop being racist by sheer force of will. We are not willing to examine the parts of White supremacy that live within us. We look for quick fixes, putting Black Lives Matter signs in our front yards, donating money to charities, supporting BIPOC businesses, and putting our kids into diverse schools. While there is nothing wrong with these gestures, they will get us nowhere if we are not willing to face our own racism.

While it is absolutely necessary for us to work toward dismantling systemic oppression through collective activism, including grassroots movements and institutional and political restructuring, the real work of overcoming racism begins with us. We need to metabolize the festering trauma, fear, and hatred to break through our complicit role in upholding White supremacy.

Otherwise, we are bound to repeat the same behaviors and pass them on to the next generation.

Try as we might, we are never going to be able to avoid racist and sexist thoughts altogether; nor is that the point. But we are responsible for changing our actions, which ultimately influence our thoughts and beliefs. Multiple books, workshop series, websites, and even "anti-racism starter kits" are out there to help us heal. While these resources are invaluable, this work is messy. No single book, method, workshop, or person has all the answers on how to unpack centuries of internalized trauma and "isms."

Depending on the individual and what stage of growth we are in, some approaches and methods are more effective than others. A highly sensitive empath requires a completely different approach than a proud White man who believes he has earned everything he has. Healing from racism requires a multifaceted approach involving daily work, as well as trial and error.

Additionally, this work requires consistent and ongoing reflection. It may feel like we need to immediately do, change, or fix something; however, the more pressure we feel to "fix it" and "fix ourselves," the less effective we become in trying to bring about change. Racism has been building inside of us over the course of a lifetime. There is no detox or cleanse to be rid of it once and for all. We must constantly work to metabolize the toxin, as well as recognize that we are *always* absorbing more, simply by virtue of living in a society that force-feeds it to us. Otherwise, we will backslide into the default programming as the toxin seeps back in. The same goes for our society as a whole.

Waging a war on racism or our own beliefs simply won't work. Overcoming racism undoubtedly requires resolve and urgency—but if we do not also take time to slow down, educate ourselves, self-reflect, and even rest and recharge, this work can and will quickly overwhelm us.

The 2020 murder of George Floyd was a racial awakening for millions of White people across the globe. However, many of the most active and vocal folks have faded into the background. Some felt like they had shown up and done their part, while countless others didn't know where to go next. It is easy to be loud and angry, but taking a deep, inward journey and becoming involved in long-term efforts against systems of oppression takes a fundamental shift in how we approach the world and ourselves.

A militant approach makes us more susceptible to burnout and fatigue, making us less effective in the long run. Verbally attacking others or ourselves for being racist, policing others on social media, or screaming at the police during a protest (all of which I have admittedly done) will often leave us feeling more confused and hopeless than when we started.

Similarly, we cannot afford to waste time navel-gazing at our Whiteness and beating ourselves up over it. Rather, our challenge lies in better understanding ourselves in order to develop a more positive, anti-racist White identity.[710]

But what does that look like, and more importantly, how do we do this?

• • •

BUILDING A NEW SELF

> "Today most White people think of themselves as having no real culture. We look at communities of color and see culture lacking in our own lives..."
> —Susan Goldberg & Cameron Levin

While there is no "right" way to combat the pain and suffering caused by Whiteness, some approaches are more effective than others. Like any big life change, we must go about it from multiple angles. We can only achieve concrete change through a mixture of consciousness raising and skill building, identity development, community and culture, along with organized anti-racist action.[711] When we combine these elements, we become not only more effective in bringing about change but also more self-aware and compassionate.

The process of reimagining Whiteness and ourselves is *not* about framing our Whiteness as positive but rather about discovering who we are in spite of our Whiteness, and who we can become when we begin to push back on it. We can achieve a much broader understanding of ourselves as well as our complex racial identities. This involves a lifelong journey of self-discovery and activism. If we want to begin healing, we need to reconstruct our understanding of Whiteness and create new identities rooted in anti-oppression.

The notion of constructing an alternative type of White identity is not a new one. Back in 2009, Susan Goldberg and Cameron Levin, members of a Los Angeles–based anti-racism organization, wrote a pivotal paper titled "Toward a Radical White Identity," centered on how to begin framing a different White identity. This involves four key elements: understanding Whiteness and White privilege, rediscovering lost ancestry and culture, grappling with complex intersecting identities, and joining an ongoing movement of White anti-racist resistance against oppression, colonial culture, and ethnic erasure.[712] For the sake of simplicity, this can be boiled down to three key elements: reflect, rehumanize, and resist.

• • •

WAKING UP

The first part of the journey is all about reflecting and (re)learning. It is centered on better understanding Whiteness and how it has shaped the world today—as well as our prescribed place within it. To begin to heal from the harmful effects of Whiteness, we must first fundamentally grasp the "cultural norms" of Whiteness and how our White identity is directly linked to power and privilege. This is effectively the phase of waking up from denial.

During this phase, we often become inundated with information through conversations, media, and experiences that challenge almost everything we thought we knew about ourselves. In this "un-brainwashing," we begin detaching from our preconceived beliefs, assumptions, and opinions about Whiteness and our racial identity. This also means diving into the history and structures of Whiteness itself, to understand how and why our racial status has been deliberately hidden from us. We begin to shed our ignorance and denial and truly see ourselves as White for the first time.

Unfortunately, because the persistent anger, pain, guilt, and shame that typically occur in this stage of discovery can become intense, this is as far as many White people choose to go on their anti-racist journey. "Guilt creates paralysis. . . . Guilt is where most White people get stuck. Guilt is the ultimate obstacle in the personal journey to being a White ally,"[713] explains Diane Flinn, a managing partner of Diversity Matters, in an interview with Learning for Justice. A sense of betrayal and disillusionment can leave us feeling disjointed, raw, and overwhelmed. While some give up, others, recognizing how much further they still have to go, try to jump ahead, assuming that hating Whiteness is the primary prerequisite to being a good ally.

Those who stop at this spiteful stage will likely end up becoming anti-White rather than anti-racist. In this stage, many of us begin to resent ourselves, resent Whiteness, and detach from anything we sense as being connected to our race. We clamor to find a new culture, a new identity, and a new sense of purpose; we often end up causing more harm in the process of trying to "fix" other White people by making them see how "evil" Whiteness is—without offering any real solutions. Even worse, our self-righteous and militant attitude tends to push other potential allies further away from anti-racist work versus bringing them in by meeting them where they are on their path. Rather than expanding the movement, we become like religious zealots holding signs on street corners that say, "Repent!" Many people want nothing to do with us, and we often end up creating further animosity in those we interact with.

The "holier than thou" approach that permeates many White progressive spaces ultimately alienates people. We must be willing to do this work with and alongside the White folks who are willing to go on this journey—no matter how misguided or clueless they may seem compared to us. It is not our job to condemn, "fix," or force them to see things our way; rather, we should try to support them in their learning and self-discovery of their own racial identity and complicity.

Because so many anti-racists in this proselytizing stage are driven by guilt and self-hate, they often cause additional harm to the very people they are trying to support. "When guilt becomes The onus is on those of us who choose to join involved in antiracist work, their work and relationships are negatively impacted," Levin and Goldberg explain. This often includes "placing people of color on an unrealistic pedestal . . . [which] can lead to cultural tourism, rejection and judgment of White people, and the inability to fully embrace all parts of oneself."[714] Many of us default to deference while trying to serve and even emulate the communities we have harmed. We try to identify more with the oppressed, wanting to think of ourselves as no longer being part of the problem.

"These feelings leave a void in White people that causes us to develop [further] oppressive solutions for filling this void,"[715] Levin and Goldberg explain. Many of us latch onto other cultures, traditions, and forms of spirituality (e.g., Buddhism, Taoism, Native American spirituality) to fill that gap—appropriating and misrepresenting something that is fundamentally not ours.

Similarly, "guilt transfers the responsibility to people of color.

Guilt continues the aspect of racism wherein white people put people of color in a situation of taking care of [them],"[716] according to Diane Flinn, managing partner of Diversity Matters. Many of us become stuck in this misguided cycle of self-rejection, comfort seeking, and cultural appropriation if we do not seek a deeper relationship with *all* people (including fellow White people) and try to better understand how Whiteness came to define our existence. We cannot create a more holistic identity that goes beyond our race until we have looked behind the curtain. Only then can we begin to move away from the "soilless culture" that has warped our understanding of ourselves and the world.

Rather than fighting against Whiteness, we must seek what has been lost or buried—while also creating something completely new. We must begin the process of rehumanization. This requires us to understand who our ancestors were before they became White.

● ● ●

RESURRECTING OUR HISTORY

Most White Americans are detached from their ancestry beyond two or three generations prior. We tend to equate our history with either suffering from, fleeing from, or benefiting from persecution. This binary thinking tells us that our ancestors were either the "good guys" or the "bad guys"—all of whom lived in relation to the monarchies of Europe and/or the Union versus the Confederacy. The reality is much more complicated.

We have created countless belief systems, structures, and institutions to keep our society confined to a hierarchy that benefits a few at the expense of others. Yet less than a thousand years ago, many of our distant ancestors were indigenous to Europe, having lived off the land for millennia in relatively small groups. Long after the rise and fall of the Holy Roman Empire around the fifth century AD, polytheism and practices of animism and mysticism were still common throughout Europe, as were healers, hallucinogens, and shamanism. Similar instances existed before and within Judaism, spanning back nearly 4,000 years.

However, at some point in our communal history, these threads of our ancestry were not only severed but also deliberately suppressed.

Before Europe colonized the globe, it had to colonize (i.e., domesticate) itself. Untold numbers of agrarian villages and tribes were either forced to convert to Christianity and toil within a feudal system or be slaughtered.[717] A few of these groups—namely the Welsh, whose ancestry in Wales traces back nearly 4,000 years— were still practicing many of their old ways as recently as the seventeenth and eighteenth centuries.

To cleanse itself of such "heathenism," Victorian England created compulsory boarding schools specifically to stamp out the last traces of non-Anglicized Protestant culture, rituals, and language[718] (a practice that would soon carry over to the Americas and Native American "education"). But the Welsh did not go down without a fight. Many continued to speak their native language and practice their customs, despite increasingly harsh consequences.

In a speech delivered to the Institute of Welsh Politics on November 16, 2009, Adam Price—the Welsh member of Parliament for Dinefwr and East Carmarthenshire—described the visceral frustration that much of England experienced in trying to rid itself of Welsh influence. In 1651, angered by the lack of progress in converting them to the Christian monarchy, a Protestant pamphleteer lamented that there were still plenty of "Indians at home—Indians in Cornwall, Indians in Wales, Indians in Ireland."[719] Like many of his contemporaries, this pamphleteer argued that rather than missionaries being sent abroad to the West Indies, they should be sent directly to Wales.

Like the Native American boarding schools in North America, the compulsory education system in the England was designed to de-indigenize the Welsh. MP Price went on to say that the primary "symbol of all of cultural imperialism in Wales . . . was a little wooden halter with the letters WN [Welsh Not] branded in it that hung around the necks of children. . . . The language was literally beaten out of [them]. . . . [C]hildren were forced not just to betray their culture but also their classmates: the ultimate mental cruelty."[720]

Unfortunately, after a few generations of cultural erasure and forced assimilation, the oppressed often take on the characteristics of the oppressor. The Welsh were no exception to this insidious cycle. MP Price explained how "English imperialism can perhaps be described as Wales's greatest and most terrible export. What was tried and tested here soon became the template for what one English historian has called the 'thousand year Reich' of the English empire." This model of conquest was emulated and adopted throughout Europe as colonialism became the backbone of its economy and of imperial expansion. This laid the framework for American expansion.

While American exceptionalism teaches that we hit a metaphorical reset with the Declaration of Independence, proudly detaching ourselves from European history, what we see today is merely an extension of this ongoing "thousand-year Reich" of imperialism. We not only suffer from its lingering trauma but also have taken on the very same supremacist beliefs and oppressive roles.

In many ways, White America suffers from a profound case of Stockholm syndrome—only we have lost track of who is emulating whom. We idolize and embody many tenets and practices of our European counterparts, fetishizing Anglo characteristics and culture because we are their progeny. White America took the torch of imperialism and has since become the most influential and dominating colonial power on the planet.

Once we recognize and grapple with this troubling reality and the paradoxes it presents, we can begin to change our understanding of ourselves as White Americans. We too are the distant descendants of people who were stripped of their culture, beliefs, and connection to the land. Without grasping this fundamental piece of how American Whiteness has been foisted upon us, we remain part of an oppressive caste system that demands our loyalty, silence, and participation in order to sustain itself.

However, the sad reality is that we will never be able to reattach our ancestral, native European roots. Unlike Indigenous Americans, who actively work to heal their roots and tend to their ancestral ways, White Americans have become too far removed from our indigeneity to pick up and rebuild what has been lost. We do not even reside on the land of our ancestors but instead have been thrust onto land illegally taken from its rightful stewards and protectors.

Where does this leave us? We clearly can't go backward, but how do we move forward?

There is still hope. If there is one thing that we can and arguably must learn from oppressed and marginalized groups in America, it is that almost *all* these communities have begun the long process of reattaching and redefining their understanding of themselves and their cultures. Many groups are even creating new shared communities and identities steeped in traditions, values, and beliefs that draw upon echoes from their past. Some have chosen to integrate multicultural and multiethnic ways of being and coexisting in solidarity.

White Americans must rise to the challenge of reconnecting to something deeper than the Constitution, our modern religions, or some nebulous belief in "individuality" and "freedom" if we want to have a shot at forging an identity that is not primarily rooted in oppression. Understanding *what* we have been assimilated into gives us the power to begin to let go and reattach to deeper parts of our identity.

There are many different layers to this ongoing process of

rediscovery and reinvention. A crucial first step is to study our ancestry and how we got here to gain a better understanding of the cultures and countries that laid our foundations. There are workshops, resources, and even communities centered around ancestry work and tracing our stories beyond America. Discovering our lineages can also help us better understand the complexities of the intergenerational trauma we are up against in our own families.

Some of us have pinpointed when our ancestors were first racialized as White—or came to see themselves as such. Some of us have also discovered relatives who actively fought against oppression and allied themselves with marginalized communities. For others, this process of rediscovery can unearth painful and difficult truths about family history, especially when it comes to enslaving other human beings. Still others date our lineage back to royalty in Europe, often adding additional layers of guilt and shame for the oppression our ancestors caused.

Perhaps the most confusing revelation for many White folks is discovering an ancestor who was not considered White. Reconciling why that information was not known or kept a secret in the first place adds multiple layers to unpacking our family history. For folks who are adopted, this work can be particularly challenging, as they may have to go above and beyond by using DNA websites or tracing birth parents or family members where possible.

While ancestry work is a critical piece of this multifaceted puzzle of anti-oppression work, this still does not provide the depth of connection that we need to sustain ourselves in the here and now. It can be helpful to know where we came from, but it is equally important to figure out where we are going.

● ● ●

GROWING NEW ROOTS

Understanding the process of rerooting and rehumanizing is no easy task. It must take place both individually and collectively.

Let's start with a basic analogy. A tree that is pulled from the ground and transplanted elsewhere must put down new roots, or it will not survive. However, it must also strengthen and sustain what remains of its existing root system, as these new roots are fragile until they have had years to thicken and strengthen.

In 2021, Harvard Graduate School began a unique project called Making Caring Common. Their mission is all about healing our society through teaching people to care about one another, seeking fairness and justice, and a willingness to put community first. In specifically seeking to combat the growing trends of loneliness, isolation, and even political divides, they advocate "working to restore our commitments to each other and the common good,"[721] acknowledging "that we have commitments to ourselves, but we also have vital commitments to each other, including to those who are vulnerable." The project also advocates "building not just our physical but our social infrastructure at every level of government and in our communities. We need to begin reimagining and reweaving our social relationships in health care, schools, and many other institutions."

One of the primary solutions is often right in front of us, yet it can be exceedingly difficult to do.

As individuals and within the community, we can create entirely new traditions, rituals, and even spiritual practices. Again, we only need to look to marginalized communities to see how important community, family, and ancestral connection can be in the process of healing and rebuilding.

To be clear, the process does not involve abandoning all elements of our culture to take pieces of others' but rather adding new layers while also resurrecting parts of our own that may have been lost. A simple example of this would be for someone with Northern European ancestry to research what the holiday of Yule originally celebrated or why many so-called "pagan" ancestors revered pine trees and decorated their homes with greenery long before Christmas became a holiday.[722] Many Jews can find similar practices and beliefs rooted in numerology, mysticism, herbalism, and Hebrew priestesses, all elements that have faded into obscurity at the hands of patriarchy and religious persecution.[723] Similarly, we can trace why there are seven days in a week, twelve months in a year, the significance of the lunar calendar, and how ancient astronomy, astrology, and pagan rituals are now hidden in plain sight amid religious and cultural symbolism.[724]

This is the part of the journey where we seek what has been buried to use the pieces to create something new. Grasping the significance of the natural world, the stars, and the planets to our ancestors' spiritual practices is about understanding how our roots can lead us to a much deeper appreciation of how we became who we are—and how we can reclaim these lost parts of ourselves. Breadcrumbs from our oppressed ancestors lay scattered around us, and all we have to do is look for them.

This is not to be done in isolation. We must remain engaged in the struggle of not only finding ourselves but also connecting with and supporting others who have suffered this same forced erasure. This brings us to perhaps one of the most fundamental parts of shifting our understanding of who we are as well as who we can become. If we are committed to real change and growth within, we must also put that same energy into dismantling racism, patriarchy, and oppression in the world around us. True anti-oppression work requires more than just healing ourselves.

It is easy to forget that not all of our ancestors were in favor of racial oppression. An ongoing multiracial struggle against racism and patriarchy is also part of America's identity and of many White people's ancestry. If we choose to take part in this struggle, we are choosing to honor the work and efforts of more recent ancestors, some of whom lost their lives seeking justice.

JOINING THE MOVEMENT

Since America was first conceived, White allies have fought against slavery and oppression. Susan Goldberg and Cameron Levin explain, "Millions of White people have stood against racism and White supremacy throughout the 400-year history of the United States. . . . [However,] the history of White people actively resisting the White supremacist system has been covered over and lost."[725] These names weren't merely forgotten; their legacies and contributions were deliberately ignored, suppressed, and often erased from history by White supremacy.

When it comes to racial solidarity, iconic images of White Americans peacefully interlocking arms with Black Americans around Dr. Martin Luther King Jr. are often the extent of the resistance we are shown. However, the idea that White America suddenly woke up to racial oppression in the 1960s is fabricated. This shows only a sliver of White resistance and multiple ongoing attempts to overthrow systems of racial oppression in America.

We are not taught that many of the laws criminalizing interracial existence were created specifically to put an end to what was already happening. There have always been White Americans who refused to abide by the tenants of racial supremacy. Countless interracial marriages, friendships, and abolitionist groups are sorely lacking mention in mainstream American history. In fact, entire pockets of multiracial communities existed from the seventeenth century onward, often comprising a mixture of escaped slaves, White indentured servants, and Indigenous peoples living together in tight-knit communities throughout early America.[726]

While some early European settlers chose to try to abandon Whiteness altogether, many others chose to fight back from within. Without the contributions of White abolitionists, we would not be nearly as far along as we are today—yet few White Americans can name a single one. William Lloyd Garrison, for example, published *The Liberator* newspaper and was a prominent leader and voice of the abolitionist movement during the 1800s. White abolitionists such as Garrison actively leveraged their positions and statuses to push back on White supremacy as well as patriarchy. But their names will not be remembered unless we seek them out and honor them.

Countless forgotten abolitionists became involved in the cause, writing publications, becoming involved in politics, and founding entire organizations, such as the American Anti-Slavery Society. Many of the most vocal—and even feared—White abolitionists were women. It is in large part *because* women played such a big role in the abolitionist movement that this chapter of America has remained in obscurity. Empowered and outspoken women who advocated for human rights—and were often more sexually liberated and progressive—did not fit the mold of the "great (White) American hero" stories we have been spoon-fed for generations.

However, women were critical to this ongoing fight for equality. Simply put, "without women the abolitionist movement would not have succeeded to the extent it did. They raised the funds to keep the movement going; their petition campaigns were critical in the political arena; and they wrote many of the pamphlets, poems and articles that provided the 'moral suasion' needed to mobilize the mainstream,"[727] describes Dr. Sharon Presley, executive director of the Association of Libertarian Feminists. "Without the contributions of the women . . . the abolitionist movement may very well have faltered and the antislavery movement set back for many more years."

However, names such as Elizabeth Margaret Chandler, Lucretia Mott, Sarah and Angelina Grimke, Lydia Maria Child, and Abby Kelley have faded to the dusty, archived shelves of

American history, only kept alive through the painstaking work of historians and biographers who have recognized their immeasurable significance.

These names should be entering mainstream knowledge by now, but the vehement pushback against teaching anything about race and racism in schools (which once again reared its ugly head in 2023) has shown why many White Americans remain viscerally afraid to confront the past—because acknowledging the existence of these abolitionists requires us to acknowledge that there was and still is something worth fighting for and against.

The onus is on those of us who choose to join this fight to resurrect these names and their struggles, and more importantly to recognize that we can carry on their legacies moving forward. To create a new sense of our Whiteness, we must find the resistance within by tapping into the strength and wisdom of those who paved the way. As Levin and Goldberg remind us, countless "individuals and groups serve as role models for White people and shining examples of resistance. . . . Learning our history gives us the ability to imagine and create new possibilities."[728] Even if our immediate ancestors were vehement defenders of White supremacy, we can choose to end the cycle of harm and abuse, just like inheritors of alcoholism. We thereby reroot ourselves in an ongoing anti-racist movement that has burned steadily alongside White supremacy's roaring flames.

We likely will never be able to fully dismantle Whiteness in our lifetime, but we can certainly loosen the stranglehold it currently has on our institutions, our nation, and ultimately our own minds, and pave the way for generations to come.

● ● ●

RECOVERY FROM WHITENESS

> "White supremacy is a hell of a drug."
> —Allison Wiltz, Anti-Racism Writer

It is often said that White people are addicted to privilege. I would argue that White people are dependent on Whiteness itself. Consciously or not, we are "hooked on" the status, comfort, safety, power, security, access, privilege, and internalized superiority that it seemingly enables us to maintain—and this includes well-meaning, progressive "anti-racist evangelicals." Even for those White folks who feel socioeconomically marginalized or left out, who don't feel like their Whiteness has granted them any material advantage, the promise of achieving some degree of access and privilege keeps them dependent on Whiteness. Moreover, if they can't achieve status, privilege, or power—as was the case with many of the European immigrants who came here over the last four centuries—there is always the hope that their children will.

While it may seem odd to compare overcoming addiction to overcoming a specific racial identity, applying "the lens of addiction helps provide perspective on the corrosive nature of racism's impact on the hearts and lives of White Americans,"[729] explains Tennessee educator Eli Foster. "An addict knows cognitively that what they are doing is wrong, but they are continually drawn to their addiction. [Many] want to be free, but the power of addiction is so strong that they sacrifice everything to maintain it." As with addiction, the lies, manipulation, and cognitive dissonance, and dehumanization required to maintain a White identity takes a huge toll on everyone.

No matter which path one takes toward overcoming an addiction, the first step is about moving out of denial and admitting that the problem of internalized White supremacy exists. It signals a surrender and admission that our dependence on Whiteness is too big of a problem for us to manage on our own or to try to solve through sheer willpower.

The process of overcoming this dependency may include joining racial affinity groups, attending workshops, or seeking the help and support of other White people on the same path. "Having [ongoing] support from anti-racist people can help . . . [but] the burden shouldn't be on Black and marginalized groups,"[730] explains writer Allison Wiltz in a 2021 Medium article about "breaking the habit" and detoxing from White supremacy. Our desire to let go of guilt and shame should never be done at the expense of others, especially if it inflicts further harm upon marginalized groups and individuals.

While we can seek support from specific BIPOC folks who are willing to support us in the process, it is critical to recognize that many are not open to subjecting themselves to further trauma and potential harm as we work through our own confusion and racial trauma. This tends to be a messy stage, often requiring us to rely on folks with whom we have already built a close relationship and who are willing to give us support, as well as challenging and honest feedback.

This ongoing process is typically done in a community with other White people who are also committed to dismantling Whiteness. There are both in-person and virtual racial affinity groups where White people can have these difficult conversations. There are even life coaches and therapists who can support us in this type of racial identity work.

To be clear, I am not advocating that we build a "sense of community" around our shared racism, but it is imperative that we put ourselves in a position where other White people can relate and empathize with us in their own process of healing. Otherwise, these thoughts, beliefs, and secrets will continue to remain in the dark, become further internalized, and get passed on to future generations.

Recovery from addiction thrives on connection and community, honesty, and self-love. These elements are key to stepping beyond a lens of internalized superiority. More importantly, they are the foundation upon which we can establish a sense of self that goes beyond a mere 300-year-old socially constructed racial identity—an identity based on a false sense of superiority, an oppressive mindset, greed, and ultimately fear.

We need to be willing to examine every nook and cranny of our Whiteness, including our entitlement, feelings of superiority, and even fears, resentments, and hostility held toward others. It will also require us to be honest about our most shameful thoughts, beliefs, actions, and secrets when it comes to our perspectives of race. This may mean putting these uncomfortable truths down on paper and working through them one by one with other white folks. This means not just admitting to but also being willing to bravely face our actions—and the consequences that have affected others and ourselves.

As described by Ijeoma Oluo, author of *So You Want to Talk about Race*, we often want to gloss over the past and the harm we have already done and just get to that shiny future. But the harm that we have caused is not gone. Oluo elaborates that without taking this necessary inventory and admitting to—if not outright making amends for—our actions, we will repeat the same mistakes. Taking this inventory allows us to make a better choice in the future when we are presented with the same issue.[731]

This has nothing to do with shaming ourselves; the process is about recognizing our faults, our errors, and our humanity—and recognizing that we will continue to make mistakes and that we need to own up to them.

Perhaps the most important thing is that supporting others on this journey is ultimately a way of helping ourselves. No matter how long one has been on this journey, we are still susceptible to the same thoughts, beliefs, and behaviors that brought us here in the first place. By continuing to engage in a process of ongoing reflection, rehumanization, and resistance, we keep learning, growing, and challenging ourselves. We are never going to become un-White, but we can act to mitigate the systemic harm and impact caused by centuries of Whiteness by supporting others in doing the same. "It took 400 years for us to form this addiction," described Eli Forster. "We will not overcome it in our lifetime, but the work to get clean now will create a better world for our children and our grandchildren."[732]

My fellow White folks, it is time to start talking about the stuff we've been keeping inside. In turning a blind eye, we remain part of a problem that is much bigger than us. Willing away our biases and stereotypes doesn't work, and pretending they are not there is inexcusable. When we hide behind the guise of our progressive ideology and desire for a better world, we never face our underlying feelings of racial superiority. Racism exists out in the open, but it thrives in secret.

Overcoming and dismantling White supremacy is neither a sprint nor a marathon. It is a relay race. Our job is to take the baton and run with it before passing it off to the next generation to continue the journey forward. If we expect to be the ones to "cross the finish the line" and "solve" racism once and for all, we set ourselves up for failure and disappointment.

We have a choice. We can either go it alone, as many often do, or admit that we need help. We didn't create Whiteness or patriarchy, nor the thoughts or beliefs that come with them, but they are now our shared responsibility to overcome. We can choose to work toward a world where Whiteness no longer holds power over our minds, our society, and other people.

To my fellow White American men, this is a call to action. The structures by which we remain in power are rapidly shifting. This remarkable new world—which is being created not by or for but rather in spite of us—is not going to wait for those who refuse to face our history, biases, prejudices, and especially unmerited power and privilege.

This work is not about attacking, destroying, and abolishing Whiteness but rather about rebuilding ourselves and overcoming the collective identity we've become imprisoned in. We have an opportunity to recognize the humanity in every individual. As our nation becomes more and more polarized, the stakes keep getting higher.

Speak up, my fellow White men. Our voices are needed here. It is time to recognize that our finite and limited worldview must extend beyond the borders of our own race and gender, and beyond our experiences in this lifetime. It is time to push beyond the world that we know, and to fight for a world no longer under *our* control. We owe it to ourselves. We owe it to future generations. More importantly, we owe it to the communities we have oppressed for far too long.

ACKNOWLEDGMENTS

I would like to express my deepest gratitude to my wife and partner, Chinmayi Bhavanishankar. Your belief and unwavering support, countless hours spent editing late into the night, and marketing expertise have transformed this book. Your honest critiques, endless patience, and unwitting role as a sounding board have shaped not only the words on these pages but also my determination to see this project through. This book simply could not, and would not, exist without you.

I would like to extend a sincere thank you to Koehler Books for your willingness to take a chance on this book. Your belief in its potential and the support of the team in bringing this project to life have been instrumental. A special mention to my editor, Hannah, who dove into every nook and cranny of the manuscript. Your keen insights and meticulous work were invaluable.

A heartfelt thank you to Meghana Doty for your tireless editing work. Your patience and dedication in sifting through numerous (not-so-polished) drafts have been instrumental in getting this book off the ground.

I am indebted to my previous literary agent, Jay Schaffer, for not only contributing the title of this book but also lending your keen editing eye to shaping the synopsis—ultimately helping me land a publisher.

A shout-out to Grand Central Bakery in Burien, Washington, for graciously providing me with the space, time, and coffee I needed to immerse myself in the writing process.

Thank you to Kristina Katayama. Your persistent encouragement and belief in my ability have been a guiding light during many moments of self-doubt. Your ongoing advocacy for my voice in social justice work has been a constant source of motivation, and has opened doors I never thought possible.

Finally, I want to express my gratitude to the numerous activists, freedom fighters, authors, historians, and scholars who have played an integral role in bringing this book to life. The knowledge contained within these pages is the result of centuries of collective research and the wisdom gained from generations of lived experiences. I'm acutely aware of the paradox and irony that my position as a white male affords me visibility on these topics, and I'm dedicated to utilizing this platform to amplify, advocate for, and empower those who continue to be marginalized and silenced.

ENDNOTES

1. Lowe, Frederick H. "The Clutch of Fear." *Chicago Reader*, August 20, 2021. https://www.chicagoreader.com/chicago/the-clutch-of-fear/Content?oid=903053.
2. Definition of White." In Merriam-Webster Dictionary. Accessed April 5, 2019. https://www.merriam-webster.com/dictionary/White.
3. "Definition of Black." In *Merriam-Webster Dictionary*, Accessed April 5, 2019. https://www.merriam-webster.com/dictionary/Black.
4. Tippett, Krista. *Becoming Wise: An Inquiry into the Mystery and Art of Living*. New York: Penguin Press, 2016.
5. Villanueva, Edgar. *Decolonizing Wealth: Indigenous Wisdom to Heal Divides and Restore Balance*. First edition. BK Currents Book. Oakland, CA: Berrett-Koehler Publishers, Inc, 2018.
6. Villanueva, Edgar. *Decolonizing Wealth: Indigenous Wisdom to Heal Divides and Restore Balance*.
7. Kimmerer, Robin. "Speaking of Nature." Orion Magazine, December 14, 2022. https://orionmagazine.org/article/speaking-of-nature/.
8. "Definition of Brown." In *Merriam-Webster Dictionary*, Accessed April 5, 2019. https://www.merriam-webster.com/dictionary/brown.
9. Tager, James, and Clarisse Rosaz Shariyf. "Reading between the Lines: Race, Equity, and Book Publishing." PEN America, January 3, 2023. https://pen.org/report/race-equity-and-book-publishing/.
10. Grossman, Page. "The Role Accents Play in Customer Service." Zendesk (blog), September 21, 2021. https://www.zendesk.com/blog/role-accents-play-in-customer-service/.
11. "Definition of Brown." In *Merriam-Webster Dictionary*, Accessed April 5, 2019. https://www.merriam-webster.com/dictionary/brown.
12. Oxford English Dictionary. "Faggot, n. & Adj. Meanings, Etymology and More." Accessed April 6, 2019. https://www.oed.com/viewdictionaryentry/Entry/67203.
13. McHugh, Jess. "The Nationalist Roots of 'Merriam-Webster's Dictionary.'" The Paris Review, March 30, 2018. https://www.theparisreview.org/blog/2018/03/30/noah-websters-american-english/.
14. "Definition of White." In Merriam-Webster Dictionary.
15. McHugh, Jess. "The Nationalist Roots of 'Merriam-Webster's Dictionary.'"
16. New World Encyclopedia. "Noah Webster." Accessed May 28, 2021. https://www.newworldencyclopedia.org/entry/Noah_Webster.
17. Noah Webster House & West Hartford Historical Society. "Noah Webster History." Accessed May 23, 2021. https://noahwebsterhouse.org/noahwebsterhistory/.
18. McHugh, Jess. "The Nationalist Roots of 'Merriam-Webster's Dictionary.'"
19. McHugh, Jess. "The Nationalist Roots of 'Merriam-Webster's Dictionary.'"
20. Editors of Merriam-Webster, "Webster's 1828 American Dictionary of the English Language," April 15, 2022, https://www.merriam-webster.com/wordplay/noah-webster-dictionary.
21. Websters Dictionary 1828. "Definition of Plantation." Accessed August 18, 2023. https://webstersdictionary1828.com/Home?word=plantation.
22. J Kendall, The Forgotten Founding Father: Noah Webster's Obsession and the Creation of an American Culture, 2011, http://ci.nii.ac.jp/ncid/BB06599004.
23. McHugh, Jess. "The Nationalist Roots of 'Merriam-Webster's Dictionary.'"
24. The National Endowment for the Humanities. "Better Living through Spelling." Accessed August 18, 2023. https://www.neh.gov/humanities/2010/marchapril/statement/better-living-through-spelling.
25. Webster, Noah. "History of the United States." Internet Archive, 1832. https://archive.org/details/historyunitedstoowebsgoog/page/n22/mode/2up.
26. Webster, Noah. "History of the United States."
27. Newsy. "How Racist History Books Spurred the Black History Education of Today." 2 News

Oklahoma KJRH Tulsa, February 18, 2019. https://www.kjrh.com/news/national/how-racist-history-books-spurred-the-black-history-education-of-today.
28. "Noah Webster and America's First Dictionary." In *Merriam-Webster*.
29. Noah Webster House & West Hartford Historical Society. "Noah Webster History."
30. Center for Documentary Studies at Duke University. "S2 Seeing White E3: Made in America," Scene on Radio. March 16, 2017. https://sceneonradio.org/episode-33-made-in-america-seeing-white-part-3/.
31. Mansky, Jackie. "The True Story of Pocahontas." Smithsonian Magazine, March 23, 2017. https://www.smithsonianmag.com/history/true-story-pocahontas-180962649/..
32. U.S. Army Center of Military History. "The U.S. Army in 1803 - Lewis and Clark," January 31, 2021. Accessed June 9, 2023. https://history.army.mil/lc/The%20Mission/the_us_army_in_1803.htm.
33. U.S. Army Center of Military History. "The U.S. Army in 1803 - Lewis and Clark."
34. Sacagawea Historical Society. "Early Life." Accessed June 9, 2023. http://www.sacagawea-biography.org/biography-early-life/.
35. National Humanities Center. "7. Slave Trade, Exploration, American Beginnings: 1492-1690, Primary Resources in U.S. History and Literature, Toolbox Library, National Humanities Center." Accessed August 18, 2023. https://nationalhumanitiescenter.org/pds/amerbegin/exploration/text7/text7read.htm.
36. Hampton History Museum. "The 1619 Landing — Virginia's First Africans Report & FAQs | Hampton, VA - Official Website." Hampton.gov. Accessed August 18, 2023. https://hampton.gov/DocumentCenter/View/24075/1619-Virginias-First-Africans?bidId=.
37. The New York Times Live Events. "The 1619 Project," August 13, 2019. https://timesevents.nytimes.com/1619NYC.
38. PBS. "Indentured Servants In The U.S. | History Detectives." Accessed August 17, 2020. http://www.pbs.org/opb/historydetectives/feature/indentured-servants-in-the-us/.
39. Costa, Tom. "Runaway Enslaved People and Indentured Servants in Colonial Virginia - Encyclopedia Virginia." Encyclopedia Virginia, June 5, 2023. https://encyclopediavirginia.org/entries/runaway-slaves-and-servants-in-colonial-virginia/.
40. PBS. "Africans in America | Part 1 | Narrative | From Indentured Servitude to Racial Slavery." Accessed August 17, 2023. https://www.pbs.org/wgbh/aia/part1/1narr3.html.
41. Jacqueline Battalora. "Birth of a White Nation," July 10, 2014. Accessed January 1, 2022. https://www.youtube.com/watch?v=riVAuCodnP4. (min 9:00)
42. PBS. "Africans in America | Part 1 | Narrative | From Indentured Servitude to Racial Slavery."
43. United States Sentencing Commission. "Demographic Differences in Sentencing," January 13, 2021. https://www.ussc.gov/research/research-reports/demographic-differences-sentencing.
44. Wikipedia contributors. "Virginia General Assembly." In *Wikipedia*, April 24, 2023. Accessed May 30, 2021. https://en.wikipedia.org/wiki/Virginia_General_Assembly.
45. Orr, Katie. "July 21, 1656: Elizabeth Key Wins Her Freedom," July 22, 2023. https://www.zinnedproject.org/news/tdih/elizabeth-key-wins-freedom/.
46. History of American Women. "Elizabeth Key," April 2, 2017. https://www.womenhistoryblog.com/2008/01/elizabeth-key.html.
47. History of American Women. "Elizabeth Key."
48. General Assembly. "'Negro Womens Children to Serve According to the Condition of the Mother' (1662) - Encyclopedia Virginia," Encyclopedia Virginia, August 17, 2021, https://encyclopediavirginia.org/entries/negro-womens-children-to-serve-according-to-the-condition-of-the-mother-1662/.
49. General Assembly. "'An Act Declaring That Baptisme of Slaves Doth Not Exempt Them from Bondage' (1667) - Encyclopedia Virginia." Encyclopedia Virginia, December 7, 2020. https://encyclopediavirginia.org/entries/an-act-declaring-that-baptisme-of-slaves-doth-not-exempt-them-from-bondage-1667/.
50. Craven, Jackie. "Mansions, Manors, and Grand Estates in the United States." *ThoughtCo*,

August 5, 2019. https://www.thoughtco.com/mansions-manors-and-grand-estates-4065236.
51. Lindert, Peter. "Table 6 . Inequality in the American Colonies 1774." ResearchGate, September 2012. Accessed August 8, 2021. https://www.researchgate.net/figure/Inequality-in-the-American-Colonies-1774_tbl3_256034285.
52. Center for Documentary Studies at Duke University. "S2 Seeing White E3: Made in America."
53. Dr. Jacqueline Battalora on her book "Birth of a White Nation" https://www.youtube.com/watch?v=riVAuCodnP4&t=240s&ab_channel=JacquelineBattalora 4 min.
54. PBS. "Africans in America/Part 1/Bacon's Rebellion." Accessed August 17, 2023. https://www.pbs.org/wgbh/aia/part1/1p274.html.
55. Center for Documentary Studies at Duke University. "S2 Seeing White E3: Made in America."
56. Center for Documentary Studies at Duke University. "S2 Seeing White E3: Made in America."
57. PBS. "Indentured Servants In The U.S. | History Detectives." Accessed January 30, 2022. http://www.pbs.org/opb/historydetectives/feature/indentured-servants-in-the-us/.
58. Assembly, General. "'An Act to Repeale a Former Law Makeing Indians and Others Ffree' (1682) - Encyclopedia Virginia," Encyclopedia Virginia, December 7, 2020, https://encyclopediavirginia.org/entries/an-act-to-repeale-a-former-law-makeing-indians-and-others-ffree-1682/.
59. Jacqueline Battalora. "Birth of a White Nation", (min. 13:50)
60. Assembly, General. "'An Act for Suppressing Outlying Slaves' (1691)." Encyclopedia Virginia, December 7, 2020. Accessed August 17, 2023. https://encyclopediavirginia.org/entries/an-act-for-suppressing-outlying-slaves-1691/.
61. Jacqueline Battalora. "Birth of a White Nation," (min. 12:06)
62. Woodson, C. G. "The Beginnings of the Miscegenation of the Whites and Blacks." *The Journal of Negro History 3*, no. 4 (October 1, 1918): 335. https://doi.org/10.2307/2713814.
63. Center for Documentary Studies at Duke University. "S2 Seeing White E3: Made in America."
64. Woodson, C. G. "The Beginnings of the Miscegenation of the Whites and Blacks." *The Journal of Negro History 3*, no. 4 (October 1, 1918): 335. https://doi.org/10.2307/2713814.
65. Center for Documentary Studies at Duke University. "S2 Seeing White E8: Skulls and Skin," Scene on Radio. May 17, 2017. https://sceneonradio.org/episode-38-skulls-and-skins-seeing-white-part-8/.
66. Menakem, Resmaa. *My Grandmother's Hands: Racialized Trauma and the Pathway to Mending Our Hearts and Bodies*. Central Recovery Press, 2017.
67. PBS. "RACE - The Power of an Illusion. Background Readings." Accessed August 17, 2023. https://www.pbs.org/race/000_About/002_04-background-02-07.htm.
68. Center for Documentary Studies at Duke University. "S2 Seeing White E8: Skulls and Skin."
69. Mitchell, Paul Wolff. "The Fault in His Seeds: Lost Notes to the Case of Bias in Samuel George Morton's Cranial Race Science." *PLOS Biology 16*, no. 10 (October 4, 2018): e2007008. https://doi.org/10.1371/journal.pbio.2007008.
70. Penn Today. "A New Take on the 19th-Century Skull Collection of Samuel Morton | Penn Today," October 4, 2018. https://penntoday.upenn.edu/news/new-take-on-infamous-Morton-skulls.
71. Center for Documentary Studies at Duke University. "S2 Seeing White E8: Skulls and Skin."
72. National Human Genome Research Institute. "Genetics vs. Genomics Fact Sheet." Genome.gov, March 9, 2019. Accessed June 18, 2018. https://www.genome.gov/about-genomics/fact-sheets/Genetics-vs-Genomics.
73. National Geographic. "Black and White: Skin Deep," April 2018. https://www.nationalgeographic.com/magazine/issue/april-2018.
74. Smith, Linda B. Decolonizing Methodologies: Research and Indigenous Peoples, 1999. https://ci.nii.ac.jp/ncid/BB10544877.
75. Schofield, Hugh. "Human Zoos: When Real People Were Exhibits." BBC News, December 27, 2011. Accessed April 22, 2021. https://www.bbc.com/news/magazine-16295827.
76. Parks, Shoshi. "These Horrifying 'Human Zoos' Delighted American Audiences at the Turn of the 20th Century." Medium, July 7, 2018. Accessed June 10, 2023. https://timeline.com/human-zoo-worlds-fair-7ef0d0951035.
77. Goldberg, Susan. "For Decades, Our Coverage Was Racist. To Rise above Our Past, We

Must Acknowledge It." Magazine, May 3, 2021. https://www.nationalgeographic.com/magazine/2018/04/from-the-editor-race-racism-history/.
78. Wamsley, Laurel. "'National Geographic' Reckons with Its Past: 'For Decades, Our Coverage Was Racist.'" NPR, March 12, 2018. https://www.npr.org/sections/thetwo-way/2018/03/12/592982327/national-geographic-reckons-with-its-past-for-decades-our-coverage-was-racist.
79. Genetics Generation. "Introduction to Eugenics - Genetics Generation," May 30, 2021. https://knowgenetics.org/history-of-eugenics/.
80. HISTORY. "Eugenics: Definition, Movement & Meaning," November 15, 2017. https://www.history.com/topics/germany/eugenics.
81. Priceonomics. "The Surprising Reason Why Dr. John Harvey Kellogg Invented Corn Flakes." Forbes, May 17, 2016. https://www.forbes.com/sites/priceonomics/2016/05/17/the-surprising-reason-why-dr-john-harvey-kellogg-invented-corn-flakes/?sh=50a488bb6997.
82. Daugherty, Greg. "Dr. John Kellogg Invented Cereal. Some of His Other Wellness Ideas Were Much Weirder." HISTORY, May 17, 2023. https://www.history.com/news/dr-john-kellogg-cereal-wellness-wacky-sanitarium-treatments.
83. Leung, Collette. "Kellogg, John Harvey." Eugenics Archive. Accessed December 14, 2020. https://www.eugenicsarchive.ca/
84. HISTORY. "Eugenics: Definition, Movement & Meaning."
85. Whitman, James. "Hitler's American Model: The United States and the Making of Nazi Race Law." International Dialogue 7, no. 1 (November 1, 2017). https://doi.org/10.32873/uno.dc.id.7.1.1148.
86. Wilkerson, Isabel. Caste: The Origins of Our Discontents. Peguin Random House, 2020. p. 81.
87. Guo, Jeff. "The Nazis as Students of America's Worst Racial Atrocities." Washington Post, April 8, 2023. https://www.washingtonpost.com/opinions/the-nazis-as-students-of-americas-worst-racial-atrocities/2017/05/19/fdbcd258-1ef9-11e7-a0a7-8b2a45e3dc84_story.html.
88. Kelly, Amita. "Fact Check: Was Planned Parenthood Started To 'Control' The Black Population?" NPR, August 14, 2015. https://www.npr.org/sections/itsallpolitics/2015/08/14/432080520/fact-check-was-planned-parenthood-started-to-control-the-black-population.
89. Oluo, Ijeoma. Mediocre. John Murray, 2021. p. 3.
90. Center for Documentary Studies at Duke University. "S2 Seeing White E8: Skulls and Skin."
91. Genographic Project. "Map of Human Migration," November 15, 2016. https://web.archive.org/web/20200408013252/https://genographic.nationalgeographic.com/human-journey/.
92. National Geographic. "Black and White: Skin Deep."
93. Center for Documentary Studies at Duke University. "S2 Seeing White E8: Skulls and Skin."
94. Saini, Angela. "Why Race Science Is on the Rise Again." The Guardian, June 6, 2019. https://www.theguardian.com/books/2019/may/18/race-science-on-the-rise-angela-saini.
95. Gibbons, Ann. "Shedding Light on Skin Color." Science 346, no. 6212 (November 21, 2014): 934–36. https://doi.org/10.1126/science.346.6212.934.
96. Krulwich, Robert. "Your Family May Once Have Been A Different Color." NPR, February 2, 2009. https://www.npr.org/templates/story/story.php?storyId=100057939.
97. Wolchover, Natalie. "What Will Future Humans Look Like?" Livescience.Com, September 18, 2012. https://www.livescience.com/34228-will-humans-eventually-all-look-like-brazilians.html.
98. National Geographic. "Black and White: Skin Deep."
99. Gerszak, Fen Montaigne; Photographs by Rafal. "The Story of How Humans Came to the Americas Is Constantly Evolving." Smithsonian Magazine, December 18, 2019. https://www.smithsonianmag.com/science-nature/how-humans-came-to-americas-180973739/.
100. Adhikari, Kaustubh. "How We Found the Genes That Control Nose Shape – and What They Say about Us." The Conversation, May 24, 2016. http://theconversation.com/how-we-found-the-genes-that-control-nose-shape-and-what-they-say-about-us-59837.

101. Nestor, James. *Breath: The New Science of a Lost Art*. Riverhead Books, 2020.
102. Adhikari, "How We Found the Genes That Control Nose Shape – and What They Say about Us."
103. The Scientist Magazine. "How Your Nose Got Its Shape." Accessed August 18, 2023. https://www.the-scientist.com/notebook/how-your-nose-got-its-shape-33101.
104. Southern Poverty Law Center. "Alt-Right," August 2023. https://www.splcenter.org/fighting-hate/extremist-files/ideology/alt-right.
105. Harvard University. "How Science and Genetics Are Reshaping the Race Debate of the 21st Century - Science in the News." Science in the News, February 27, 2019. http://sitn.hms.harvard.edu/flash/2017/science-genetics-reshaping-race-debate-21st-century/.
106. Heid, Markham. "Neanderthal DNA Could Be Messing With Your Health." *Vice* (blog), November 7, 2017. https://www.vice.com/en/article/43n7dm/neanderthal-dna-could-be-messing-with-your-health.
107. National Geographic. "Black and White: Skin Deep."
108. The Smithsonian Institution's Human Origins Program. "Ancient DNA and Neanderthals." Accessed August 18, 2023. http://humanorigins.si.edu/evidence/genetics/ancient-dna-and-neanderthals.
109. Science.org. "Africans Carry Surprising Amount Neanderthal DNA," January 2020. https://www.science.org/content/article/africans-carry-surprising-amount-neanderthal-dna.
110. Betti, Lia, Francois Balloux, Tsunehiko Hanihara, and Andrea Manica. "The Relative Role of Drift and Selection in Shaping the Human Skull." *American Journal of Physical Anthropology*, January 1, 2009, NA. https://doi.org/10.1002/ajpa.21115.
111. Adhikari, "How We Found the Genes That Control Nose Shape – and What They Say about Us."
112. Harvard University. "How Science and Genetics Are Reshaping the Race Debate of the 21st Century - Science in the News."
113. National Geographic. "Black and White: Skin Deep."
114. Norton, Heather L., Ellen E. Quillen, Abigail W. Bigham, Laurel N. Pearson, and Holly Dunsworth. "Human Races Are Not like Dog Breeds: Refuting a Racist Analogy." *Evolution: Education and Outreach* 12, no. 1 (July 9, 2019): 17. https://doi.org/10.1186/s12052-019-0109-y.
115. Laroche, Tony, and University of Rhode Island. "Researchers Refute Widespread Racist Analogy Comparing Human Races to Dog Breeds." Accessed August 18, 2023. https://phys.org/news/2019-07-refute-widespread-racist-analogy-human.html.
116. Norton et al., "Human Races Are Not like Dog Breeds: Refuting a Racist Analogy" July 9, 2019.
117. Dickey, Bronwen. *Pit Bull: The Battle over an American Icon*. First Vintage Books edition. New York: Vintage Books, a Division of Penguin Random House LLC, 2017.
118. Bronwen. *Pit Bull: The Battle over an American Icon*.
119. Norton et al., "Human Races Are Not like Dog Breeds: Refuting a Racist Analogy," July 9, 2019.
120. Nair, Yasmin. "Racism and the American Pit Bull | Current Affairs." Accessed July 10, 2020. https://www.currentaffairs.org/2016/09/racism-and-the-american-pit-bull.
121. Nair, Yasmin. "Racism and the American Pit Bull."
122. The Faculty Lounge. "Are Pitbulls the Black People of Dogs?" Accessed July 10, 2020. https://www.thefacultylounge.org/2008/02/are-pitbulls-th.html.
123. Linder, Ann. "The Black Man's Dog: The Social Context of Breed Specific Legislation." Animal Law Review 25, no. 1 (January 1, 2018). https://lawcommons.lclark.edu/alr/vol25/iss1/4.
124. Coraldrake. "Why Are There so Many Pit Bulls and Chihuahuas in Shelters? - Rescue Dog Home." Rescue Dog Home, March 24, 2023. https://rescuedoghome.com/why-are-there-so-many-pit-bulls-and-chihuahuas-in-shelters/.
125. City Journal. "Scared of Pit Bulls? You'd Better Be!" Accessed July 22, 2022. https://www.city-journal.org/article/scared-of-pit-bulls-youd-better-be/.
126. Laroche, "Researchers Refute Widespread Racist Analogy Comparing Human Races to Dog

Breeds."
127. Lee, Megan. "Engineering Mankind: The Sociopolitical Impact of Eugenics in America," Voces Novae: Vol. 11, Article 3. Chapman University Digital Commons. (2019) https://digitalcommons.chapman.edu/cgi/viewcontent.cgi?article=1127&context=vocesnovae
128. Harkinson, Josh. "Meet the White Nationalist Trying to Ride the Trump Train to Lasting Power." *Mother Jones* (blog). Accessed August 18, 2023. https://www.motherjones.com/politics/2016/10/richard-spencer-trump-alt-right-White-nationalist/.
129. Psychology Today. "Canine Intelligence—Breed Does Matter." July 15, 2009. https://www.psychologytoday.com/us/blog/canine-corner/200907/canine-intelligence-breed-does-matter.
130. Editorial, Chewy. "Why Were Pugs Bred?" BeChewy, January 1, 2019. https://be.chewy.com/the-purpose-of-pug/.
131. American Kennel Club. "Becoming Recognized by the AKC." Accessed August 3, 2023. https://www.akc.org/press-center/articles-resources/facts-and-stats/becoming-recognized/.
132. Harvard University Internet Archive. *Noah Webster. History of the United States: To Which Is Prefixed a Brief Historical* ...Wilcox, Dickerman, 1832. http://archive.org/details/historyunitedstoowebsgoog.
133. Statista. "Share of NFL Players by Ethnicity 2022" Accessed June 21, 2021. https://www.statista.com/statistics/1167935/racial-diversity-nfl-players/.
134. Hawkins, Billy. "The Black Student Athlete: The Colonized Black Body." *Journal of African American Men* 1, no. 3 (1995): 23–35. https://www.jstor.org/stable/41819389.
135. Carvalho, John. "Sports Media Is Still Racist Against Black Athletes." Vice (blog), October 3, 2014. https://www.vice.com/en/article/4x987d/sports-media-is-still-racist-against-black-athletes.
136. Carvalho, "Sports Media Is Still Racist Against Black Athletes."
137. Carvalho, "Sports Media Is Still Racist Against Black Athletes."
138. Lawrence, Andrew. "How the 'natural Talent' Myth Is Used as a Weapon against Black Athletes." The Guardian, October 2, 2018, sec. Sport. https://www.theguardian.com/sport/2018/oct/02/athletes-racism-language-sports-cam-newton.
139. Sports Injury Predictor. "Marshawn Lynch Injury History and Analysis," February 25, 2020. https://web.archive.org/web/20200225225713/https://sportsinjurypredictor.com/player/marshawn-lynch/7786.
140. Pantuosco, Jesse. "Richard Sherman Had Been Battling Depression, Suicidal Thoughts since December." www.audacy.com, August 6, 2021. https://www.audacy.com/national/sports/sherman-had-been-battling-suicidal-thoughts-since-december.
141. Steinberg, Leigh. "5 Reasons Why 80% Of Retired NFL Players Go Broke." Forbes. Accessed August 18, 2023. https://www.forbes.com/sites/leighsteinberg/2015/02/09/5-reasons-why-80-of-retired-nfl-players-go-broke/.
142. Ingraham, Christopher. "Analysis | NCAA Rules Allow White Students and Coaches to Profit off Labor of Black Ones, Study Finds." Washington Post, September 8, 2020. https://www.washingtonpost.com/business/2020/09/07/ncaa-student-athletes-pay-equity/. | Karimi, Faith. "What the NCAA Ruling Really Means for Student Athletes." CNN, June 23, 2021. https://www.cnn.com/2021/06/23/us/ncaa-supreme-court-ruling-explainer-trnd/index.html.
143. Karimi, "What the NCAA Ruling Really Means for Student Athletes."
144. Ingraham, "NCAA Rules Allow White Students and Coaches to Profit off Labor of Black Ones, Study Finds."
145. Garthwaite, Craig, Jordan Keener, Matthew J. Notowidigdo, and Nicole F. Ozminkowski. "Who Profits From Amateurism? Rent-Sharing in Modern College Sports." Working Paper. Working Paper Series. National Bureau of Economic Research, August 2020. https://doi.org/10.3386/w27734.
146. Frontline Medical Communications Inc. "NFL Players Have High Mortality Rate from Alzheimer's Disease and ALS." MDedge Neurology, October 2012. https://www.mdedge.com/neurology/article/73622/alzheimers-cognition/nfl-players-have-high-mortality-rate-

alzheimers-disease.
147. McIntosh, Kimberly. "Why Are Black People Desirable as Entertainment in Clubs but Not as Clientele?" *The Guardian*, June 13, 2018, sec. Opinion. https://www.theguardian.com/commentisfree/2018/jun/13/black-people-clubs-drama-rihanna-drake.
148. Nair, Yasmin. "Racism and the American Pit Bull."
149. Lawrence, Andrew. "How the 'natural Talent' Myth Is Used as a Weapon against Black Athletes." *The Guardian*, October 2, 2018, sec. Sport. https://www.theguardian.com/sport/2018/oct/02/athletes-racism-language-sports-cam-newton.
150. Jim Crow Museum. "The Jezebel Stereotype - Anti-Black Imagery." Accessed March 31, 2021. https://jimcrowmuseum.ferris.edu/jezebel/index.htm.
151. Jim Crow Museum. "The Jezebel Stereotype - Anti-Black Imagery."
152. Jim Crow Museum. "The Jezebel Stereotype - Anti-Black Imagery."
153. Redpath, James. "The Roving Editor: Or, Talks with Slaves in the Southern States.,My Second Trip., Page 141." by Tufts University and Gregory Crane. Accessed August 18, 2023. https://www.perseus.tufts.edu/hopper
154. Jim Crow Museum. "The Jezebel Stereotype - Anti-Black Imagery."
155. Jim Crow Museum. "The Jezebel Stereotype - Anti-Black Imagery."
156. Gordon, T. A. The Fancy Trade and the Commodification of Rape in the Sexual Economy of 19th Century U.S. Slavery. (Master's thesis). (2015) Retrieved from https://scholarcommons.sc.edu/etd/3636
157. Gordon, T. A. "The Fancy Trade and the Commodification of Rape in the Sexual Economy of 19th Century U.S. Slavery."
158. White, D. G. (1999). *Ar'n't I a woman? Female slaves in the plantation South* (Rev. ed.). New York, NY: W. W. Norton. (page 188)
159. Jim Crow Museum. "The Jezebel Stereotype - Anti-Black Imagery."
160. Hirsch, Afua. "'As a Black Woman I'm Always Fetishised': Racism in the Bedroom." *The Guardian*, January 13, 2018, sec. Life and style. https://www.theguardian.com/lifeandstyle/2018/jan/13/black-woman-always-fetishised-racism-in-bedroom.
161. Perry, Barbara, and Mike Sutton. "Policing the Colour Line Violence Against Those in Intimate Interracial Relationships." *Race, Gender & Class* 15, no. 3/4 (2008): 240–61. https://www.jstor.org/stable/41674663.
162. Hirsch, Afua. "'As a Black Woman I'm Always Fetishised': Racism in the Bedroom."
163. Calabrese, Sarah K., Valerie A. Earnshaw, Manya Magnus, Nathan B. Hansen, Douglas S. Krakower, Kristen Underhill, Kenneth H. Mayer, Trace S. Kershaw, Joseph R. Betancourt, and John F. Dovidio. "Sexual Stereotypes Ascribed to Black Men Who Have Sex with Men: An Intersectional Analysis." *Archives of Sexual Behavior* 47, no. 1 (January 2018): 143–56. https://doi.org/10.1007/s10508-016-0911-3.
164. Hirsch, Afua. "'As a Black Woman I'm Always Fetishised': Racism in the Bedroom."
165. Hirsch, Afua. "'As a Black Woman I'm Always Fetishised': Racism in the Bedroom."
166. Hirsch, Afua. "'As a Black Woman I'm Always Fetishised': Racism in the Bedroom."
167. Morris, Natalie. "Racial Fetishisation: Why It's Racist to Say You 'have a Thing' for Black Women." *Metro* (blog), December 22, 2020. https://metro.co.uk/2020/12/22/what-is-racial-fetishisation-and-why-is-it-a-form-of-racism-13762955/.
168. Morris, Natalie. "Racial Fetishisation: Why It's Racist to Say You 'have a Thing' for Black Women." *Metro* (blog), December 22, 2020. https://metro.co.uk/2020/12/22/what-is-racial-fetishisation-and-why-is-it-a-form-of-racism-13762955/.
169. McIntosh, Peggy. "How to Recognize Your White Privilege — and Use It to Fight Inequality." TEDxTimberlaneSchools, October 2012. https://www.ted.com/talks/peggy_mcintosh_how_to_recognize_your_white_privilege_and_use_it_to_fight_inequality/transcript?language=en.
170. Weir, Kirsten and American Psychological Association. "Inequality at School: What's behind the Racial Disparity in Our Education System?" *Monitor on Psychology* Vol 47, no. No. 10 (November 2016): 42. https://www.apa.org/monitor/2016/11/cover-inequality-school.
171. Joffe-Walt, Chana, Julie Snyder, Sarah Koenig, Neil Drumming, Ira Glass, Eve L. Ewing, Rachel Lissy, and Stowe Nelson. "Episode One: The Book of Statuses." *The New York Times*,

July 26, 2022. https://www.nytimes.com/2020/07/30/podcasts/nice-white-parents-serial.html?showTranscript=1.
172. Institute of Medicine. "*Unequal Treatment: Confronting Racial and Ethnic Disparities in Health Care.*" 2003. Washington, DC: The National Academies Press. https://doi.org/10.17226/10260.
173. Egede, Leonard E. "Race, Ethnicity, Culture, and Disparities in Health Care." *Journal of General Internal Medicine* 21, no. 6 (June 2006): 667–69. https://doi.org/10.1111/j.1525-1497.2006.0512.x. https://www.ncbi.nlm.nih.gov/pmc/articles/PMC1924616/
174. Institute of Medicine. "*Unequal Treatment: Confronting Racial and Ethnic Disparities in Health Care.*" 2003.
175. Egede, Leonard E. "Race, Ethnicity, Culture, and Disparities in Health Care."
176. American Heart Association. "High Blood Pressure and African Americans." www.heart.org, Access Date: February 9, 2022 https://web.archive.org/web/20220209233850/https://www.heart.org/en/health-topics/high-blood-pressure/why-high-blood-pressure-is-a-silent-killer/high-blood-pressure-and-african-americans.
177. American Heart Association. "High Blood Pressure and African Americans."
178. Center for Drug Evaluation and. "Preventable Adverse Drug Reactions: A Focus on Drug Interactions." FDA, June 9, 2021. https://www.fda.gov/drugs/drug-interactions-labeling/preventable-adverse-drug-reactions-focus-drug-interactions.
179. Farrell, Stephan. "African Americans At Greatest Risk of Vitamin D Deficiency." The Cooper Institute, September 24, 2009. https://www.cooperinstitute.org/blog/african-americans-at-greatest-risk-of-vitamin-d-deficiency.
180. Harris, Susan S. "Vitamin D and African Americans." *Journal of Nutrition* 136, no. 4 (April 1, 2006): 1126–29. https://www.sciencedirect.com/science/article/pii/S0022316622082153?via%3Dihub.
181. Johns Hopkins. "What Is Sickle Cell Disease?" *hopkinsallchildrens*, September 10, 2020. https://www.hopkinsallchildrens.org/ACH-News/General-News/What-is-Sickle-Cell-Disease.
182. Rozenbaum, Mia. "How Sickle Cell Protects against Malaria." Understanding Animal Research, September 6, 2019. https://www.understandinganimalresearch.org.uk/news/research-medical-benefits/how-sickle-cell-protects-against-malaria-a-sticky-connection/.
183. Ashorobi, Damilola, Adam Ramsey, Siva Naga S. Yarrarapu, and Ruchi Bhatt. "Sickle Cell Trait." In StatPearls. Treasure Island (FL): StatPearls Publishing, 2023. http://www.ncbi.nlm.nih.gov/books/NBK537130/.
184. CDC. "Data & Statistics on Sickle Cell Disease." Centers for Disease Control and Prevention, May 2, 2022. https://www.cdc.gov/ncbddd/sicklecell/data.html.
185. Noisette, Laurence and American Academy of Pediatrics. "Can Biracial Children Get Sickle Cell Disease?" HealthyChildren.org, August 21, 2019. https://www.healthychildren.org/English/tips-tools/ask-the-pediatrician/Pages/Can-biracial-children-get-sickle-cell-disease.aspx.
186. Yudell, Michael, Dorothy E. Roberts, Rob DeSalle, and Sarah A. Tishkoff. "Taking Race out of Human Genetics." Science 351, no. 6273 (February 5, 2016): 564–65. https://doi.org/10.1126/science.aac4951.
187. Farrell, Philip. "Tracking down the Origins of Cystic Fibrosis in Ancient Europe." Smithsonian Magazine, September 10, 2018. https://www.smithsonianmag.com/science-nature/tracking-origins-cystic-fibrosis-ancient-europe-180970238/.
188. Withrock, Isabelle C., Stephen J. Anderson, Matthew A. Jefferson, Garrett R. McCormack, Gregory S. A. Mlynarczyk, Aron Nakama, Jennifer K. Lange, et al. "Genetic Diseases Conferring Resistance to Infectious Diseases." Genes & Diseases 2, no. 3 (September 1, 2015): 247–54. https://doi.org/10.1016/j.gendis.2015.02.008.
189. Farrell, Philip. "Tracking down the Origins of Cystic Fibrosis in Ancient Europe."
190. Brott, Armin A., and Jennifer Ash. *The Expectant Father: Facts, Tips, and Advice for Dads-to-Be.* 2nd ed. New York: Abbeville Press, 2001.
191. Mayo Clinic. "Tay-Sachs Disease - Symptoms and Causes - Mayo Clinic," January 21, 2022. https://www.mayoclinic.org/diseases-conditions/tay-sachs-disease/symptoms-causes/syc-

20378190.
192. Withrock et al., "Genetic Diseases Conferring Resistance to Infectious Diseases," September 1, 2015.
193. National Library of Medicine. "Phenylketonuria Genetics." MedlinePlus. Accessed August 15, 2023. https://medlineplus.gov/genetics/condition/phenylketonuria.
194. Norton et al., "Human Races Are Not like Dog Breeds: Refuting a Racist Analogy" July 9, 2019.
195. Withrock et al., "Genetic Diseases Conferring Resistance to Infectious Diseases," September 1, 2015.
196. Yudell, Michael, Dorothy E. Roberts, Rob DeSalle, and Sarah A. Tishkoff. "Taking Race out of Human Genetics."
197. Norton et al., "Human Races Are Not like Dog Breeds: Refuting a Racist Analogy," July 9, 2019.
198. Hochschild, Jennifer, and Brenna Powell. "Racial Reorganization and the United States Census 1850-1930: Mulattoes, Half-Breeds, Mixed Parentage, Hindoos, and the Mexican Race." *Studies in American Political Development* 22, no. 1 (2008): 59–96. https://scholar.harvard.edu/jlhochschild/publications/racial-reorganization-and-united-states-census-1850-1930-mulattoes-half-br.
199. Hochschild, "Racial Reorganization and the United States Census 1850-1930: Mulattoes, Half-Breeds, Mixed Parentage, Hindoos, and the Mexican Race."
202. US Census Bureau. "Decennial Census of Population and Housing Questionnaires & Instructions." Census.gov, November 23, 2021. https://www.census.gov/programs-surveys/decennial-census/technical-documentation/questionnaires.1790_Census.html.
203. Hochschild, "Racial Reorganization and the United States Census 1850-1930."
204. Hochschild, "Racial Reorganization and the United States Census 1850-1930."
205. US Census Bureau. "Decennial Census of Population and Housing Questionnaires & Instructions." Census.gov, November 23, 2021. https://www.census.gov/programs-surveys/decennial-census/technical-documentation/questionnaires.1840_Census.html.
206. Little, Becky. "The Most Controversial Census Changes in American History." HISTORY, May 23, 2023. Accessed June 13, 2021. https://www.history.com/news/census-changes-controversy-citizenship.
207. US Census Bureau. "Decennial Census of Population and Housing Questionnaires & Instructions." Census.gov, November 23, 2021. https://www.census.gov/programs-surveys/decennial-census/technical-documentation/questionnaires.1870_Census.html.
208. US Census Bureau. "Decennial Census of Population and Housing Questionnaires & Instructions."
209. Paul Wolff Mitchell, "The Fault in His Seeds: Lost Notes to the Case of Bias in Samuel George Morton's Cranial Race Science," *PLOS Biology* 16, no. 10 (October 4, 2018): e2007008, https://doi.org/10.1371/journal.pbio.2007008.
210. Little, Becky. "The Most Controversial Census Changes in American History."
211. US Census Bureau. "1850 Census Instructions to Enumerators." Census.gov, October 8, 2021. Accessed June 12, 2021. https://www.census.gov/programs-surveys/decennial-census/technical-documentation/questionnaires/1850/1850-instructions.html.
212. US Census Bureau. "1870 Census Instructions to Enumerators." Census.gov, October 8, 2021. Accessed June 12, 2021. https://www.census.gov/programs-surveys/decennial-census/technical-documentation/questionnaires/1870/1870-instructions.html.
213. Kennedy, Lesley. "Building the Transcontinental Railroad: How 20,000 Chinese Immigrants Made It Happen." HISTORY, April 28, 2023. Accessed June 13, 2021. https://www.history.com/news/transcontinental-railroad-chinese-immigrants.
214. US Census Bureau. "1900 Census Instructions to Enumerators." Census.gov, October 8, 2021. Accessed June 11, 2021. https://www.census.gov/programs-surveys/decennial-census/technical-documentation/questionnaires/1900/1900-instructions.html.
215. US Census Bureau. "1900 Census Instructions to Enumerators."
216. US Census Bureau. "1900 Census Instructions to Enumerators."
217. Little, Becky. "The Most Controversial Census Changes in American History."

218. US Census Bureau. "1930 Census Instructions to Enumerators." Census.gov, October 8, 2021. Accessed June 11, 2021. https://www.census.gov/programs-surveys/decennial-census/technical-documentation/questionnaires/1930/1930-instructions.html.
219. Kiviat, Barbara. "Should the Census Be Asking People If They Are Negro?" TIME.com, January 23, 2010. https://web.archive.org/web/20210818060300/http://content.time.com/time/nation/article/0,8599,1955923,00.html.
220. Consumer Compliance Handbook. "Federal Fair Lending Regulations and Statutes Fair Housing Act." Accessed August 15, 2023. https://www.federalreserve.gov/boarddocs/supmanual/cch/fair_lend_fhact.pdf.
221. Kiviat, Barbara. "Should the Census Be Asking People If They Are Negro?"
222. US Census Bureau. "1940 Census Instructions to Enumerators." Census.gov, October 8, 2021. Accessed June 11, 2021. https://www.census.gov/programs-surveys/decennial-census/technical-documentation/questionnaires/1940/1940-instructions.html.
223. US Census Bureau. "1970 Census Instructions to Enumerators." Census.gov, October 8, 2021. Accessed June 11, 2021. https://www.census.gov/programs-surveys/decennial-census/technical-documentation/questionnaires/1970/1970-instructions.html.
224. United States Census Bureau. "Programs Surveys: 1980 Short Questionnaire." census.gov. Accessed June 6, 2021. https://www.census.gov/content/dam/Census/programs-surveys/decennial/technical-documentation/questionnaires/1980_short_questionnaire.pdf.
225. United States Census Bureau, "Race: U.S. Census Bureau, American Community Survey (ACS)," census.gov, accessed March 29, 2020, https://web.archive.org/web/20200329214708/https://www.census.gov/quickfacts/fact/note/US/RHI625218.
226. United States Census Bureau. "Race: U.S. Census Bureau, American Community Survey (ACS)."
227. United States Census Bureau. "Facts for Features: Hispanic Heritage Month 2018." Census.gov. September 13, 2018. https://www.census.gov/newsroom/facts-for-features/2018/hispanic-heritage-month.html.
228. U.S. Department Of Commerce Economics and Statistics Administration. U.S. Census Bureau. "2020 Census Informational Bilingual Questionnaire." census.gov. Accessed June 13, 2021. https://web.archive.org/web/20230806095647/https://www2.census.gov/programs-surveys/decennial/2020/technical-documentation/questionnaires-and-instructions/questionnaires/2020-informational-questionnaire.pdf
229. United States Census Bureau. "2020 Census Questionnaire." census.gov. Accessed July 14 13, 2020. https://web.archive.org/web/20200714014044/https://my2020census.gov/.
230. Kambhampaty, Anna Purna. "At Census Time, Asian Americans Again Confront the Question of Who 'Counts' as Asian. Here's How the Answer Got So Complicated." Time, March 12, 2020. https://time.com/5800209/asian-american-census/.
231. Ishisaka, Naomi. "Why It's Time to Retire the Term 'Asian Pacific Islander.'" The Seattle Times, December 1, 2020. https://www.seattletimes.com/seattle-news/why-its-time-to-retire-the-term-asian-pacific-islander/.
232. Zhou, Li. "The Term 'Asian American' Doesn't Serve Everyone It Covers." *Vox*, May 5, 2021. https://www.vox.com/identities/22380197/asian-american-pacific-islander-aapi-heritage-anti-asian-hate-attacks.
233. Ishisaka, "Why It's Time to Retire the Term 'Asian Pacific Islander.'"
234. Pew Research Center's Social & Demographic Trends Project. "Poverty Rate of Cambodian Americans," September 8, 2017. https://www.pewresearch.org/social-trends/chart/u-s-cambodian-population-living-in-poverty/.
235. Zhou, "The Term 'Asian American' Doesn't Serve Everyone It Covers."
236. Zhou, "The Term 'Asian American' Doesn't Serve Everyone It Covers."
237. Zhou, "The Term 'Asian American' Doesn't Serve Everyone It Covers."
238. Zhou, "The Term 'Asian American' Doesn't Serve Everyone It Covers."
239. Budiman, Abby, and Neil G. Ruiz. "Key Facts about Asian Origin Groups in the U.S." *Pew Research Center* (blog). Accessed August 19, 2023. https://www.pewresearch.org/short-reads/2021/04/29/key-facts-about-asian-origin-groups-in-the-u-s/.
240. United States Census Bureau. "2020 Census Questionnaire." census.gov. Accessed July 14

13, 2020. https://web.archive.org/web/20200714014044/https://my2020census.gov/.
241. U.S. Department Of Commerce Economics and Statistics Administration. U.S. Census Bureau.
242. Gholami, Samira. "Gholami: White on Paper, Brown in Public: Issues with the Census Race Question - The Daily Utah Chronicle," June 1, 2020. https://dailyutahchronicle.com/2020/06/01/gholami-white-on-paper-brown-in-public-issues-with-the-census-race-question/.
243. Center for Documentary Studies at Duke University. "S2 Seeing White E8: Skulls and Skin."
244. Center for Documentary Studies at Duke University. "S2 Seeing White E8: Skulls and Skin."
245. Brace CL. "Race" is a four-letter word: the genesis of the concept. New York: Oxford University Press; 2005.
246. Smith. "United States District Court for the Eastern District of South Carolina." *Harvard University* In re Dow, 213 F. 355 (April 15, 1914). https://cite.case.law/f/213/355/.
247. Batalova, Jeanne, Laura Harjanto. "Middle Eastern and North African Immigrants in the United States." migrationpolicy.org, January 12, 2022. https://www.migrationpolicy.org/article/middle-eastern-and-north-african-immigrants-united-states.
248. United States Census Bureau. "2020 Census Questions: Race." census.gov. Accessed July 15 13, 2020. https://web.archive.org/web/20200714014044/https://my2020census.gov/ https://2020census.gov/en/about-questions/2020-census-questions-race.html.
249. US Census Bureau. "1850 Census Instructions to Enumerators." Census.gov, Accessed September 17, 2021. https://www.census.gov/programs-surveys/decennial-census/technical-documentation/questionnaires/1850/1850-instructions.html.
250. Jaye Bell, Zenobia Desha. "African-American Nomenclature: The Label Identity Shift from 'Negro' to 'Black' in the 1960s." *University of California*, 2013. https://escholarship.org/content/qt1j12q56x/qt1j12q56x_noSplash_7fc074a369bc6684f13e6ca33c085193.pdf?t=n2oha3.
251. Collier-Thomas, Bettye, and James Turner. "Race, Class and Color: The African American Discourse on Identity." *Journal of American Ethnic History* 14, no. 1 (1994): 5–31. https://www.jstor.org/stable/27501932.
252. Collier-Thomas, Bettye, and James Turner. "Race, Class and Color: The African American Discourse on Identity."
253. Collier-Thomas, Bettye, and James Turner. "Race, Class and Color: The African American Discourse on Identity."
254. Kennedy, Randall. "Nigger: The Strange Career of a Troublesome Word." washingtonpost.com, January 11, 2001. https://www.washingtonpost.com/wp-srv/style/longterm/books/chap1/nigger.htm.
255. Brown, Tanya Ballard. "No More 'Negro' For Census Bureau Forms And Surveys." NPR, February 25, 2013, sec. America. https://www.npr.org/sections/thetwo-way/2013/02/25/172885551/no-more-negro-for-census-bureau-forms-and-surveys.
256. Starr, Barbara. "Army Says Word 'Negro' OK to Use." First on CNN: CNN Politics, November 5, 2014. https://www.cnn.com/2014/11/05/politics/army-says-word-negro-ok-to-use/index.html.
257. Starr, Barbara. "Army Says Word 'Negro' OK to Use."
258. Jaye Bell, Zenobia Desha. "African-American Nomenclature: The Label Identity Shift from 'Negro' to 'Black' in the 1960s."
259. Mende, Moise. "Should We Say Black Or African American?" The Observer, April 30, 2022. https://fordhamobserver.com/30133/opinions/should-we-say-black-or-african-american/.
260. Sandra E. Garcia, "BIPOC: What Does It Mean?" The New York Times, June 17, 2020, https://www.nytimes.com/article/what-is-bipoc.html.
261. Sandra E. Garcia, "BIPOC: What Does It Mean?"
262. Priority Magazine. "BBIA: Being Black In America," May 3, 2017. https://prioritymag.com/bbia-an-intro-to-being-black-in-america/.
263. Desjardins, Jeff. "All of the World's Money and Markets in One Visualization." Visual Capitalist, January 25, 2021. https://www.visualcapitalist.com/all-of-the-worlds-money-and-markets-in-one-visualization-2020/.

END NOTES | 453

264. Vine, David. "The United States Probably Has More Foreign Military Bases Than Any Other People, Nation, or Empire in History."
265. Engelhardt, Tom. "America's Empire of Bases." TomDispatch.Com, April 23, 2021. https://tomdispatch.com/best-of-tomdispatch-chalmers-johnson-on-garrisoning-the-planet/.
266. Cooper, Helene. "African-Americans Are Highly Visible in the Military, but Almost Invisible at the Top." *The New York Times*, October 18, 2021. https://www.nytimes.com/2020/05/25/us/politics/military-minorities-leadership.html.
267. Full Diversity Partners Global (FDP Global). "Courageous Leaders Summit." wmfdp.com. 2022. https://wmfdp.com/courageous-leaders-summits/.
268. "Definition of Privilege." In Merriam-Webster Dictionary, Accessed June 6, 2021. https://www.merriam-webster.com/dictionary/privilege.
269. Hutcherson, Lori Lakin. "What I Said When My White Friend Asked for My Black Opinion on White Privilege." The on Being Project, July 23, 2016. https://onbeing.org/blog/what-i-said-when-my-White-friend-asked-for-my-black-opinion-on-White-privilege/.
270. Mohr, Tara Sophia. "Why Women Don't Apply for Jobs Unless They're 100% Qualified." Harvard Business Review, August 25, 2014. https://hbr.org/2014/08/why-women-dont-apply-for-jobs-unless-theyre-100-qualified.
271. Gruver, Jackson. "Racial Wage Gap for Men." Payscale, May 7, 2019. https://www.payscale.com/data/racial-wage-gap.
272. Horst, Megan, and Amy Marion. "Racial, Ethnic and Gender Inequities in Farmland Ownership and Farming in the U.S." *Agriculture and Human Values* 36, no. 1 (October 28, 2018): 1–16. https://doi.org/10.1007/s10460-018-9883-3.
273. MacBride, Elizabeth. "White Men Are Now The Minority Of Business Owners In The United States." *Forbes*, May 23, 2021. https://www.forbes.com/sites/elizabethmacbride/2021/05/23/white-men-are-now-the-minority-of-business-owners-in-the-united-states/?sh=5b83c2e91582.
274. Mercado, Darla. "Closing This Wealth Gap Could Take 228 Years." CNBC, August 9, 2016. https://www.cnbc.com/2016/08/09/closing-this-wealth-gap-could-take-228-years.html.
275. Statista. "Property Crime in the U.S. by Type and Race 2021." Accessed September 8, 2021. https://www.statista.com/statistics/252486/number-of-property-crimes-in-the-us-by-type-and-race/.
276. Horn, Chris. "Racial Disparities Revealed in Massive Traffic Stop Dataset." University of South Carolina, June 12, 2020. https://sc.edu/uofsc/posts/2020/06/racial_disparities_traffic_stops.php#.YUZri55Kho4.
277. Wagner, Meg and Kyle Blaine, Jessica Estepa, Melissa Macaya Fernando Alfonso III. "Final 2020 Presidential Debate Fact Check and News Coverage." CNN, October 23, 2020. https://www.cnn.com/politics/live-news/presidential-debate-coverage-fact-check
278. NBC News. "Trump: I've Done More for Black People than Anyone, Maybe Lincoln." July 22, 2020. https://www.nbcnews.com/now/video/trump-says-he-has-done-more-for-black-people-than-anyone-with-possible-exception-of-lincoln-88141381811.
279. Janey, David W. "Black Parents Give Their Kids 'The Talk.' What If White Parents Did, Too?" Cognoscenti. WBUR.Org, August 12, 2021. https://www.wbur.org/cognoscenti/2021/04/12/the-talk-racism-black-parents-children-david-w-janey.
280. Kuperinsky, Amy, "Tenafly Police Chief Praises Cops in Caren Turner Video: They Handled It 'Perfectly.'" NJ Advance Media for nj.com. April 26, 2018. https://www.nj.com/news/2018/04/tenafly_top_cop_talks_about_the_video_that_put_a_p.html
281. Kuperinsky, Amy, "Tenafly Police Chief Praises Cops in Caren Turner Video: They Handled It 'Perfectly.'"
282. Kuperinsky, Amy, "Tenafly Police Chief Praises Cops in Caren Turner Video: They Handled It 'Perfectly.'"
283. Walz, Tim. "'I Got A Ticket For Driving While Black': Video Released Showing Rep. John Thompson's Traffic Stop," CBS News Minnesota Local. *cbsnews.com*. July 13, 2021. https://minnesota.cbslocal.com/2021/07/13/i-got-a-ticket-for-driving-while-black-video-released-showing-rep-john-thompsons-traffic-stop/.
284. Waxman, Olivia. "The Birth of the U.S. Police Force." *Time*, May 18, 2017. https://time.

com/4783934/the-birth-of-us-police-force/.
285. Waxman, Olivia. "The Birth of the U.S. Police Force."
286. Hutcherson, Lori Lakin. "What I Said When My White Friend Asked for My Black Opinion on White Privilege."
287. Lichter, Robert "Prime-time Prejudice: TV's Images of Blacks and Hispanics" Public Opinion 10. (1987). Accessed September, 26, 2021. pp. 13–16. https://en.wikipedia.org/wiki/Representation_of_African_Americans_in_media#cite_ref-2
288. Parrot Analytics. "The Impact of Talent Diversity on Audience Demand for Television," Accessed August 5, 2023. https://www.parrotanalytics.com/insights/the-impact-of-talent-diversity-on-audience-demand-for-television/.
289. Wolchover, Natalie. "Why Do News Anchors All Talk the Same?" NBC News, www.nbcnews.com, October 1, 2011. http://www.nbcnews.com/id/44740700/ns/technology_and_science-science/t/why-do-news-anchors-all-talk-same/#.XoJRvNNKh04.
290. "Midwest Intonation." Interview by Diana Page Jordan, July 7, 2021.
291. Lopate, Leonard. "The 46 Seconds When Non-White Actors Speak In 'Lord Of The Rings'" The Leonard Lopate Show, New York Public Radio. wnyc, August 19, 2015. https://www.wnyc.org/story/46-seconds-when-non-white-actors-speak-lord-rings/.
292. Dahlen, Sarah Park. "Picture This: Diversity in Children's Books 2018 Infographic." *Sarah Park Dahlen, Ph.D.* (blog), June 19, 2019. https://readingspark.wordpress.com/2019/06/19/picture-this-diversity-in-childrens-books-2018-infographic/.
293. Villanueva, Edgar. *Decolonizing Wealth: Indigenous Wisdom to Heal Divides and Restore Balance.*
294. Diamond, Anna. "Inside a New Effort to Change What Schools Teach about Native American History." *Smithsonian Magazine*, September 18, 2019. https://www.smithsonianmag.com/smithsonian-institution/inside-new-effort-change-what-schools-teach-about-native-american-history-180973166/.
295. Black History Studies. "15 Facts on the Moors in Spain." July 24, 2018. https://blackhistorystudies.com/resources/resources/15-facts-on-the-moors-in-spain/.
296. Sullivan, Kevin, and Lori Rozsa. "DeSantis Doubles down on Claim That Some Blacks Benefited from Slavery." *Washington Post*, July 24, 2023. https://www.washingtonpost.com/politics/2023/07/22/desantis-slavery-curriculum/.
297. Pruitt, Sarah. "Why the King James Bible of 1611 Remains the Most Popular Translation in History." *HISTORY*, July 13, 2023. https://www.history.com/news/king-james-bible-most-popular.
298. Levy, Joel J. and Center For Jewish History. "How the King James Bible Came to Be." *Time.Com*, June 19, 2017. https://time.com/4821911/king-james-bible-history/.
299. Pruitt, Sarah. "What Did Jesus Look Like?" HISTORY, March 22, 2021. https://www.history.com/news/what-did-jesus-look-like.
300. Dolsten, Josefin. "Jews of Color Are Chronically Undercounted, Researchers Find." *Jewish Telegraphic Agency* (blog), May 30, 2019. https://www.jta.org/2019/05/30/united-states/jews-of-color-are-chronically-undercounted-researchers-find.
301. Dolsten, Josefin. "Jews of Color Are Chronically Undercounted, Researchers Find."
302. De Witte, Melissa. "Consequences of Perceiving God as a White Man." Stanford News, January 31, 2020. https://news.stanford.edu/2020/01/31/consequences-perceiving-god-white-man/.
303. De Witte, Melissa. "Consequences of Perceiving God as a White Man."
304. De Witte, Melissa. "Consequences of Perceiving God as a White Man."
305. Mitchell, Travis. "About Three-in-Ten U.S. Adults Are Now Religiously Unaffiliated." *Pew Research Center's Religion & Public Life Project* (blog), December 14, 2021. https://www.pewresearch.org/religion/2021/12/14/about-three-in-ten-u-s-adults-are-now-religiously-unaffiliated/.
306. Bowens, Tracy and Elisabeth Cook. "27+ English Phrases Call Center Representatives Can Use Over and Over Again." *FluentU Business English Blog*, June 26, 2023. https://www.fluentu.com/blog/business-english/call-center-english/.
307. Peterson, Amber. "Literacy Is More than Just Reading and Writing." *National Council of*

Teachers of English, April 6, 2020. https://ncte.org/blog/2020/03/literacy-just-reading-writing/.
308. Peterson, Amber. "Literacy Is More than Just Reading and Writing."
309. Peterson, Amber. "Literacy Is More than Just Reading and Writing."
310. "What You Need to Know about Literacy." *UNESCO*, June 29, 2023. https://www.unesco.org/en/literacy/need-know.
311. Heath, Shirley Brice. *Ways with Words: Language, Life and Work in Communities and Classrooms*. 1983, Stanford: Cambridge UP. ISBN 9780511841057.
312. "Definition of Black." In *Merriam-Webster Dictionary*, Accessed April 5, 2019. https://www.merriam-webster.com/dictionary/Black.
313. Baugh, John. "American Varieties, African American English: Ebony + Phonics." pbs.org. Accessed October 10, 2021. https://www.pbs.org/speak/seatosea/americanvarieties/AAVE/ebonics/.
314. Luu, Chi. "Black English Matters." JSTOR Daily, February 20, 2020. https://daily.jstor.org/black-english-matters/.
315. Baugh, John. "American Varieties, African American English: Ebony + Phonics."
316. Baugh, John. "American Varieties, African American English: Ebony + Phonics."
317. "Ebnonics." Senate Hearing 105-20 39-641 Cc. U.S. Government Publishing Office, 1997. Accessed October 16, 2021 https://www.govinfo.gov/content/pkg/CHRG-105shrg39641/html/CHRG-105shrg39641.htm.
318. "Ebonics Controversy Comes To City, Stirs Lively Debate." courant.com. January 12, 1997. Accessed October 16, 2021. https://www.courant.com/news/connecticut/hc-xpm-1997-01-12-9701120168-story.html.
319. "Ebonics Controversy Comes To City, Stirs Lively Debate."
320. "Ebnonics." *Senate Hearing 105-20.*
321. "Ebnonics." *Senate Hearing 105-20.*
322. "Ebnonics." *Senate Hearing 105-20.*
323. Luu, Chi. "Black English Matters."
324. Editors of Merriam-Webster. "The Double Negative: It's Not Unusual (Sometimes)," May 19, 2020. Accessed October 22, 2021. https://www.merriam-webster.com/words-at-play/double-negative-not-adjective-litotes.
325. Ravelhofer, Barbara. "William Shakespeare: Twelfth Night. Ed. Keir Elam. The Arden Shakespeare: Third Series. London: Cengage Learning, 2008.
326. Meraji, Shereen Marisol. "Why Chaucer Said 'Ax' Instead Of 'Ask,' And Why Some Still Do." NPR, December 3, 2013. Accessed November 9, 2021. https://www.npr.org/transcripts/248515217.
327. Meraji, Shereen Marisol. "Why Chaucer Said 'Ax' Instead Of 'Ask,' And Why Some Still Do."
328. Meraji, Shereen Marisol. "Why Chaucer Said 'Ax' Instead Of 'Ask,' And Why Some Still Do."
329. StudyLight.org. "Matthew 7:7 - MCB - Axe, and It Shalbe Geuen You: Seke, and Ye Shall Fynde: Knocke, and It Shalbe Opened Vnto You." Accessed August 19, 2023. https://www.studylight.org/bible/eng/mcb/matthew/7-7.html.
330. Meraji, Shereen Marisol. "Why Chaucer Said 'Ax' Instead Of 'Ask,' And Why Some Still Do."
331. Baugh, John. "American Varieties, African American English: Ebony + Phonics."
332. Billings, Andrew C. "Beyond the Ebonics Debate: Attitudes about Black and Standard American English." Journal of Black Studies 36, no. 1 (2005): 68–81. http://www.jstor.org/stable/40027322.
333. Wikipedia contributors. "Accent Reduction." Wikipedia, July 15, 2023. Accessed November 12, 2021. https://en.wikipedia.org/wiki/Accent_reduction.
334. Poulton, Jay Alexander. "Dialect Coach, Accent Reduction, Speech Coach, Voice Acting." The Accent Coach, Accessed November, 11, 2021, https://www.theaccentcoach.com/.
335. Accent Advisor. "Learn to Speak with an American Accent." Accessed November 12, 2021. https://english.accentadvisor.com/.
336. Anderson, Samantha, Samuel D. Downs, Kaylene Faucette, Josh Griffin, Tracy King, and Staci Woolstenhulme. "How Accents Affect Perception of Intelligence, Physical Attractiveness, and Trustworthiness of Middle-Easter-, Latin-American-, British- and

Standard-American-English-Accented Speakers." *BYU Undergraduate Journal of Psychology* 3, no. 1 (2007). https://scholarsarchive.byu.edu/intuition/vol3/iss1/3.

337. Anderson et al., "How Accents Affect Perception of Intelligence, Physical Attractiveness, and Trustworthiness of Middle-Easter-, Latin-American-, British- and Standard-American-English-Accented Speakers."
338. Anderson et al., "How Accents Affect Perception of Intelligence, Physical Attractiveness, and Trustworthiness of Middle-Easter-, Latin-American-, British- and Standard-American-English-Accented Speakers."
339. English Language Institute. "English for Academic Purposes." February 1, 2022. https://sites.udel.edu/eli/programs/iep/tracks/eap/.
340. Colorín Colorado. "What Is the Difference between Social and Academic English?," December 19, 2019. Accessed November 14, 2021. https://www.colorincolorado.org/article/what-difference-between-social-and-academic-english.
341. The Glossary of Education Reform. "Academic Language Definition," August 29, 2013. https://www.edglossary.org/academic-language/.
342. English Language Institute. "English for Academic Purposes," February 1, 2022. https://sites.udel.edu/eli/programs/iep/tracks/eap/.
343. English Language Institute. "English for Academic Purposes."
344. Baugh, J. (2004). Standard English and Academic English (Dialect) Learners in the African Diaspora. Journal of English Linguistics, 32(3), 197–209. https://doi.org/10.1177/0075424204268228
345. Irfan, Sameen. "A Brief History of the English Language." Oxford International English Schools, October 22, 2020. https://www.oxfordinternationalenglish.com/a-brief-history-of-the-english-language/.
346. Irfan, Sameen. "A Brief History of the English Language."
347. Editorial Staff. "The English Renaissance: An Introduction to the Cultural Revival That Inspired an Era of Poetic Evolution." Poetry Foundation. Accessed November 14, 2021. https://www.poetryfoundation.org/collections/154826/an-introduction-to-the-english-renaissance.
348. Andrei, Mihai. "Why Shakespeare's 'Much Ado About Nothing' Is a Brilliant Sneaky Innuendo." ZME Science, May 9, 2023. Accessed November 14, 2021. https://www.zmescience.com/science/why-shakespeares-much-ado-about-nothing-is-a-brilliant-sneaky-innuendo/.
349. Irfan, "A Brief History of the English Language - Oxford International English Schools." October 22, 2020.
350. The Glossary of Education Reform. "Academic Language Definition."
351. Baugh, John. "Standard English and Academic English (Dialect) Learners in the African Diaspora." *Journal of English Linguistics* 32, no. 3 (September 2004): 197–209. https://doi.org/10.1177/0075424204268228.
352. Fussell, Sidney. "What the SAT's Adversity Score Means for Its Racist Past." The Atlantic, May 18, 2019. https://www.theatlantic.com/technology/archive/2019/05/college-board-sat-adversity-score/589681/.
353. McCluney, Courtney L. "The Costs of Code-Switching." Harvard Business Review, January 28, 2021. https://hbr.org/2019/11/the-costs-of-codeswitching.
354. McCluney, Courtney L. "The Costs of Code-Switching."
355. Hewlin, Patricia Faison. "Wearing the Cloak: Antecedents and Consequences of Creating Facades of Conformity." *Journal of Applied Psychology* 94, no. 3 (May 1, 2009): 727–41. https://doi.org/10.1037/a0015228.
356. Walton, Gregory M., Mary C. Murphy, and Ann Marie Ryan. "Stereotype Threat in Organizations: Implications for Equity and Performance." Annual Review of Organizational Psychology and Organizational Behavior 2, no. 1 (April 10, 2015): 523–50. https://doi.org/10.1146/annurev-orgpsych-032414-111322.
357. McCluney, Courtney L. "The Costs of Code-Switching."
358. Durkee, Myles I., Elizabeth R. Gazley, Elan C. Hope, and Micere Keels. "Cultural

Invalidations: Deconstructing the 'Acting White' Phenomenon among Black and Latinx College Students." *Cultural Diversity & Ethnic Minority Psychology* 25, no. 4 (October 1, 2019): 451–60. https://doi.org/10.1037/cdp0000288.
359. TIME.com. "Top 10 Joe Biden Gaffes," March 23, 2010. Accessed January 30, 2021. https://web.archive.org/web/20210127051602/http://content.time.com/time/specials/packages/article/0,28804,1895156_1894977_1644536,00.html.
360. TIME.com. "Top 10 Joe Biden Gaffes."
361. Sullivan, Eric Bradner, Arlette Saenz,Caroline Kenny,Kate. "Biden Defends Comments about Segregationist Senators: 'There's Not a Racist Bone in My Body' | CNN Politics." CNN, June 20, 2019. https://www.cnn.com/2019/06/19/politics/joe-biden-segregationists-cory-booker/index.html.
362. "Definition of Black." In *Merriam-Webster Dictionary*, Accessed April 5, 2019. https://www.merriam-webster.com/dictionary/Black.
363. Gaither, Sarah E., Ariel M. Cohen-Goldberg, Calvin Gidney, and Keith B. Maddox. "Sounding Black or White: Priming Identity and Biracial Speech." Frontiers in Psychology 06 (April 20, 2015). https://doi.org/10.3389/fpsyg.2015.00457.
364. Libit, Daniel. "Transcribers' Agony: Frustrated Not by What Trump Says but How He Says It." CNBC, August 18, 2016. https://www.cnbc.com/2016/08/15/transcribers-agony-frustrated-not-by-what-trump-says-but-how-he-says-it.html.
365. HBS Working Knowledge. "Minorities Who 'Whiten' Job Resumes Get More Interviews," May 17, 2017. http://hbswk.hbs.edu/item/minorities-who-whiten-job-resumes-get-more-interviews.
366. NBER. "Employers' Replies to Racial Names." Accessed November 11, 2021. https://www.nber.org/digest/sep03/employers-replies-racial-names.
367. NBER. "Employers' Replies to Racial Names."
368. HBS Working Knowledge. "Minorities Who 'Whiten' Job Resumes Get More Interviews." Accessed November 11, 2021. https://hbswk.hbs.edu/item/minorities-who-Whiten-job-resumes-get-more-interviews
369. HBS Working Knowledge. "Minorities Who 'Whiten' Job Resumes Get More Interviews." Accessed November 11, 2021. https://hbswk.hbs.edu/item/minorities-who-Whiten-job-resumes-get-more-interviews.
370. HBS Working Knowledge. "Who Has Potential? For Many White Men, It's Often Other White Men," May 10, 2021. https://hbswk.hbs.edu/item/who-has-potential-for-white-men-its-usually-other-white-men.
371. HBS Working Knowledge. "Minorities Who 'Whiten' Job Resumes Get More Interviews."
372. Waziyatawin. "Understanding Colonizer Status." *Unsettling America: Decolonization in Theory & Practice*, September 6, 2011. Accessed February 1, 2021. https://unsettlingamerica.wordpress.com/2011/09/06/understanding-colonizer-status/.
373. Victor, Daniel. "What, Congressman Steve King Asks, Have Nonwhites Done for Civilization?" *The New York Times*, July 19, 2016. https://www.nytimes.com/2016/07/19/us/politics/steve-king-nonwhite-subgroups.html.
374. Cuncic, Arlin, MA. "What Is Cultural Appropriation?" *Verywell Mind*, November 8, 2022. https://www.verywellmind.com/what-is-cultural-appropriation-5070458.
375. Johnson, Maisha Z. "What's Wrong with Cultural Appropriation? These 9 Answers Reveal Its Harm." Everyday Feminism, August 14, 2020. https://everydayfeminism.com/2015/06/cultural-appropriation-wrong/
376. Writing the Other. "My Culture Is Not A Trend: A Dialogue About Cultural Appropriation," August 2018. Accessed November 19, 2021. https://writingtheother.com/wp-content/uploads/2018/08/On-Reverse-Cultural-Appropriation.pdf.
377. Madarang, Charisma. "This Is How Lucky Charms Have Transformed Over 50 Years." Foodbeast, March 6, 2014. https://www.foodbeast.com/news/how-lucky-charms-marshmallow-shapes-have-changed-over-the-past-50-years/.
378. Lewis, Danny. "How Did the Six-Pointed Star Become Associated with Judaism?" *Smithsonian Magazine*, July 6, 2016. https://www.smithsonianmag.com/smart-news/how-did-the-six-pointed-star-become-associated-with-judaism-180959693/.

379. Gelman, Lilly. "The Star of David: Between Judaism and Zionism." Moment Magazine, June 26, 2019. https://momentmag.com/the-star-of-david-between-judaism-and-zionism/.
380. Dutt, Yashica. "A Cultural History of White Girls Wearing Bindis." *Vice* (blog), October 16, 2015. https://www.vice.com/en/article/xye97d/a-cultural-history-of-white-girls-wearing-bindis.
381. Banyan Botanicals. "Brahmi Oil (Coconut)." Accessed August 6, 2023. https://www.banyanbotanicals.com/brahmi-oil-coconut/.
382. Dutt, Yashica. "A Cultural History of White Girls Wearing Bindis."
383. Dutt, Yashica. "A Cultural History of White Girls Wearing Bindis."
384. "Royalty." Netflix, July 23, 2021. Accessed October 27, 2021. https://www.netflix.com/title/80216752.
385. World Population Review. "GDP Ranked by Country 2023." Accessed November 20, 2021. https://worldpopulationreview.com/countries/countries-by-gdp.
386. KCTS9. "Treasures of the World | Taj Mahal." pbs.org. Accessed August 20, 2023. https://www.pbs.org/treasuresoftheworld/a_nav/taj_nav/tajnav_level_1/3building_tajfrm.html. https://www.tajmahal.org.uk/legends/theft-in-taj.html.
387. Harari, Yuval N. Homo Deus: A Brief History of Tomorrow. First U.S. edition. New York, NY: Harper, an imprint of HarperCollins Publishers, 2017.
388. Krikorian, Stephanie. "The Cash Is Always Greener: Hamptonites Are Shelling out 6 Figures to Keep Lawns Lush." *Vanity Fair*, July 18, 2023. https://www.vanityfair.com/style/2023/07/hamptonites-are-shelling-out-six-figures-to-keep-lawns-lush.
389. Boissoneault, Lorraine. "The True Story of the Koh-i-Noor Diamond—and Why the British Won't Give It Back." *Smithsonian Magazine*, August 30, 2017. https://www.smithsonianmag.com/history/true-story-koh-i-noor-diamondand-why-british-wont-give-it-back-180964660/.
390. Boissoneault, Lorraine. "The True Story of the Koh-i-Noor Diamond—and Why the British Won't Give It Back."
391. Smith, Nicholas. "Henry Cole and the Koh-i-Noor Diamond." V&A Blog, August 22, 2017. https://www.vam.ac.uk/blog/caring-for-our-collections/henry-cole-and-the-koh-i-noor-diamond.
392. Frayer, Lauren. "Why the Kohinoor Diamond Won't Make an Appearance at King Charles III's Coronation." *NPR*, May 4, 2023. https://www.npr.org/2023/05/04/1173260412/kohinoor-diamond-coronation-charles-camilla-crown.
393. Frayer, Lauren. "Why the Kohinoor Diamond Won't Make an Appearance at King Charles III's Coronation."
394. New Delhi Television. "Kohinoor Diamond Will Stay Put in Britain: David Cameron to NDTV (July 2010)," April 18, 2016. https://www.youtube.com/watch?v=aAun-xH2UB0.
395. Historic Royal Palaces. "See the Crown Jewels," Accessed August 8, 2023. https://www.hrp.org.uk/tower-of-london/whats-on/the-crown-jewels/.
396. International Gem Society LLC. "What Is the British Coronation Regalia and How Much Is It Worth?" gemsociety.org, April 27, 2023. https://www.*gemsociety.org*/news/2023/04/20/british-coronation-regalia-worth/.
397. Monbiot, George. "Trashing the Planet and Hiding the Money Isn't a Perversion of Capitalism. It Is Capitalism." The Guardian, October 7, 2021. https://www.theguardian.com/commentisfree/2021/oct/06/offshoring-wealth-capitalism-pandora-papers.
398. Arundhati, Baitmangalkar. "How We Can Work Together to Avoid Cultural Appropriation in Yoga," Yogainternational.Com, February 26, 2021. https://yogainternational.com/article/view/how-we-can-work-together-to-avoid-cultural-appropriation-in-yoga/.
399. The Editors of Encyclopedia Britannica. "Yoga | Benefits, History & Types." Encyclopedia Britannica, July 20, 1998. https://www.britannica.com/topic/Yoga-philosophy.
400. Heibel, Christa. "A Short History of Yoga in India." Replenish Living | International Falls, Minnesota, May 10, 2023. https://www.replenishliving.com/a-short-history-of-yoga-in-india/.
401. Hammond, Holly. "The Timeline and History of Yoga in America". Yoga Journal. 2018. Accessed November, 20, 2021. https://en.wikipedia.org/wiki/Yoga_in_the_United_States

402. "Ida Craddock." In Wikipedia, June 6, 2023. Accessed November 6, 2021. https://en.wikipedia.org/wiki/Ida_Craddock.
403. Mishra, Debashree. "Once Upon A Time: From 1918, this Yoga institute has been teaching generations, creating history." Mumbai: Indian Express. July 3, 2016. Accessed November 20, 2021. https://en.wikipedia.org/wiki/Yoga_in_the_United_States
404. Farmer, Jared. Review of AMERICANASANA, by Mark Singleton, Stefanie Syman, and Robert Love. *Reviews in American History* 40, no. 1 (2012): 145–58. Accessed November 26, 2021 http://www.jstor.org/stable/41348960
405. Farmer, Jared. "Review of AMERICANASANA."
406. Farmer, Jared. "Review of AMERICANASANA."
407. Arundhati, Baitmangalkar. "How We Can Work Together to Avoid Cultural Appropriation in Yoga."
408. Farmer, Jared. "Review of AMERICANASANA."
409. "Cover Page," *Om Yoga Magazine*. Issue 113. January, 2021. https://www.ommagazine.com/magazine/issue-113-january-2021/.
410. "Stewart Gilchrist – Authentic Radical Yogi," *Om Yoga Magazine*. Issue 113. January, 2021. Accessed March 4, 2021, https://www.ommagazine.com/stewart-gilchrist-authentic-radical-yogi/.
411. "Buddha Pants" *Om Yoga Magazine*. Issue 113. January, 2021. Accessed February 2, 2021, https://www.ommagazine.com/buddha-pants/
412. Walton, Alice G. "How Yoga Is Spreading In The U.S." Forbes, March 15, 2016. https://www.forbes.com/sites/alicegwalton/2016/03/15/how-yoga-is-spreading-in-the-us/?sh=1fdee42e449f.
413. Johnson, Nicole. "60+ Insane Yoga Statistics: Why Yoga Is the Fastest Growing Industry," July 22, 2023. https://bookretreats.com/blog/yoga-statistics.
414. Anjali, Joshi. "Why a Bindi Is NOT an Example of Cultural Appropriation." HuffPost. Huffington Post, April 15, 2014. Accessed July 22, 2023, https://www.huffpost.com/entry/why-a-bindi-is-not-an-exa_b_5150693?guccounter=1.
415. Morris, Wesley. "Why Is Everyone Always Stealing Black Music?" The New York Times, November 9, 2021. https://www.nytimes.com/interactive/2019/08/14/magazine/music-black-culture-appropriation.html.
416. Morris, Wesley. "Why Is Everyone Always Stealing Black Music?"
417. Jackson, Ashawnta. "The Conservative Christian War on Rock and Roll." JSTOR Daily, February 3, 2021. Accessed August 7, 2023, https://daily.jstor.org/the-conservative-christian-war-on-rock-and-roll/.
418. Haines, John. "The Emergence of Jesus Rock: On Taming the 'African Beat.'" Black Music Research Journal 31, no. 2 (2011): 229–60. https://doi.org/10.5406/blacmusiresej.31.2.0229.
419. Jackson, Ashawnta. "The Conservative Christian War on Rock and Roll."
420. Wall, Mick. *When Giants Walked the Earth: A Biography of Led Zeppelin*. 1st U.S. ed. New York: St. Martin's Press, 2009.
421. Ross, Michael E. "The Rolling Stones' '(I Can't Get No) Satisfaction': A History, PopMatters." PopMatters, July 30, 2015. https://www.popmatters.com/195573-satisfaction-a-history-2495505454.html.
422. Iasimone, Ashley. "Billboard." Billboard, March 18, 2017. https://www.billboard.com/articles/columns/rock/7728708/chuck-berry-tribute-mick-jagger-rolling-stones.
423. Beal, James. "Rolling Stones Axe Brown Sugar from US Tour Set List over Slavery and Rape Lyrics..." *The US Sun*, October 13, 2021. https://www.thesun.com/entertainment/3851514/rolling-stones-axe-brown-sugar/.
424. Beal, James. "Rolling Stones Axe Brown Sugar from US Tour Set List over Slavery and Rape Lyrics."
425. Naledi Ushe Usa. "Appropriation or Appreciation? How 'Elvis' Highlights His Complicated History with Black Music." *USA TODAY*, September 2, 2022. Accessed August 7, 2023, https://www.usatoday.com/story/entertainment/music/2022/06/30/elvis-presley-complicated-relationship-black-music/7746069001/.

426. Setaro, Shawn. "Here's Why Post Malone Is a Problem." Complex, May 20, 2023. https://www.complex.com/music/2017/11/post-malone-and-racism.
427. Setaro, Shawn. "Here's Why Post Malone Is a Problem."
428. "Definition of Wigger." In Merriam-Webster Dictionary, Accessed February 1, 2021, https://www.merriam-webster.com/dictionary/wigger.
429. Penn II, Michael. "Post Malone Tries to Go Post-Racial in America," Vinyl Me, Please, February 24, 2016, https://magazine.vinylmeplease.com/magazine/post-malone-tries-to-go-post- racial-in-america/.
430. Penn II, Michael. "Post Malone Tries to Go Post-Racial in America."
431. Penn II, Michael. "Post Malone Tries to Go Post-Racial in America."
432. Association of Research Libraries. "Copyright Timeline: A History of Copyright in the United States," December 18, 2020. Accessed August 7, 2023. https://www.arl.org/copyright-timeline/.
433. Johnson, Maisha Z. "6 Ways Well-Intentioned People Whitesplain Racism (And Why They Need To Stop)." The Body Is Not an Apology, August 3, 2021. https://thebodyisnotanapology.com/magazine/6-ways-well-intentioned-people-whitesplain-racism-and-why-they-need-to-stop/.
434. Facing History & Ourselves. "Killing the Indian in the Child," September 20, 2019. Accessed November 26, 2021, https://www.facinghistory.org/stolen-lives-indigenous-peoples-canada-and-indian-residential-schools/chapter-3/killing-indian-child.
435. Callimachi, Rukmini, and Sharon Chischilly. "Lost Lives, Lost Culture: The Forgotten History of Indigenous Boarding Schools." *The New York Times*, November 17, 2021. https://www.nytimes.com/2021/07/19/us/us-canada-indigenous-boarding-residential-schools.html.
436. Williams, Samantha. "Native American Boarding Schools: Some Basic Facts and Statistics." May 8, 2020. https://www.samanthamwilliams.com/blog/native-american-boarding-schools-some-basic-facts-and-statistics.437. Facing History & Ourselves. "Killing the Indian in the Child."
438. Williams, Samantha. "Native American Boarding Schools: Some Basic Facts and Statistics."
439. Little, Becky. "How Boarding Schools Tried to 'Kill the Indian' through Assimilation." *HISTORY*, July 11, 2023. https://www.history.com/news/how-boarding-schools-tried-to-kill-the-indian-through-assimilation.
440. Cleveland, Claire. "Legacy Of Indigenous Boarding Schools In Colorado Includes Unmarked Graves And Generational Scars." *Colorado Public Radio*, August 6, 2021. https://www.cpr.org/2021/08/02/indigenous-boarding-schools-colorado-unmarked-graves-generational-scars/.
441. Cleveland, Claire. "Legacy Of Indigenous Boarding Schools In Colorado Includes Unmarked Graves And Generational Scars."
442. Facing History & Ourselves. "Killing the Indian in the Child."
443. Raz, Guy. "Famous Dave's: Dave Anderson." How I Built This. NPR, November 2020.
444. Callimachi, Rukmini, et al. "Lost Lives, Lost Culture: The Forgotten History of Indigenous Boarding Schools."
445. Callimachi, Rukmini, et al. "Lost Lives, Lost Culture: The Forgotten History of Indigenous Boarding Schools."
446. United States Senate "Indian Reform School; Rules and Regulations; Consent of Parents to Placing Youth in Reform School." In United States Code. Vol. Title 25. Indians Chapter 7. Sec. 302. U.S. Government Publishing Office: www.gpo.gov, Accessed February 8, 2021 https://www.rounds.senate.gov/imo/media/doc/Summary%20of%20RESPECT%20bills.pdf.
447. Facing History & Ourselves. "Killing the Indian in the Child."
448. The Canadian Encyclopedia. "Residential Schools in Canada," Accessed February 8, 2021. https://www.thecanadianencyclopedia.ca/en/article/residential-schools.
449. Facing History & Ourselves. "Killing the Indian in the Child."
450. Anthony, Craig. "Indigenous Education," Martinez Fellowship Seminar. Technology Access Foundation. 2020.

451. U.S. Department of the Interior. "Indian Affairs." Bureau of Indian Education (BIE), Accessed November 26, 2021, https://www.bia.gov/bie.
452. Alden, Woods. "Lessons Lost: The Federal Government Gives Native Students an Inadequate Education, and Gets Away with It." *ProPublica*, August 10, 2020. https://www.propublica.org/article/the-federal-government-gives-native-students-an-inadequate-education-and-gets-away-with-it.
453. Writing the Other. "My Culture Is Not A Trend: A Dialogue About Cultural Appropriation,"
454. Moreno, Johan. "Black Google Product Manager Stopped By Security Because They Didn't Believe He Was An Employee." *Forbes*, September 23, 2021. https://www.forbes.com/sites/johanmoreno/2021/09/23/black-google-associate-product-manager-detained-by-security-because-they-didnt-believe-he-was-an-employee/?sh=7284d5f22349.
455. American Civil Liberties Union. "Know Your Rights | Students' Rights | ACLU," June 23, 2023. https://www.aclu.org/know-your-rights/students-rights.
456. Chico, Beverly. "Hats and Headwear around the World: A Cultural Encyclopedia." *Choice Reviews Online* 51, no. 09 (April 22, 2014): 51–4787. https://doi.org/10.5860/choice.51-4787.
457. Emdin, Christopher. *For White Folks Who Teach in the Hood... and the Rest of y'all Too: Reality Pedagogy and Urban Education*. A Simmons College/Beacon Press Race, Education, and Democracy Series Book. Boston: Beacon Press, 2016.
458. PBS Online. "Only A Teacher - Schoolhouse Pioneers: Horace Mann (1796-1859)." Accessed November 11, 2021. https://www.pbs.org/onlyateacher/horace.html.
459. Caito, Pam. "How Schools Operated in 1830." Johnson County Public Library. Accessed November 27, 2021. https://www.pageafterpage.org/how-schools-operated-in-1830.s
460. Austin, Jensen. "The Education of Upper Class Young Men." BYU Presents Pride and Prejudice, February 1, 2014. https://byuprideandprejudice.wordpress.com/2014/02/05/the-education-of-upper-class-young-men-2/.
461. Race Forward. "Historical Timeline of Public Education in the US." Accessed November 27, 2021. https://www.raceforward.org/research/reports/historical-timeline-public-education-us.
462. Emdin, Christopher. *For White Folks Who Teach in the Hood... and the Rest of y'all Too: Reality Pedagogy and Urban Education*.
463. Okun, Tema. "(Divorcing) White Supremacy Culture: Coming Home to Who We Really Are." White Supremacy Culture. Accessed August 20, 2023. https://www.whitesupremacyculture.info/.
464. Centre for Community Organizations. "White Supremacy Culture in Organizations: By Dismantling Racism Works." *coco-net.org*. Accessed November 27, 2021. https://coco-net.org/wp-content/uploads/2019/11/Coco-WhiteSupCulture-ENG4.pdf.
465. Denning, Steve. "Reinvent Education As Well As Creating Greater Access." Forbes, June 28, 2020. https://www.forbes.com/sites/stevedenning/2020/06/28/reinvent-education-ahead-of-creating-greater-access/?sh=5f93899e61ed.
466. Local Futures. "Derek Rasmussen: Stemming The Tide of De-Indigenization" The Economics of Happiness. March 30, 2015. https://www.youtube.com/watch?v=cr87shQNnYA.
467. Denning, Steve. "Reinvent Education As Well As Creating Greater Access."
468. Dahmer, David. "The Harsh Truth about Progressive Cities." Madison365, September 3, 2015. https://madison365.com/what-no-one-wants-to-talk-about-race-and-progressive-cities/.
469. Zane, Zachary, and Calen Razor. "Here's How Often Men and Women Really Think about Sex." *Men's Health*, November 2, 2021. https://www.menshealth.com/sex-women/a28483383/how-often-think-about-sex/.
470. Lander, Christian. *Stuff White People like: The Definitive Guide to the Unique Taste of Millions*. New York: Random House Trade Paperbacks, 2008.
471. Desjardins, Jeff. "All of the World's Money and Markets in One Visualization." Visual Capitalist, May 27, 2020. https://www.visualcapitalist.com/all-of-the-worlds-money-and-markets-in-one-visualization-2020/.

472. McIntosh, Peggy. "How to Recognize Your White Privilege — and Use It to Fight Inequality."
473. Heidler, Jeanne T., and David S. Heidler. "Manifest Destiny | Summary, Examples, Westward Expansion, & Significance." Encyclopedia Britannica, August 11, 2023. https://www.britannica.com/event/Manifest-Destiny#ref1253055.
474. Smithsonian American Art Museum. "Manifest Destiny and U.S Westward Expansion," August 2014. https://americanexperience.si.edu/wp-content/uploads/2014/08/Manifest-Destiny-and-U.S-Westward-Expansion.pdf.
475. Knowing Jesus. "149 Bible Verses About Nature." Accessed December 17, 2021. https://bible.knowing-jesus.com/topics/Nature.
476. Bible Hub. "Matthew 28:19 - The Great Commission." Accessed December 27, 2021. https://biblehub.com/matthew/28-19.htm.
477. Smithsonian American Art Museum. "Manifest Destiny and U.S Westward Expansion."
478. Smithsonian American Art Museum. "Manifest Destiny and U.S Westward Expansion."
479. Evans, Eli T. "A Shining City on a Hill." Bible Study Magazine, September 2015. Accessed December 17, 2021. https://web.archive.org/web/20210429064800/https://www.biblestudymagazine.com/septoct-2015-a-shining-city-on-a-hill.
480. Evans, Eli T. "A Shining City on a Hill."
481. Goddard, Taegan. "City on a Hill." *In Political Dictionary*. Accessed December 12, 2021. https://politicaldictionary.com/words/city-on-a-hill/.
482. White, Jeremy B. "When Reagan Dared to Say 'God Bless America.'" POLITICO Magazine, July 17, 2015. https://www.politico.com/magazine/story/2015/07/reagan-god-bless-america-120286/.
483. White, Jeremy B. "When Reagan Dared to Say 'God Bless America.'"
484. Utt, Jamie, and Shelly Tochluk. "White Teacher, Know Thyself: Improving Anti-Racist Praxis through Racial Identity Development." *Urban Education 55*, no. 1 (May 16, 2016): 125–52. https://doi.org/10.1177/0042085916648741.
485. Kreitner, Richard. Break It up: *Secession, Division, and the Secret History of America's Imperfect Union*. First edition. New York: Little, Brown and Company, 2020.
486. National Humanities Center. "Observations on the Disunity of the American Colonies, 1722-1764." Accessed December 3, 2021. http://nationalhumanitiescenter.org/pds/becomingamer/american/text4/unionofcolonies.pdf.
487. National Humanities Center. "Observations on the Disunity of the American Colonies, 1722-1764."
488. Facing History & Ourselves. "Statistics from the Civil War," August 12, 2022. https://www.facinghistory.org/resource-library/statistics-civil-war.
489. Walsh, Joe. "U.S. Just Surpassed 650,000 Covid Deaths—These 8 States Have The Highest Fatality Rates." *Forbes*, September 8, 2021. https://www.forbes.com/sites/joewalsh/2021/09/08/us-just-surpassed-650000-covid-deaths-these-8-states-have-the-highest-fatality-rates/?sh=415614e03161.
490. Kreitner, Richard. Break It up: *Secession, Division, and the Secret History of America's Imperfect Union*.
491. Kreitner, Richard. Break It up: *Secession, Division, and the Secret History of America's Imperfect Union*.
482. Cremers, Jurriën. "Lessons Learned: American Diplomats in the Netherlands, 1780-1801." Thesis for the Research Master in History. Leiden University, 2012.
493. Kreitner, Richard. Break It up: *Secession, Division, and the Secret History of America's Imperfect Union*.
494. Butterfield, Lyman H. "Dr. Rush to Governor Henry on the Declaration of Independence and the Virginia Constitution." Proceedings of the American Philosophical Society 95, no. 3 (1951): 250–53. https://www.jstor.org/stable/3143062.
495. Kreitner, Richard. Break It up: *Secession, Division, and the Secret History of America's Imperfect Union*.
496. Kreitner, Richard. Break It up: *Secession, Division, and the Secret History of America's Imperfect Union*.

497. Kreitner, Richard. *Break It up: Secession, Division, and the Secret History of America's Imperfect Union.*
498. Stevens, Jason, ed. "On the Constitution and the Union: William Lloyd Garrison." Teaching American History. Accessed August 20, 2023. https://teachingamericanhistory.org/document/on-the-constitution-and-the-union-2/.
499. Wise, Tim J., ed. *White like Me: Reflections on Race from a Privileged Son; the Remix.* Rev. and Updated. ed. Berkeley, Calif: Soft Skull Press, 2011.
500. Cillizza, Chris. "Trump's 'shithole' Comment Is His New Rock Bottom." CNN Politics. January 11, 2018. https://www.cnn.com/2018/01/11/politics/trump-rock-bottom/index.html.
501. HuffPost. "10 Ironic 'Speak English' Signs (photos)," September 23, 2012. https://www.huffpost.com/entry/13-ironic-speak-english-signs_n_1906008.
502. De Witte, Melissa. "When Thomas Jefferson Penned 'All Men Are Created Equal,' He Did Not Mean Individual Equality, Says Stanford Scholar." Stanford News Service, July 1, 2020. Accessed December 4, 2021. https://news.stanford.edu/press-releases/2020/07/01/meaning-declaratnce-changed-time/.
503. De Witte, Melissa. "When Thomas Jefferson Penned 'All Men Are Created Equal,' He Did Not Mean Individual Equality, Says Stanford Scholar."
504. National Archives. "Declaration of Independence: A Transcription," January 31, 2023. Accessed December 3, 2021. https://www.archives.gov/founding-docs/declaration-transcript.
505. Foresi, Tiffany. "'The Absolute Right to Rule' – The Divine Right of Kings." Royal Central, May 28, 2019. https://royalcentral.co.uk/features/the-absolute-right-to-rule-the-divine-right-of-kings-40465/.
506. Foresi, Tiffany. "'The Absolute Right to Rule' – The Divine Right of Kings."
507. Foresi, Tiffany. "'The Absolute Right to Rule' – The Divine Right of Kings."
508. Center for Documentary Studies at Duke University. "S4: Seeing White E1: Rich Man's Revolt" Scene on Radio. January 28, 2020. https://sceneonradio.org/the-land-that-never-has-been-yet/.
509. Miller, Marion Mills, ed. *Great Debates in American History: Slavery from 1790 to 1857; with an introduction by C. F. Adams.* Volume 4 of *Great Debates in American History: From the Debates in the British Parliament on the Colonial Stamp Act (1764-1765) to the Debates in Congress at the Close of the Taft Administration (1912-1913).* New York: Current Literature Publishing Company, 1913. P. 59 Accessed December 3, 2021 https://books.google.com/books?id=wfGLdz2NMfUC&pg=PA59&lpg=PA59&dq=%22.
510. Writers, Fiusm Contributing. "How Military Recruitment Targets Low-Income Schools, And Why That's A Problem." *PantherNOW*, July 29, 2020. Accessed April 17, 2021 http://panthernow.com/2020/07/27/how-military-recruitment-targets-low-income-schools-and-why-thats-a-problem/.
511. Keyes, Allison. "Military Recruiters Target Blacks, Hispanics." NPR, August 16, 2005, sec. Race. Accessed April 17, 2021. https://www.npr.org/templates/story/story.php?storyId=4801610.
512. Camacho, Roberto. "Military Recruiters Are Increasingly Targeting Latinx Students for Enlistment." *Prism*, September 19, 2022. https://prismreports.org/2022/09/19/military-recruiters-target-latinx-students/.
513. Caffier, Justin. "The US Army Somehow Thought This Rap Recruitment Video Was a Good Idea." *Vice* (blog), February 27, 2019. https://www.vice.com/en/article/nexq4d/look-upon-this-cringey-us-army-rap-recruitment-video-and-despair.
514. Alston, Christopher. "The Army Field Band Now Has Its First Rappers." NPR, July 26, 2023, sec. National. https://www.npr.org/2023/07/26/1190327589/the-army-field-band-now-has-its-first-rappers.
515. Stewart, Phil, M.B. Pell, and Joshua Schneyer. "The Military's Racial Reckoning: U.S.Troops Battling Racism Report High Barrier to Justice." *Reuters Reports,* September 15, 2020. https://www.reuters.com/investigates/special-report/usa-military-civilrights/.

516. Creitz, Charles. "Rep. Waltz Slams West Point 'White Rage' Instruction: Enemy's Ammo 'Doesn't Care about Race, Politics.'" *Fox News*, April 9, 2021. https://www.foxnews.com/politics/rep-michael-waltz-slams-west-point-white-rage-instruction-enemys-ammo-doesnt-care-about-race-politics.
517. National Alliance to End Homelessness. "People of Color Make Up a Disproportionate Share of the Homeless Veteran Population - National Alliance to End Homelessness," January 16, 2019. https://endhomelessness.org/resource/people-color-make-much-larger-share-homeless-veteran-population-general-veteran-population/.
518. Dunne, Eugene M., Larry E. Burrell, Allyson Diggins, Nicole Ennis Whitehead, and William W. Latimer. "Increased Risk for Substance Use and Health-Related Problems among Homeless Veterans." *American Journal on Addictions* 24, no. 7 (September 11, 2015): 676–80. https://doi.org/10.1111/ajad.12289.
519. VHA Office of Mental Health. "Veterans Experiencing Homelessness." US Department of Veteran Affairs. va.gov, February 27, 2018. Accessed April 17, 2021. https://web.archive.org/web/2021
520. Bryan, Jami L. "Fighting For Respect: African-American Soldiers in WWI." *The Army Historical Foundation,* February 15, 2018. https://armyhistory.org/fighting-for-respect-african-american-soldiers-in-wwi/.
521. Equal Justice Initiative. "Lynching In America: Targeting Black Veterans," 2017. https://eji.org/wp-content/uploads/2019/10/lynching-in-america-targeting-black-veterans-web.pdf.
522. Equal Justice Initiative. "Lynching In America: Targeting Black Veterans."
523. Equal Justice Initiative. "Lynching In America: Targeting Black Veterans."
524. Morley, Jefferson, and Jon Schwarz. "More Proof The U.S. National Anthem Has Always Been Tainted with Racism." *The Intercept*, July 25, 2023. https://theintercept.com/2016/09/13/more-proof-the-u-s-national-anthem-has-always-been-tainted-with-racism/.
525. American Battlefield Trust. "The British Corps of Colonial Marines," May 16, 2021. https://www.battlefields.org/learn/articles/british-corps-colonial-marines.
526. American Battlefield Trust. "Cornerstone Speech: Savannah, Georgia, March 21, 1861," Accessed February 4, 2022. https://www.battlefields.org/learn/primary-sources/cornerstone-speech.
527. Hyphenated America. "Making Immigration Laws and Policies Easier to Understand." Accessed June 6, 2021. https://web.archive.org/web/20201102004904/https://www.hyphenatedamerica.org/.
528. Times, New York. "Roosevelt Bars the Hyphenated; No Room in This Country for Dual Nationality." The New York Times, October 13, 1915. Accessed June 20, 2021. https://www.nytimes.com/1915/10/13/archives/roosevelt-bars-the-hyphenated-no-room-in-this-country-for-dual.html.
529. Ignatiev, Noel. *How the Irish Became White*. Routledge Classics. New York: Routledge, 2009.
530. Ignatiev, Noel. *How the Irish Became White*.
531. Slayton, Robert. "When Did Jews Become White?" *Jewish Currents*, September 21, 2021. https://jewishcurrents.org/when-did-jews-become-White/.
532. Kaplan, Karen. "DNA Ties Ashkenazi Jews to Group of Just 330 People from Middle Ages - Los Angeles Times." *Los Angeles Times,* September 9, 2014. https://www.latimes.com/science/sciencenow/la-sci-sn-ashkenazi-jews-dna-diseases-20140909-story.html.
533. Slayton, Robert. "When Did Jews Become White?"
534. Center for Documentary Studies at Duke University. "S4: Seeing White E6: A New Deal" Scene on Radio. March 17, 2020. https://sceneonradio.org/the-land-that-never-has-been-yet/.
535. Dean, David. "Roots Deeper than Whiteness." White Awake, January 31, 2023. https://whiteawake.org/2018/10/27/roots-deeper-than-whiteness/.
536. Dean, David. "Roots Deeper than Whiteness."
537. Dean, David. "Roots Deeper than Whiteness."
538. Center for Documentary Studies at Duke University. "S4: Seeing White E6: A New Deal"

539. Lipsitz, George. *The Possessive Investment in Whiteness: How White People Profit from Identity Politics*. Rev. and Expanded ed. Philadelphia: Temple University Press, 2006.
540. Roediger, David R., ed. *Black on White: Black Writers on What It Means to Be White*. 1st ed. New York: Schocken Books, 1998.
541. Wilkerson, Isabel. Caste: The Origins of Our Discontents. p. 48
542. LeVine, Mark. "Abolishing Whiteness Has Never Been More Urgent." Racism | Al Jazeera, November 17, 2019. https://www.aljazeera.com/opinions/2019/11/17/abolishing-whiteness-has-never-been-more-urgent.
543. Aderet, Ofer. "The Uncomfortable Truths of Jewish Life in the U.S. South - U.S. News." *Haaretz.Com*, June 22, 2021. https://www.haaretz.com/us-news/.premium.MAGAZINE-slave-owners-confederates-and-wrestlers-jews-of-the-u-s-south-in-the-showcase-1.9928841.
544. Aderet, Ofer. "The Uncomfortable Truths of Jewish Life in the U.S. South - U.S. News."
545. Aderet, Ofer. "The Uncomfortable Truths of Jewish Life in the U.S. South - U.S. News."
546. Butler, Pierce "Judah P. Benjamin." American Crisis Biographies." Philadelphia: George W. Jacobs & Company. 1907. P. 118-119 https://en.wikipedia.org/wiki/Judah_P._Benjamin
547. Aderet, Ofer. "The Uncomfortable Truths of Jewish Life in the U.S. South - U.S. News."
548. Aderet, Ofer. "The Uncomfortable Truths of Jewish Life in the U.S. South - U.S. News."
549. James, Baldwin. "Negroes Are Anti-Semitic Because They're Anti-White." New York Times Archives, April 9, 1967. Accessed December 18, 2021. https://archive.nytimes.com/www.nytimes.com/books/98/03/29/specials/baldwin-antisem.html?_r=1.
550. James, Baldwin. "Negroes Are Anti-Semitic Because They're Anti-White."
551. Strom, Adam. "Benjamin Franklin and German Immigrants in Colonial America." Re-Imagining Migration (blog), October 3, 2019. https://reimaginingmigration.org/benjamin-franklin-and-german-immigrants-in-colonial-america/.
552. Strom, Adam. "Benjamin Franklin and German Immigrants in Colonial America." *Re-Imagining Migration* (blog), October 3, 2019. https://reimaginingmigration.org/benjamin-franklin-and-german-immigrants-in-colonial-america/.
553. Strom, Adam. "Benjamin Franklin and German Immigrants in Colonial America."
554. Little, Becky "When German Immigrants Were America's Undesirables." *HISTORY*, April 2, 2019. https://www.history.com/news/anti-german-sentiment-wwi.
555. Siegel, Robert. "During World War I, U.S. Government Propaganda Erased German Culture." NPR, April 7, 2017. https://www.npr.org/2017/04/07/523044253/during-world-war-i-u-s-government-propaganda-erased-german-culture.
556. Siegel, Robert. "During World War I, U.S. Government Propaganda Erased German Culture."
557. Siegel, Robert. "During World War I, U.S. Government Propaganda Erased German Culture."
558. Resnick, Brian. "White Fear of Demographic Change Is a Powerful Psychological Force." *Vox*, January 28, 2017. Accessed January 2, 2022. https://www.vox.com/science-and-health/2017/1/26/14340542/White-fear-trump-psychology-minority-majority.
559. Resnick, Brian. "White Fear of Demographic Change Is a Powerful Psychological Force."
560. Bonitatibus, Steve. "How White Supremacy Returned to Mainstream Politics," *Center for American Progress*, June 5, 2023, https://www.americanprogress.org/issues/security/reports/2020/07/01/482414/white-supremacy-returned-mainstream-politics/.
561. Coates, Ta-Nehisi. "Donald Trump Is the First White President." *The Atlantic*, May 22, 2018. Accessed March 30, 2020. https://www.theatlantic.com/magazine/archive/2017/10/the-first-white-president-ta-nehisi-coates/537909/
562. Center for Documentary Studies at Duke University. "S2: Seeing White E1: Turning the Lens." Scene on Radio. February 15, 2017. https://sceneonradio.org/episode-31-turning-the-lens-seeing-white-part-1/.
563. Dyson, Michael Eric. *Tears We Cannot Stop: A Sermon to White America*. First edition. New York: St. Martin's Press, 2017.
564. "H. R. 40, Naturalization Bill, March 4, 1790 | U.S. Capitol - Visitor Center." Accessed August 12, 2023. https://www.visitthecapitol.gov/artifact/h-r-40-naturalization-bill-

march-4-1790.
565. Office of the Historian. "Milestones: 1921–1936." Accessed August 12, 2023. https://history.state.gov/milestones/1921-1936/immigration-act.
566. Wilkerson, Isabel. Caste: The Origins of Our Discontents. p. 50
567. Abad-Santos, Alex. "What "Fresh off the Boat" Means to Asian-Americans." *Vox*, January 16, 2015. Accessed January 28, 2022. https://www.vox.com/2014/5/15/5717046/what-fresh-off-the-boat-means-to-asian-americans.
568. Yoshida, Kate Shaw. "Not yet Gone, but Effectively Extinct," Ars Technica, July 12, 2013, https://arstechnica.com/science/2013/07/not-yet-gone-but-effectively-extinct/.
569. Cupp, S. E. "What Laura Ingraham Said Was Awful. And Unsurprising." CNN, August 9, 2018. https://www.cnn.com/2018/08/09/opinions/laura-ingraham-awful-immigrant-remark-cupp/index.html.
570. Barr, Jeremy. "The Hollywood Reporter." *The Hollywood Reporter*, May 28, 2019. https://www.hollywoodreporter.com/news/trump-2020-campaign-sponsored-fox-news-host-laura-ingrahams-podcast-1214078.
571. Acosta, Brian Stelter Dana Bash and Jim. "Laura Ingraham Being Considered for White House Press Secretary Post." CNN Money, November 14, 2016. Accessed December 18, 2021. https://money.cnn.com/2016/11/14/media/laura-ingraham-press-secretary/.
572. "Conserve Definition - Google Search." Accessed April 9, 2021. https://www.google.com/search?q=conserve+definition.
573. "Definition of Conserve." In *Merriam-Webster Dictionary*, August 9, 2023. Accessed April 9, 2021. https://www.merriam-webster.com/dictionary/conserve.
574. Bonitatibus, Steve. "How White Supremacy Returned to Mainstream Politics." *Center for American Progress*, June 5, 2023. https://www.americanprogress.org/issues/security/reports/2020/07/01/482414/white-supremacy-returned-mainstream-politics/.
575. Reimann, Nicholas. "'It's Hurtful': McConnell Says Comment Suggesting Black Voters Aren't 'Americans' Was Accidental." *Forbes*. January 21, 2022. https://www.forbes.com/sites/nicholasreimann/2022/01/21/its-hurtful-mcconnell-says-comment-suggesting-black-voters-arent-americans-was-accidental/.
576. Bonitatibus, Steve. "How White Supremacy Returned to Mainstream Politics."
577. Lavender, Paige. "David Duke Threatens To Expose Other Politicians With White Supremacist Ties." *HuffPost*, January 2, 2015. Accessed February 22, 2021. https://www.huffpost.com/entry/david-duke-steve-scalise_n_6406844.
578. Southern Poverty Law Center. "David Duke." Accessed April 10, 2021. https://www.splcenter.org/fighting-hate/extremist-files/individual/david-duke.
579. Ballotpedia. "David Duke." Accessed April 10, 2021. The Encyclopedia of American Politics. https://ballotpedia.org/David_Duke.
580. Benen, Steve. "Scalise's Vote against MLK Day Gains New Relevance." msnbc.com, December 30, 2014. Accessed April 10, 2021. https://www.msnbc.com/rachel-maddow-show/scalises-vote-against-mlk-day-gains-new-relevance-msna494891.
581. Lavender, Paige. "David Duke Threatens To Expose Other Politicians With White Supremacist Ties."
582. Domonoske, Camila. "Trump Fails To Condemn KKK On Television, Turns To Twitter To Clarify." NPR, February 28, 2016. https://www.npr.org/sections/thetwo-way/2016/02/28/468455028/trump-wont-condemn-kkk-says-he-knows-nothing-about-white-supremacists.
583. Nagourney, Adam. "Reform Bid Said to Be A No-Go For Trump." The New York Times, February 14, 2000. Accessed April 10, 2021. https://www.nytimes.com/2000/02/14/us/reform-bid-said-to-be-a-no-go-for-trump.html.
584. Domonoske, Camila. "Trump Fails To Condemn KKK On Television, Turns To Twitter To Clarify."
585. Jackson, Abby. "Former KKK Leader David Duke Strikes out at Trump for Condemning a White Nationalist Rally: 'It Was White Americans Who Put You in the Presidency.'" Business Insider, August 12, 2017. https://www.businessinsider.com/david-duke-strikes-out-at-trump-for-condemning-charlottesville-rally-2017-8.

586. Jackson, Abby. "Former KKK Leader David Duke Strikes out at Trump for Condemning a White Nationalist Rally: 'It Was White Americans Who Put You in the Presidency.'"
587. Center for American Progress. "How White Supremacy Returned to Mainstream Politics," July 1, 2020. https://www.americanprogress.org/article/white-supremacy-returned-mainstream-politics/.
588. *The Guardian*. "Who Is Steve Bannon and What Has He Been Charged With?" August 20, 2020, sec. US news. https://www.theguardian.com/us-news/2020/aug/20/who-is-steve-bannon-charges-we-build-the-wall-trump.
589. Gore, Leada. "Who Is Stephen Miller? Controversial Ex-Trump Advisor Joins Mo Brooks to Announce Alabama Senate Run." al, March 22, 2021. https://www.al.com/news/2021/03/who-is-stephen-miller-controversial-ex-trump-advisor-joins-mo-brooks-to-announce-alabama-senate-run.html.
590. Opsahl, Robin. "Steve King Says All Cultures Do Not Contribute Equally, to Claim Otherwise Is to Devalue the 'Founding Fathers.'" *The Des Moines Register*, May 29, 2019. Accessed March 31, 2021. https://www.desmoinesregister.com/story/news/politics/2019/05/28/steve-king-culture-white-nationalism-supremacy-great-replacement-mexican-iowa-facebook-controversy/1264866001/.
591. Opsahl, Robin. "Steve King Says All Cultures Do Not Contribute Equally, to Claim Otherwise Is to Devalue the 'Founding Fathers.'"
592. Coaston, Jane. "The Scary Ideology behind Trump's Immigration Instincts." Vox, January 18. 2018. https://www.vox.com/2018/1/18/16897358/racism-donald-trump-immigration.
593. Talbot, Haley and Sahil Kapur. "Democratic Lawmaker Reacts to 'America First Caucus' Recruiting on 'Anglo-Saxon Political Traditions.'" NBC News. April 16, 2021. https://www.nbcnews.com/politics/congress/hard-right-republicans-forming-new-caucus-protect-anglo-saxon-political-n1264338.
594. Greene, Marjorie Taylor. "America First Caucus Policy Platform." America First Caucus, 2021. Accessed April 17, 2021. https://punchbowl.news/wp-content/uploads/America-First-Caucus-Policy-Platform-FINAL-2.pdf.
595. Cupp, S.E. "What Laura Ingraham Said Was Awful. And Unsurprising."
596. Fitzpatrick, Kevin. "In Racist Tweet, Trump Tells Congresswomen of Color to 'Go Back' to 'the Totally Broken and Crime Infested Places From Which They Came.'" Vanity Fair, July 14, 2019. https://www.vanityfair.com/news/2019/07/ trump-congresswomen-go-back-country.
597. Congress.gov. "Members of the U.S. Congress: 93rd-118th Congress (1973-2024)." Accessed August 17, 2023. https://www.congress.gov/members.
598. Schaefer, Katherine. "The Changing Face of Congress in 8 Charts: Race, Ethnicity, Gender, Generation, Immigrant Status, Education and More." Pew Research Center, Accessed January 22, 2022. https://www.pewresearch.org/fact-tank/2021/03/10/the-changing-face-of-congress/.
599. Gramlich, John. "The 2020 Electorate by Party, Race, Age, Education, Religion: Key Things to Know." Pew Research Center, October 26, 2022. Accessed January 22, 2022. https://www.pewresearch.org/fact-tank/2020/10/26/what-the-2020-electorate-looks-like-by-party-race-and-ethnicity-age-education-and-religion/.
600. Gramlich, John. "The 2020 Electorate by Party, Race, Age, Education, Religion: Key Things to Know."
601. NPR. "Director Raoul Peck: James Baldwin Was 'Speaking Directly To Me,'" February 14, 2017. Accessed February 26, 2022. https://www.npr.org/transcripts/515196224.
602. Datil, Ariane, Stephanie Wilson, and Tolu Oluwadiya. "TIMELINE: From a Presidential Speech to Insurrection, Here's How the Capitol Riots Evolved." wusa9.com, January 11, 2021. Accessed April 16, 2021. https://www.wusa9.com/article/news/national/capitol-riots/timeline-rioters-breach-us-capitol-minute-by-minute/65-b3ee849a-d322-4050-bcf7-467dc4622b2e.
603. "The Gettysburg Address: November 19, 1863" Historical Documents. *ushitory.org*. https://www.ushistory.org/documents/gettysburg.htm.
604. United Nations. "Population." March 1, 2021. Accessed March 1, 2021 https://web.archive.

org/web/20210301155951/https://www.un.org/en/sections/issues-depth/population/index.html.
605. United Nations. "Population." March 1, 2021.
606. Counter Extremism Project. "Great Replacement Theory." Accessed December 30, 2021. https://www.counterextremism.com/content/great-replacement-theory.
607. Manjoo, Farhad. "Opinion | The White-Extinction Conspiracy Theory Is Bonkers." *The New York Times*, March 21, 2019. https://www.nytimes.com/2019/03/20/opinion/new-zealand-great-replacement.html.
608. Coaston, Jane. "The White Genocide Conspiracy Theory, Explained." *Vox*, November 7, 2018. https://www.vox.com/2018/1/18/16897358/racism-donald-trump-immigration.
609. Coaston, Jane. "The White Genocide Conspiracy Theory, Explained."
610. Grant, Madison, and Jared Taylor. The Passing of the Great Race: Or, The Racial Basis of European History. Nachdr. Abergele: Palingenesis Project, 2012
611. Southern Poverty Law Center. "James Mason," Accessed January 2, 2022. https://www.splcenter.org/fighting-hate/extremist-files/individual/james-mason.
612. Wilson, Andrew F. "#whitegenocide, the Alt-Right and Conspiracy Theory: How Secrecy and Suspicion Contributed to the Mainstreaming of Hate." *Secrecy and Society* 1, no. 2 (February 16, 2018). https://doi.org/10.31979/2377-6188.2018.010201.
613. Moses, A. Dirk. "'White Genocide' and the Ethics of Public Analysis." *Journal of Genocide Research* 21, no. 2 (April 3, 2019): 201–13. https://doi.org/10.1080/14623528.2019.1599493.
614. Counter Extremism Project. "Great Replacement Theory." Accessed January 2, 2022. https://www.counterextremism.com/content/great-replacement-theory.
615. Devlin, F. Roger. "Global Demographics and White Survival: What Is to Be Done? Part II." American Renaissance, October 4, 2018. https://www.amren.com/commentary/2017/10/over-population-kaibab-deer-foreign-aid-f-roger-devlin/.
616. Rasmussen, Derek. "Qallunology 101: A Lesson Plan for the Non-Indigenous." Edited by Dru Oja Jay. Buddhist Peace Fellowship, April 27, 2013. Accessed January 7, 2022. https://web.archive.org/web/20220120203833/https://buddhistpeacefellowship.org/qallunology-101-a-lesson-plan-for-the-non-indigenous/.
617. Norris, Michele L. "Visualizing Race, Identity and Change." *Photography*, May 4, 2021. https://www.nationalgeographic.com/photography/proof/2013/09/17/visualizing-change/.
618. Strom, Adam. "Benjamin Franklin and German Immigrants in Colonial America." Re-Imagining Migration, January 14, 2022. https://reimaginingmigration.org/benjamin-franklin-and-german-immigrants-in-colonial-america/.
619. National Geographic. "Black and White: Skin Deep."
620. Khan, Razib. "Why There Will Not Be a Beige Future: Skin Color, Genetics, Race and Racism." Areo, November 29, 2018. https://areomagazine.com/2018/11/28/why-there-will-not-be-a-beige-future-skin-color-genetics-race-and-racism/.
621. Khan, Razib. "Why There Will Not Be a Beige Future: Skin Color, Genetics, Race and Racism."
622. Khan, Razib. "Why There Will Not Be a Beige Future: Skin Color, Genetics, Race and Racism."
623. Bahrampour, Tara. "They Considered Themselves White, but DNA Tests Told a More Complex Story." *Washington Post*, February 9, 2018. https://www.washingtonpost.com/local/social-issues/they-considered-themselves-white-but-dna-tests-told-a-more-complex-story/2018/02/06/16215d1a-e181-11e7-8679-a9728984779c_story.html.
624. Bahrampour, Tara. "They Considered Themselves White, but DNA Tests Told a More Complex Story."
625. Thompson, Krissah. "Obama's Purported Link to Early-American Slave Is Latest Twist in Family Tree." *Washington Post*, May 19, 2023. https://www.washingtonpost.com/politics/purported-obama-link-to-first-american-slave-is-latest-twist-in-presidents-family-tree/2012/07/30/gJQAYuG1KX_story.html.
626. Peralta, Eyder. "Genealogists Say Obama Likely A Descendant Of First American Slave."

NPR, July 30, 2012. https://www.npr.org/sections/thetwo-way/2012/07/30/157597233/genealogists-say-obama-likely-a-descendant-of-first-american-slave.
627. Stolberg, Sheryl Gay. "Obama's Mother Had African Forebear, Study Suggests." The New York Times, July 29, 2012. https://www.nytimes.com/2012/07/30/us/obamas-mother-had-african-forebear-study-suggests.html.
628. Krulwich, Robert. "Your Family May Once Have Been A Different Color."
629. Parker, Laura. "143 Million People May Soon Become Climate Migrants." Science, May 4, 2021. https://www.nationalgeographic.com/news/2018/03/climate-migrants-report-world-bank-spd/.
630. Center for Documentary Studies at Duke University. "S4: Seeing White E8: The Second Redemption." Scene on Radio. April 15, 2020. https://sceneonradio.org/the-land-that-never-has-been-yet/.
631. Hillman, Melissa. "Whiteness Is a Disease," July 12, 2016. bittergertrude.com (Blog) https://bittergertrude.com/2016/07/08/whiteness-is-a-disease/.
632. Wise, Tim J. "White like Me: Reflections on Race from a Privileged Son." p. 194
633. Wise, Tim J. "White like Me: Reflections on Race from a Privileged Son." p. 194.
634. Wilkerson, Isabel. Caste: The Origins of Our Discontents. p. 49.
635. National Geographic. "Black and White: Skin Deep."
636. Skillings, Judith H., and James E. Dobbins. "Racism as a Disease: Etiology and Treatment Implications." *Journal of Counseling and Development* 70, no. 1 (September 10, 1991): 206–12. https://doi.org/10.1002/j.1556-6676.1991.tb01585.x.
637. Pyke, Karen D. "What Is Internalized Racial Oppression and Why Don't We Study It? Acknowledging Racism's Hidden Injuries." *Sociological Perspectives* 53, no. 4 (December 1, 2010): 551–72. https://doi.org/10.1525/sop.2010.53.4.551.
638. Villanueva, Edgar. *Decolonizing Wealth: Indigenous Wisdom to Heal Divides and Restore Balance*. Chapter 5
639. Black is Beautiful. "The African Americans: Many Rivers to Cross" PBS. Accessed January 26, 2023. http://www.pbs.org/wnet/african-americans-many-rivers-to-cross/video/black-is-beautiful/.
640. Poupart, Lisa M. "The Familiar Face of Genocide: Internalized Oppression among American Indians." *Hypatia* 18, no. 2 (2003): 86–100. https://doi.org/10.1111/j.1527-2001.2003.tb00803.x.
641. Demsas, Jerusalem, and Rachel Ramirez. "How Racism and White Supremacy Fueled a Black-Asian Divide in America." Vox, March 16, 2021. https://www.vox.com/22321234/black-asian-american-tensions-solidarity-history.
642. Okonofua, Benjamin Aigbe. "'I Am Blacker Than You': Theorizing Conflict Between African Immigrants and African Americans in the United States." *SAGE Open* 3, no. 3 (July 1, 2013): 215824401349916. https://doi.org/10.1177/2158244013499162.
643. Okun, Tema. "(Divorcing) White Supremacy Culture: Coming Home to Who We Really Are."
644. Equal Justice Initiative. "Segregation Forever." *eji.org* Accessed August 17, 2023 https://segregationinamerica.eji.org/report/segregation-forever-leaders.html.
645. Peck, M. Scott. *The road less traveled: A new psychology of love, traditional values and spiritual growth*. Simon & Schuster. New York. 1978. p. 35
646. Goldberg, Susan B., and Cameron Levin. "Towards A Radical White Identity." AWARE in Los Angeles, awarela.org. November 4, 2009. Accessed March 26, 2022. https://static1.squarespace.com/static/581e9e06ff7c509a5ca2fe32/t/588d4ff3414fb55621d5d0f1/1485656053135/Toward+a+Radical+White+Identity.pdf.
647. Goldberg, Susan B. et al. "Towards A Radical White Identity."
648. Van Der Valk, Adrienne, and Anya Malley. "What's My Complicity? Talking White Fragility With Robin DiAngelo." Learning for Justice, May 2, 2019. https://www.learningforjustice.org/magazine/summer-2019/whats-my-complicity-talking-white-fragility-with-robin-diangelo.
649. DePino, Melissa. "The Nightmare of the Newly Woke - Melissa DePino - Medium." Medium, December 31, 2021. Accessed September 26, 2022. https://depinomelissa.medium.com/

the-nightmare-of-the-newly-woke-1f4d6dc8f27b.
650. Alliance of White Anti-Racists Everywhere. "Alliance Building and Accountability." awarela.org. Accessed March 26, 2022. https://static1.squarespace.com/static/581e9e06ff7c509a5ca2fe32/t/58f25f1486e6c05c3a8202f3/1492279061056/04+AWARE-LA+Accountability+and+Alliance+Building.pdf.
651. Taylor, Chris. "How One Woman's Yard Sign Became a Rallying Cry for Allies," *Mashable*, October 29, 2021, https://mashable.com/article/in-this-house-we-believe-black-lives-matter-kindness-is-everything-sign/.
652. Garcia, Sandra E. "Black Boys Feel Less Safe in White Neighborhoods, Study Shows," *The New York Times*, August 14, 2018, https://www.nytimes.com/2018/08/14/us/black-boys-white-neighborhoods-fear.html.
653. Blake, John. "How 'Good White People' Derail Racial Progress." CNN, August 2, 2020. https://www.cnn.com/2020/08/01/us/white-liberals-hypocrisy-race-blake/index.html.
654. Jealous, Ann Todd, and Caroline T. Haskell, eds. *Combined Destinies: Whites Sharing Grief about Racism*. Lincoln: Potomac Books, an imprint of the University of Nebraska Press, 2014. p. 45
655. Menakem, Resmaa. *My Grandmother's Hands: Racialized Trauma and the Pathway to Mending Our Hearts and Bodies*. p. 59
656. McGlynn, Sean. "Violence and the Law in Medieval England." *History Today* 58, no. 4 (April 2008). https://www.historytoday.com/archive/violence-and-law-medieval-england.
657. Menakem, Resmaa. *My Grandmother's Hands: Racialized Trauma and the Pathway to Mending Our Hearts and Bodies*. p. 60
658. Kallam, Sushma. "Walls and the Tiger," Documentary. 2015. https://wallsandthetiger.com/.
659. Dean, David. "Roots Deeper than Whiteness."
660. Menakem, Resmaa. *My Grandmother's Hands: Racialized Trauma and the Pathway to Mending Our Hearts and Bodies*. p. 60
661. Dean, David. "Roots Deeper than Whiteness."
662. Klein, Christopher. "Why Did the Pilgrims Come to America?" *HISTORY*, November 13, 2020. https://www.history.com/news/why-pilgrims-came-to-america-mayflower.
663. Klein, Christopher. "Why Did the Pilgrims Come to America?"
664. Mann, Charles C. "Native Intelligence." *Smithsonian Magazine*, December 1, 2005. Accessed December 12, 2021. https://www.smithsonianmag.com/history/native-intelligence-109314481/.
665. Dean, David. "Roots Deeper than Whiteness."
666. Dean, David. "Roots Deeper than Whiteness."
667. Klein, Christopher. "Why Did the Pilgrims Come to America?"
668. Plimoth Patuxet Museums. "Mayflower and Mayflower Compact," August 9, 2023. Accessed December 11, 2021. https://plimoth.org/for-students/homework-help/mayflower-and-mayflower-compact.
669. "John Rolfe," *HISTORY*. October 28, 2019. https://www.history.com/topics/exploration/john-rolfe.
670. Mann, Charles C. "Native Intelligence."
671. Mann, Charles C. "Native Intelligence."
672. Klein, Christopher. "Why Did the Pilgrims Come to America?"
673. Klein, Christopher. "Why Did the Pilgrims Come to America?"
674. Mann, Charles C. "Native Intelligence."
675. Mann, Charles C. "Native Intelligence."
676. Mann, Charles C. "Native Intelligence."
677. Klein, Christopher. "Why Did the Pilgrims Come to America?"
678. Dean, David. "Roots Deeper than Whiteness."
679. Lacayo, Richard. "Blood At The Root." TIME Vol. 155 No. 14 Visions 21 (April 10, 2000). https://web.archive.org/web/20010210025206/http://www.time.com/time/magazine/article/0,9171,42301,00.html.
680. Lacayo, Richard. "Blood At The Root."

681. Jealous, Ann Todd, et al. *Combined Destinies: Whites Sharing Grief about Racism.*
682. Jealous, Ann Todd, et al. *Combined Destinies: Whites Sharing Grief about Racism.*
683. Lacayo, Richard. "Blood At The Root."
684. Wilkerson, Isabel. Caste: The Origins of Our Discontents. p. 94
685. Menakem, Resmaa. *My Grandmother's Hands: Racialized Trauma and the Pathway to Mending Our Hearts and Bodies.* p. 61
686. Rasmussen, Derek. "Qallunology 101: A Lesson Plan for the Non-Indigenous."
687. Cashin, Ali. "Loneliness in America: How the Pandemic Has Deepened an Epidemic of Loneliness — *Making Caring Common*." Making Caring Common, October 20, 2022. https://mcc.gse.harvard.edu/reports/loneliness-in-america.
688. Centers for Disease Control and Prevention. "Loneliness and Social Isolation Linked to Serious Health Conditions," April 29, 2021. Accessed May 7, 2022. https://www.cdc.gov/aging/publications/features/lonely-older-adults.html.
689. Jensen, Brennen. "New Research Links Isolation in Old Age to Negative Health Outcomes." The Hub, June 21, 2023. https://hub.jhu.edu/magazine/2023/summer/elderly-isolation-study-aging/.
690. Wise, Tim J., ed. *White like Me: Reflections on Race from a Privileged Son.* p. 101
691. American Foundation for Suicide Prevention (AFSP). "Suicide Statistics," January 2018. Accessed December 12, 2021. https://web.archive.org/web/20180106063345/https://afsp.org/about-suicide/suicide-statistics/.
692. Statista. "Mass Shootings by Shooter's Race in the U.S. 2023." *Statista.org* August 1, 2023. https://www.statista.com/statistics/476456/mass-shootings-in-the-us-by-shooter-s-race/.
693. Noriega, David, and Tess Owen. "Nearly All Mass Shooters Since 1966 Have Had 4 Things in Common." Vice (blog), November 19, 2019. https://www.vice.com/en/article/a35mya/nearly-all-mass-shooters-since-1966-have-had-four-things-in-common.
694. The Violence Project Research Center. "Most Comprehensive Mass Shooter Database - The Violence Project." The Violence Project, July 27, 2023. https://www.theviolenceproject.org/mass-shooter-database/.
695. Jones, Dustin. "What Is the 'great Replacement' and How Is It Tied to the Buffalo Shooting Suspect?" *NPR*, May 16, 2022. https://www.npr.org/2022/05/16/1099034094/what-is-the-great-replacement-theory.
696. Counter Extremism Project. "Great Replacement Theory." Accessed August 20, 2023. https://www.counterextremism.com/content/great-replacement-theory
697. Noriega, David, et al. "Nearly All Mass Shooters Since 1966 Have Had 4 Things in Common."
698. Sinnar, Jayashri Srikantiah & Shirin, and Stanford Law Review. "White Nationalism as Immigration Policy." *Stanford Law Review*, March 11, 2019. Accessed August 13, 2023. https://www.stanfordlawreview.org/online/white-nationalism-as-immigration-policy/.
699. Noriega, David, et al. "Nearly All Mass Shooters Since 1966 Have Had 4 Things in Common."
700. Education Week. "School Shootings in 2021: How Many and Where." March 1, 2021, sec. Leadership, School Climate & Safety. https://www.edweek.org/leadership/school-shootings-this-year-how-many-and-where/2021/03.
701. Doxsee, Catrina, Seth G. Jones, Jared Thompson, Kateryna Halstead, and Grace Hwang. "Pushed to Extremes: Domestic Terrorism amid Polarization and Protest," November 29, 2022. https://www.csis.org/analysis/pushed-extremes-domestic-terrorism-amid-polarization-and-protest.
702. Mayo Clinic. "Post-Traumatic Stress Disorder (PTSD) - Symptoms and Causes." Accessed August 20, 2023. https://www.mayoclinic.org/diseases-conditions/post-traumatic-stress-disorder/symptoms-causes/syc-20355967.
703. Jealous, Ann Todd, et al. *Combined Destinies: Whites Sharing Grief about Racism.*
704. Covert, Bryce. "The Myth of the Welfare Queen." The New Republic, August 21, 2023. Accessed February 26, 2022. https://newrepublic.com/article/154404/myth-welfare-queen.
705. Weil, Simone "Uprootedness." Atlas of Places. (564ES) Accessed August 21, 2023. https://

atlasofplaces.com/essays/uprootedness/.
706. Rasmussen, Derek. "Qallunology 101: A Lesson Plan for the Non-Indigenous."
707. Villanueva, Edgar. *Decolonizing Wealth: Indigenous Wisdom to Heal Divides and Restore Balance.*
708. Dean, David. "Roots Deeper than Whiteness."
709. Menakem, Resmaa. *My Grandmother's Hands: Racialized Trauma and the Pathway to Mending Our Hearts and Bodies.*
710. Utt, Jamie, et al. "White Teacher, Know Thyself: Improving Anti-Racist Praxis through Racial Identity Development."
711. Alliance of White Anti-Racists Everywhere. "Alliance Building and Accountability."
712. Goldberg, Susan B. et al. "Towards A Radical White Identity."
713. Learning for Justice. "White Anti-Racism: Living the Legacy." Accessed April 23, 2022. https://www.learningforjustice.org/professional-development/white-antiracism-living-the-legacy.
714. Goldberg, Susan B. et al. "Towards A Radical White Identity."
715. Goldberg, Susan B. et al. "Towards A Radical White Identity."
716. Learning for Justice. "White Anti-Racism: Living the Legacy."
717. Mackenzie, Laura. "Who Were the Normans and Why Did They Conquer England?" History Hit, May 15, 2018. Accessed April 16, 2022. https://www.historyhit.com/who-were-the-normans-and-why-did-they-conquer-england/.
718. Price, Adam. "Wales, the First and Final Colony." Institute of Welsh Politics. walesonline. November 16, 2009. http://www.walesonline.co.uk/news/wales-news/wales-first-final-colony---2070487.
719. Price, Adam. "Wales, the First and Final Colony."
720. Price, Adam. "Wales, the First and Final Colony."
721. Cashin, Ali, Richard Batanova, Milena Weissbourd, Virginia Lovison, and Eric Torres. "Loneliness in America: How the Pandemic Has Deepened an Epidemic of Loneliness." *Making Caring Common*, February 2021. https://mcc.gse.harvard.edu/reports/loneliness-in-america.
722. Puiu, Tibi. "The Origin and History of the Christmas Tree: From Paganism to Modern Ubiquity." *ZME Science*, April 30, 2023. Accessed April 17, 2022. https://www.zmescience.com/science/history-science/origin-christmas-tree-pagan/.
723. Hammer, Jill, and Taya Shere. *The Hebrew Priestess: Ancient and New Visions of Jewish Women's Spiritual Leadership*. Teaneck, New Jersey: Ben Yehuda Press, 2015.
724. Cobb, Frank Dunkle David. "Paganism In Christianity." United Church of God, October 22, 2011. https://www.ucg.org/vertical-thought/paganism-in-christianity.
725. Goldberg, Susan B. et al. "Towards A Radical White Identity."
726. Goldberg, Susan B. et al. "Towards A Radical White Identity."
727. Presley, Sharon. "White Women Abolitionists: More 19th-Century Freedom Fighters." *Libertarianism.org*. March 9, 2016. Accessed April 23, 2022. https://www.libertarianism.org/columns/white-women-abolitionists-more-19th-century-freedom-fighters.
728. Goldberg, Susan B. et al. "Towards A Radical White Identity."
729. Foster, Eli. "White Americans Should Treat Racism as an Addiction to Overcome." *Nashville Tennessean*, August 15, 2020. Accessed April 24, 2022. https://www.tennessean.com/story/opinion/2020/08/15/white-americans-should-treat-racism-addition-overcome/5587838002/.
730. Wiltz, Allison. "White Supremacy Is a Hell of a Drug - An Injustice!" Medium, January 7, 2022. https://aninjusticemag.com/white-supremacy-is-a-hell-of-a-drug-893ffaaa34ad.
731. Oluo, Ijeoma. *So You Want to Talk about Race*. First edition. New York, NY: Seal Press, 2018.
732. Foster, Eli. "White Americans Should Treat Racism as an Addiction to Overcome."

www.ingramcontent.com/pod-product-compliance
Lightning Source LLC
LaVergne TN
LVHW091652070526
838199LV00050B/2155